Getting Off At Edge Hill – The Tracks Of My Years 1

There have been 'friends' who have sailed away in 'ships' to desert you on a deserted island whereas lasting 'friendships' bond together setting a united passage across life's treacherous seas!

To Absent Friends

Chapter Headings

1. Where Do You Go Too (My Lovely)…
2. Pal of my Cradle Days…
3. In My Liverpool Home…
4. Our House…
5. Everybody Was Kung Fu Fighting…
6. Knock Three Times on the Ceiling if You Want Me…
7. Riding Along on my Pushbike Honey…
8. Games Without Frontiers…
9. Seasons in the Sun…
10. Everybody's On Top Of Top Of The Pops…
11. Talk Talk…
12. Get Down On It…
13. Summer The First Time…
14. Billy the Mountain…
15. Singing The Blues …
16. Just Be Good To Me…
17. Live It Up…
18. Eton Rifles…
19. From A Jack To A King…
20. Living in the past…

Chapter One

Where Do You Go To (My Lovely)…

Hello, my names Dave, these are my words and this is my book and from the start I just want to say that I'm forty six years of age, I'm married to Sue, I have two wonderful kids and I am stoutly proud of the fact that I am a scouser!
'Is right' as us scousers would say and it may be of interest to know that the word 'scouse' refers to a stew made up of leftovers and believed to have originated from Scandinavian sailors who docked in Liverpool but you probably know that's one of the many tidbits of information I shall bestow on you from time to time. Hope you don't mind?
I will also spill my very soul on this narrative of my life and I will perhaps reveal too much about myself; my inner passions and thoughts will be laid before you to then dissect.
I'm relaxed about that actually as this is a 'warts and all' account but let me begin by pointing out that I feel a smidgen uncomfortable writing about myself as this would suggest that I'm wrapped up in my own ego. Perhaps I am, so lets reserve judgement for now but for years I've come to realise that I like telling stories and I like the imaginative world.
You see I realise I have a creative side to my character simply hankering to evolve, I like the way the mind works and how the written word can conjure up images, thoughts and ideas unique to that person and how they were feeling at the time.
It would be a stretch to say I'm a prolific reader but when I do get the urge to read a book, usually in some sunny clime, I prefer crime novels with Lee Childs being my favourite author at the moment and I also like the sharp northern wit of Stuart Maconie. His collection of books is very funny and by all accounts a dam good read.
I like the way a book can take you to another part of you, another world, another time, another ego, another…well, I'll stop there but all this got me thinking about my childhood and in doing so I was reminded of a phrase I first heard at College when I was studying to become a Social Worker the career I ended up falling into, I say this because I never

planned on working with children and families. Anyway I think the phrase went something like this. 'Give me the boy till he's seven and I will give you the man'.

Now excuse the male bias but I think the Jesuit Monks first coined this phrase and I remember musing over this revelation and thinking, yes probably right but I'd respectfully challenge those robed philosophers and say 'hey monk I agree but what about Secondary School, ones teenage years, friends and influences, fashion and music'. Weren't they all equally as influential and as you will soon discover in my case I believe they certainly were?

See, as I see it we're social animals, evolving all the time, most definitely beyond our seventh birthday and we become who we are because of learning and experiences, influenced by the plethora amounts of data our brain absorbs on a daily basis, which as we know continues throughout ones life until our very last breath.

Take music for example, someone else's ability to create a tune has without doubt played an enormous part in my life, still does actually and for every memory 'pogoing' around my brain I can usually attach a particular track that brings life to that moment.

So to help me rummage through the alcoves of my mind, hey isn't that a song, I don't know but I will pause a 'beat' and 'tune' into a track associated with that memory or from that period of my life as it helps me transport back in time.

On a cautionary note I will recall some wonderful classic tracks as I am sure you will agree and some guilty pleasures too but there will be some that are down right painful to the ears but you may think differently. Like any art or media, music is a personal thing which is why it excites me so much and if you 'bop' to the end of the book you will see that I've certainly amassed a sizeable back catalogue of favourite tracks with the year when it was released.

I am also slightly perturbed with the possibility that I might have unwittingly fallen foul of some copyright infringement law so I did my own research into this and I could not find a definitive answer other than track names are not copyrighted, so they remain, whereas lyrics are not allowed even under 'fair use' as they are protected. I understand why of course as someone somewhere has created the lyrics but I grudgingly had to get the red pen out and I ended up massacring my final edited version for fear of being sued and as a failsafe I will use *italics* to emphasise a track to prevent any confusion.

I would have used the term song or tune but the 'songs or tune of my years' doesn't fit easily into the title of this book and with that let me

Getting Off At Edge Hill – The Tracks Of My Years

sheepishly explain why I used 'Getting Off at Edge Hill' as my title. I'll talk more about Edge Hill Station later but all trains you see would stop at Edge Hill at the entrance to the tunnel to Lime Street Station given rise to the euphemism for 'coitus interruptus' and as I see it the meaning behind this Latin phrase is best translated into scouse. If you were ever 'lucky' with a girl the next day a mate would ask; 'did yer gerrof at Edge Hill den'.

I'll leave the rest to your imagination but a famous saying round our way and also a useless Catholic contraception method I may add so kids don't ever get the train without putting a rain jacket on as life can get very bumpy nine months later down those prenatal tracks!

Thankfully Dad forgot his coat back in July of 1965, strange how I had never done the maths before today and 'didn't get off at Edge Hill' and so you now understand the reason why I titled this book, *'Getting Off At Edge Hill – The Tracks of My Years'*.

Moving gingerly on, please also bear in mind dear reader that my memory is as good as the next person but I can't claim to recall every detail so I will include data I researched off the internet and especially Wikipedia. Yes today the kids and me can research facts and information for this book or homework or just for fun whilst watching telly, instantly and on various electronic gizmos whereas we relied upon teachers, word of mouth standing with your mates in the cold, seeing something in the newspaper, catching something on the telly, verbal wisdom passed down by elders or if all else fails the local library if we wanted to 'know!' Our library was Picton Road Library in Wavertree but I rarely entered unless escaping the rain if truth were told.

Anyway, it's also not for me to judge whether this book is a gripping read in the genre of Mr Maconie et al as this prose is neither a thriller nor fictional but it is simply a book of memories and ill try and be as factual as my wayward mind will recall but above all its a personal adventure, just like my musical tastes.

In some respects though it doesn't really concern me if you stop at the first page, although having spent a large chunk of my life buried in this book I would be disappointed with you and in any event it would be such a thrill to see my ramblings published. That would certainly be a huge achievement for me after falling out of school with no qualifications and me thinks 'one in the eye' for my English teacher's. Indeed if you're reading this as a book then in the words of Baldrick from the excellent 'Black Adder' comedy series, my 'cunning plan' came up trumps as I've discovered that you can self publish using Amazon. I have no doubt ordered several copies for family and friends for keepsake to then gather dust in the attic next to old toys, unused camping gear and naff ornaments, but my real motivation is not about making money but a desire to record my childhood for the benefit of my children and their children and maybe even their children. Who knows?

So what's this fascination with the past you may ask, as I don't think I've had a particularly interesting life? Perhaps I've been watching too many 'Who Do You Think You Are' episodes on telly but the obvious question is where does the inspiration come from? Telly by the way is a shortened version of television, obvious I know but you may not understand my accent from time to time.

I suppose its about asking yourself the question; wouldn't it be fantastic to have in your possession a diary or a biography written by the hand of a relative from a bygone age giving you an awareness, an insight into their life story, family births for example, deaths, ancestral struggles and perhaps celebrations and accomplishments? In other words *The Things the Grandchildren Should Know'*, a track penned by the wonderful Mr E from 'the Eels' and I'd also recommend his biography! Inspirational! How wonderful and revealing that would be and I think the answer has to be a resounding yes unless you're some criminal on an FBI witness protection programme who was forced to erase their past for personal safety reasons and with that let's give a nod to Kid Creole's track from the eighties, 'Stool Pigeon', ah cha cha cha!'

Yes indeed, I think I have been reading one to many American novels sprinkled with a few Mafia thrillers like the brilliant Sopranos, which reminds me of the track *'Don't Stop Believing'* by 'Journey', as it was played in the final instalment from Tony Soprano and an ending that leaves you with more questions than answers. Please please make another series.

I think you'll agree in any event, how could you not. No matter what part of the world you come from elders will pass down stories by word of mouth to the next generation and although I find stories interesting like I said before and particularly wearing this adult suit, as a child I'd sit politely but with glazed eyes; usually preoccupied with the outside world but in truth bored as any respectful kid would be.

Children have an eye on the present but mainly on the future in their quest to grow up, but rarely the dull past as each generation believes it holds a unique position and understanding of the world. I would go as far as to say children of the past, today also and in the future believe they created childhood and its bigger sister, adolescences, they believe they have a moratorium on its very existence, only realising this isn't the case when they hit their twenties and beyond as they then pass the baton on

to the next generation, sometimes reluctantly if you consider the desire to remain *'Forever Young'*. A splendid track by the equally splendid 'Bob Dylan.'
Sadly many a family memory ends up on the cutting floor of life and will simply fade away to the sound of mother time, see the clever use of the female bias to balance things up and did you spot the one before?
Decades pass and with them fascinating stories are forever lost or they become distorted over the passage of time.
Family stories rarely go beyond the last generation, or possibly the next in my experience and you find yourself becoming reliant upon your Mum or Dad retaining the precious story from their parent like a delicate rose and then passing it on to you but as with anything passed orally, the story gets chewed up, massed around a bit in the mangle of life and it will naturally evolve and can become diluted over time.
The petals fall away with the passing wind but this is not the case with everyone of course. Those who are famous or born with blue blood have their every move chronicled by the media especially in this day an age when the world seems a much smaller and reachable place than it did in the seventies when I was a kid. The need to know what's going on in the lives of famous people is aided by modern technologies such as Twitter and Facebook and I challenge you to name me one young person, who is 'not' on Facebook and I will say 'surely a weirdo' as this is the way children communicate and network today.
Actually, although not a young person myself as you might have gathered, I must be a weirdo as I've resisted the temptation thus far to tell the world my every move. Who cares what kind of day I am having, do I take one sugar or two, or what I had for tea? Mind-boggling if you ask me but perhaps I'm just very old, I certainly feel it these days.
Anyway, it seems society has an insatiable appetite for more and more morsels of information and like sheep, we follow celebs be them A, B or bloody Z listers. In fact society has become a community of stalkers in my view and some internalise their obsessions and become crazed fans such is societies fascination with knowing the business of people in the limelight, who themselves seem to crave the attention.
You only have to look at celebs that twitter their every move, why I ask myself if not to publicise that your still out there and want to be listened too. Popularity is based on how many people you have following you, not genuine relationships, or how many friends you have when in reality most are friends of friends of friends. I am old aren't i?
Windows into the life and times of regular Joe or Josephine's like you and me, gender balance restored, are lost forever. Ashes to ashes, dust to

dust so the saying goes as we watch teary-eyed as our dearly beloved pass to the other side hoping to see the pearly gates and past loves; to the sound of 'We'll Meet Again' or some other favourite passing over tune but not mine so no italics this time. In fact I'd choose one of two tracks, the theme tune to the Archers, I'm with Billy Connolly as this should be the countries National Anthem, or *'(Don't Fear) The Reaper'* by The 'Blue Oyster Cult' for obvious reasons and a wonderful track to boot, so bear that in mind should I pass any day soon.

Family members take with them their memories and stories, perhaps leaving grainy photographs to be photo shopped or if you're really lucky, a video recording for any budding genealogist in the family to try and piece together.

There's a thought do people still say 'make sure you video the Sopranos', or worst still 'tape that for me', if you do, then hello and welcome my fellow forty something friend, remember kids 'record' today.

Anyway I'm guessing you agree, well I hope so, I don't see how you couldn't and I also hope this book captures your imagination a bit and inspires you to jot down your childhood memories like I'm about to do. Still with me, just thought I'd tell you were well past page one, good, so now I've got you hooked a bit let me tell you where this all begin.

I'm a busy individual, with work, the family and my beloved golf and badminton, I don't really have the time for this but in truth writing this book became a labour of love, my hobbyhorse so to speak.

I found the whole experience to be very cathartic, perhaps my mid life crises, I don't know, should have bought a Harley Davidson me thinks, would have been easier, but I felt really inspired to delve into my past to hopefully make sense of my future as it scares the bejesus out of me right now.

I began by jotting down some one liner ideas in the spring of 2011 and most weekends I would spend an hour or so adding to my book. Some would say that *'Everyday I Write the Book'*, ouch that hurt and please excuse the alarmingly poor grammar but this is a brilliantly crafted track by the exceptionally talented Elvis Costello worthy of a mention.

I would let my mind wander and as I delved further one memory would unlock another and like tumbling dominoes I would find myself going off on a seventies tangent deep into the murky recesses of my mind.

Yes, although born in the sixties I am a child of the seventies, a decade of changes without doubt, if you don't believe me then please read on as I try and analyse what's gone before by comparing to what we have now.

It's also amazing what junk you have stored up there ready to be unlocked, trust me and I found the key to unlocking the past is to let your mind meander back in time and to immerse yourself and to try and transcend into the memory with both feet.

You don't need a personal guru sitting cross legged next to you in case that image has just popped into your brain but I would try and meditate backwards in time and I would visualise the area, the characters I met along my life path and I would try and recall what I was thinking, how I felt and what I was observing at the time, I realise now I was an impressionable and suggestible inner city kid who has a substantial library of useless information win zipped throughout my grey matter.

At this stage of the book I think I need to add a further cautionary note before I delve further. See, I will of course make reference to my mates and their parent's and other adults that were around me but I feel the need to offer a sincere apology if my memory offends anyone as you might know me or know of me. This would of course be true if you are part of my family, unless, I'm this long dead relative who's passed over by now, don't forget the Archers!

Hope I had a good turn out but indeed a scary thought! Actually I'm not that precious about my memories, this is about personal perceptions and I therefore accept without apology that my memories may clash with people who knew me back in the day. I can just hear my sisters for example, an old friend perhaps or indeed an old foe in my head saying, 'now I don't remember it being like that', or 'I never realised Dave was thinking that way, how odd?'

The brain is an amazing organic piece of kit, so intricate by design as we know but its not totally reliable in my view and I may get some names and places wrong as memories can become discoloured over time, I think this is understandable especially as I get older with the dreaded onset of age and advancing greying temples.

So I ask you dear reader to bear with me and I hope you don't lodge a grievance or a challenge to my story, I shall await the writs, as this is clearly a personal account. I shall therefore use a bit of a default system so as not to offend people and I may use pseudonyms at times particularly for people who are sadly not with us anymore.

I'm going to say a big thank you to my youngest son Adam, his real name by the way, at this point as he's 'one' reason why I started all this. We were sprawled out on the couch watching the Gadget show on telly, eating crisps and this must have been sometime mid February 2011. I'd had a hard day at work as I recall and I think it must have been about 8pm. Bloody hell sounds like I'm about to break into singing the Abba track, *'The Day Before You Came?'* A good track by the way but a guilty pleasure.

Anyway, the presenter with the shaven head was demonstrating the merits of this very futuristic go kart; it was really cool and was made out of slick sixties aluminium, sprayed silver and it could travel effortlessly at break neck speed as it sped down the hill with the presenter screaming out loud with delight. 'Wouldn't that be good', said Adam and we then had a conversation about how my mates and me would sometimes make go-karts when we were kids but we called them 'steeries'. Not quite as good as the one before my eyes granted but same principle applied and certainly the same thrill down a hill! Hey that rhymed!

I could see that Adam was very interested and he asked me if I could make one for him. Unlike my eldest son, Kieran, a typical grunting teenager, probably takes after me; Adam still thinks I'm cool and interesting. At the risk of sounding like a lazy sod, again it's been said before, so I'm egotistical and lazy thus far, please keep that in mind, I explained to Adam that I'm in a different place now without the essential materials to make a steerie, most prams are moulded plastic in any case and the wheels are way too small you'd hit all the speed bumps that seem to be bloody everywhere these days, or indeed, I haven't got the time but quizzically I have the time to write this book, I know a clear contradiction.

I told my sister Tina about this book and what inspired me and she laughed and said she once bought a pram from a jumble sale and I pinched the wheels. For what it's worth I'm sorry sis and if I had apologised back in the day I would have said 'soz Tina'. Tina would have replied 'ar eh', meaning 'oh no'.

Perhaps I am being lazy but this then got me thinking about my childhood and all the street games we played as kids and how I should really make an effort and record stuff such as how to make a steerie for prosperity amongst other things because kids have lost a section of their brain marked imagination and ingenuity.

Over the next few days and weeks the imagination section in my brain sparked into life and memories began to ricochet round this head of mine and I just had to write down my thoughts. I was inspired and I would wake up at night or I would be out and about and suddenly I would think of a memory and I would tap away on my I phone with a silly smile on my face thinking about preserved thoughts long since buried.

I would bore work colleagues with stories, close friends, my mate Neil on the golf course; I would read and recount snippets out loud from my book to see if they were interesting. People were generally polite but I'm also guessing people thought I was bonkers.

Now I'm not sure if you have the same problem but I really struggle with a biro, perhaps modern technology is to blame, as I don't practice much these days and I'm such a messy writer. Most of the time I can't even understand my own writing, it's like I have a pet spider deliberately spoiling my words coupled with this mischievous apparition nudging and hovering over my hand as I write.

When I write in my mother tongue, God it's like a game of gender tennis this, my own vernacular, my strong scouseness, the sentence, 'me and my mate', would result in a green squiggly line ordering me to write 'my mates and me'. So if you see a sentence with 'my mate', blame the drop down tool menu at the top of my I Mac and my inability to rebel or ignore those better at grammar than us!

I must have dozed off during English lessons, perhaps the 'code' was taught when I was in hospital having my appendix out when I was eleven or perhaps as a result of moving school when I was thirteen, all shall be revealed later, but I go into a bit of a panic when I write certain words.

Let me give you a few examples, should I type 'to' or 'too', 'of' or 'off', 'your' or 'you're', I think you get the picture? The track *'Too Much Too Young'* by 'The Specials has certainly helped me over the years with 'too' and Adam has since explained the theory that has evaded the section of my brain where correct grammar is stored but I guess I will still make the odd mistake or too, ha ha!

Then we have typo mistakes. No matter how hard I concentrate if I type 'from' it often reads 'form' and likewise 'for' becomes 'fro' and annoyingly 'the' becomes eth, all words that evade the squiggly line spellchecker so good luck spotting them, I' sure there are many hidden from these tired scrutinising eyes.

I'm not dyslexic but some words also become 'fuzzy' so I write phonetically just to record my thoughts in case they fade away. Thank God for grammar and spell check but even with Mr Gate's gratefully received help I'm sure, dear reader, you will find quite a few mistakes as you read on, probably in the opening paragraph or even the opening sentence, probably this sentence, oh no I'm now being paranoid, so go and add that to the list.

But again this doesn't really concern me as it's the content that I hope catches your interest and not the grammar but do please feel free to pick up your own red pen if you are particularly inclined to do so but be warned I would then accuse you of being an anal so and so.

You won't be the first I can tell you and definitely not the last, so that's egotistical, lazy, paranoid and bad at English and while I think on I'm not encouraging you to deface the printed book, as I really hate that but there again, if my Baldrick Amazon plan worked, you could be reading this on a Kindle so you couldn't correct my mistakes in any case, so a big raspberry to you.

Oh just before we move to the next chapter and perhaps reflecting my mind and how it works, I must warn you however that I will jump around from topic to topic as I found it too tasking and laborious to follow a time line as common sense would suggest, a chronological approach. I'm not that good an author you see, author, me, no sir, not possible.

I will also make reference to names at different points throughout this book and I'm hoping it will all make sense by the end? Fingers, legs and everything else crossed.

This book also has to have an ending so I've decided to stop around nineteen, no not page nineteen that would be a Kindle sample version of this book, I wish, no I mean the age of nineteen when I became a young independent adult with the world at his feet, or so I assumed.

Hey, maybe I have a second book in me covering my adult life, now there's a thought but I fear a sequel will be more of a dull read and I am not suggesting my adult life has been boring, no just less dramatic than my childhood I think, so it's one book and one book only.

One of the first lines I wrote when I begun this book was: every one of us has a good book in them so they say; I hope this is mine, so with that in mind I now invite you dear reader to probe into my soul and what childhood experiences shaped me, my personality, my values, and my hopes and aspirations, the relationships I had, in essence my book. Unashamedly using the words from Peter Sarstedt superb memoire track *'Where Do You Go to (My Lovely)*, you can have the back streets of Naples any day my lovely, me, I get off at Edge Hill, now come with me and let me first tell you all about my family and how I came to be, then my house, my street, my area, my friends, my education, my musical journey and I'll add in a few train journey's to spice things up!

Chapter two

Pal of my Cradle Days...

Now this chapter is very personal endeavour so it will probably only be of interest to any genealogists in my family and I do warn you the opening segments are very slushy to say the least so unless you're part of my clan or devoid of a sick bucket, I really don't blame you if you flick on by to the next Chapter.
Still here, good, so where do I begin? My Dad by passed Edge Hill Station like I said, obviously, as I wouldn't be here recording my distant childhood memories so let me dedicate a few pages to what loins introduced me to this world, my Mum and Dad, a bit about my slightly annoying sisters then my extended family.
Now before I embark on this journey and at the risk of sounding unashamedly sentimental, here's another entry to my burgeoning list, I have kick-started this chapter with the 'toe curling' track *'Pal of my Cradle Days'* by Ann Breen. This track you see, isn't really a favourite of mine but will always remind me of my Mum, which isn't surprising if you give this track a spin and I first heard it on Billy Butler's Radio Merseyside Show in the early eighties. I would later howl out the lines from the top of my ladder when I worked as a decorator and for what its worth Mum, I think the girls made your hair silver not me?
On the subject of hair my Mum now has what I consider to be the typical 'mature' lady look that I see shuffling through the precinct most Saturday's; yes she is a fully signed up member of the 'short blonde just been the hairdressers, pastel coloured fleece and legging wearing brigade sometime pushing a trolley'. Tickles me and from behind they all look the bleeding same or is this just a scouse thing?
Anyway Mum and Dad, perhaps you should take this opportunity sit down whilst I take a gulp, I don't say this very often but I do love you both and I thank you for all the sacrifices you have made and being the best parent's a son could ever want. There I said it, which isn't very often, a googolplex of gushiness I know and with that let me meander on and tell you more about my family.

14 David Griffith

Being a kid born in the sixties Mum's and Dad's round our way didn't invent stupid names for their kids like Kiora or Amber, no we were usually named after more traditional names and usually after a favoured relative, names that have seen a resurgence lately it seems. Mum and Dad for example, are called Pat and Len and I have two sisters, Tracy and Tina, although come to think of it neither is named after an Aunt or a Gran, I wonder why?

My lasting memory of my sisters from my childhood is that they had this twin thing going on for a few years despite them being born two years apart and they constantly bickered and argued and they still do if left in a room for too long.

Tracy is two years younger than me she was born in 1968 and she is now married to David and they have a son called Tom. Tina is two year's younger again and she was born in 1970 and she is married to Eric and they have two daughters, Bethan and Cerys.

Was that good family planning by Mum and Dad I wonder seeing as we were born two years apart or was Mr Stork on a well-earned sabbatical from Edge Hill? Who knows, but my first memory of Tina was standing at the front door watching Mum walking towards me with my new baby sister.

I was aged four, it must have been May and I am guessing Dad must have kept me informed and I must have known Mum was pregnant on account that she would have had a bigger belly but I can't recall thinking 'where's Mum' when she went to the hospital after her waters broke. There again Mum was a big woman when I was a child so she might have hid her pregnancy and in my vague memory Tina just appeared one day bathed in a white shawl on a hot May Day and swaddled in Mum's arms!

Tina was the youngest in our family but in a matter of months she soon caught Tracy up and before too long they were kitted out in harmonizing outfits befitting of doppelgangers. It's amusing to see them now as they are so different, when they were little they had similar platinum blonde hair whereas these days they are both dark, although Tracy would have you believe her dyed blonde hair is 'not' from a bottle. Sorry sis your secrets out and long blonde hair on a forty something year old woman isn't a good look but neither is gelled greying hair on a man in his late forties I hear you say! Touché.

On the subject of hair I also recollect my Mum weaving torn stripy pyjama strips into my sisters hair to create bouncy curls in the morning and she would do this on a Sunday night after the weekly bath and I think the strips were called ringlets?

Getting Off At Edge Hill – The Tracks Of My Years

In the mid seventies my sisters had the 'Perdy' haircut in reverence to the kicking female lead actress from the seventies telly programme 'The Avengers'. Most girls had this haircut actually and they would dress in long flowing flowery Maxi skirts as I recall or hip hugging flares.

Like many little girls up and down the land my sisters idolised the Scottish boy band 'The Bay City Rollers'; they were absolutely huge and fashion suddenly took on a Scottish bias. Flared jeans would be hemmed with red tartan and shirts would have tartan cuffs and collars and it was cool to be Scottish and my sisters also had an album by the band. The album I have since discovered was called 'Rollin' and reached number one in 1974.

'Rollermania' as it became known, gripped the country for a year or so and on the inside sleeve cover of the album was the bands likes and the dislikes, which fed the tartan army of girls with snippets of information leaving them with the impression that they really knew their idols. I do confess to liking the tracks '*Bye, Bye, Baby*' which I have since discovered was a cover of a 'Four Season' track and it stayed at number one for six weeks in the spring of 1975.

My sisters then moved onto David Sole and conversations amongst girl's on the playground turned to who was more dishy, 'Starsky or Hutch' from the same titled cop series from the States. Whereas us lads preferred the 'Sweeney' or better still, 'Professionals', you see they drove a Ford Capri Ghia, 'the' classic seventies car and the show had masses of action, countless rolling around scenes in run down factories, shootouts with bad guys, fist fighting and screeching car chases.

Bodie was the scouse hard man, Doyal, or was it Kevin Keegan moonlighting after his Brute advert, separated at birth perhaps; anyway he was the curly haired gentleman. Whilst Cowley was the Sargent major type and he would bark out orders in his authoritarian Scottish twang. For apparent reasons this all reminds me of the terrific track '*Watching the Detectives*', another new wave master class from the ever so talented Mr Costello. Talking of Mr Keegan, a favourite telly programme us boys would watch was Superstars. Each week famous sports personalities of the day would compete against each other in this cheap version of the Olympics and the part I remember the most was when Keegan fell off his bike and went flying over the handle bars. We've all been there and I still have the grit in my knees to prove it.

Would you like to hear a string of jokes I remember from when I was a kid to do with detectives, no well I'm going to tell you anyway. So using the voice of Lesley Neilson from the brilliant 'Police Squad'. 'My names 'Bud' because they say I'm weiser' than the average private detective;

16 David Griffith

you see I'm a private dick. I was once working on this case, couldn't afford a desk you see. When this tall blonde walks on by, I knew she was tall as we were on the second floor.

She came into my office; she was a stunner with long blond hair down her back, none on her head mind you but loads down her back. She rolled her eyes at me so I picked them up and rolled them back. She said hurry there's been a murder on Fifty-second Street lets get the lift. I said 'my dear what's the lift done to you'. We got out of the lift, made our way through the lobby and this taxi pulled up with a jerk, the jerk got out so we got in. To pass the time away the blonde then said 'you know Bud I have one very clever pussy'. With one eyebrow raised fearing this Bud was about to get frothy, I cautiously asked 'how come' and she replied, 'when I ask my pussy to shut the door she says 'meow'.

Slightly relieved the taxi gathered pace and was speeding down Fourth Avenue when this cop rides along side us and mouths 'pullover', I reply 'no I'm wearing a fetching cardigan actually'. We pull over so as not to break the law and the cop escorts us blue lights flashing funny enough going meow meow, to the scene of the crime. We find a male sprawled on the floor of this abandoned warehouse covered in cornflakes, rice crispies and clutching a broken Weetabix. I turn to my blonde companion, 'this is surely the work of a cereal killer!' my companion looks puzzled, 'my names not Shirley but yes he's dead' she replies.

Sorry where was I? Oh yes family stuff. My Mum was a proud woman and I can recall holding onto my sister's big blue 'Silvercross' pram whilst out shopping and my Mum telling passing friends that I had lovely eyes as I looked away all coy.

Mum was the primary parent in our house due to Dad working shifts but when he came home or when he got out of bed after working nights, Dad was never too tired to play silly games with my sisters and me. Dad would run around the house with my sisters on his shoulder for example, not at the same time I might add although I do recall him balancing Tracy and Tina on opposite shoulders like he was carrying bags of cement. I challenge you to try doing that now Dad!

On the subject of things Dad cant do now, I also remember holding on to my Dad's leg like he was a giant and standing on his foot with him walking round the house like he had a painful limp. I was clearly a lot smaller back then and I think Dad would like that memory gift, as he's a good six inches smaller than me now!

Dad loved to play 'horses'; he would sit on a chair with his legs crossed over and I would then sit on his knee facing the other way. Dad would hold onto my shirt collar, top button undone to avoid choking me of course and once steady, we were off and Dad would bounce his knee up and down as if I was on the most famous of all seventies horses, 'Red Rum', jumping over fences at Aintree. I'd have nothing to hold onto and would fall about from side to side whilst Dad would do his best to steady me by holding on tightly which added to the fun. What comes around goes around I guess as I remember playing the very same game with my kids and perhaps a paragraph mention in their very own memoire book?

Another favourite Dad game from when I was a toddler was 'round and round the garden'; a traditional nursery rhyme known nation wide I know and a funny game accompanied by various actions. Dad would lightly stroke small circles using his index finger on the upturned palm of my hand, then with each step he'd walk his finger up my arm and after a short pause, to gain maximum effect, he would tickle me under the arm. You knew what to expect but still very funny on each occasion and again, I do confess to playing this childhood favourite with my kids when they were little, where's my originality?

Come to think of it as I write these lines two other 'similar nursery rhymes' from when I was a little boy have just popped into my head. First of all we have 'Incy Wincy Spider' but this time Dad would use his thumb and finger to imitate a spider walking up and down my arm as if it was a drainpipe before tickling me under the arm. Very funny and it might interest you to know that this rhyme is also known as 'Itsy Bitsy Spider' in other parts of the country according to Wiki.

Then we have another treasured memory from when I was a young child; Dad playing 'This Little Piggy' on my toes after having a bath curled up on his lap with a towel around me. Now because this nursery rhyme originates from around 1728, thanks again Wiki, I am actually okay to quote the words verbatim, so here goes. *'This little piggy went the market, this little piggy stayed at home, this little piggy had roast beef, this little piggy had none, and this little piggy went wee wee wee all the way home.* I loved this game and Dad would count out the piggy's on my toes climaxing in him tickling the underneath of my foot when he got to the 'wee wee wee' section. I'd know what was coming and I'd kick out trying to escape and maybe these games are why as an adult I become hysterically paralysed whenever someone tickles me? Oh no my secrets out!

As for jumping on the bed, every child must have done this at some point thinking they were on trampoline and I also remember running into my Mum and Dad's room in the middle of the night and squeezing between them because I had just had a bad dream. I can still sense the relief after avoiding the monster that had crept into my dreams despite me trying to think of nice things like footy and cream cakes. I had found a safe haven, a place of sanctuary in an otherwise dark creepy house with ghouls hiding in the shadows or in the wardrobe waiting to pounce if I looked away and the bed always felt warm and cosy.

My sisters and me attended the same primary school, more shall be revealed about school later. Tracy was probably the cleverest in our family and the only one to pass the eleven plus, a test to filter out the cleverest kids, so she was rewarded with a place at Notre Dame Catholic Grammar School in Woolton, a school that pops up all over this book. Tina could match Tracy in the brains department but like me she sadly lacked confidence when it came to taking exams and she ended up attending St Margaret Clitherow's, a Secondary school near Sefton Park.

We had pets when I was a kid, mainly cats, do you remember the *'Year of the Cat"*, just thought I'd mention it because it's a good track, to chase after any invading mice seeking shelter in our house. When I was very small we had this ginger cat, funny enough I think said cat's name was 'Ginger' but I don't know what happened to him or her. Probably moved home, most cats in my experience choose their owner and I probably got on its nerves being a grabbing toddler.

When I was in Primary School we had this black and white cat called 'Tiddle's', she was my favourite pet and a cat never to be replaced and she would sit on my lap when I watched telly. At night Tiddle's would follow me upstairs and would curl up at the bottom of my bed and I would drift off to sleep listening to her purring and sometimes I would walk around the area with Tiddle's inside my coat with her head popping out every now and then to see what was happening.

Tiddle's was a very clever cat too, she would wee down the bath plughole and I know that sounds disgusting and unhygienic but the upshot was we must have saved heaps of money on smelly cat litter so not such a bad thing and thankfully she never did a number two inside, told you she was clever, I wonder if she could shut a door. Should have asked!

Tiddle's sadly died, she just left one day to ascend to feline heaven down some back entry and we replaced her with Ebony, not very original I know but this was because she was an all black cat. She wasn't the friendliest of cats either as I recall, I think I was about thirteen as she would lash out or scratch you and certainly not as clever as Tiddle's.

We had a budgie called 'Budgie Malone'; named after the film 'Bugsy Malone' that I had seen at the cinema, you know the kids gangster film with Jodi Foster and where all the characters are played by kids who fight with cream pies and drive around in pedal cars.

Anyway, Malone had a cage and this hung down from under the stairs attached to a hook and Ebony would sit hypnotised at the tasty dish perched up high and she would stare for hours and hours working out an attack strategy. Thinking about it we should have called her Sylvester and Malone should have been Tweetypie after the cartoon we often watched.

In a moment of lunacy Ebony would sometimes take a leap of faith and she would pounce and with her claws out she would hang from the bottom of the cage but would be thwarted by the iron bars and as a result Malone was never allowed out of her cage unless her cage was being cleaned which wasn't very often as we would forget she lived up above. Heaven knows how but Malone lived for years and died of old age in her free from flight sandpapered floored prison and looking back now this all sounds so heartless and cruel.

If pressed to choose a particular track from my early childhood then I would choose 'George Harrison's' song '*My Sweet Lord*'. I remember this with unbending fondness, it simply captivates me, the lyrics are plainly heaven sent and etched me thinks from Georges yearning heart. The song is painlessly easy for a child of the seventies to learn and sing along too and the track still evokes an emotion in me that catapults me back in time, to a time when life was far less complicated. I'd go as far as to say this is a modern masterpiece to match anything written by men in wigs with quills from centuries past and the most complete song I have ever heard. I simply love it, love it, love it even if George was later done for copyright infringement by some Motown girl band.

My Mum wasn't named after anyone in particular and she would sometimes joke that she never wore a T shirt with her name printed proudly on the front for fear that someone would misinterpret her name as a command. I know this is an awful joke but there you have it, a family joke that probably influenced my naff sense of humour and please feel free to use it if your name just so happens to be Pat but probably works best with girl Pat's unless you're a bloke who likes having his man boobs fondled!

My Mum and Dad met in a district called Speke in Liverpool, this is a large working class council estate on the outskirts of the city where I currently work. My Dad's family originally lived by Chevasse Park in town and my Dad has a black and white picture showing the area and the place looks like a scene from a Dickens' novel.

It must have felt like progress when my Dad's family then moved to the Dingle area, near to where the drummer Ringo's ancestral home and

near Wellington Road before moving to Speke under some council regeneration scheme to help families live in better accommodation.
I mention this as Dad attended Wellington Road Senior School and Dad would tell us stories about playing as a kid on a playground that was on the roof. We assumed he was fibbing and being a footy mad kid I would wonder what would happen if you kicked the ball over the fence, who would go for the ball should someone toe end it out of sight?
Couldn't be true surely. We would moan if we had to scale a fence to reclaim our ball but to descend several floors, now that's simply not on and no wonder Dad's not a gifted footy player as he probably spent half his time running up and down those stairs. Probably explains why he's 'fit as a butchers dog' though.
Soon after qualifying as a Social Worker in the mid nineties I got my first job with Liverpool and coincidently I worked out of Wellington Road School as it had by then become a social services district office. Before it became a school then a social services office I think it was a hospital when it was first built, so Dad proclaims.
It turns out Dad was telling the truth as I ended up taking Dad to his old stomping ground on a nostalgic tour of his old school. Sadly the roof playground was closed off and we didn't have a ball in any event but the classroom layout remained pretty much the same. My desk was in one of the many classrooms on the ground floor level, it still had that smell you get in school made from decades of bleach and polish. We still had the same noisy plumbing and our staff room for meetings was the Head Teacher's old office and Dad could remember ascending the steps to his room to be told off. You don't think that your parents were ever naughty at school do you?
As with a lot of historically significant buildings the school has since gone through yet another transformation and is now completely renovated into swanky flats with a penthouse instead of a play area and no doubt wondrous views across the Mersey of Camell Lairds and the Welsh Mountains opposite!
My Mum's family originated from Garston, near Speke as it happens and Mum would tell us that Nan would remark all snooty like that she wasn't from Liverpool but from Garston Village as if it was some small posh hamlet near Liverpool where riff raff lived in workhouses, in other words my Dad's family!
Nan's maiden name was McKenna and Mum said my Nan's Mum's name was Burke and she had four girls, Bridgette, also known as Sissy, Winnie, my Nan, Mary and Lilly who ended up living in Scotland. Mum said her maternal family, like so many scousers it seems, came from

Speke and when my Dad told her Betty was out she then left to meet with another girlfriend.

Mum was stood outside the pub and Dad, the old dog, sensed an opportunity and arrived a few minutes later; he casually suggested that they go in and have a drink together. Oh the charm, I wonder how long he had held his secret feelings for Mum?

They consumed several drinks it seems and Dad later walked Mum to the bus stop and he 'sealed' his destiny with a 'stolen kiss' from Mum, who was shocked as they had always been just friends. It may be of interest to know that Bobby Vinton sang the connecting track *'Sealed With a Kiss'*.

I was told Dad then asked Mum out on a date, they went to the Bluebell Pub on Prescott Road in Liverpool of all places, why I wonder as the pubs miles away from Speke and the rest, as they say, is history. Mum said they had a somewhat clandestine relationship for weeks, probably explains why the went the Bluebell and they would hide their feelings for each other from their pals, just like the track, *'Like Sister and Brother We'll Wait for Each Other'*.

This went on for a while and Mum plucked up the courage and eventually confessed to Betty who was shocked and Betty apparently warned Mum to treat her brother well as he was a 'nice lad' and he was and still is. Betty has passed on now and Ill come to that in a bit but if you're looking down on us Betty I think my Mum treated Dad well, most of the time that is!

One of the earliest childhood memories I have is when I was at my Nan and Granddad's flat on my Mum's side. My Granddad was called Tommy, a family name passed from generation to generation it seems and my Nan was called Winnie, short for Winifred. Before I forget Tommy was born on the 18th November 1911 and died 1st January 1990 and Winnie was born on the 2nd April 1915 and she died in 1979 on the 21st May.

My Mum's parents had left their tenement flat in Speke by the time I arrived and they lived in a high rise flat in Halewood off Mackets Lane and I remember crawling behind the couch and coming out the other end as if I'd been through some magical time travelling tunnel. I'd do this for hours amusing myself as the adults chatted and cooed over Tracy who, I'm surmising, would have been a baby at the time.

Senses are an important part of anyone's imagination don't you think and if I had to describe the flat using the sense of smell, I'd say musty old folk smell, mixed with a whiff of sterilised milk! Not an unpleasant odour I may add but a lived in smell as my Granddad was actually a bit of a stickler for cleaning up, unlike my Mum! Just thinking do the likes of Tescos or Asda sell steri milk anymore given we have fridges to keep milk fresh; I must check sometime and actually thinking about it my grandparents had this big old yellow fridge but old habits from a bygone age die hard I guess?

My Mum reckons I took my first steps at my Nan's. She recalls my Nan exclaiming; "I didn't know our David was walking Pat" to which my Mum, so I'm led to believe, said "neither did I", as I probably stumbled across the room between the adult knees reaching out to steady myself like toddlers do.

As for when this happened I'm guessing it must have been around the spring of 1967, a year or so after my birth, a time when man had embarked on space flights and a time when human's would soon take their first steps on the moon unless that is, you believe in conspiracy theories. There was me in my sodden nappy oblivious to such future wonderment's of course, taking my first steps on the earth, on my Nan's gold cord carpet! Really wish we had a cine camera back then like middle class families seem to have, how cool would that have been to see me rise and fall to the astonishment of my Nan but cameras were beyond my families reach.

So why, years later, did I miss the same opportunity as I regrettably never captured Adam or Kieran's first steps and the annoying thing is we do and did have a digital camera at my disposal and I should have kept it on permanent standby! Sorry kids and note to self; be more organised should I be a Dad again, which is, if you don't mind me saying, medically impossible if you get my drift as I had the snip after Adam was born so scrap that note. I am an official 'Jaffa', yes I am 'seedless' and I guess I just have to wait for the grandchildren! Brhhhh perish the thought!

I have many memories of Nan and Granddads but I don't recall my grandparents ever liking music as enthusiastically as my Mum but I'm sure they must have had a favourite old tune or two from the thirties, some swinging jazz number, who knows but I do remember my Granddad liking the melodic sound of the Carpenters. He had the album; it was 'Yesterday Once More', my Mum bought it for him and I do confess to humming the words to *'It's a Kind of Hush (All Over the World)'* on more than one occasion.

My Nan went blind not long after my first steps on this earth; in fact I think it was me and possibly Tracy whom she ever saw as Tina was born after us. She had diabetes you see amongst other illnesses and I'm told her blindness was caused by cataracts in her eyes and sadly for her I'm

told this condition can be operated on if she went blind today!
Mum used to attend the eye hospital just in case she inherits the same problem as she also has adult diabetes like my Nan! Hope I'm spared but I fear this could be a hereditary thing so any generations from my family reading this beware, you really should watch your diet and sugar intake. Uncrossing my fingers as you do let's head back to my memory. We would travel to Nan and Granddads on the Corpie's green number seventy eight bus most weekends leaving rows upon rows of soot entombed terraced houses where we lived, passing through suburban semi detached houses in leafy Gateacre and Woolton on the way.
I remember gazing out of the window in wonderment making steamy finger patterns on the window whilst fantasising that one day when I was older I would buy a house with a garden and a big drive to park my Ford car on just like the fortunate people who passed my gaze, who seemed happy and content in their clean suburban homes. I always wanted a Ford and life for those passing images seemed less of a struggle and something to aspire too. I got there in the end as it happens and my dream came true as I now have a semi detached in leafy South Liverpool and I've nearly paid my mortgage to boot before my fiftieth birthday, now lets add smug to the egotistical, lazy and bad at English list.
I wasn't very good at travelling as a kid and I would always suffer with motion sickness, still do, especially on boats, that makes me think of lovely relaxing track I've had the pleasure of hearing recently called *'Rollin Sea'* by this folk band called 'Retiva'. Anyway, like clockwork I would beg my Mum to take me off the bus the stop 'before' the one we should have disembarked. Mum would be fuming I can tell you, which is understandable of course and she would no doubt think I was doing this for attention as I would manage to keep my nausea under control till near the end of the ride.
I wasn't kidding Mum, honest, could have been a Pavlovian response for all I know but she would struggle off the bus with me yelping knowing she had to push the pram with my sisters in it for a mile or so and me strolling by her side puffing and panting.
She also knew the extra walk was a price worth paying as I would have been sick otherwise and Mum needed the exercise in any event, sorry Mum, as she wasn't the slimmest back then. Unlike now I might add, after attending the roller coaster ride called weight watchers for several years.
On the subject of fatty foods, I remember a fond routine we looked forward to as we approached Nan and Granddads. Mum would buy my sisters and me a cake each as a treat from Sayers at the concourse of

shops by the flats on occasion. One time and after much pondering at the row of cakes, nose pressed against the glass again, anticipating the taste explosion, I remember choosing a delicious cream slice, the kind that has lashings of artery clogging cream oozing from every side when pressed together with pink icing on top.

I asked Mum if I could demolish it as we climbed the steps to the flat's as it was far too appealing to a snotty nosed kid. I think I had inherited my Mum's 'temptation bug'.

Mum said no, be patient but she relented after a few Bart Simpson moans and huffs and I opened the greaseproof paper bag with my cream slice. I excitedly ran up the concrete stairs, as was the custom, taking two steps at a time but to my utter horror the cake slipped from my hand and it landed splodge like in excruciating slow motion on the dirty floor!

Being a kid I was so tempted to pick out the many pieces of grit and bits, as this was a real treat lost and I remember welling up! Clearly a painful memory as its there in the forefront of my mind which may explain why it remains and I probably had to watch my sisters eat their cake all smug like and I can't recall whether anyone cared to share their bounty with me? Probably did but I can't remember and I don't think I would have shared my cake if the tables had been turned, okay now add selfish.

Like I said my grandparents lived in a high rise concrete flat and I can't remember what floor my Nan and Granddad lived on, think it was the seventh but it was certainly high up and you could see for miles right across Woolton Golf Club and beyond.

On a sunny day you could see as far as the Welsh mountains through the cityscape haze and my blue nose Evertonian brethren. I'd look over the edge as people went about their ways below feeling the effects of vertigo whilst having a strange fascination with the madcap questions; what would it feel like to jump over the barrier, how long would it take for me to hit the floor, would Superman save me before I splatted.

I shall attempt to merge two disparaging tracks into this paragraph loosely related to the aforementioned lines; *'Oh Superman'*, by Laurie Anderson with the hypnotic minimalist half sung half spoken words and no track to do with flight would be complete without the brilliant *'Free as a Bird'* by the Beatles.

The irony being that I could see Woolton and other Beatles landmarks from Nan and Granddad's flat and it may be of interest to know that this track started out as a John Lennon demo tape made in 1977, re-mastered by the surviving Beatles with help from Geoff Lynn from ELO as the producer. Now I come to think of it I was probably looking out over the edge as a ten year old little boy when John was conceiving this brilliant track in the Dakota buildings thousands of miles away in New York. How spiritually cosmic and serendipish is that?

I remember running through the corridors and dodging the hundreds of Daddy long legs, I think they're called horse flies; that took sanctuary in the flats. They freaked me out I can tell you because they flew around aimlessly and stupidly like they were drunk on life, blind like my dear old Nan I guess, banging into the wall and me if I wasn't quick enough or careful!

After dodging the army of long kegs we'd get into the lift and I can still recall the smell, a mixture of urine and bleach I think! I'd run out as soon as the doors opened, not because of the smell but because I wanted to race my sisters to the front door that was always open, to be first was a game and we would shout, "It's us". Times have changed I suppose as old folk could leave their doors ajar back in the seventies in case people called and they couldn't hear as that was the hospitable thing to do. People were probably more trusting and less worried about thieves and in any case folk like my grandparents had nothing to steel so no point in modern security devices.

Whilst the adults talked I would sit and wonder what Nan was thinking in her dark world and how it must feel like for her being blind and almost totally reliant on my Granddad? Being the inquisitive type I tried to find out once and I tied my school tie round my eyes and it was really hard to walk for fear of hurting your shins so I didn't do this for very long. God knows how anyone is able to function in the world without seeing, probably the most important sense of all if you ask me!

Nan sadly passed away in 1979 when I was thirteen. This is a dark memory for me not just because Nan had died of course but how I dealt with being told. In my defence I was a moody teenager and we know teenagers are notoriously selfish and I was certainly no exception to the rule. I remember coming downstairs to get dressed for school and Mum was sitting at the table looking very upset smoking a Regal cigarette. I was useless and after being told the sad news I think I said something inappropriate like, 'I'm sorry Mum', gave her a hug and off I popped to school like nothing had really happened.

Mad really as I hated school by then, ill reveal more about that later dear reader and as for why I didn't take the day off even if I had liked school to mourn Nan and to support and help my Mum, is beyond me. But that's what life's like when you're a teenager isn't it, an array of complicated decisions, please say yes as I am still trying to make sense of this grim selfish episode in my life? I remember sitting in class switched off to what was happening around me which wasn't unusual and thinking how sad that I'd never see my Nan again and was she looking down on me from above whilst pondering as to whether her sight would have been restored by the all forgiving God.

This was actually the first time I had experienced the death of a close family member and it made me question mortality and the meaning of life, great early eighties film by the way by Monty Python.

To this day I don't do death very well, I don't like endings or goodbyes and I know no one really does do death very well but I'm useless with grief. Okay now add useless at grief to that list but to my eternal shame I never grieved properly or attended the funerals of any of my Grandparents who passed in quick succession through the eighties! Having done a bit of psychology I now realise that this is an important part of the grieving process and I should have made an effort but in my teenage way I just wanted to shut myself off from the world like an ostrich and what was happening around me in the hope I would wake up and every thing would be back to normal. Truth is I'm not at all impressed with my younger buried in the sand self and I'll allow you to call me selfish once again.

I took this lad called Graham, a fleeting schoolmate of mine, to my Granddads one rainy afternoon at the weekend! Granddad had this wooden moneybox he'd had for years and in it he kept old pennies, I think Mum's still got the box. Isn't it funny how my kids today have tax free ISA saving plans encouraging the next generation the value of saving for the future whereas I had a piggy bank, emptied frequently but I did have a post office account when I was twelve.

Anyway, we shared the contents of the box out whilst examining the smudged dates and royal figureheads caused by years of sweaty defacing fingers. Granddad said we could take them home to keep and to my annoyance Graham spotted the oldest one, dated 1803! I protested that first dabs were with me as the pennies were a family heirloom but Graham wouldn't part and Granddad didn't intercede either. Oh well what will be will be I guess but those pennies got me into coin collecting which I'll talk about later and can I suggest you listen to a lovely track about someone writing a book coincidently and giving it to a friend called *'Copper Coin'* by the magnificent 'Mark Olson!'

When I was sixteen, I can say that with some confidence as I was on a Youth Training Scheme or YTS as it became known and if my maths is right it must have been around 1983. I'll talk more about my first job in the penultimate chapter to this book but YTS's were basically slave labour and the Conservatives attempts to keep us inner city kids occupied; to discourage mischief whilst at the same time allowing employers to line their greedy pockets by exploiting the nations youth to do work for £25. I know we're talking decades ago but still an ungenerous sum!

The reason why I mention this is because of my Great Uncle George. Hope this all makes sense but Great Granddad Tommy Kearns was killed during the First World War leaving his wife Emily and four children. Emily's maiden name was Freeman and the children were called Billy, Tommy, who was my Granddad, Ethel and George.

It must have been really hard for Emily, this is an era before Bevan's welfare state and she must have struggled as a single parent so she ended up meeting a bloke called Billy Leigh. Together they had a son and his name was Arthur and the family including Granddad and his siblings lived on Raglan Street before moving to Clarence Grove in Garston.

Sadly Emily died not long after having Arthur so my Granddad and his full siblings became destitute, they were orphaned children and Mum said they then lived a transient childhood between various relatives who also lived in Garston. Arthur stayed with his Dad Billy.

It must have been a devastating blow to Granddad and his siblings loosing your parents and the security that naturally comes with being part of a family and if that wasn't bad enough my Granddad also had polio as a kid leaving one leg shorter than the other.

Mum said George ended up becoming a delinquent child which isn't surprising and he was sent to Borstal for his many misdemeanours. When he was fourteen the Government came up with a forced deportation policy resulting in thousands of children emigrating to distant lands to become part of the Commonwealth to stamp a sense of 'Britishness' in the colonies I assume. George was sent to Canada and some years later he came back to the United Kingdom as a young adult when he served in the Canadian Air Force but this was a brief visit and the last time Granddad had seen his brother.

Now, my Mum's half cousin, Arthur, met his wife Dot, a Scottish lady whilst serving in the Royal Navy. Arthur and Dot had two sons, Barry and Ronnie and they moved to Australia under yet another scheme, the ten-pound ticket scheme I think it was called, to encourage families to emigrate, probably for the same reason. Barry followed in his Dad's footsteps it seems and he joined the Australian Navy, whilst Ronnie became the Director of Education in Tasmania, I wonder if he saw any devils?

Anyway Arthur traced George through the Salvation Army and he telephoned my Granddad to tell him the good news. Now there's a thought, if Arthur was looking for George today he might have began his search by typing George Kearns into Google or other search engines. Might have been quicker, who knows he might have even had a Facebook account?

George eventually spoke with his only surviving sibling, my Granddad and he insisted on visiting his hometown to meet up with his brother after forty years of not seeing each other. Now I'm not sure how but the Daily Mirror Paper got wind of this and they sent a reporter and a photographer to my Granddads flat passing the long legs en route I guess, wonder if they succumbed to the lure of Sayers and did they buy a cake? So many questions?

We were all there and I remember having my picture taken with the rest of my family and George in my YTS donkey jacket and wedge hair cut as was fashionable at the time. I was at the back as I had sprouted to a skinny six foot by then and we made the papers centre pages the next day, my families claim to fame and Mum still has the cut out somewhere in her loft!

Sadly George died within days of meeting his brother, he didn't look at all well and we later discovered that his poor wife had begged him not to travel, as she feared the worst. Mum said Granddad had to phone Doreen, our neighbour, because we didn't have a phone at the time, to say he had found poor George dead in bed and he hadn't even unpacked his suitcase.

The desire to meet with his long lost brother before ascending the celestial stairway was too much of a pull for dear old George and he simply had to travel to his home town of Liverpool one last time to say goodbye. I felt so sorry for his wife and I remember all the fuss Uncle Tommy had to go through in re-patronising George to his family in Canada and questions upon questions about whether he should have travelled. We felt very guilty.

Strange thing this but George had one daughter like my Grandparents and her name was the same as my Mum's, Patricia Anne Kearns, I wonder if she wore a T shirt with her name on it? Mum kept in touch with her namesake for a few years but as with most families it seems they have since drifted apart. She had problems with her ex husband and at one point was planning on escaping to Liverpool! The irony's not lost on me, someone thinking of returning to Liverpool from the new world and I wonder what George and Tommy would say about that from above.

Just before I end this segment about George, Mum said his wife was his second wife as he had been married before and he told Granddad that he had three sons whom my Mum has never met but we presume they live in Canada, if indeed they are still alive.

My Granddad's sister, Ethel, married a man from Malta called Joe Tubbs and they had two children Pam and Joe. Pam keeps in touch with my Mum and she lives in Luton and she's interested in getting in touch with me as she has researched the family tree. Mum had a close relationship with her cousin Joe as they were of a similar age and Joe ended up being a very successful businessman accustomed to travelling the globe. Joe left Liverpool when he became an adult, that emigration gene strikes once more, what were they all escaping from I wonder, to make his fortune in engineering.

Mum said he invented and patented a videophone and that's how he made his money but I'm not sure whether this is an exaggeration but cool thought nonetheless. Anyhow, Joe was clever, he could play the piano, see a city full of musical talent and Mum said although she and Joe were close as kids he wasn't meant to live in Garston, his place of birth; he was destined for bigger things in another world. Joe would travel the world on business and would sometimes visit us with dollar bills and other Yankee stuff, by then he had settled in Canada before moving to the States with his wife and family. When in Liverpool he always made it his business to visit Granddad, his favourite uncle.

In 1995 his son, Chris, I think he's now a DJ in the States, carried on this tradition and visited us when he was travelling across Europe on a gap year. In fact Joe and his grandson, nice lad called Ryan, visited Liverpool in May 2012 and we all went for a family meal together.

I spoke with Joe and he's a charming spritely seventy one year old with an inner jest for life befitting of a younger man and I asked him if home was here or the States. Joe said in his American twang 'the States'. Joe said my granddad was a mentor to him as a youngster more so than his own father and when my granddad died in 1991 Joe had to board Concord otherwise he would have missed the funeral. Some measure of how my granddad influenced people and how much he was respected and I too looked up to him as a child.

Joe said he lives in Virginia in a town in the middle of nowhere called Lynchburg and he invited us over to stay. Who knows one day perhaps but this got me thinking about how different in many aspects he was to me and my family but we shared a family lineage that binds us together in a blood related way. We spoke and looked differently, we were from different cultures and no doubt had differently values but family ties us across the miles, across the ocean and people feel grounded knowing they have a past.

And with that back to the past. Granddads older brother, Billy married a woman called Ivy and they had four children; he was a significant member of the Blue Union on the docks in Gartson. Lawrence was an architect and now deceased, Jimmy is also deceased, Billy junior joined the Navy and Ivy still lives in the same house in Garston off St Mary's Road.

At the same meal with Joe I also met my Mum's cousin Ivy who I hadn't seen for years and her daughter, Christine was there too with her daughter Catherine and they now live in Hale in Cheshire. I remember attending Christine's wedding when I was about thirteen at the Orange Lodge Hall in Garston and Christine said this was in 1979. I told her that I remember wearing a yellow Fred parry T-shirt with matching brown jumper and bronze coloured jumbo cords, funny how trivial things like that stick in my mind and the strange thing is she works at Tesco's on the till and if I was ever passing her way in rural Hale, I wouldn't have had the foggiest idea that we are related?

Like I said before Mum has a brother and it's worth mentioning Tommy at this point, named after his Dad. Mum and Tommy did have a little sister called Anne but sadly Anne died when she was three and Mum said her Mum lost many babies. Mum had miscarried three babies herself and I could always sense that Mum had never really gotten over the death of Anne, which isn't surprising. How awful that must that have been to loose someone so close when only a child but I guess infant mortality was higher in the fifties, this must have been very upsetting time for my family.

Tommy is thirteen years younger than my Mum and he would sometimes sleep at our house when he was on a night out in Liverpool. One Sunday morning I got up to play footy, you can read more about my footy talents when I talk about school and I had to navigate around and over Tommy and his new girlfriend who were sleeping on the floor under a blanket on cushions.

Tommy later married this girlfriend and when he first introduced me to his future wife, I swear he said here's 'teacher' and for months I thought she taught kids as she did indeed look like a typical teacher. My hearing, her name is Leticia and she's a lovely woman but she still looks like she would be comfortable standing in front of a chalkboard!

Tommy's a staunch Liverpool supporter and Leticia originates from Manchester of all places, a bit of a mixed marriage thing going on there and for years Tommy's has had to endure friendly banter from Leticia's side of the family. Leticia has two daughters to a previous marriage, Rebecca and Michaela and I first met them when they were little girls in

Runcorn where Leticia and Tommy lived. Together they had Lucy and there is no doubting she is has the Kearns gene running through her body, as she is uncannily just like my Mum in the looks and personality department and full of life. The girls are all married and they have several children between them but I couldn't begin to name them all, see the retention of names is something I am not very good at although I know Lucy has a daughter called Evie.

Before the 'teacher' Tommy lived in Kirkby with his then wife, I think her name was Maureen and she had long dark brown hair and looked like a throw back to the sixties, a real life hippy with big thighs as I recall! This marriage didn't last very long, don't know why, that's Tommy's business of course but from the divorce we got a fancy glass bookshelf and a matching glass table when they split up.

Months later however I ended up smashing said table when I tried walking across it playing keep the kettle boiling, one of my many house games I discuss elsewhere!

Tommy's always been the best kind of Uncle a kid could have but I wouldn't exactly say I looked up to him, not in the physical sense that is and I say this because I quickly grew taller than Tommy by some inches. Tommy would struggle with his weight when he got older and for years Mum would warn me to watch my diet or I'd end up like Tommy, she could talk, as I would devour everything in sight although I would always remain slim no matter how calorie enriched my diet was!

This is a tad unfair actually as Tommy's content with his weight as far as I know however the same could not be said for his short legs. Tommy would always bemoan to me that he wished he'd gotten my Granddads long legs and not Nan's as she was only just over five foot tall.

Sorry Tommy them are the genetic deals in life and I'm sorry you never took after your Dad in stature but if its any consolation you took after Granddad in name and in character though. Just like you he was a top bloke, very intelligent as I recall and he never had an unkind word to say about anyone.

Who needs long legs anyway unless you're a shelf stacker or goalie, which is why granddad was reputedly very good between the posts, and I followed his footsteps by becoming s decent goalie myself and I'll tell you more about that later? Indeed Granddad had large hands as I recall and he could play the piano but sadly I never had the pleasure of hearing him play.

I was actually average in the height department through my primary school years but it was when I was about fourteen that I began to grow taller by the week like I had slept in a grow bag, capping at six foot one when I was about sixteen. My height change was very dramatic and my Mum took me to this clinic on Hartington Road for tests.

I took all my clothes off down to my Y fronts and once disrobed I was then ushered into an adjacent room for a thorough examination. Now lets pause and picture the scene, I am a very body conscious skinny pubescent teenager with the onset of hairy parts, so I walk in naturally cupping my genitals but to my horror I was confronted by a dozen or so examining eyes. They were mainly female nurses and that made it worse and they looked me up and down from head to toe as if I was some cattle at the market and I felt violated, he doctor should have asked.

I quickly got dressed when they were done with staring at my body and I hadn't paid much attention because I was in shock but my Mum later told me that the doctor was worried about the curvature of my spine and my right shoulder seemingly slopes lower than my left.

I believe I had childhood scoliosis, not too severe to cause me discomfort over the years or to require treatment but I think this is the reason why I have never been able to touch my toes. I mention all this because I've just been diagnosed with scoliosis and degenerative arthritis in my back probably caused by years of playing badminton. The gel like substance between my vertebrae has thinned causing me back pain and I am hoping it wont get worse.

Moving on let me now tell you more about my Dad's family. Dad's Mum was called Florence May, her maiden name was Opie and she was born on the 14th September 1913 and his Dad was called Frank and he was born on the 16th February 1907. Nan died 8th March 1985 and Granddad died 9th September 1989. Dad's Granddad on the Griffith side, so my great Granddad was called Ralph Peter and he was born 1st October 1876 and Dad's Nan was Elizabeth Trevor and she was born in 1871. Dad's Grandfather on his mother's side was Joseph Barnes Opie and he was born 1875 and died in 1945, Dad's Nan on his mother's side was a lady called Sarah Jane Hamlin born in 1874 and died in 1940. I mention all this just in case you're a distant relative researching my family tree.

Dad had several siblings. From the top down you had Frank junior, Betty, Dad, Ralph and Anne. I remember Frank being a drinker, he led a chequered life it seems and I believe he had several kids and eventually lived in Kirkby.

We've lost touch with Frank, I couldn't tell you if he's still '*Alive and Kicking*', a great anthemic track by Simple Minds by the way, but I remember his daughter Donna staying with us when we were kids, she was a few years older than me. I think life at our house was marginally better than life with her Mum and Dad, I think she must have had it

really tough but she knew she felt safe living with my family.
Betty had Paul and Lynn and they lived in Dovecot. Betty sadly died in 2010 like I said before, after suffering with Alzheimer's disease for a few years. She was in a nursing home and her illness got that bad she didn't recognise my Mum and Dad when they visited her. Mum found this very upsetting, as she had lost 'her Betty' by then and I think they decided not to visit her wishing to remember Betty as a very funny, lovely and caring person. Paul and Lynn are very close and neither has children.

Anne has two children, Lisa and Chris, to different fathers but that's not to suggest she was or is some kind of 'slapper', far from it Anne's a principled and well respected member of the community.

Lisa's father was a rogue I believe, I don't think I ever met him and Lisa now lives with her partner and she has one child and a new-born baby. Chris has also recently had a baby to his girlfriend and her name is Ava and we recently attended her Christening. Anne still lives in Speke with Peter her partner of many years; Chris's Dad and they live round the corner from where my Mum and Dad live, which is good as I know Dad's very close to Anne.

When I was eleven we went to live with Ann when my Mum was in hospital and I'll refer to the reasons why under my primary school chapter. Like Ann, Ralph never left Speke and he lived with my Nan and Granddad for most of his life and Dad said he was often sent to his room. Ralph has died now and he was a lovely man as I recall and Dad said he started having emotional difficulties after being jilted by his first love and this resulted in him acting very bizarrely.

Ralph suffered with depression and he ended up having moderate mental health problems for the rest of his life and he was hospitalised on occasions in Rainhill. Dad said he would sometimes visit his brother and he was shocked by the patient's behaviour on the ward and Ralph had even endured the barbaric electro shock treatment. Anne was very close to Ralph and she would support and watch over him throughout his life and she became his carer. Anne's a star sent from heaven.

Nan and Granddad lived on Clough Road, which, somewhat paradoxically, is the same road where my Mum and Dad currently live and I'll talk more about how and why they left my spiritual home in a bit. The house was a council house and Granddad loved gardening. He was always out in the garden whenever we called up, just like my Dad, which is why he had dark creased suntanned skin, just like Dad as it happens but so far, less creases.

As for my Nan she looked like a stereotypical Native American squaw as she was dark skinned too and would wear her long grey hair tied back. I say this because Nan's maiden name was 'Opie' and Dad grew up believing we descended from Native Americans and this story was then reiterated to us as kids.

My Dad remembers going to his Granddads as a child and he remembers seeing all kinds of Indian artefacts and headdresses in his house brought by the family when they moved from the States to Liverpool and he believed them to be genuine. Me and my Dad and his siblings have dark features like his parents and we have dark eyes, sallow skin and we therefore believed that Nan's maiden name confirmed once and for all that we were from Native American ancestral stock. I can't grow a decent beard either and I read somewhere that some tribes could grow some facial hair but not a full beard just like me.

As an adult I became more interested in this and some years back I emailed the Hopei tribe believing the name came from their tribe and had been anglicised over time. They sent me a very nice email telling me this was probably untrue as most tribal members rarely leave the tribe or the area of their birth but I wasn't convinced, as I felt an affiliation by then, an attachment to an identity I craved.

That was to all end as we then discovered that the name Opie originates from a small area of Cornwall and indeed there's a famous artist who bears this name. Could the celebrated 'John Opie' be related to my family, after all I did get a grade C in my art O'Level?

Tracy and my Dad have more information on this as they did a bit of research into the families past when my Dad retired from the building trade and they learnt that the Opie family lived in Cornwall but then travelled to America searching for work we believe, so some truth in the story and they arrived in New York where they lived for a few years. They were stonemasons by trade and worked in a quarry in Cornwall and they came to Liverpool via New York looking for work and actually worked on the Anglican Cathedral.

It may be of interest to know that this is the largest Anglican Cathedral in the World and work first started in 1904 so I'm surmising they disembarked in my City at the turn of the century.

Liverpool is of course famed for having two Cathedrals, the Catholic one is affectionately known as 'Paddy's Wigwam, which, thinking out loud, would have been a more appropriate building for my paternal ancestors to have worked on!

As a kid some other kids would call me the N word, which I really hate so I won't even write it down in this book and they would say I wasn't white like them. Typical of me but rather than laugh off these ridiculous comments I would take them to heart as I wanted to belong and I did begin to wonder why I was darker than my mates, like most kids I hated being different. Some years later in the eighties when the fashion was to have an all over St Tropez golden tan, I came to realise that being dark was an advantage when it came to looking hip and cool, so one in the eye for all you racist dickheads who ridiculed me. Now calm down Dave.

Having believed I was dark skinned due to my family coming from a Native American background I have to say I was a disappointed to find out that this wasn't true as I had romantic images of me riding bare back across the plains patting my hand against my mouth to make the Indian chant we did as kids whilst chasing buffalo with a spear.

Just goes to show you though unless stories are written down they can become confused and embellished a bit which I guess is one of the reasons why I'm happily tapping away now so as my kids know the truth. Truth, as far as I know it that is?

We would visit Nan and Granddad on occasion but not as much as we visited my Mum's parents. Not sure why but it could have had something to do with having to catch two busses to Speke from Edge Hill and therefore two chances of me being sick! Dad told me recently that he would save money by making us walk to Ullet Road to catch the number eighty bus, which was a bit of a walk, and then a further long walk to Nan and Grandddads house when we got to Speke. That's Dad for you always thinking about how to save money and how to keep us fit!

Talking of long walks, a much-loved day out for my family and me was a trip to New Brighton on the Ferry across the Mersey. We would board at the Pier Head jumping across the creaking wooden gangway to find our bench upstairs so as we could look at the Liver Buildings as we sailed away and I remember watching the seagulls dipping in and out of the water as it frothed up in the Ferry's wake. We would then disembark at Seacombe with the throngs of fellow scousers looking forward to a day out and we would walk up this long tunnel to a ticket collector at the top.

Turning right 'the throng' would begin the long and arduous walk to New Brighton that seemed to go on and on and annoyingly I believe the Ferry once docked at New Brighton.

When we arrived Mum and Dad would buy us fish and chips and we would sit on the beach watching the tide hit the sand and we would go for a paddle. There was an inside fun fair and Mum and Dad would let

38 David Griffith

me and my sisters have a go on the dodgems and the haunted house and I can still hear the hooters and bells that randomly sounded out, pure magic and I loved the place.

Outside you had 'Perch Rock' which I'll talk about later and I remember being frozen with fear at the top of the 'Big Wheel'. My most cherished memory though was the superb Helter Skelter and memories of descending down the spiralling slide on the outside of this huge tower on straw mats hoping to catch up with my sisters to give them a thud in the back with my stocking feet. To then excitedly run up the internal stairs and to do it all again.

What absolute joy and I must heap buckets of praise in the direction of the Beatles for their track *'Helter Skelter'* released in 1968, apparently written by Paul McCartney in response to critics accusing him of being a one trick pony ballad writer. He wanted to prove he could write a more raunchy gritty song and if this was an assignment I think he passed with distinction.

Like most scousers our summer holidays, when Mum and Dad could afford it, were spent in caravans in North Wales when I was a kid and I vaguely remember spending a week in this tiny caravan with Mum and Dad when I was a toddler.

I also remember one year meeting up with aunty Betty, uncle Harry and my cousins Paul and Lynn and we stayed in a caravan in Rhyll. Dad had an old red Hillman Hunter car with a cracked window, accidently broken by my mate Grant on the day we got the car.

I remember running home after evening mass knowing the car was outside my house and I knocked at Grants house, as I wanted to boast about our good fortune. We never had much back then so a bit of gloating was acceptable and none of my mates parents had a car besides Jeanette's who I mention in a bit. Grant and me twiddled with the various levers taking turns to sit behind the wheel imagining we were driving at Silverstone. We then sat in the back and Grant lifted a shelf and in doing so this bolt that we hadn't spotted scraped across the window casing the crack. We sat there shocked, I was mortified and good enough Mum and Dad never gave me a good hiding, they realised it had been an accident but I felt so guilty.

I have to say the Hillman was bought for fifty pounds borrowed from my Granddad so it was a bit of a banger and I remember the cost as Mum made me cycle to my Granddads with my mates to pick up the money and I remember taking a detour away from Woolton Golf Club as we spotted this gang clambering over a wall and we feared they were after us knowing we were carrying cash. They were probably evading the green keeper!

Dad learnt to drive when he worked as a bread deliveryman before he settled down with my Mum. I don't recall many people owning a car in our street as this was seen as a luxury but I recall my Dad having at least three cars in total, when he was working that is. They were mainly rust buckets. In addition to the Hillman we had two sky blue Vauxhall Viva cars at different times, bought from some mechanic called 'Totty', and I remember the first one being stolen and then looking around the area trying to spot it. This car was never seen again, probably burnt out on some waste ground.

Thinking of cars, here's two tracks to salivate over, firstly we have the terrific road rage inspired *'Cars'*, which was Gary Numan's attempt to record a more chart friendly single. Then we have *'The Sounds of the Suburbs'* by the Members' and wondrous lyrics about washing cars and cooking Sunday dinner. A superb track in my view but thinking about it we were more 'Sound of the urbans', Mum would cook Sunday dinner as was customary, boiling repugnant cabbage most of the time but Dad would more likely be fixing a smashed window than buffing up his car. In fact the onset of soapy suds would have resulted in Dad's cars falling apart as the rust was the thing that kept them together! Anyway back to one such car, the Hillman. We took my cousin Lisa away with us on holiday and Lisa took one look at the car, folded her arms in disgust and said 'I'm not going anywhere in that' and she sulked off down the road. We sat in the car thinking hurry up you spoilt brat whilst poor old Mum and Dad had to persuade Lisa to stop being silly. She eventually relented and full to the brim with holiday clothes and rashes of bacon and other food supplies we headed off to the Birkenhead Tunnel to make our way to Sunny Rhyll. Rhyll was always sunny back then.

Lisa's negativity must have rubbed off on Dad's rusty car though as it broke down several hundred yards after leaving home on Smithdown Road. The engine was in the back and we could see smoke bellowing out from underneath the suitcases probably cooking the bacon and Dad had to pull over. Or was he wearing a cardigan? 'Totty' fixed the car, I think Dad ran round to his garage but we left with trepidation fearing we'd never get through the tunnel but thankfully we did.

Just so happens my on and off girlfriend from when I was a kid, Jeanette and her family were also going on holiday to North Wales. For some reason I think of the track *'That's the Way I like It'* by KC and the Sunshine Band, when I think of Jeanette for no apparent reason other than I remember my mates and me listening to this song being played on

a tape recorder in her loft. Her Dad was quite handy with wood and he had done a cheap loft conversion and I certainly did like it, the conversion that is, although that was to change some years later so keep reading!
Anyway where was I, oh yes, I knew they were leaving a few hours after us and her Dad had a beige three-wheeler Robin Reliant. Our journey took an eternity as we navigated through villages and towns and I remember descending down this steep Welsh meandering road and as we stopped at the junction praying the breaks would work, who should drive by but Jeanette and her family. I hid in shame but hoping we'd bump into her during the holiday but sadly we didn't and my dreams of my first holiday romances faded away.
Anyhow and in spite of the dubious start and Lisa's grumbles we did make it in one piece and we did have a wonderful time in Rhyll. The caravan was kitted out with all the things we had at home but newer and we had a swing park nearby. I remember Paul, who was a year or so older than me, sliding down the slide and catching a coin in his side pocket and ripping his trousers.
Each day Mum and Dad would give me a pound and I knew this had to last me all day. Full of independent freedom Paul and me would make our way over a railway bridge to the fair most of the time; attracted by the glitzy lights and supplementary pumping music inviting us to come and find out what was happening over the tracks.
Talking of tracks, the tracks that reminds me of this holiday is Bony M's song *'Ma Baker'* and I now know this was released in 1977 so I must have been eleven. I also remember Donna Summers suggestive track *'Love to Love You Baby'* but having no idea that it was so sexually explicit. I heard recently that Donna has died of cancer.
We would jump off and on various rides and I remember an old wooden and very rickety rollercoaster as being very fast and scary. The fair had the normal dodgem cars and the waltzes' but my favourite was this strange attraction called 'the Rotter'. The first time we had a go I recall Paul and me standing in a circular room and wondering what would happen next and some greasy bloke from up above in cut down denims shouted down at us, 'stand next to the wall kids'.
Next thing the room started to spin faster and faster and the floor fell away from our feet but somehow we stayed glued to the wall and I realise this is centrifugal force but to a young kid this was so amazing and we felt like Spiderman chasing the Green Goblin.
On other days we would wander down to the beach avoiding the kiss me quick hats and we would spend our pennies in the arcade machine

on the front. The place would be heaving of people on holiday, mainly scousers; Paul and me would try and dislodge the many-perched two pence pieces hanging over the edge and sometimes you won but most of the time you left with less money. We would loiter and watch over other punters shoulders trying to second-guess the machine that would give the next big pay out and jump in as soon as they moved on. Oh the fun I hear you mutter.

I remember Rhyll as being the place where I first leant to roller-skate. Paul and me got talking to these local girls in the arcade and they suggested we meet up the next day at the open-air rink over the road. Suppose it was my first proper date and we got there early to practice as neither of us had any desire to look like a 'divvy' which is scouse for stupid. You never wished to appear a 'div'!

Before too long and after a few scrapes, we became proficient enough to do a whole circuit without falling over and I can't remember if we impressed our new found female friends who arrived later but we had a good day nonetheless, otherwise I wouldn't have remembered all of this. I do recall holding 'my girls' hand not to steady myself but because this felt like a thrill and I wonder whatever happened to them, I cant remember their names or how they looked and when I try and recall the memory in more detail all I can conjure up is a feint outline of two girls wearing flared jeans and with dark bobbed hair.

I've been away with my Mum and Dad since but our last 'family holiday' was when Mum and Dad scraped together enough money to pay for a week's holiday to Butlins in Pwellhi in North Wales, another popular holiday destination for scousers.

We caught a coach from town and I was aged seventeen by then and thinking I was all grown up, I had pestered Mum for a chalet of my own and I ended up having my own room next door. Mum said this cost a lot of money, money she didn't really have!

I was on my own but this didn't stop me going to the onsite club and I remember becoming friendly with these charming girls from Chepstow in South Wales. This didn't escalate to 'train travelling romance', not for the want of trying I might add but I would write to them for a few months after the holiday.

I also remember kissing this scouse girl on top of a child's slide in the early hours of the morning and she tried to persuade me stay a few days and 'bunk' in her chalet rather than return home the next day. The raging hormones in me made me contemplate this but I knew I would have no way of getting home and thought better not, Mum would have been furious.

Mum remembers this holiday and she will often talk about passing me bacon butties through my window, as I was often too hung over to get up for breakfast. Mum said by the end of the holiday she had no more money left in her purse and she said I ended up buying dinner on the way home for the family as I had a few pounds left over. The least I could do all things considered.

When we got home Dad's Irish mate, Joe told Dad that he had been finished up from his 'cash in hand' labouring job and once again *'A Hard Rains A Gonna Fall'* on our family, a protest track about the Cuban missile crises in the sixties by Bob Dylan, later covered by Bryan Ferry and 'belts' were once again tightened.

Chapter Three

In My Liverpool Home…

In writing this book I come to realise that I was greatly aided by modern gizmos and technology that probably featured on the gadget show at some point and that got me thinking about how the world has changed beyond recognition to what it was like when I was a kid and who knows what the future will look like and the continual impact technology will have on our lives.
At the moment I'm more fascinated with the past particularly the comparisons and differences between the decades and I can only speak from personal experience, I confess to having a 'scouse centric' view of the World but this view, my eccentricity was clearly shaped by my childhood experiences and what was happening around me.
I'm very proud of the fact that I originate from Liverpool you see, I think that's a tad obvious and for those of you unfamiliar with Liverpool don't believe the hype, were not scroungers, were not thieves, well sometimes perhaps, were not football hooligans and we don't all don shady perms and seventies moustaches or play music but scousers are largely and fiercely proud of our city, its people, its achievements and its multi cultural roots.
So there I was looking at some grainy pictures of skinny me when I was a kid stored in this battered looking photo album that Mum has to decide what picture to use on the cover of this book. Looking at the pictures I had a prodigious sense of nostalgia tinged with a degree of wistfulness but I realised I was interested in what I looked like of course, how my face and body has changed over time but I'd also look past me beaming at the camera and I'd spot houses, cars and people in the background, people I had known.
The buildings looked so different to now, original brickwork before being painted, wooden framed windows and paint flaking windowsills. The clothes looked tatty too and, well, retro I guess and as for the cars, they were up to date at the time of course but the shape and the size of them seem to come from a far less sophisticated, drab and bulky era.

This was the seventies and I'd say I was a typical seventies inner city kid and therefore most of this book is set in this era but as you will discover large chunks of these memories spill into the eighties.

For me this was a period of time that was defined by ch ch ch *'Changes'* as Bowie would beautifully warble and in every aspect of our lives but particularly in music and fashion, political unrest and huge changes to how we lived.

In fact Bowie embodied the social and cultural transformation that was rife at the time and boundaries were pushed further when *'Ziggy Stardust'* hit the charts. An alien from above had descended; an alien in a dress and it wasn't just his music that appealed to the youth of the day but Bowie's overall chameleon image and attitude.

Bowie proved you were free to change your hair, your style and even your name, not to mention his declaration that he was bi sexual and this coming only a few years after the decriminalisation of homosexual acts. I always thought he was slightly bizarre as I was a bit too young to appreciate his artistry at the time but I realise now how he was very courageous and clearly a trailblazer.

I do recall the decade with fondness and like I said with a tint of nostalgia but in truth the seventies were a struggle at times, partly due to the power struggle that gripped the nation and the uncertainty that came with factories closing down up and down the country.

We never knew it was a struggle of course as most people were in the same boat so to speak and in any event through adversity came opportunity and I guess that's the essence of this book as life goes on and on and on. Bit like me, I hear you mutter.

I've often day dreamed about time travel, who hasn't, Dr Who being a favourite telly programme I'd watch as a kid and I am reminded of the classic kids knock knock joke. For those of you from planet Zogg here goes. 'Knock knock, whose there, Dr! Dr Who! Exactly!' So funny to a child's ear.

By the way Tom Baker will always be the best Dr as far as I'm concerned as he was 'alive' when I was a kid, although Mat Smith, the latest Dr, has something about him. If the kids and me were able to hitch a ride in the Dr's Tardis, or as Iggy Pop would say, to become a *'Passenger'*, to when I was a kid, would they cope or survive without all the modern stuff they have become accustomed too?

They'd see cars that were manly petrol blue and rusty, cobbled uneven streets and rows upon rows of cramped terraced houses and people, mainly women I cautiously add, standing on doorsteps talking about this and that, what did Mum's talk about back then?

People had houses to retreat too but as I recall they communicated with neighbours and they seemed more interested in what was going on beyond their front door and people seemed more community orientated, friendlier and more hospitable back when I was a kid.
They'd smell chips, boiling cabbage sometimes and dust from all the houses that were being demolished making way for new council estates or ring roads. They'd feel odd in their skinny jeans when everyone was wearing flares and tight checked buttoned at the collar shirts and they'd stand out. I can visualise people passing them by and enquiring with frowned and inquisitive faces, 'what e dem kids from France doin over ere'. I'm speculating they would look so out of place if not a little continental.
Everything evolves with time of course, as do technological advances and I guess the same could be said if I pushed the Dr aside and cranked the wrong lever in the Tardis and found myself in the fifties when my Mum and Dad were teenagers. I remember reading somewhere that the concept of teenagers is actually a modern phenomenon and defines the passage from childhood to adulthood. I think this is so true, prior to my Mum and Dad's generation children became adults with no in between bit and were sent off to work in the factories when they hit their teens. They seemingly dressed like their parents and had the same tastes and wants and it all looked very grey back then but I think that's because colour telly was some years off.
Anyhow, such is the pace of life in this so called modern society I believe the changes would be felt to a lesser extent as I think the social and cultural differences are far greater and more polarised when comparing now with the seventies to that of the seventies to the fifties. Hope that makes sense, I could be wrong as I wasn't there of course, the Dr never arrived you see, but what I'm trying to say is that things we take for granted today will seem old hat in a matter of years as opposed to decades.
You buy a new flat screen telly for example and you know Sony, Samsung, Panasonic, Toshiba, LG and other techno companies from distant lands would have made an even better telly waiting to unleash it, to astound the world and you will try and resist but you know you will have to upgrade in a few years if it hasn't gone bust beforehand.
We live in a consumer led throwaway society now unlike in the seventies and I'm convinced gadgets are made with a limited shelf life to force you to replace them before you've even had time to dispose of the bloody packaging. Back when I was a kid, stuff lasted for years and we only had the likes of K Tell or Ronco to woo us with the latest gadgetry.

I watched a documentary on the telly recently and I learnt that Britain's first party with green credentials, 'The Peoples Party', first came to prominence in 1973. We've become accustomed to recycling it would seem but in the frugal seventies ordinary families were warned that the fragile ecology of spaceship earth was doomed if we continued to exploit it's natural riches, so nothings changed there then.
Living off the land became popular as a result and the 'Good Life' on telly epitomised those who opted out of the rat race to embrace a life of self-efficiency, a life of knitted jumpers and organic food, a life of recycling.
This was mainly the life style choice of middle class families with gardens of course who had a little put aside but my family did their bit to lesson the families outgoings when we got an allotment at the back of our house and I'll talk more about that later dear reader.
Remember the rat like 'Womble's' on telly and their relentless pursuit of gathering stuff from the common long before recycling became popular. Visionaries it seems but when I think about it we were already schooled in the 'waste not want not' attitude you see today. We returned milk bottles and beer bottles to the shop for example and the shop sent them back to the plant to be washed, sterilised and refilled, so it could use the same bottles over and over again. Parents would wash baby's nappies because they didn't have the throwaway kind and we tended to dry clothes on a line after going through a mangle, not in some energy-guzzling machine.
I didn't because I was the only boy in the family and the eldest but kid's got hand-me-down clothes from their brothers or sisters without a second thought as to whether said garment was still in fashion and if you did object Mum just told you it would be fashionable again so wear it!
We drank from the tap when we were thirsty instead of drinking from a plastic bottle of water shipped from the other side of the world that has reputedly seeped through some volcano for thousands of years gathering essential minerals to make you feel alive and healthy but with an expiry date! All I'm saying is one such seller, Evian, is 'naïve' spelt backwards!
We never wasted food when I was a kid and there was no such thing as a sell by date stamped on products forcing you to restock if you left it too late. We never died if food looked old or rotten and if cheese went mouldy then the green bit would be cut off and if you burnt the toast you scraped away the scorched bit accepting it would taste like charcoal. People took the bus everywhere and kids rode their bikes to school or,

like my sisters and me, they walked. Now most kids rely on a twenty-four hour taxi service run by Mum and Dad.
People shopped nearby and daily instead of driving to some large supermarket on the edge of town once a week to stack up on food as if the World was about to end in Armageddon and in the process squeezing out the local shop on the corner into bankruptcy as they simply can't match the two for one deals or the variety.
Sorry about this but let me just pause a beat to mention a superb track that I simply adore more than most, *'World Without End'* by AA Bondy, a recent addition to my I Tunes collection and I urge you to shut your eyes and listen to the lyrics, they move me to tears. Bondy is a superb singer songwriter with an alluringly smooth melodic voice equalled by few.
Ill do that a lot I'm afraid, flicking from decade to decade, subject to subject, sorry. Where was I? Large multi national corporations, technology and globalisation of brands like McDonalds and Microsoft have made our world feel smaller don't you think and the world is being forever squeezed and not just on the High Street.
It's happening *'All Around the World'* as 'The Jam' would chant and cultures are blending into one, arguably loosing individualism a long the way and what is fashionable on the streets of Japan is equalling appealing to some kid in London and it seems we are all being influenced and driven by mass media and celebratory like I alluded too before.
We retain some differences such as language and tradition but fashion, music and trends seem to gain in popularity across the globe in my view, spreading and influencing people wherever they may live. They become viral. Some places are more ahead than others and they will cast a snooty eye at their neighbours in the knowledge they will soon follow.
Liverpool felt like that in the eighties, probably far from the truth but we had this egocentric outlook and swagger on life, what we started other people would follow, or so we thought and I'm ashamed to say I remember lad's from Liverpool travelling abroad returning with bags full of sport branded T shirts stolen from some poor retailer on the continent.
Talking of travel, such changes may also be as a result of people being able to travel without much fuss and thereby able to leave an impact on distance lands.
Foreign destinations have become reachable with the likes of Easyjet and Ryanair and within an hour or so you can be sipping wine in some back street bar in Naples looking out for Mr Sarstedt or dancing on a beach in

David Griffith

Ibiza. Yes indeed it has become a *'Small World'* as the brilliant Roddy Frame would say.

In the seventies a trip abroad was unheard of for the likes of my family and I longed to do the *'Spanish Stroll'*, which is a superb track by 'Mink De Ville'. The middle classes were never going to holiday in Rhyll with the likes of us, no they jetted off to 'stroll' in places like St Tropez, the Costa del Sol to the sound of *'This Year I'm Off to Sunny Spain'* by the captivating Swede known as Sylvia and other exotic sounding places. The telly would show lucky families jetting off happily together and I would 'wish I was there' and women would board the plane with matching hats and gloves.

Of course as a kid from inner city Liverpool I wouldn't have been aware of this but I read somewhere that this was partly due to the government relaxing the rules on taking money out of the country, so Brits flocked abroad and got drunk on sun, sea, sex and exotic hedonism and returned with sombreros, sangria and tacky Donkey souvenirs. Tell me what do you call a three-legged Donkey? Wait for it! A 'wonkey! Tickles me every time that joke!

It seems buttoned up inhibitions melted away in the heat and even the 'Carry On' crew famed for spending weeks camping and frolicking in Skegi got in on the act with 'Carry on Abroad'.

The traditional British seaside was transported to sunny climes with an array of pubs called the 'Duke of Wellington' and the 'Hare and Hounds', fish and chip shops sprung up and you could eat a full English breakfast all along the Costa's. Mass-market tourism ebbed back home though with people being introduced to foods like spaghetti, garlic bread, lasagne for the first time and wine and I read somewhere that in ten years the average wine intake in the UK had doubled by the end of the seventies.

Granted shelves were limited to 'Blue Nun, Black Tower and Mateus' when I was a kid but they did represent sophistication, affluence and that you were well travelled but truth is my Mum and Dad remained loyal to good old Stout!

Things have changed and foreign holidays have become affordable to the masses and as with my family they have become a contemporary must do each summer and thousands flock from regional airports in search of sun. Sun soaked resorts like Benidorm have replaced rainy Rhyll, which is now fighting for its life and has become a bit of a relic from past times when people wanted thrills and candy floss and not all over golden tans.

Getting Off At Edge Hill – The Tracks Of My Years

Some more fortunate souls holiday twice a year now and have city breaks at the weekend just because they can. In fact if you're prepared to hop on a plane at some ungodly hour on some fuel guzzling plane, the cost is about the same as a taxi home from Town after a good night out and probably at about the same time of the day! Doesn't make sense to me but at least I'm spared having to leave a tip with the captain although we do end up paying extras for baggage, I suspect we'll have to [ay to go the loo on a plane before too long.

We live in a society now where people want the latest gadget no matter what the costs and this is why 'certain' shops have sprung up in precincts up and down the country enticing people to buy the latest stuff at extortionate interest rates. They know people are addicted to whatever is fashionable today but the clever thing is they also know it will become old tomorrow and you only have to think of how mobile phones have evolved as an example.

True when I was a kid Mum would buy clothes from the Freemans catalogue especially at Christmas and she would takes ages to pay it off but generally speaking people would put aside a pound or two a week if they wanted something. Now there's a memory, sneaking a look when Mum and Dad went out at scantly clad women advertising sexy lingerie in Freemans. Okay and add perv to the list but I bet I wasn't the only lad to do this?

Actually that's not all together true now I come to think of it as Mum would often pawn Nan's rings bequeathed to her following my Nan's death when she was strapped for cash. Those rings certainly rebounded back and forth like a yo yo on one too many occasions and Nan must have been spinning in her grave like the yo yo?.

Mum would also borrow money from the 'Provi man' who worked for the 'Provident' to pay for Christmas and I remember this friendly bloke visiting our house weekly to collect the money she owed. Bit like a friendly money lender with low interest rates and he got on really well with my Mum and Dad as I recall and would stand and chat for a few minutes to get warm before moving on to another neighbour who was also saving.

Families in the seventies where I lived borrowed this way rather than borrow from a High Street Bank. I suppose trends have changed, back then workers were paid weekly in cash, in little brown envelopes with a little plastic window and I recall many robberies reported on the news. I remember being paid this way when I worked as an apprentice painter and this continued until employers insisted on payments being made into a Bank account and most people are now paid monthly. I'm

guessing Banks have made many billions investing said wages and families are forced to budget their money over the month, myself included, as thirty odd days was and still is a long time to wait!
People now use credit cards, which first became popular in the seventies as it happens with the likes of Access. People get loans for a new car, a holiday or the latest gadget and this has resulted in most people carrying thousands upon thousands of pounds in debt. It's become an illness and they call this the 'afluenza society', people believing their more affluent than they really are, many borrow on the 'never never'. This would have stressed many a folk out in the past but it seems the safety in numbers principle applies here whereby people take solace knowing others are in the debt mire too, trying to pay off things they bought yesterday so as they can begin the whole process again tomorrow!
This is consumerism, this is the rat race I suppose and I am not suggesting I am any different of course but this for me is the big shift in societies psyche when compared to life when I was younger and more innocent and perhaps explains why the nation, indeed the world, is in debt.
Our eating habits have changed beyond recognition too. Take away food back then was limited to fish and chips from the Chinese wrapped up in last nights newspaper and we had never heard of Pizza Express, McDonald's, KFC, Subway or Nandos.
All companies who began their empires in far of exotic lands and like rampaging marauders their bloody everywhere. If you wanted a brew whilst out and about shopping with Mum she would drag you past the statue affectionately known as Dickey Lewis to scousers, he was naked you see and literally stood 'proud' inviting you into Lewis's café for a cup of tea and a lemonade. There's an unlocked memory. When I was about eight and somewhat weirdly, I would sip tea to the very last drop from a tablespoon and it would take me ages!
Back to 'Dickey'. Most women couldn't resist a peak I guess and Mum said she and her mates took a trip to Town to see the stature soon after it's 'glory' was revealed and they sat on the upstairs deck to get a better look! Shame on you Mum and the statute is immortalised by the Liverpool jumper wearing folk band 'the Spinners' in their song *'In My Liverpool Home'*, with the unusual but accurate couplet; *'we speak with an accent exceedingly rare, meet under a statue exceedingly bare'*.
That's unless we were shopping up Wavertree Road when Mum would take me into Freemans for a brew, the department store not the catalogue, now there's a thought, real semi naked life models... steady! Now you can get all manner of drinks, cappuccino and skinny

cappuccino for those watching their waistline, lattes and espresso coffee. Too much choice for me and we certainly never had Starbucks or Costa bloody fortune.

Where I grew up we had Mr Lee's chippy, short for chip shop in case you don't know, on the corner of our street and where you could get a bag of chips for six pence. Mr Lee was Chinese but I don't recall ordering meals like 'Chicken and Black Bean' from a list behind his head that ran into the hundreds, no the meals seemed far simpler and my favourite snack was potato scallops or fish cakes.

Not the healthiest of snacks I can tell you but back then we weren't preoccupied with diets and calorie counting and in any case they were bloody delicious and very filling. Everywhere you look now there's a product, a pill, the latest diet or a spot of nip and tuck surgery that is guaranteed to take years off you or correct the mistakes Mother Nature has seemingly made.

One of my earliest memories was waiting for my order of chips when I was about six and running my finger across Mr Lee's counter then licking the spilt salt with my finger. Yuck I know but my taste buds craved salt and I was usually bored. I remember Mr Lee changing the focus of his business some years later to that of a takeaway with a hatch, that mainly catered for the late night revellers from the nearby Spoffy pub at kick out time. He had spotted a gap in the market the wiry old fox and had the audacity to raise his price of chips to a staggering eighteen pence! Extortionate at the time and this resulted in me having to travel further afield to Manny's chippy on Earle Road for my salt addiction. Manny was also a good mate.

When I was about twelve me and my mates were kicking a ball against a house wall, probably annoying its occupant again, when we witnessed three burly men attempt to crow bar Mr Lee's side door open. This was a break in and although Mr Lee had increased his prices we liked him so we ran over and shouted get lost and they ran away.

Coincidently as I write this I've just had a chat with Adam about how he can improve his footy skills. Adam's got potential but his kicking is weak and he has no left foot to speak off. I told him, when I was a kid I'd find a wall and would spend hours kicking the ball at a painted on goal. We'd learn how to trap the ball and quick pass and suggested he could always practice kicking ten shots at a time with his left foot only.

You don't see that these days but street footy is without doubt a brilliant way to improve ones skills and I think this is why places with economic problems do better at footy because kids literally have a ball taped to their feet when they're growing up. Look at where great footy players

like Best, Messi or even Rooney came from?
Anyway where was I? Oh yes, back in the seventies shops would close at 6pm and didn't open at the weekends but somehow we didn't starve to death and we certainly didn't panic buy at Christmas despite the shops closing for the holiday.
I remember my Mum sending me to the shops when I was barely out of my nappies but I guess it felt like we grew up in a safer era back then. Mum said she would find me crawling to the shop on the corner of a street where Webster Road met the junction of Spekeland Road and Spofforth Road and I've since done a bit of research into this to discover the name of the shop was 'Kirkwood's' but when I was a kid the owner was called Mr Pope and he also owned the fruit and veg shop opposite. A family called Bakers owned the veg shop before Mr Pope and Sara Baker lived in our street so Mum tells me.
The streets opposite the Spofforth Pub were later demolished, we got a big field to play footy on, bye, bye wall, and I'll talk about that later and opposite the field our local shop was Ali's to begin with. Then Foddle too over the shop, Foddle was a scouse Asian bloke he sold all manner of things and forgive the obvious stereotype about Asian shopkeepers but Foddle was a workaholic and he became part of the community and he took the earth shattering decision to stay open till 10pm. The first convenience store round our way selling all sorts, our open all hours store.
True, Charlie's at the top of Cranborne Road sold everything from spuds to Sayers cakes but he closed around sevenish as I recall. Now there's a memory. Buying my first 'Cinder Bar' from Charlie's, delicious honey combed candy in a see through plastic wrapper that would last all day and would annoyingly get stuck in your teeth. Didn't detract from the enjoyment though!
Seemingly we have become the fifty-third State of the USA. This wasn't always the case as the seventies was an era before the telly mad Americanisation and strangle hold on our British culture. For example we've been introduced to compensation and ambulance-chasing lawyers promising you a quick buck, see I'm even using dollars, for a fall telling you no win no fee. Some firms offer money up front and I even spotted a solicitor offering an I pad if you made a claim with them. I've only ever been involved in one minor traffic accident; yes I'm touching wood with one hand whilst typing with the other hand. I had a minor prang in my car in 2009, I crashed into the back of a car and it was my mistake, no quibble from me as I wasn't concentrating but no one was hurt, or so I thought.

I later discovered that the woman in question had claimed a thousand pound for a sore neck, there was nothing wrong with her and the insurance people said this has become standard practice. This really grates on me, as she was very angry and said this is the second time in a week someone had hit her and she was actually in a hire car. Still, I'm guessing when she had eventually calmed down and did the maths; her pain was softened knowing that she had made double the money in one week. Two thousand pound, not bad eh?

This explains to me why rates have rocketed and I feel so sorry for young people nowadays who go in search of insurance deals that cost more than the bloody car. So after paying, lets say two thousand a year for an insurance policy, you have a crash knowing they'll get about five hundred pounds back to replace their battered fiesta.

The arithmetic simply doesn't stack up for me and I know I sound like a grumpy old man but I also object to the higher rates us scousers have to pay when searching for insurance deals. If your postcode starts with an L for Liverpool you will be hit hard and you're not telling me other areas such as Mosside in Manchester or Brixton in London are safer areas to live with a lower crime rate. I think this is a complete exploitation of scousers and totally bollocks if you ask me.

The whole insurance business seems so immoral. When I was a kid if you got hurt it was your fault for being so bloody clumsy and compensation was unheard of. Still wouldn't mind an I Pad though. Now there's a thought, only kidding.

Actually being a child of the seventies and having the name 'Dave' how could I ever forget public information adverts warning us of the dangers of modern life? Let me jog your memory a bit, do you remember the 'learn to swim cartoon', it seems Dave could do anything besides swim and I would ardently protest to the obvious tease from mates, 'I can bloody swim and bloody well and I have my bronze medallion award to prove it!' We would also watch out for a Humphrey encouraging us kids to drink gallons of fresh milk to give us much needed calcium and we were told to ration water during the blistering heat in 1976.

Do you remember the slightly disturbing 'Charlie the Cat' warning or should I say scaring us in his translated cat voice not to walk off with strangers and did you know the comic come radio presenter, Kenny Everett did the voiceover?

Then we had the Green Cross Code man. Did you know the avocado coloured actor played Dark Vader in Star Wars but you'd never have guessed though as he permanently wore his black suit just like the advert, must have been really ugly! Remember Clunk Click with every trip for those luckily enough to posses a car; the recently departed Jimmy Saville was the narrator I think.

Smoking was the norm in homes, shops workplaces and pubs up and down the country and it was seen as fashionable on telly, in films and my Mum and her peers chain-smoked. Dad gave up smoking in the sixties probably for monetary reasons as opposed to health ones.

Mums also drank alcohol ignorant to the dangers whilst pregnant and they even ate blue cheese, loads of bacon and processed meat and one has to ask if all this did us any harm?

Cots in the seventies were covered with brightly coloured lead-based paints enticing babies to gnaw away at the wooden frame and I don't recall the use of safety stair gates until well into the eighties. It didn't take much to open medicine bottles and doors or cabinets were never child proof, in fact they would lure us like a blue light to a fly to look inside. Now there's a decent Punk track to mention at this point, *'I am the Fly'* by 'Wire'.

Were the seventies I enquire, really that dangerous a time to live in? It didn't feel like it at the time although I do remember returning home one day thirsty as hell after playing footy all day and taking a desperately needed swig from a plastic bottle not realising it was bleach pilfered from Mum's work. I ran to the kitchen sink for a gulp of good old-fashioned non-volcanic tap water. Taste was horrible.

We tended to ride our bikes without helmets or pads and if it could be climbed then it shall be climbed was our motto. We would climb trees to the top; we scaled buildings and dared each other to walk along high walls. We would treat whole areas as some kind of army assault course just like the one in the Krypton Factor on telly and whoever reached the top of whatever we climbed, would majestically chant the triumphant ditty; 'I'm the king of the castle, you're a dirty rascal'.

You would share a can of coke with a mate and no one actually died from this. We never thought of germs or microorganisms and do you remember 'last on'. Whoever was last on would get the dregs, which were horrible and then they had the ignominy of having to dispose of the bottle or the can. Actually there's another unlocked memory. Cans had ring pulls that came away from the can as opposed to cans now and we would pull them apart so as we could flick the ring part at a mate and you would see dozens of discarded rings on the floor.

This may come as a surprise but we seldom threw our rubbish to the ground, we were proud of our area, Mum or Dad or a neighbour would give you a ticking off if you did and we certainly weren't litterlouts. I hate it when people say, its okay to throw litter on the floor as it keeps someone in a job, referring to street cleaners. No it bloody well doesn't and it only encourages vermin or possibly the Womble's if you're lucky because they would make something out of your laziness.

The other month I was walking through Sefton Park with my family and hoards were out enjoying the sun after some Royals wedding. Two lads and a girl walked past me and threw an empty bottle of beer into the grass. I wasn't happy I can tell you and with complete disregard for my own personal safety and I guess that of the family I ran after the lad and shamed him into going back and picking up the bottle and putting it into a bin conveniently situated no more than thirty drunken steps from where he threw it. 'Pet hate' of mine that and they weren't from Liverpool I may add, they didn't have a scouse twang.

When I was a kid we actually collected old pop bottles, not for safety or environmental reasons but to cash them in at the corner store. You don't see that anymore but this is how we made a few shillings for sweets. We weren't completely innocent though as we would sometimes make money by scaling the factory wall and nicking bottles of pop from Minsters Brewery to sell them back to the shop after drinking its contents. Sorry about that kids but this is a warts and all account.

I don't think we ever bought milk from a shop or some huge supermarket with our groceries; no, the milkman delivered it with a red top. You would hear the electric motor of the float in the morning and the clanging of bottles, like a local alarm clock telling all in sundry it was nearly time to get up, as the milkman arranged the bottles on our doorstop. I think redtop bottles were full fat, they had cream at the top as I recall, in fact I don't think healthier semi skimmed milk had even been thought of back then? It was simply one variety of milk if you don't include steri that is.

I even remember milk being delivered by a horse and cart when I was really small and I can recall some huge beast peering down through our window! The dairy I've since discovered after speaking with Dad was on Spofforth Road and the name of the dairy was Thwaites.

On the subject of horses, every two or three weeks you would hear 'any old iron, any old iron' and that was the yodelling cry of the rag and bone man. You would run in and ask Mum if she had any scrap or old clothes' as you would be rewarded with a cheap brightly coloured toy in exchange. A bit like a McDonalds Happy Meal I guess but without the nuggets.

On the subject of clothes how did Mum and Dad cope with the weekly washing before washing machines? We've become really complacent I think but thankfully this has put to bed such an arduous weekly task

that I remember as a kid. I dreaded the 'baggy', a place where Mum would drag you too kicking and screaming to wash our clothes, mostly on a Sunday afternoon I think, the bag wash, the launderette.
You'd sit there staring at the clothes spinning round in the drum like you were watching telly, feeling utterly bored and listening to Mum gossiping with the other women whilst sharing and smoking a ciggy. Then I'd help Mum put the sodden clothes into the spinner to try and hurry the process up, once spun then the dryer. I'd feel a bit relieved as we were nearly done and I would hope she would run out of ten pence pieces or better still topics of conversations with her fellow gossipers. Then it would be a matter of folding the clothes into neat piles to be put into the plastic washing basket to then tie to the shopping trolley to be taken home.
Sounds very complicated and the only good thing about the baggy was that it was guaranteed to be a place that was warm but no good in summer though for obvious reasons!
We would buy teeth breaking toffees and gobstoppers. We'd chew on bubble gum for hours and I remember dipping the liquorish into the sherbet dip and 'flying saucer sweets' that stuck to your upper mouth. I remember pyramid shaped frozen orange drinks called 'Jubbly's and the best bit was at the end when the juice had melted but I also remember being annoyed on more than one occasion after pushing the ice too hard to see it pop out and fall to the floor, usually in slow motion. Talking of orange juice that reminds me of a joke I thought off when I was in Primary School and I was convinced I had made it up and no I hadn't read it in a cracker. Oh you want to hear it do you, well okay. Why did the orange stop rolling down the road? Because it ran out of juice. Sorry you've heard it? One must assume like a global epidemic it must have went viral once I had unleashed it on the world!
We either ate white bread or Hovis bread, bread was served with every meal, medium or thick, there was little choice when I was a kid; we had never heard of fancy but delicious croissants and pastries. We would spread Echo margarine on our butties but if Mum and Dad had a few extra shillings they would go more upmarket and buy Stork Margarine and when really flushed they would get a block of butter in. I remember placing a buttercup under someone's chin to reveal a yellow reflection and if that happened, which it always did of course, then he or she had revealed a liking for butter.
Mum would buy her cheese from the corner shop cut into slabs using a wire and it was always cheddar, we didn't have the choices we have today and there was only the one strength. Mum would also buy two

ounces of boiled ham from the butches as a treat. I remember loving golden syrup that came in a round tin and licking the spoon after placing some on a buttie. Basically a sugar buttie!

In fact in the seventies we drank soft drinks saturated with sugar from the Alpine Man who would deliver drinks weekly from an open top truck, dandelion and burdock was my favourite and none of this diet stuff but we weren't overweight as we would play outside like I said and we would burn off the many calories we consumed! Get ready for a spurious track link; do you remember '*Sugar Baby Love*' a debut single by the pop band 'the Rubettes'. A great song from my childhood.

I think kids today have big bums and matching big thumbs as a result of playing on console games for hours at a time and I was watching this telly programme about kids playing out and apparently forty per cent of kids play outside these days compared to seventy two per cent in the seventies. Well I was one of the seventy-two crew but when I did succumb to the allure of the telly for too long my Dad would say 'eh square eyes go n play out'. I did unless it was teaming down and we would leave home in the morning and play out all day on our bikes or we would be climbing something or playing footy or whatever was popular at the time. We had daily adventures and Mum wouldn't worry as long as we were back when the streetlights came on. We didn't have mobiles and no one could reach us all day but that was okay as we were safe and enjoying our own adventures and in a bit I will tell you more about the antics we got up to.

Everyone seemed to be on strike in the seventies, except for schoolteachers annoyingly and I remember electricity being 'rationed'. Many a night we would sit in the dark around the shimmering light and warmth from a candle and I read somewhere that the reason for this was partly due to the Miners as they had become very disgruntled with their lot and led by the shouting Arthur Scargill, Flying pickets choked the coal supply to Britain's power stations.

The price of oil rocketed filling the Saudi's pockets as it did, the three-day week was introduced to preserve electricity and inflation shot up increasing food prices tenfold and ordinary families felt the pinch.

I remember Mum and Dad struggling but everyone found it hard and Mum said it felt like Britain during the war when everybody pulled together during the blitz.

The sunny optimism of the must have sixties faded and with it came poverty and cutbacks not seen for decades and I remember the party political broadcast that called on families to think of SOS; 'Switch Of Something'. The telly would close down at night and we had to invent house games to pass the time away but this drew the family together, imagine that happening today?

I also remember the Ford Factory in Halewood going on strike knowing that my mates Dad's were on the picket line. I now know the strike was over pay and the management at Ford's eventually conceded; workers won a whopping seventeen per cent pay rise.

The news would broadcast stories about other factories going on strike like striking dominoes but I remember Liverpool having a reputation as being particularly militant, a socialist backwater bent on breaking the government.

I've also talked to social workers that worked during the seventies to be told that the government cut the pay of public sector workers and millions went on strike.

I also read about the lorry drivers who transported commodities and food around the country demanding pay rises and the country was brought to its knees. There were many justifiable strikes but 1978 in particular will always be remembered as a cold harsh winter and as a result of all the strikes and hardship it became know as the 'winter of discontent'.

I was about thirteen and I remember feeling like the world had gone mad and the chaos was epitomised by startling images of rubbish building up in large piles splashed on the news every night and other stories of council gravediggers refusing to bury the dead. Seemingly Britain was seen as an off shore industrial slum imploding on itself with workers striking for a variety of reasons, some justified, health and safety reasons as in the construction industry, or pay as in women's rights struggle for equal pay but I was also aware of 'silly strikes' because the grade of loo roll was 'crap'.

The car company British Leyland became emblematic of this and the nightly news would have you believe that workers walked out over trivia issues, spelling disaster for the British car industry and resulted in an influx of imported foreign cars onto the streets of Britain.

The Thatcher machine seized the moment, public opinion had swung against the unions to the right away from Labour and with a slick marketing campaign run by Saatchi and Saatchi, Thatcher gained a slim majority but enough to snatch power. The Sun newspaper aided and abated her success, a paper that remained neutral most of the time but this time it ran a front page editorial urging its working class readers to vote Tory to rid the country from the union stranglehold that had reputedly caused a life of misery.

I remember Mum and Dad vowing to never buy the Sun again and we remained loyal to the Mirror.

For those that don't know Thatcher became the first woman Prime Minister and I remember Mum telling me the reason for this was because many women trustingly voted for her believing she would be more sympathetic to women and more adept at balancing the countries finances because most women ran the family budget after the blokes had handed over their brown envelopes. Bit sexist I know but working class men in the seventies were mainly the 'bread winners'.

In fact she did more to dismantle the women's rights movement that began in the seventies than any male predecessor pushing women back into the home by reducing nursery places during economic hard times and I also remember Thatcher lamenting in her soft condescending but carefully rehearsed voice, 'of course I'm working class, I work bloody hard. Try digging a trench in the rain or cleaning a classroom for a few quid Maggie then you can call yourself working class.

The winter of discontent was cold as I recall but thinking back my Dad was probably 'less' discontent than Mum with the occasional energy inconvenience as the fifty pence meter would stop swirling round, preventing a dent his pocket.

Dad remembers when he was a child his Mum and Dad placing a house brick into the fire as it would retain the heat and then the brick would be wrapped in paper and placed at the end of the bed to keep you warm. An early version of a hot water bottle but must have hurt your toes if you involuntarily kicked out!

In fact Dad had several favourite money saving related phrases from when I was a kid and I can still hear him through the mists of time pecking away at my brain like a relentless money saving woodpecker. First of all he would say 'money doesn't grow on trees ye know' whenever he thought we were being 'wasteful' like when we left the telly or a light on when not in the room. He'd tell us to turn the 'big light off' which is the strangest of sayings; I don't remember Dad pointing to the lamp and saying turn the 'little light off' but come to think of it I can't recall if we ever had a lamp, I blame my fading memory.

Dad would say 'warm ye hands on the kettle if ye cold', see it had to be near artic conditions if Dad turned the fire on and when he did it would be closely monitored and turned off once the chill had been 'taken out' of the room. But we also knew this was Dad's attempt to get one of us to make him a brew as he loves his cup of tea, very strong so as the tea spoon could virtually stand up in his brew and always in a big mug.

Mum and Dad would make cups of tea using a teapot with loose tealeaves encased in a knitted tea cosy to keep the tea warm, unlike now when we have the more convenient tea bags and I even remember pyramid tea bags but this didn't catch on. When we did use teabags, usually Tetley tea bags, Dad would get at least three cups of tea out of one bag, 'waste not want not' should be engraved on his gravestone! I remember drinking Camp coffee, no not a drink for gay men, which was thick dark syrup like and was poured from a bottle to then mix with hot water. We didn't have the huge selection of coffee grains or instant coffee you see today but when we did it was the foul tasting chicory kind.

Dad would also say 'put ye jumper on if ye cold' rather than turn the gas fire up and isn't it funny how you become your parent as I go round the house turning lights off and I even tell my family to wear something warm even though I can afford the bills.

Those Jesuit monks were probably right but that said kids don't take liberties as I like to think my miserly imposition is for environment reasons and not 'necessary' something nurtured into me by Dad, honest and at times it feels like a battle of wills. See I'm sure my eldest leaves lights and the telly on when not in the room to deliberately annoy me as kids are predisposed to do because he's never had to worry about whether Mum and Dad have money to pay the bills or why is the phone cut off.

I'd rather have it that way of course and I do confess to sometimes forgetting to turn lights off myself and Kieran takes pleasure in telling me that I have double standards. I then remind him that his Mum and me pay the bills so if I want to leave things on then that's my choice but secretly thinking 'drat he's right of course' and what would Dad say? God I have become my Dad and this reminds me of the track *'Son of My Father'* by 'Chicory Tip' and for all you synth fans out there did you know this track was co-written by Giorgio Moroder and was the first number one single to prominently feature a synthesizer!

Now I'm not having a go at my Dad as he was obviously influenced by his childhood and his Dad so on that basis perhaps my kids will be influenced by me, so beware kids I will remind you of that fact when you're older.

Dad was working class to the core and a proud man, always willing to work even if that meant forfeiting benefits when others would bemoan, 'I'm not workin for ten quid more den me dole'. Well my Dad 'would' work and he was not a scrounger as many up and down the country think of us scousers, he had a strong unyielding work ethic and a sense

of self-responsibility and a need to provide for his family. Salt of the earth he is, as is my Mum in case she thinks I'm neglecting her role and contribution to my life and I'd be happy if my kids feel 'half' the affection and admiration for me as I did for my Dad.
He wasn't always unemployed and I remember Dad working shifts at a factory called Dunlop's in Speke when I was little but this was our families bad luck story.
You see, the seventies economic decline that I mentioned before struck Liverpool very hard and over a period of fifteen years 40,000 jobs were lost as many of the cities largest employers laid off staff, relocated or closed. Liverpool's reputation had been blighted as a city of wingers; jobless men and woman felt powerless and simmering political issues and social tensions ended in rioting on the streets in Toxteth in 1981, or 'Tocky' as we knew the area by. Liverpool was often used by the media as the example of inner city issues and we have been tarnished with this brush ever since.
The irony is my Dad could have worked for Fords like my Mum did for a while when I was a baby but he chose Dunlop's due to my Granddad working at the factory in a minor senior role. With hindsight this was a far-reaching bad move and like a lot of good men his pride and independence was torn away from him by redundancy in the mid seventies. The somewhat morose but fabulous track *'Ghost Town'* by the Specials typifies how we felt and all this coincided with the onset of Thatcherism when Dad was made to feel like a dole scrounger, a blight on society and this was unreservedly unfair.
Dad had become *'One in Ten'* as proclaimed by UB40 and we would watch Bleasdale's 'Boys from the Black Stuff' on telly and although comical at times and brilliantly written, the story lines ran all too true for us, Dad even had the 'Yosser Hughes' moustache. You see, Dad 'had' to work 'on the side' as he needed to provide for his family and the only employment he could find was that of an unskilled but an accomplished labourer.
Being a proud man it was very disheartening watching Dad slip out the back door as if he was doing something wrong like a fraudster and this was a very stressful time for my family as we lived one day at time hoping better times would pop up soon. Mum and Dad would stretch our meals and go without sometimes so as we kids could eat and anything that wasn't eaten would be recycled and fried the next day. I remember eating jam butties a lot and although it wasn't exactly rationing like during the war these times were nevertheless harsh economic times for my family.

David Griffith

I remember Dad living in a secret world, a world where people became very insular and frightened. Dad had an abundance of untapped energy and to stifle the onset of boredom when not in work he would go on long walks and he even took up jogging to keep healthy before jogging had become popular but he never wore a head sweatband.

It's fair to say we grew to hate Thatcher and all her middle class postulating as she epitomised those with money, those with prospects, those who only jogged to look good, those who had good lives and secure employment and as for the 'get on your bike' mantra from Norman Tebbit insinuating that people should look harder for work and travel like he did in his day, this really stuck in my throat I could almost baulk over his baldy cross combed head and I would have done if he had passed my way. To us in the jobless Labour voting North, the South seemed like another world full of Tory voting Daily Mail and Sun reading, upper crust hooray Henry's exemplified by Harry Enfield's 'Loads a Money caricature on telly.

With the onset of a new decade I remember the country being divided and everyone could see that and Thatcher's popularity was on the decline as she neared the end of her first term in power. Her bacon was saved though when the 'Argies' 'conveniently' invaded the Falklands, suddenly she was the armed forces pin up girl sitting aloft on some Sherman tank, she became Boudicca and Britannia rolled into one, the Sun loved her, naturally and she could do what she liked. She won the next election and remained in power and continued to dismantle the Welfare State with her laissez faire capitalism crusade!

My family feared the worst and we literally felt like we had no hope! That said I do find myself slightly admiring Thatcher's determination and single-mindedness as she followed an individualism path that she never swayed from and in doing so she purposely sold the countries crown jewels and I for one and I'm sure many others to, will 'not' mourn her death when it eventually comes.

Sorry if this is unsympathetic especially to her family but she was simply hated and loathed for creating a class divide that still exists if you ask me and assumed people were on the take. In fact the track *'We Don't Need This Fascist Groove Thang'* by 'Heaven 17' not only sent a stark warning that the rise of right wing politics was spreading across the land with Maggie's darling, Mr Reagan leading the battle charge from across the water but this track doubled up as a mighty fine track to strut ones tush too. Indeed as I write these words I see that a film has been released with Meryl Streep playing the Iron Lady and I wonder how many empty seats there will be in Liverpool's multiplexes.

Talking of the cinema, I went too the Woolton Picture House recently, which is near to where I now live, and they had an intermission for choc-ices. It felt like I was transported back in time, the original paint was pealing off the walls if you looked close enough and they even had Pearl and Dean's music playing prior to telling me to try out the local Indian curry house opposite the cinema. More intimate and cosy I guess but the popcorn was still too expensive but they aren't alone though as its big brother's eight screen version charge way too much too.

When I was a kid I remember thinking that all this privatisation was a clever trick to make the populous think it had become middle class and therefore more likely to vote Tory with the other Thatcher zombies. We all got sucked into it and many invested in private pension, some even bought their council house in the belief they were moving up the class ladder; I think they refer to this as embourgeoisment theory as I later discovered in sociology.

Would you like to hear something rather curious? I wrote the aforementioned paragraph before reading Stuart Maconies book of his memoires, 'Cider and Roddies' and he makes reference to teaching this theory to unemployed factory workers in Skem. I ask the question, what are the chances of me using this obscure word that spellcheck has apparently never come across before and to then read it a few weeks later in a similar context?

Blew my mind away that but I thought I'd get this in just in case Maconie thinks I'm ripping him off but he does uncannily tap into other aspects of my life that resonate with me, such as babysitting and music which I'll talk about later. As if Maconie would ever read this book? Anyway, the government sold of British Gas and other nationally owned organisations and the whereabouts of 'Sid' seduced some into buying shares for the first time. I'd never even heard of shares before and the forever savvy Brad, more about him later, took the lead from his Bluecoat educated brother, Adam, and bought shares and then sold them years later for a tidy profit. Credit to Brad and others for making a profit, I don't wish to appear jealous but this seems wrong somehow selling the nations treasures, albeit they were in downfall mode.

The seventies began the process but the eighties continued with the social changes, a decade of denationalisation, a decade of individualism and a decade of capitalism typified by the grotesque 'yuppie'? Back then my family aligned ourselves more to Mr Hatton's militant party believing the rest of the country had it in for us Liverpudlians so we should stick together. Liverpool people became defensive and unapologetic in its battle against Madame Thatcher and her cronies and it has taken years for Liverpool to improve its tarnished image as a city full wingers.

I guess I will always consider myself to be a socialist at heart but like Mr H I may have sold out too as I now live in a semi-detached house in the suburbs. I have all the trappings that suggest I'm doing okay; I have a drive to park my two cars on and a back garden with a trampoline, so no need to jump on the bed and being a social worker I have a professional qualification, we have two incomes and mandatory holidays abroad at least once a year. God I even Podcast and listen to the Archers now which is why I like the tune! Where did it all go wrong Dad but has it gone wrong I ask myself as surely my life is better now compared to Mum and Dad's struggles and why should I be ashamed for making a better life for my family and me?

One things for certain though, my life now and that of my kids is so different from when I was last in school shorts with grazed knees and dirty finger nails. We did have a telephone mind you, beige one with a ringer you pushed round with your finger but we needed to make sacrifices in the late seventies and the phone was disconnected and it stood as a poignant reminder of better times.

I remember taking some girl back to my house when I was about nineteen and she asked if she could phone a cab after a night of fondling and kissing on the couch. I went red and had to confess to said phone being a relic and obsolete, like an ornament and I never did see her again, she was from Woolton so it was to be expected and for some unfathomable reason she never bought a train ticket!

Chapter Four

Our House…

So let me tell you about my house but before I do a few words about the surrounding area where I grew up. Edge Hill is an inner city area of Liverpool first developed in the late eighteenth Century and according to Wiki its most notable resident was this rich philanthropic guy called Joseph Williamson.
He was a tobacco magnate who was responsible for much of the housing development in the area during the early nineteenth Century that resulted in rows upon rows of terraced houses crisscrossing the area with Smithdown Road and Picton Road being the main thoroughfare through to the better heeled Wavertree.
Mr Williamson is remembered around our way as the 'Mole of Edge Hill' because he also employed hundreds of men, men who had returned from the Crimean War I think with no work or prospects, to construct a network of tunnels beneath the Edge Hill area. Tunnels now open to the public as a tourist attraction and to my shame a place I've never visited and we grew up knowing this, it became folklore to us kids and gained almost legendary status until they opened up the catacomb of tunnels as proof in the eighties as I recall. How I wished my mates and me had discovered them foraging about in the corner of some wasteland, the fun we would have had running around in this secret world beneath the ground in the dark!
Anyway, Edge Hill Station, the focus of this book, was built in 1830 but little remains of the original building and I read that the current station dates from 1836 when the main city terminus was moved to Lime Street station. Here's a fact you may wish to lodge in your brain. The station buildings remain in use and these buildings are the oldest in the world still open to the public at a working railway station. How cool is that, makes one feel very proud and my brother in law works there as a ticket collector.
The Station is also famously known for Stephenson's steam powered Rocket; the first locomotive of its kind and one of the main reasons as to

why the industrial revolution gathered pace as commerce had to be ferried from factory to factory. Imagine growing up in the North West of England where many an invention was made that drove through better ways of making stuff that also resulted in huge social mobility.
I read somewhere that prior to the industrial revolution people lived and died within a thirty mile radius on average but with trains came the opportunity to travel further afield, probably looking for work so no different to when I was a teenager as many including myself, left Liverpool in search of work too.
I now realise that most people tend to outgrow places as you spread out in search of other horizons but my childhood area has certainly left a lasting imprint on my mind that now spans the decades. If you asked me to draw the streets and the dwellings for example, I could effortlessly design the buildings I walked by as if they were outside my window now instead of the swaying trees in my garden that has kept me inspired these past few months.
I can visualise street after street, shops selling bread and sweets, pubs with patrons laughing inside and some houses standing sublimely in my memory. I can see shadows caused by the sun as it descended over the rooftops and I can smell, taste and feel the area as if I was there now.
So where about in Edge Hill did I live, well my street was called Galloway Street, probably named after some Lord, a simple non-descript Street similar to others but unique to me because it was my home, it housed my mates and I shall never forget where I grew up for as long as I walk this earth.
I lived in number seventeen not far from the middle so I would look left and right when I opened my door, but before I tell you more let me just pause to mention a bit of a connection with a guilty pleasure of mine, the track '*7teen*' by the Regents and then we have another fab track, the melancholy folky track '*Seventeen*' by Janet Ian. Are there anymore seventeen tracks out there, letters in writing too…?
Anyway being a big softy I confess to taking a nostalgic walk around the area from time to time and somewhere in my mind I can hear the running steps, the laughter and the shouts of excited kids playing outside and I have stopped and looked at window sills I have perched on, lampposts I have shimmied up and walls I have kicked a ball against. My reminiscing must have looked very peculiar indeed to people staring out of their windows, probably looked like an undercover policeman and I've often wanted to stop at my house to ask the current occupier if I could have a look inside. Can I see where we sat in the living room and where I slept all those years ago.

That aside I thought of yet another important question I had never asked Mum and Dad before; why did they move to Edge Hill of all places seeing as they were from Speke, situated about ten miles away. See, Edge Hill will always have a special place in my heart like I said but you wouldn't really choose to live there but I suppose I am guilty of looking at this from a contemporary perspective and not from another decade when my parents were weighing up their options with limited resources. The place looks run down and grubby now and some houses are empty with plywood covering the windows to stop kids gaining access. Wouldn't have stopped my mates and me though!

So I got to ask this question recently and Mum told me they wanted to escape the area where they lived and they first rented a flat by Sefton Park and this was a very dingy flat and they had to share a bathroom with other residents.

Was Mum still trying to hide her relationship with Dad, who knows but according to Mum, Dad was still working shifts in Dunlop's and Mum was working at Fords at the time and being of the nervous disposition, Mum refused to sleep in the flat when Dad worked nights so she would sleep at her Mum and Dad's. I wonder if Tommy still charged entry if Mum was late?

Eventually Nan suggested they move in with them and into Tommy's room and he had to bunker down with my Nan and Granddad but that's what families did back then, they made do but he must have been particularly miffed. Nan didn't charge rent and this then allowed Mum and Dad to save up a hundred pound deposit on a house and they found my house in the Liverpool Echo Newspaper in the classified ads and decided to move into what was to become my birth house, Galloway Street. Probably all they could afford at the time, as I believe the place was a right wreck.

My Grandparents and I guess their parents rented their homes and I think my Mum and Dad were the first in my family to buy their own place. I read somewhere that the seventies created a tremendous sea change when it came to property. Freedom first felt in the swinging sixties resulted in more opportunities and more money and certainly at the start of the seventies there seemed to be ample work, a decent welfare system and the country was relatively wealthy.

The Bank of England relaxed its lending laws and High Street Banks could then offer affordable mortgages to the populous and the upshot was ordinary families like mine began to have expectations, they wanted a home of their own, not a rented one and New Towns were built to rehouse those used to living in slums and dilapidated houses.

David Griffith

Thankfully we remained in our crumbling Liverpool home but the dream of owning your own home, your own castle certainly blossomed in the seventies and according to this telly programme I watched recently, house prices went up seventy per cent in a mere two years such was the effect of market forces.
Thinking musically, I would say the track *'Our House'* as opposed to the Madness version, by 'Crosby Stills and Nash' evokes dreams of domesticity and warm tranquillity and sought of sums this period up for me, a period when people began to embrace consumerism.
In fact by 1980 the average house was worth ten times its value from the start of the decade. That's if you lived in better parts of the country me thinks as my Mum and Dad ended up giving away our house to get out of the area in the late nineties as by then most of their friends had either moved away or died and the street had lost its community spirit.
New arrivals to the street from lands afar don't seem as concerned with keeping their home or the area in good order. Less of a community spirit and Mum and Dad felt threatened by the solitude that comes with feelings insecure and suspicious of ones neighbour, neighbours from a different culture.
Mum and Dad wanted out and some lucky sod with an eye on the market bought our house for about nine thousand pound! Certainly never made 'ten times' and I've often wondered why I never bought the house myself with my credit card not just for sentimental reasons of course but for profit as the house must be finally worth ten times after all these years!
Putting aside my lack of entrepreneurial insight, I'll skip back to the past and I'll do my best to help you with a little visualisation of my home from when I was a kid.
Our Street was not too dissimilar to the famous cobbled street you see on telly three nights a week at the other end of the M62, Coronation Street, but the difference being our house didn't have a bay window or a pub at the end. Incidentally scousers tend to use the term 'alehouse' and 'bevey' when referring to the pub and having a drink, as in 'yer goin de alehouse for a bevey' and if someone had one too many 'bevey's' then we would say 'ees bladdered'.
Our alehouse was round the corner and was called the Spoffy, short for the Spofforth, again another Lord I guess and unlike on telly I don't recall everyone having a quick half and a chat at the Spoffy. I know it's been said many times by social commentators but how on earth do those who live in the area of soapsville afford such luxuries on a daily basis

especially with rocketing beer prices? I think the writers have got it wrong an dare stuck in the past.

Thinking out loud, I suppose most cities have their own version of Coronation Street with rows and rows of terraced houses jam-packed together. I say most, as I somehow don't see Hilda Ogden living in the City of Westminster or Bath for that matter! Still, a funny thought though.

Neil S's Mum and Dad lived at number twenty-seven and they had stone cladding however Billy and Doreen bore no resemblance in any shape or form to the Duckworth's. That said Jack Duckworth amongst other jobs, was a window cleaner and he would no doubt have ran up and down a fair few ladders in his time, when not in the boozer of course. Billy had a green company van and he pasted posters on huge bill boards as a job, so similar to window cleaning and some weekends Billy, me and his son Neil would drive round the North West in his little green van hanging advertisements for Embassy Cigarettes and stuff like that and it felt like a proper day out! I must have been about eight I think.

The nights were so dark when I was a kid and I realise we had less lights and cars in the city in the seventies and in these days of austerity cut backs and ecological concerns why not turn back time and turn the lights off or dim them after twelve? I think I'm about to answer my own question as I suppose we would worry about crime and opportunity for youths to run amok like the recent riots up and down the country in summer 2011. Which incidentally had nothing to do with poverty or racism as I see it but to do with pure gluttony and greed by youths who saw an opportunity to steal?

They were simply bored kids and worrying some were adults and had been spoon fed on violent desensitising games such as 'Call of Duty' and 'Grand Theft Auto' and I think the line between reality and fantasy has arguably become blurred.

Opposite to the entrance to the street we had a large field where rows upon rows of terraced houses previously stood built by the aforementioned Williamnson. I remember these streets with affection but they were bulldozed in the late seventies and I'll talk more about why a bit later and the opportunities for adventures and rummaging that came with advancement of roaring JCB's.

It was 1981 and I remember stopping footy on the field one late summers day and we all looked at the red sky thinking good were in for a sunny day tomorrow, which meant more dreams of playing for Everton! The sky was crimson you see and we knew the phrase, 'red sky at night

shepherds delight' usually meant it would more likely be a warm one when you got out of bed.
Groups of men then started to appear from different corners of the field interrupting our game as they walked hypnotised towards the brilliant red mist and smelling of booze and you could smell burning in the air like it was bomb fire night!
I later realised, as it was reported on the News, that these men had piled out of pubs in search of male testosterone excitement wishing to plunder, wanting to fight the law and certainly not in search of sheep and hot summer days!
Toxteth was ablaze you see, you could see the smoke and I couldn't believe all this was happening on my doorstep and you could hear explosions and sirens in the distance. Frustrations over unemployment and anger about unfair policing had exploded into violence, I was aged fifteen and 1981 was the year of the riots.
This was a dark chapter in Liverpool's history and regardless of the reasons why the riots erupted the riots served to add to people's fears and beliefs that Liverpool was a lawless and anarchistic place to live. It never felt like that and people generally got a long knowing most people were going through the same economic struggles although I do accept that political tensions overflowed fuelling people with extremist tendencies to take on the police head on.
I remember how the police would randomly stop and search people and they were accused of targeting mainly black youths and I recall being stopped on more than one occasion and asked to open up my kit bag by a 'bizzie'. Bizzie was the term we used when talking about the police as in 'de bizzie station', or 'quick, leg it ere comes de bizzies'.
I wandered up Upper Parliament Street to have a look at the aftermath and the place resembled a war zone with bricks, burnt cars and scorched buildings, some of which had to be demolished like the iconic Rialto Building.
Not long after the riots, Michael Heseltine, who was the Conservatives Environmental Minister, was appointed the tsar for Liverpool due to my city being seen as a city in decline and in need of a makeover. Mr H had his faults by the very fact he was a Tory and he had a wicked fringe but there's no doubting that he is partly responsible for regenerating the Albert Dock into an apartment and shopping complex, before which the Dock had stood as a derelict eyesore and a reminder of a time when trade passed through Liverpool, when Liverpool was glorious!
He is also famously remembered for planting trees everywhere to make the place look more green but in reality we got goal posts on our field

and he is also remembered for the International Garden Festival that opened for six months on The 2nd May 1984.
This was the Conservatives attempt to generate jobs to appease social unrest and to ultimately attract tourists and at the time we thought this was politically condescending and supercilious but I actually think we should thank Mr H not only for having a decent wedge hair cut but for his visionary concepts as he certainly earmarked the start of Liverpool transforming to a world class cosmopolitan city I see today.
Brad worked at the Britannia Pub at the Festival over the summer of 1984 and he would talk about the many foreigners he served at the bar and I remember visiting soon after it opened. I can remember catching the train to Aigburth Station or 'Aigy' as we called it, pronounced 'eggy' by the way and then walking round various gardens. The most impressive being the oriental gardens with a pagoda and I remember this slide shaped like a dragon.
I remember the train that ran around the site and the Festival Hall that later became Pleasure Island Amusement Park and I once went there with Sue to have a go at the laser quest and ten pin bowling in the nineties with Brad and Jean.
I also remember walking through a house built by Barrat's I think giving us an insight into how houses would be built in the future and indeed most housing estates you see today are mirrored versions of what I had seen at the Festival. Small square and non-descript houses with no soul or heart.
Although short lived the Festival was viewed as a success but when it closed the site lay dormant and overgrown for three decades tucked away behind security fences and the Festival Hall was demolished as it had became a bit of a carbuncle that attracted vandals and vagrants.
The current owners and I believe there have been many, were at a loss as to how to develop the land, they were going to build new houses at one point and there was even talk of Everton Football Club building a stadium on the site but the infrastructure didn't fit.
Some thirty years on and the Garden Festival has gone through a multi million pound restoration and recently I went with the family to have a look and retraced some of the steps I would have taken when I was eighteen. Looks lovely now and worthy of a visit and the good thing is, unlike back in its heyday, it's free and yes even the car park!
Returning to the past, young black people were harangued more and they felt especially powerless and the riots raised questions about race relations in Liverpool. In fact the riots coincidently began thirty years ago as I write these lines and although it erupted as a race issue, it struck

me the men who interrupted our kick about on our filed were mainly White men! Just thought I'd mention that fact as historians often portray it as a black issue only.
I did my own research into this to discover that in the seventies the Black community represented about eight per cent of Liverpool's population. Housing policy, stereotyping, prejudice and discrimination meant that the majority of Black people lived in Liverpool eight, Toxteth and often felt separated from other communities.
When I was a kid Edge Hill was a largely a White area and although we had some Black friends I'm sad to say there was a noticeable divide between races and cultures that began and ended at Lodge Lane up the road from my house. This isn't the case now but back when I was young the community in Toxteth seemed more introspective and insular. People generally kept to themselves.
If I'm being honest I would feel slightly uneasy walking along the Lane as a kid; it felt like an intimidating place for no other reason than my misplaced and stereotypical fear that I stood out. I didn't really as the area was multi cultural, it was actually a fascinating and vibrant area with people whose ancestry could be traced from all four corners of the world. In fact gangs of kids never enquired why I had strayed into their area and I was never afforded a second glance in truth, it was simply my youthful paranoia.
You had the likes of Kwik Save and the Co-Op but the shops looked more exotic and sold tins and fruit I'd never heard of before. I opened a savings account at a Post Office on the Lane, not sure why, there was a Post Office on Lawrence Road near to where I lived and here's a lovely memory that's just popped into my head, a memory stored in the 'wish I could do that again' recess of my mind.
Mum had won some money at bingo, my sisters and me were on our school holiday's and we were given a share of the bounty, a small share granted but a pound was a lot of money when I was very young and we were told that we could spend it on whatever we wanted. So why on earth did my sisters and me end up in the Post Office on Lawrence Road instead of TJ's but putting that aside we did leave with a plastic bag full of plastic toys and we almost cleared the shop of its plastic! Certainly didn't buy stamps or Hallmark stationary, as one would expect!
On the subject of saving Mum and Dad put a little aside for us kids in a savings policy and I remember Mum slipping up and telling me that my sisters had been paid out on their eighteenth birthday. Now at the risk of sounding jealous and ungrateful did I get my insurance, no I bloody well didn't and I still rib my Mum about this all these years later. I honestly

don't mind but Mum still squirms when I throw this into the conversation.

Anyway, when I was a kid Mum and me would sometimes shop on the Lane and my Mum still attends the same Bingo, the Pivvy and she and her Speke friends are taken by bus to gamble away their pensions conveniently run by the Pivvy!

When I was about twelve my Mum joined a music club at a shop on the Lane and every now and again she would let me pick a single and sometimes an album, which is one reason why I began to like music so much.

I would study the charts and would work out what singles I would buy and I remember excitedly walking up Smithdown Road to buy my records but feeling very nervous but I soon realised I had nothing to fear but fear itself and before long I happily trekked up the Lane and beyond realising people are all the same but with differences and this is something we should celebrate. Sounds like a contradiction but I know what I mean but when you're a kid the unknown can be very scary and sometimes you just have to immerse yourself to conquer any misconceptions you may hold and thankfully that's what I did.

Let me take you back to my street. A much-loved nocturnal pastime we enjoyed as kids was stargazing and we would lie on our backs and stare at the stars and I could show you should you ever find yourself lying next to me on the floor which isn't going to happen I know but just a thought.

I now know that the most recognisable and one of the brightest consolations in the night's skies are known as the stars of Orion, or Orion's belt. We didn't know them as that; being a Catholic I guess but we knew them as the three kings and just below the kings are the expectant Mary and her hubby, Joseph waiting to be visited.

To the right of Orion's belt is the 'seven sister' consolation, a collection of distant stars visible back in the seventies but barely detectible to the naked eye due to the light pollution in Liverpool. All I can see these days is a distant smudge and only when the night is very clear and below the sisters at dawn you can spot Venus then Jupiter on the horizon.

I read up about the belt and found that different cultures picked out the Orion consolation just like me and my mates did way back in the day and I find that fascinating as people from the past must have looked up in amazement like me and my mates did. The Egyptians for example associated it with Osiris the god of death and rebirth; a Native American tribe called the three stars of the belt the three footprints of the flea god, wonder if they were 'Opie's, get over it Dave, whilst an aborigine tribe in Australia called it the canoe.

Little did I know it at the time but this is all so absorbing, see them same stars are linked to Maths, the code in nature that lets us understand the patterns, the laws that govern and command the universe. This is known as Newton's law of universal gravitation that predicts the passage of the stars into the future and how they appeared in the past! Guess whose been watching the Discovery Channel on telly or better still I urge you to catch the very funny 'Big Bang Theory?'

Are you impressed? Well, here's more. Orion is mentioned in the wonderful *Romeo and Juliet* track by 'Dire Straits' that I loved as a teenager but least said about the naff video. Orion's belt would have also looked different to our ancestors thousands of years in the past and likewise the belt will appear different to people in the future and we know this because of an apple hitting Mr Newton's Barnett!

I somehow don't think the sky looks any different forty odd years later however but that's the point isn't it. Time moves on at a blistering paste but in the greater scheme of things my life and your life is a mere microdot in the passage of time. Well that's enough of the astronomy lesson just thought it was interesting to know should you find yourself in a pub quiz or on Egg Heads on telly.

We would study the stars and look for shooting stars and we'd convince ourselves that a UFO would pass us by so we dare not look away, someone would often shout 'did ye see dat' so you dare not blink! I think this was because Close Encounters was on at the cinema and we were hooked on the possibility that life existed elsewhere, it seemed to make sense given how many stars are up there, billions and billions.

I somehow knew that a star twinkled just like the song but planets did not and Venus was the brightest object in the night sky as I recall and we would dream of distant galaxies with strange beings when in truth going through the Mersey tunnel with Neil's Dad was indeed like another world! The Wirral is an odd place don't you think?

Recently I was walking home after a night out and perhaps I had enjoyed one too many drinks but I noticed three flickering lights in the distant night sky and I was excited and intrigued and I was taken back in time to when I was a kid. Before I tell you more and for transparent reasons, this reminds me of a superb track ive had the pleasure of hearing recently by the Eels called *Blinking Lights (For Me)* about a bloke who is out of sorts with life.

Back to my 'inebriated encounters'. The lights drifted from left to right at a good pace and then disappeared and I was just about to carry on with my inebriate journey home pondering what I had seen when I spotted several more flickering lights coming from the same direction. I decided to sit down as I did as a boy and I must have looked like a proper drunk unable to get home without staggering but I wasn't and I counted about twenty-five lights in total.

Now before you add sci-fi nut to my ever increasing character list, I'm sure there's a rational explanation, Chinese lanterns perhaps as they seem to be the craze these days, but I tell you they did look convincingly UFO like, it was about three in the morning and I kept thinking about how me and my mates would have responded back in the seventies. Well I can tell you how, we would have been beside ourselves with excitement and we'd no doubt have ran home to tell our parents with Bowies '*Star Man*' running through our head and humming the tune from Spielberg's film. Oh before I go any further have you noticed how my Dad's generation pronounce the word film as filim, why is that, or is that just a scouse thing?

Anyway, I was mucking about on YouTube recently and I came across this clip taken by someone in Russia claiming the lights above were UFO's. They were 'exactly' like the ones I saw in size, formation and speed, so who knows eh perhaps I did see something out of the ordinary, where's my mates when I needed them?

Talking of all things celestial I remember being told at cubs that the sun was in the South when it was midday. This was one of many cool tips I learnt at the Cubs and I have many memories from when I was a member. The Cubs was about having fun but you also learnt stuff at the same time and back then membership was restricted to boys and I joined the Cubs when I was about seven. I recall the two-fingered solute and proudly wearing a deep green sweatshirt, my green cap and yellow necktie. All kids should attend the cubs or whatever its called these days in my view and it may interest you to know that Baden Powell founded the Cubs in 1916 to cater for younger boys wanting to join its bigger brother, the Scouts.

Our Cub pack met in St Dunstan's Church Hall, which I will talk about many more times throughout this book as it plays a reoccurring feature in my life. We would start the session by standing in neat rows like we were on parade to be inspected by the leader of the pack, a large formidable woman as I recall, who we referred to as Akela.

Each line would have a different coloured toggle, it would be competitive and you worked towards being rewarded badges for doing good deeds and different things such as successfully tying a knot should you be on a boat and you had to swear allegiance to the Queen! I even remember going on parade walking along the road with huge banners paying homage to the protestant faith and the Queen, I must have been very confused!

Setting that aside as I'm certainly not a royalist and I was a Catholic you see, knowing the sun's path was indeed useful to know. As I looked out of my house the sun would take a path across the terraced slate roof that faced my front door and midday would be pretty much in the middle. To my left meant many more hours of fun, a central position meant pop home for a quick 'jam buttie', to my right meant it was nearly time to stop playing too far from home, as it would be dark soon.

This was Mother Nature's way of saying you need to be home kid, teas up and you have school tomorrow but all this would depend on what time of year it was of course. I remember getting my first 'grown up' watch at Christmas for my tenth birthday but I overwound the dial and it broke before I had even digested my bloody turkey. Oh well back to the roof sundial abetted by ones rumbling belly.

Now seeing as *Our House* was literally in the 'middle of our street' as the Madness track goes, let me expend a few paragraphs reminiscing about my home. I love the line by the way about sister having a mood on in her bedroom, not quite the lyrics for fear of infringement and I reckon Suggs wrote the song as a tribute to all terraced houses up and down the country?

Anyway, our house began as a two up two down Victorian built terraced, I've just done the Suggs look up then down expression he does in the video, which probably catered for Liverpool's expanding population in the nineteenth century rippling through the likes of Wavertree, Aigburth, Old Swan and other areas.

Ready for an interesting fact. Did you know Liverpool has the largest concentration of terraced houses in the country when compared to other cities and was the first corporation in Britain to build homes for its inhabitants? I leant that Liverpool built flats as part of its clearance of 'slum' housing, the first of these, St George's Cottages opened in 1869. See we are truly trailblazers!

In our house space was certainly a premium, not quite like a slum but cramped nevertheless. My sisters and me would sleep in the back room and being a boy I was fortunate to have my own bed whereas my sisters had to sleep 'top and tail'. I was aware as a kid that Mum had miscarried three babies', as did a lot of mothers I guess and I cannot begin to imagine how we would have all shoehorned into that box of a house if my unborn sibs had survived or would Mum and Dad have disembarked that train after three? Just a thought, I would have loved to have more siblings and I suppose we would have coped like other families did but clearly Dad needed to get to Lime Street by passing Edge Hill Station on more than one occasion!

My sisters and me would talk into the night and one of our favourite games was trying to guess when the headlights from passing cars would travel around the room. Oh the fun we had as kids I hear you shout but we made a game out of everything and anything as you will discover and we were able to use our imagination.

Also goes without saying if I played the game today we'd never had got any shut eye on account of the many cars on the road and the room would have been constantly lit up. Dad would have used his one of many one-liners the next day; 'hey sleepy ed dya need matchsticks to keep ye eyes awake'.

I think the City Council handed out home improvement grants to help improve the area and we and some other neighbours had extensions built when I was about ten. We lived in a house opposite our house for a few months at noon, the house under the sun, should have called it *'the House of the Rising Sun'* and the lady owner, what's her name again, damn you fading memory, lived on her barge during this period which was very generous of her given the upheaval.

Although I never really appreciated it at the time most properties were beyond their best before date and were drastically in need of modernisation and restoration if they were to make it into the twenty first century and Dad told me recently the place was full of rot and he often had to fix the slates on the roof. One time Dad said the ceiling collapsed as it had been raining heavily and he had to get on the roof to fix it in the middle of the night. That must have been very scary and thankfully he wasn't scared of heights.

The extension all happened before the demise of Dunlop's and it felt like we were finally moving up the bourgeois ladder. My sisters were rewarded with their very own bed for the first time and I got my own brand new pink plastered bedroom and I was so pleased with myself and my newfound independence and solitude.

I could fart in bed without moans from my sisters, I felt liberated shutting the door after me when I went to bed but never satisfied I do remember feeling lonely sometimes and talking to Tracy and Tina through the door about what I had learnt in school that day. I was and still am a gabber when the need arises.

I felt lucky but I soon realised all was not as it seemed and at the risk of sounding ungrateful to the Council, whoever drew the plans and my Mum and Dad; the room was barely big enough for a single bed and a small wardrobe and I am guessing I could now touch both side of the room if I stretched my arms.

This became more evident over the years as I grew bigger and bigger till eventually my feet and head banged against headboard. Would have suited Tommy though and perhaps that's why my spine curved like I said before, no room to grow you see, so whom do I send my compensation claim too, perhaps an I Pad awaits?

I'm not saying the room was cold but when you opened the door the light came on and I christened my room 'de fridge'! See we may have gained an inside toilet but central heating wasn't for the likes of us unlike my mates house and in the depths of winter you could literally scrape the ice off from the inside of my window. Good for creating artistic patterns, ill give you that, but bloody freezing.

I did have an electric heater and although he disputes my frost bitten memory my Dad banned me from using it. Fifty pence piece in the meter wouldn't last all night it seems and I would really dread the nine o'clock news as that would signify bedtime and I'd run though my sisters room to my room covering my eyes.

Downstairs I would literally lie in front of the fire barricading others from the warming gas flames in an attempt to somehow store up enough heat like the brick my Dad used when he was a kid, to help me make it through the cold night like a lizard does, queue Gladys Night and her Pips, but I would quickly cool down by the time I got bellow the blankets.

I would open my fridge door and the cold would clout me in the face and I'd hastily jump into bed fully clothed, socks and all! We never had fancy duvets back then, no we had layers and layers of blankets and I'd pull mine over my face forming an escape hole just big enough to breathe through.

Dad was all heart sometimes; he wouldn't tell me to 'turn de eater on son' in case your thinking he was in the money from time to time, no, he would try and warm me up by placing his donkey jacket on my bed for extra insulation. Thanks for that Dad and I can still smell the oil and grease from a days graft and that jacket will reappear later in this story. Top marks awarded if you spot where.

Through the moonlight shining through the curtain you could actually see my breath escape from my shivering mouth to the sound of my teeth chattering! Do you feel sorry for me yet, am I going on too much? No, well you should and trust me bedtime was not a pleasant experience in my house in winter and I've often wondered why my Mum and Dad never read me a story in bed after the extension was built! I know dear reader I'm one step ahead of you; this surely explains and excuses my atrocious spelling and grammar if you add in a bit of Slade? Please read on.

With the extension came a bathroom and an emersion heater to dry your clothes and a cool place to hide. I think it must have been expensive though as we were only ever allowed to share the mucky water once a week on a Sunday before school and Dad would, with accurate precision, run a bath that barely went above your hips when you laid down horizontally.

I can still recall feeling warm and snug below the surface of the water but cold above and I also remember lying in the foetal position trying to remain warm on one side before the water cooled down, then turning over like I was being cooked.

There always came a tipping point when you would stay in the bath to keep warm rather than face the cold outside and thinking back my sisters must have loathed bath time more than me as I would be far grubbier than them as I would have been playing out all day on the field or in bombed out houses and I would leave the bath with a grimy sludge mark as proof of my adventures. An oil spill and I'm guessing I was told to be the last in?

My sisters played out but you don't really get that dirty tossing up or throwing two balls to some girly chant against the wall do you. Some skill involved though, throwing a ball over arm, under arm and between your legs. Keep this to yourself okay but I was able to do a handstand against the wall like my sisters and I even tried 'two balls' a few times when my mates were in having their tea. Should I really speak so honestly, who cares?

Still, having a white plastic bath was seen as a luxury and signified opulence. Before the bathroom we had a back living room come kitchen and once a week on a Sunday Mum would bring the tin bath in from the yard that hung on the wall and after several kettle runs boiled on the gas ring we would all take turns and have a good scrub before school!

I remember pushing my sister Tina into the bath after the usual fall out and resulting tantrum and her pyjamas ringlets fell out, sorry sis. When we were very little we would squeeze into the sink for a quick wash taking care not to be scolded on the overhanging hot tap attached to a water heater and Dad would use 'carbolic soap' to wash behind our ears! Later in the seventies we got the fancy 'Life Boy' soap that was then supressed by the even more extravagant 'Imperial Leather', I remember the advert on telly and the brilliant conception of hanging soap on a rope usually given as a prezzy at Christmas and I remember shampooing my hair using washing up liquid when we ran out of Vosene in the eighties. Talking about parental cleaning when out with my Mum if I had a 'mucky' face she'd get the dreaded hankie out and in spite of my protestations and pulls away she would precede to spit on the hankie and would attack me knowing I'd do my best to wriggle away! 'The tides in' was a phrase used to describe dirty necks and used to accompany this assault!

Most houses had a parlour room and like the neighbours up and down the street and before the extension our parlour was at the front. You entered our house through the parlour but you rarely sat in the parlour as it was kept neat and tidy for guests, a room to show off your favourite China and collection of brass ornaments but no bigger than ten foot square.

Now there's a memory, polishing little elephants and other shelf animals on last nights Echo with Brasso from an orange tin on a Sunday afternoon with Mum and Dad till you could see the image of your face. I can still recall the smell in my nostrils, a really nice memory evoking and comforting seventies smell.

When the extension was done the dividing wall was knocked down creating a through room, roughly twenty by ten foot but this was still a small room but at the time it seemed expansive and I lost a place to sit in private with my mates.

One year Dad hung anaglyptic wallpaper to hide the cracks and the room was decorated with an array of family pictures showing us kids at various stages of our life and my Mum still has the same pictures on her landing wall. I remember one time when Dad decided the room needed a make over and he stripped the paper off and before hanging the wallpaper we all drew pictures on the bare wall with dates so when it came to redecorate some years later we could see what we had written. This all backfired however as the pen penetrated right through the paper and Dad had to emulsion over the 'graffiti'. Dad remembers his Dad using flour and water instead of wallpaper paste and this would attract roaches that would creep out of the wall and he remembers the wall bubbling with insects!

Before the extension we had an outside 'bog', which meant the toilet, and this would be a wooden bench with a hole in it. Pinned to the wall was last night's Echo Newspaper to wipe your bum just in case the tracing paper toilet paper pilfered from Mum's work, had ran out when you needed an 'Eartha', as in Eartha Kitt. The news back then was literally full of… There's an unlocked memory; making 'Nelson' sailor hats from old newspapers and playing army with sticks but for the life of me I

can't recall how we made them, the hat that is. Do you?
In fact the newspaper had many uses as I recall. It would be used to wrap around your chips, for privacy when cleaning the curtains, to clean the windows with and I still use newspaper dipped in water with a splash of vinegar, to be placed on the floor to stop dirt being trampled into the house, even as a table cloth sometimes when 'brasso-ing' and I even remember Christmas decorations being made from newspaper. If I had a hole in my shoe I remember Dad using a piece of cardboard to block the hole.
Now some of you may refer to the bog as the privi, short for private for obvious reasons. Should you visit the new museum by the Pier Head in Liverpool you will see a good replica of an outside bog and inside the mock house is a roughly plastered room with wooden slats, just like my house in the seventies in fact and I remember picking away at a hole in my bedroom wall once and finding the same type of slats.
Our bog was very cold and icy in winter and full of huge scary spiders in the summer! I hated going for a 'slash' or a 'jimmy riddle', as in piddle, in the middle of the night, as that would involve unlocking the back door and facing the cold then the spiders. So our family had a pee bucket on the landing for convenience, literally a convenience I guess, and yes I know, so unhygienic and where did we wash our hands?
I also remember Mum going the bingo one night and Dad decided to take down the chimneybreast in the living room to gain a foot or so extra room. Why I don't know, was he bored and did it make any difference? Mum was furious when she returned home not because lady luck had evaded her again but because everything was covered in dust and soot even her cherished brass ornaments. Dad had made me and my sisters help with moving the bricks and the soot and we were filthy, like characters from a Dickens novel. In fact Dad made my sisters wear their swimming costumes, as he knew they would get very dirty and unlike me they didn't have any 'old' clothes to wear, or should I say clothes that could be thrown away. Dad must have been in the doghouse for a while but we didn't have a dog, no we had a cat. Whatever!
Now for a few words about how we ate in our house. One Sunday Mum and Dad were late getting back from my Granddad's and Hattie and Peter, my mate Brad's Mum and Dad, invited me to stay for dinner. We all squeezed round the table, this was our table tennis table which I'll talk about later and Hattie, not her real name, had Peter running round stacking the table with all sorts of food stuff; spuds, mashed potato, sweet corn, carrots, gravy, sprouts and an assortment of meats!

Hattie had high hopes for her children, which is admirable of course. Adam for example, was the eldest child and he went to the Bluecoat School, a very posh school steeped in history and you needed to pass an entrance exam to gain a place. You still do, my Adam sat the exam last year but never made the top two hundred but did very well in his end of term SATS!

Hattie worked with my Mum as a cleaner in Webster Road Primary School, Peter, was a quiet, gentle family man and he worked at Fords like most Dad's. Peter was a bit hen pecked in truth as he would appear to be at the 'beck and call' of Hattie who like my Mum was a heavy set woman as were most women in the seventies as I recall.

A really nice friendly couple though and always very hospitable and welcoming and Hattie would never see anyone go hungry and I remember Brad taking plated Sunday dinners covered in tin foil to an old guy on Earle Road.

Brad's family were Protestants and they attended St Dunstan's Church every Sunday and they did a lot for the community but never wanted anything in return. Brad had four brothers and a sister and they all lived in a small terraced house on Spofforth Road by the pub and like my family they had an extension built to ease the cramp conditions but there's was bigger.

You may recall the fictional family a few years back in the eighties called the Boswell's from the sitcom Bread, well Brad's family reminds me of the Boswells and how they lived and functioned together and this is why I called Brad's brother, Joey after the main character, although he never wore leather trousers, in fact I can never recall anyone wearing leather trousers that wasn't on the telly!

You see, they were a typical inner city extended family, a second and possibly third generation family that lived in the Edge Hill area and they all chipped in and sure they fought and bickered sometimes, usually the eldest child bullying the next one down but they were a close-knit family and they all looked out for each other.

A strong bond existed and I was jealous in a way as I only had two younger sisters and no big brother to stand up for me and I guess growing up with boys toughened you up but if picked on I would imagine saying; I'll get our Tom onto you and most scuffles would have been negotiated to a peaceful end without a punch being swung? Bit like NATO, my very own deterrent.

Yes I would have liked an older brother and his name would have been Tom as I'm guessing that's the name Mum and Dad would have picked as Tommy, like I said, is a family name, Thomas actually.

Brad's family always ate well and Henry the eighth would have been impressed with the feast that lay before my eyes but I was actually a bit apprehensive; do I wait for someone to make me up a plate of grub, how big a portion do I spoon out if left to me, what is the etiquette in this hospitable Medieval family?
See I'd never seen so much food; my family rarely sat at the table and all that was missing was a dancing minstrel prancing about playing Green Sleeves and did you know Henry the Eighth is credited with penning this clever tune so its centuries old.
Everyone tucked in and I followed the family protocol; I enjoyed the feast but I was fit to burst I can tell you but very grateful nonetheless and there were other times when I would call for Brad on our way to the pub when we were older and I would have a bacon buttie whilst I waited for Brad who was always late.
In my house we ate well most of the time, particularly when Dad was working but meals were mainly plated up in the small galley like kitchen when we got the extension, prior to that the kitchen was a sink and cooker in the back room against the wall.
Anyway, I would always finish my meal by soaking the remainder with the crust from my bread or I would lick the plate dry, don't recall doing either at this banquet!
We would eat our meals on our laps except at Christmas when more of a fuss was made and when Granddad would visit, there's another memory unlocked. One Christmas Granddad staggered to the loo, the inside one, after having had one too many drinks and he fell in the bath! Shouldn't laugh I know but Granddad never really got drunk and all the merriment that festive year must have gone straight to his head! He was unscathed thankfully and this is a fond family memory for my sisters and me!
I remember 'Tupperware' being popular in the seventies and we had various plastic storage containers although I don't recall my Mum attending Tupperware parties with her pals, parties were someone earned commission concealed by a steady flow of drinks and silly party games.
As for the food, in our house it was a case of what would you like with your chips for tea and I remember having Findus pancakes at least once a week! Delicious, must get them in some time served with a dollop of HP sauce. Adam told me recently that Mum told him she would fill the HP sauce bottle up with cheap brown sauce hoping I wouldn't notice but I would always guess what she had done and I would turn my nose up. I never realised that HP stood for Houses of Parliament until I was an

adult and it all seems so bleeding obvious now as the front of the bottle has a picture of Big Ben.
I loved beans but it had to be Heinz Baked Beans and one of my favourite dishes was beans and mash. I would mix the contents forming an orange coloured mash of spuds and beans and then I would tuck in. spam was another deliciously simple meal we would have at least once a week, out of a square shaped tin opened with a key and best eatedn with sauce like with most meals.
I had never been introduced to sweet corn as a kid and I ate my first mushroom when I was in my early twenties and to this day I'm not a great lover of vege although I will at least try green food now, back then I was very picky indeed, bit of a pain in the backside I think but I guess it was a mixture of not trying different foods and changing taste buds! My sisters were different they ate all their vegetables, including onions!
We had scouse sometimes but not 'blind scouse', the vegetarian version without the meat. I love scouse particularly when it's covered in HP sauce and eaten with the obligatory buttie but taking care not to spill it down your top!
In contrast Dad would make 'corn beef hash', basically mincemeat and spuds mashed together and I really hated this meal and I would steadfastly refused to eat, it was too bland and had 'visible' onions and I hated onions. I remember Dad on one occasion being furious with me having spent all day cooking 'hash' and we entered into a stalemate, a battle of culinary wills.
Mum was out as I recall and he demanded that I eat up or I'd have to stay in for the rest of the day, which wasn't on for an adventurer like me but I realised I had no other option and I'd chew on small amounts wishing we had a dog under the table or a meat eating plant to discard this horrid dish! Should have trained Tiddle's to eat from my hand instead of going the loo! I think Dad gave up in the end but I never did get to play out that night, I was sent to bed with a flea in my ear and probably a good kick up the backside!
We had buttered bread with everything, still do in fact and we called them butties. I even remember making a pie buttie with HP sauce of course and worse still a pizza buttie when I was a teenager! Very unhealthy I know but delicious. Do you remember the funny track '*A Little bit of Toast*' from the late seventies? Here's a bit of trivia for you, did you know the track was by the 'Streetband', fronted by Paul Young before he began leaving his hat everywhere!
When times were tough Dad would make fish cakes, which we really liked but we knew not to ask for sweets as this meant that Mum and Dad

were struggling for money! Dad learnt how to make fish cakes in the army as a conscripted cook and the earliest picture we have of Dad is a black and white picture of him in his whites looking very thin. He must have been about eighteen I think, sad really as I have no idea what my Dad looked like as a child or a baby but I'm guessing I looked like him but I will never know. Guess I could do with the Dr's help again!

In contrast Mum has many pictures of her as a nipper, she looks just like my sisters, whereas Dad has none as his family were very poor and the taking of pictures was not the done thing and I'm guessing they never possessed a camera.

Dad wasn't a culinary expert but he was a dab hand at peeling spuds and making the tastiest fish cakes ever. He'd mash fish with potato and onion and would fashion them into burger shapes and would cover them with crunched cornflakes. We loved them and he would bake dozens at a time and we'd have them for dinner, tea and supper but not breakfast as that was reserved for cornflakes! I know the irony is not lost on me either!

You know Dad; you really should make my family and me some fish cakes. I can still smell them if I sniff hard enough and predictably I loved to smother them with HP Brown Sauce.

Dad knew he had to chop the onions up very small whatever he was making and I've often wondered why I hated onions so much. Had Dad battered me with an onion as I am told they are very tasty and a vital ingredient in most meals but to me I have an almost phobic reaction to them. My sister's grew up knowing this, they love pickled onions too, another major dislike of mine and they're even more despicable as they stank to high heaven. They knock me sick!

If I annoyed Tracy or Tina and trust me I often did, they would seek revenge on me by realising the satanic odour and chasing me through the house and sometimes into the street with a pickled onion breathing ghastly foul smells from some demonic world into my face. I was rendered powerless you see and the only thing I could do was run like the clappers like my life depended upon it.

Chapter Five

Everybody Was Kung Fu Fighting...

I did warn you that this book of my memories would veer off from topic to topic, from early childhood to teenage years and back again so with that in mind I will now talk about my school days beginning with my Nursery education but before I do so I think it's worth jotting down a few lines about me being raised a Catholic and how this influenced my childhood.
Just like our sister city Glasgow, who incidentally have their very own 'coitus interruptus' but they refer to 'getting off at Paisley' and I know this because I lived in Glasgow for a while as an adult; Liverpool can appear very polarised at times; you're either a red or a blue, from north or south Liverpool, Paul or John, a Liberal or Labour supporter, rarely a Tory unless your Neil and a Catholic or Protestant.
Most Evertonian's are reputedly Catholic although not all of them and Kopites are mainly Protestant or 'proddy dogs' as we called them.
I knew of other religions of course but rarely came face to face with anyone who was not a Christian and religious studies at school almost entirely focused on the doctrine of Christianity and the teachings of the bible. I guess we weren't so enlightened back then or more likely those in power wanted to protect the sanctity of the old ways.
Mum was a Catholic, Dad was a Protestant, a mixed marriage I guess and I was raised a Catholic not because my Mum won the coin toss as they weren't particularly religious but because of the school they wished to send me too, probably the nearest. St Hugh's was the school and every Monday morning in class those who went to St Hugh's Church would be asked to sit down leaving the heathens to shamefully stand up and face ridicule and looks of condemnation from whatever teacher we had.
You soon began to realise that God was everywhere, omnipresent as they say and you knew not to lie or to steal for fear that a bolt of lightening from above would surely strike you down.

In fact God had a clever trick up his heavenly sleeve; her name was Miss Sutton, God rest her sole as she was ancient back then and yes I've just done the sign of the cross. She would ask what the priest was wearing for those not so cursed with Catholic guilt as I was just in case you dared to try and con her into believing you had attended mass. Mates would ask what the Priest had worn and for fun you would sometimes tell them red when you knew he had worn green.

Ms Sutton was particularly keen to know whom her favourite kids were and who would end up on the naughty table destined to fail in her class! In fact I pretty much complied with all the righteous Catholic reinforcement, I wouldn't exactly say willingly, you just did because you dare not question why and I ended up becoming an alter boy and a choirboy at the same.

By that I don't mean I would happily sing hymn number 453, All Things Bright and Beautiful at the same time as assisting the good father Daley with the mass, the 453 is a guess by the way! That would be silly; no I'd attend Church twice on a Sunday and often during the week when not practicing some hymn in Latin with Mr Lovelady in the vestry, attached to the prestbury with other boys I may add just in case you are making assumptions about abuses in Church.

I came to realise that mass mainly followed the same script recited 'religiously' for many a moon but with slight adjustments throughout the year and of course we had the priest's sermon preached to the faithful about the topic of the day. I often wondered if the priest had made his sermon up as he went along, a religious adlib or was this rehearsed after spending hours labouring over a cup of tea about what he would say. However it was conceived he certainly had the unyielding attention of his devotees as they would stare and hang on his every word.

Then we have the Creed. To this day I can chant the Creed and in my head I ring the bell whenever the priest blesses and raises the bread to the heavens. Old habits and that was such an honour as an alter boy as was waving the incense during Stations of the Cross. The smell would waft around the cold stale Church searching for the nostrils of those who wanted to be cleansed and the smell was strangely intoxicating but I guess that was the point.

The best part of mass for me was going around the Church as the crowd dovetailed outside to shake hands with the priest, leaving me with a long pole to reach up and distinguish the candles. At Christmas the priest would give us kids fifty pence for being so helpful all year.

As for the choir, I wasn't devout and pious as you might think or particularly good at singing for that matter, I just fancied scaling the turning steps to the raised section where the choir sat as they always appeared so cool and you could look down on people. It seemed like an honour to be asked to wear the cloak the choir kids wore and I guess I wanted to be on that pedestal again. Mr Lovelady would play the organ with his back to us boys and when he wasn't looking we'd gaff around but being careful not to get caught, as he could be very stern when he wanted to be. Girls weren't allowed to join the choir!

I remember being asked to do the solo part of a hymn at mass on Sunday, this was an honour and we practiced for a few weeks. In truth another choirboy would have been asked first as he had the better voice but he was off school sick and I was his deputy, his *'Substitute'*, a guilty pleasure track by the South African band 'Clout', which was out about the same time. I was all prepared but said boy came back to school, he had been ill and Mr Lovelady decided to go with his initial instinct and I was 'asked' to step down. That really hurt Mr Lovelady.

I remember learning Christmas carols in school and during choir practice and using this to my advantage for many nights leading up to Christmas. Me and my mates would go carol singing you see, took a bit of courage mind you and someone would always sheepishly stand at the back and the best singers would be ushered to the front to look all angelic and pious.

Sometimes curtains would twitch and no one would answer so we'd move on to the next house but when they did you would belt out a chorus or two of 'Away in the Manger' or We Three Kings' in the hope you would be given a few pence for bestowing your talents on your unwitting benefactor.

Sometime occupants would give you money to send you on your way rather than stand in the cold listening to a group of snotty nosed kids trying to harmonise a classic carol and you were always mindful to other kids getting to streets where you knew houses that would pay up most nights. At the end you would 'divvy' out the money and arguments would start about who really contributed or not.

This is indeed a dangerous activity as we were never accompanied by a protective adult waiting in the wings and I notice these days kids sometime knock at my house carol singing but all they muster is a couple of lines then expect to be paid, wouldn't have happened in my day I can tell you! Humbug!

Anyway back to the past. One day I remember attending church at 6pm and as I walked up to take Holy Communion my mind wandered to thoughts about supper when I got home. My Mum always made sandwiches on a Sunday night with cake and other goodies! Anyway my palms were clasped together but facing down, this wasn't a conscious act as I shuffled nearer and nearer to the priest but a subconscious mistake. Mass ended and I made my way through the parishioners who were normally ancient to me and thereby very slow and cumbersome, apologising en route but with one thought on my mind, I needed to get home, cake and the Muppets awaited!

I remember getting to the front and there to my surprise was the priest. I can't recall his name but we had two Irish priests at the time, father Daley was a kind gentle man, this one was his opposite, he was very strict and scathing. I wondered how he had defrocked so quickly in the vestry and how did he get to the front in quick time. Had he magic powers? He always grimaced and he had a face like a 'farmers arse on a frosty morning' and then he said, 'Griffith here, now', finger pointing to his feet! He was on a heavenly crusade I guess and of course I did what I was told, you never refused a man of the cloth but I kept thinking what now don't you realise I have cake waiting.

I was about ten with a head full of junk never imagining that I had done anything wrong! His face twisted, he reached out and he held my side burns with one hand, my arse head hair was longer then and he pulled me up until I was stretching up on my tiptoes!

He glared and said in a threatening Irish accent, 'don't you ever pray to the devil again in my Church' referring to my hands pointing to the fiery south? As an adult I've often thought what a stupid thing to say in any case, surely his evilness would not be allowed to ply his dastardly trade below Gods own house! Doesn't seem right does it.

His action brought tears to my eyes I can tell you and I ran home with tears in my eyes and cursing the priest with no name. Feel terrible mentioning this just in case I'm being watched by father whatever his name was, after all a priest must surely have made it past the pearly gates; a one way ticket up the divine escalator unless you fiddled with kids that is! At least I hope he got to heaven.

Once a Catholic always a Catholic they say but I lost my faith from that point and although I have attended Church on occasion I turned slightly away from the faith. In fact engrained in my thoughts to this day when I do attend Holy Communion is the mantra keep your bloody palms up lad, keep your bloody palms up and when I shake the Priests hand, no longer having cake to run home to of course or young sprightly legs, I cant help think 'are you honing in on my sideburns? Don't even think about it?

Confession was also a strange event for us Catholics. I either missed the lesson or fell asleep at school, which taught us what to say at confession and for months I avoided spilling out my sins but eventually managed to pluck up the courage as I was by then racked with guilt.
Perhaps father whatever his name presided over events and stored this thinking I will have my hands on those sideburns once more but I remember attending one Saturday morning in utter fear, my stomach turned as I opened the wooden door to the small private room, I was so petrified of the consequences!
I knelt down gingerly and said, 'please forgive me for I have sinned but I can't remember what comes next father'. That in it self was a sin and I waited with baited breath to hear the wrath of God descend on me and at the very least I expected the curtain to twitch. Seconds did pass, the curtain twitched slightly but thankfully the priest simply talked me through the ritual, he must have sensed my trembling.
He was having a good day me thinks, might have felt guilty for pulling my sideburns but I felt so relieved and cleansed but with all this Catholic angst I plum forgot to think about sins I had actually committed which was the very reason why I was there! I found myself making up sins like I had not been very helpful round the house or I was nasty to my sisters, that kind of family stuff, I might have been but I was blatantly lying which is a sin in itself and so the guilt goes on and on and on.
God this Catholic guilt is all too much sometimes and even saying God is a bloody sin! Tonight I just might say three Our Fathers and ten Hail Mary's to cleanse my dammed soul but thinking about it Church wasn't so bad though, it gave me a good sense of morality that I take with me into adulthood and some funny memories too! I really liked the Hymn 'Give Me Peace in My Heart' and I only wish I still had the falsetto voice to still sing it but that vanished when my 'bollocks dropped!'
Like I said before my Mum and Dad's friends from back then were Marie and Joe and being from 'God's own country', Ireland, made sense that Joe would be my 'Confirmation' mentor when I was thirteen. Joe helps maintain St Hugh's Church where I attended but now attends Mass at St Clare's off Lawrence Road. Joe told Mum that St Hugh's had its final Mass in July 2012 due to plummeting parishioner numbers and what a shame that is, sharing a parody with the demise of many local boozers around the area, both places of worship and there must be many wonderful gothic Churches standing idol and lonely, a standing testament to another time!
With that let me now tell you all about my education. One of my earliest memories of school, one of my earliest memories of all time, was my first

day at nursery and I think this day is etched into my memory as I remember it being a somewhat traumatic experience.

The nursery was an annexe building at the back end of St Thomas A Becket on Spekeland Road, the secondary school I attended when I was aged eleven. I must have been about four I guess, so it's the start of the seventies, a new decade of optimism and I can vividly remember my Mum releasing me from her skirt and ushering me forward into the classroom so as she could get back home to put her feet up or to rearrange her rollers under her scarf that she wore all the time.

Just pausing a beat. You don't see women with rollers under scarfs these days do you although I notice that the wearing of 'big' rollers' for added bounce has become fashionable for young women who one must assume are advertising the fact that they are popular as they have a night out later.

Some scouse ladies even wear pyjamas whilst out and about shopping which for many reasons should not be done and I understand some women have PJ's as we called them for sleeping in and PJ's for shopping, how peculiar and how 'chavy' as my son would say. As for lads with their hands permanently down their tracksuit pants, well that just isn't right and I don't recall ever doing that in the seventies even after my bollocks had dropped?

Anyway back to the nursery. I was mortified you see and I cried my guts out till I had no more tears and other boys soon followed my lead and we all cried in unison like some frog chorus. We were without doubt, wimps. The girls casually walked in as I recall probably wondering what all the fuss was about whilst happily waving goodbye to their Mum's telling them to get back to whatever was the Jeremy Kyle equivalent show on telly.

I suppose it's worth mentioning a track that sums up my insecurities from around this time; *'Where's Your Mamma Gone'* by 'Middle of the Road'. This track was more commonly known as the 'Chirpy Chirpy Cheep Cheep song' and a break from the protest tracks that dominated the charts around then and I still get butterflies in my stomach when I hear the opening warble and I instantly think of my dear old Mum, so much so it was a toss up between this track and *'Pal of My Cradle Days'* as to what track should head up the chapter about my family.

Come to think of it I think I had attachment issues not wishing to leave the sanctuary of home and Mum's bosom and I also suspect Freud would call this the Oedipus complex which theorises that us boys want to consume our Mum's until we realise we have dangly bits just like our Dad's. The theory goes that Mum must have had hers castrated but at

four you hadn't quite got to grips with that concept so tears it was.
The only other two things I can remember about my nursery days was that this was the first time I had made friends with kids who would join me through primary school and who didn't live in my street and the magical cardboard box, the wonderful adventures we had in it and the imagination it would conjure up!
Sure the nursery had the normal array of toys, mainly wooden in design and painted in led based paint I guess but we boys would have hours of fun with a simple painted cardboard box with a circular hole that resembled a washing machine. One day it would be a spacecraft as it was the dawn of the space-age, then a tank, the war was still on peoples minds, then a pirate ship and then a racing car and like sardines we could fit two inside, sometimes three at any one given time. I guess we must have been very small or maybe budding Houdini's and the teacher would have to decide whose turn it was next.
After a year in the nursery I then attended St Hugh's Roman Catholic Infants and Junior School, as did my sisters and even though I spent several years in the infants I can't put a face or a name to the teachers that taught me. The aforementioned Mrs Sutton and Mr Lovelady taught me in Junior School.
I find that bizarre as I must have spoken about what I had done that day when I got home from school and it seems to me that memories fade the older one gets so on that basis will things I did when I was in my twenties become lost the closer I get to retirement age? Will I forget writing this book if I make it to eighty, maybe I should! It does make you wonder doesn't it?
Ms, Mrs or Mr whatever your name aside, I do remember a cake made out of cardboard that was rolled out to celebrate birthdays to the tune of happy birthday and feeling jealous of my peers because my birthday occurred without fail during the Easter holidays; I never did get my turn and that still hurts whoever you are!
I also remember the infants as mainly being a messy but joyful period of my life on account we would have fun playing in this raised sandpit at the back of the classroom with various buckets and spades. Kids would elbow jostle to play in the sand and when not dreaming of buried treasure on some tropical beach we would play with different shaped wooden blocks creating walls and castles to then knock down.
I remember small circular Frisbee shaped paints in smudged white trays and painting big brush strokes on large pieces of paper attached to an easel.
Yes I loved painting and I would create pictures of rainbows over a tent

pitched in a green field or a ship sailing on a stormy sea with seagulls hovering above, whilst meticulously dipping my brush into a jam jar of dirty water between strokes. I would then stand back to admire my work before flipping the paper over to start again hoping to create a masterpiece to show my teacher.

I'm sure we must have learnt about rudiment mathematics and the letters of the alphabet but I shall always remember my infants education with affection, when all you had to worry about was who would get to the front of the line first at the end of break and whether Ms, Mrs or Mr would give you a gold star in your exercise book.

Yes a gold star was the zenith of achievement whereas other coloured stars were seen as okay but gold was another level bestowed to kids that had managed to write a sentence neatly, remaining in a near perfect horizontal line as opposed to something that resembled the plummeting stock exchange!

I also remember the class taking turns to read the story of the *'Ugly Duckling'* and then listening to this lovely song that still causes the onset of a lump in my throat as I always found it to be a sad tale although I know it has a happy ending but the journey was still painful to a little boys ears.

Just thought of another track that reminds me of my infant years. *'Puff the Magic Dragon'* and I now realise that this track was sung by 'Peter, Paul and Mary' from 1963 but hey you lot, where on earth is Honah Lee, Hawaii perhaps, I have a shirt ready? I loved this acoustic track as a nipper and I know I sound like a right crier but again this song would tug at my heartstrings and would make me feel so sad and sorry for Jackie Paper. He was little boy, so I had some affinity to Jackie, who grows up and loses interest in the imaginary adventures of childhood and leaves Puff alone and depressed; a bit like this book I guess but no dragon just the odd mate or two and of course Mrs Sutton!

Primary school felt like a relatively self-haven for me and I was accepted and reasonably popular. I was usually on the top table and I think I was a studios pupil eager to please my teachers and my Mum and Dad. Mum and Dad supported my sisters and me but in truth we were self-motivated kids probably influenced by Dad's determination to provide for his family and wanting to better ourselves and I think being brought up a Catholic had something to do with trying to be of the erudite sort as you dare 'not' pay attention.

I know this soon wears off but when you're very small looking for praise and approval you would willingly do jobs for the teacher to please them believing you had been especially chosen because you could be trusted. I

remember being the 'milk monitor' for example, which basically meant handing out cold cartons of milk to thirsty peers and sometimes Ms or Sir would ask the class if anyone wished to wipe the blackboard and the whole class would quickly raise its hands hoping to be picked.
In our school, in the old building, we had the break bell and whoever rang said bell was destined for bigger things, they were the chosen one, and this was the ultimate honour to bestow on a fledgling ugly duckling.
At the end of the year each class would put on a show and I recall it being a competitive affair. I remember singing Beatles songs standing on benches but the lasting memory I have of our attempt to please Sister Francesca, our Head, was this girls Irish dancing. We'd stand and admire her back and heels as she kicked across the stage with her arms glued to her side and I guess we had an advantage as she was a little dancing angle from Ireland where Sister came from, or at least second generation, possibly third. She was our trump card.
Another end of year event was the Schools Sports Day and for some unknown reason we would have our Sports Day on Sandown Lane footy pitches which is the other end of Wavertree, a couple of miles away. Teachers appeared more relaxed and made a fool of themselves in front of parents and it was always in July, always very hot and we were always thirsty and gasping for drinks.
The egg and spoon race was my favourite, although having long thumbs gave me an advantage should I be inclined to cheat and the sack race was always funny as was the three legged race. Especially when the parent's took part then it would become even more competitive!
I remember one time being on the playground but having one of my 'does anybody know I exist moments'. I was a right sulk sometimes. The playground was heaving and my mate Leather came over and asked me to be in a band. There's a point why do boys always use surnames or a shortened, bastardisation versions of your name. I was always called Griff, which was short for Griffith of course and this name was used until I was an adult. When people call me Griff today in jest, I'm jettisoned back in time to another body, another waistline, another haircut, another time.
Sometimes you'd knock for your mate and his Mum would answer and you'd say 'is yoey in' for example, side stepped trying to compute his first name. You knew it of course but you were so used to using his street name you were sometimes caught out and unsure what to say.
Back to the playground. Five brave souls were required and only four mates were up to the task. I sat there looking forlorn but secretly wanting so much to have the courage to take to the stage, I secretly

craved the limelight and the attention and I could sing a bit. Leather was a platinum blonde mate of mine; all the girls fancied him and he eventually persuaded me to join our version of the Osmond's. I think he promised to pick me first when it came to playground footy sides, you see he was a very good footy player as well and normally the captain. I should have hated him but he was a nice kid actually.

It may seem odd this but to be picked first or near the first was another honour at school and sadly this didn't occur very often in my case as I would sometimes be the last player or if not, I was near the last picked behind the kid with two left feet or the resident geek. That is until I discovered I had feline skills, a safe pair of hands and the agility to dive to my side; I'll tell you more about my goalie antics a bit later.

Now I know I must have been about six as the Osmond track we decided to sing was '*Crazy Horses*' and I have since worked out that this charted in 1972. Never knew it at the time but did you know this track actually has an eco friendly message as it's about gas guzzling cars and not about my Opie forefathers stampeding on a mad four legged beasts galloping across the prairie as I naively thought and dreamt about. I think I was Wayne, my mates became Merrill, Alan, Donny and Jay and yes for those who can remember the badly choreographed appearance on TOTP, we did the strange knee-tapping dance done by the brothers Mormon.

I played a pretend air guitar, I had practice on a tennis racquet at home in front of the mirror so I was pretty skilled and we all sang or should I say screamed out loud which is actually befitting of the track. Throats croaked for days afterwards.

Adoring fans surrounded us; mainly girls I might add and if my memory serves me correct they had their chin in their hands, they screamed back at the five of us pretending they were at the actual concert but mainly focused on my blonde mate. Dam you Leather. I loved the attention though; it was nice being popular, being part of the in crowd, trust me it didn't happen very often.

The playground was certainly an education in itself and Mr Attenborough, a man my Mum had a crush on as a little girl, sorry Mum, should have spent time on our yard to study anthropology rather than glaring at some big hairy brute in a sweaty jungle or some fish bloated penguin in the frosty Antarctic.

We didn't have apes or flightless birds but we had older tough lads, usually skilful at footy and whatever sport they turned their hand too, they would take charge of areas only teachers would dare enter and if they did, they usually only did so in pairs.

96 David Griffith

Thankfully said kids would leave fourth year to once again take their place at the bottom rung of the ladder in bigger school and so the whole evolution process would start again. Take note Mr Attenborough and you knew one day it would be my mates and me but for now we simply wanted to enjoy our time on the yard in control and in relative harmony. Why and when did we revert to years one to eleven and don't get me started on competitive school tables, Secondary Schools becoming High School or even Academy's. As for the introduction of end of year proms, huge limos and ball gowns, where are we in the UK or on the set of Greece where the actors are nearer bloody thirty than seventeen.

In fact I overheard some woman the other day talking about the cost of decking out her daughter for her prom; not that I'm accustomed to 'gegging' in on other peoples conversations but she seemingly spent a fortune on a dress, her child's hair and makeup and the limo and she justified it all by saying its something to remember when she's older! Aren't I glad I only have boys!

The playground was also a very dangerous place; well it certainly was for me. One of our favourite games was running up to the wall and reaching high. St Hugh's Church wall served as the perimeter to one side of our yard and it had a sand stone ledge about waist high and the game was to see who could reach the highest but this would involve sprinting toward the wall and jumping like those street jumpers you see on telly. I did this day in and day out, rain or shine but one day I got it painfully wrong. I mistimed my leap just as I made it to the wall; I slipped and cut my forehead open on the sandstone Church wall. Oh yes another head cut, another scar visible below my eyebrow, another bucket load of tears. That'll teach me to be so daring I guess and I remember the teacher, God what was her name, having to take me home all covered in blood that had dripped onto my new shirt to boot.

The phone was either not installed or disconnected again and we had to find my Mum at her school, she was a cleaner in the school next door called Webster Road.

Now there's a memory, Webster Road Primary was where I learnt to swim. We would march in pairs and hand to hand in case anyone suddenly had an urge to run under a passing truck, it was a safety thing, to Webster Road School. You knew you were getting closer to the pool on entry to the old black and white building as your nose would follow the smell of bleach as you descended the stairs deep down into the basement where you would find an old compact Victorian swimming pool.

Getting Off At Edge Hill – The Tracks Of My Years 97

Order would be maintained by teachers like Mr Lovelady, who incidentally is remembered for having nicotine stained yellow fingers from years of smoking and a chewed pair of specs. Girls and boys would undress in separate rooms and we would hang our uniforms on coat hangers with colourful animal pictures like squirrels and foxes to help us avoid wearing a mate's pair of undies. When did I first start wearing boxing shorts, I have no idea but I do remember wearing off white baggie Y fronts for years.

The pool was a perfect square shape and very small but for a little lad it was all very exciting. We would march into the pool area, taking care not to slip and we would sit on the edge. Following Mr yellow fingers command we would each take our turn to do the doggy paddle from one side to the next.

To begin with we would use square rubber floats that always had some other kids teeth marks round the edge that was either very scared or hungry and with outstretched arms we would kick away trying to move forward but usually staying still but causing a wash of bubbles.

This pool didn't have signs telling us not to smooch or bomb as we had teaches to ruin our fun and we would return to class with sodden hair and wet backs because Mum wasn't there to dry us off.

Mum would tell us she took up her cleaning job to get pin money as they used to call it but most of the time she was the main 'bread winner' and years later she still worked at the school and she eventually became the caretaker.

This brought with it other opportunities and I remember my Mum allowing me to use the baths on my own as a fifteen year old but this time two strokes was enough to reach the other side. Floats not needed but I did sometimes try the doggy paddle just for nostalgic fun. It was a bit spooky though being down there all on your own and I cannot begin to imagine how many children had splashed around in the pool and learnt to swim since it was first built in the 1800's.

After school I would sometimes call round to see my Mum to have a chat with her and her workmates chain smoking and shoehorned in to their rest room. Like I said Mum and her mates were rather rotund women if that's not too insulting to them and it seemed a bit of a squeeze at times. I remember using the art material in the school, paper, water paint and brushes to do my homework as we couldn't afford the material but we also didn't have the space.

When not with school or popping in to say hello to Mum, we would play footy on Webster Road School yard as it had this opening, probably used as stables in the past but we used it as a goal albeit bigger than your average goal, to play 'goalie V'. Now there were two unofficial ways into the School playground. The first involved scaling this big fence by Sandhead Street, an element of danger, as the wire meshing would sway as you toppled over.

The other entrance involved squeezing through the green iron barred railing near the entrance. Someone had discovered that the builders of the railing from another century had not used a uniformed approach and two bars were slightly wider than the others. Everyone knew this and I remember it being a tight crush and some big kid convincing me that if you can get your head through, like a cat, then your body should slip through with a bit of effort.

I remember daring myself and pushing my head through, feeling the bars rub against my ears whilst all the time thinking I'd get stuck and someone would have to call the fire brigade.

I then turned my shoulder inwards to discover that I could indeed prize my skinny body through but then realising that I'd have to do this again to get out, oh I forgot about that!

I tended not to do this very often because I grew bigger and therefore increased my chances of getting lodged so I decided to take my chances climbing over the swaying fence.

Webster Road School had other places that appealed to an adventurer looking for a dare and my mates Grant, Alan and me would go searching for places of discovery. Running along the side where the school boarders Sandhead Street for example was the same green railing and the other side was a fifteen foot drop to probably the same level as the swimming baths inside. I might be exaggerating the depth but it felt really big at the time to someone with short legs and this fete took some courage, as there was no railing to squeeze through. You had to climb and once over the fence you would stand on the limestone mantel and you would walk along gripping the railing looking for a place to 'drop' from.

The bottom had an array of pipes and other smaller brick buildings and after running around for a bit these would allow you to get a sound footing to climb back out again once it was time to go home. I'd ask Grant or Alan for a 'shimmy up', you did this by locking your fingers together and a mate would stand on your hands, then on the count of three you'd be hoisted up to cling on to the railing. Once there you would then reach down to help your mate clamber up, unless you wanted to torment them a bit, using their feet against the wall otherwise they were stuck!

All things considered Webster Road was a funtastic place for my mates and me for many years when I was in primary school and an earlier version of a play house but without the protective padding, slides and ball pool but more fun me thinks!

Sadly this wonderful example of a Victorian School has been demolished in the name of urban modernisation again and all that's left are fond memories, an open piece of land with a football pitch and a fenced perimeter, a more sturdier fence I might add, to stop people fly tipping. In school we knew that boys were different than girls, they had long hair but not much longer, it was the seventies after all and like I said before us boys mainly had 'arse heads' on account we had centre parts like a hairy bum! I sometimes had a straight fringe.

Boys in Catholic schools wore grey shorts; probably a form of penance for being naughty as they were very cold in winter, girls wore skirts. 'Proddy dogs' wore long pants and I remember thinking this was so unfair, why make us feel the cold air rush around our skinny grazed legs? Another give away was ear piercing, back then earrings were exclusively for girls, not like now and as for nose piercing.

Ashamed to say it but one of my favourite games was catch the 'girl kiss the girl'. Simple enough game, we boys would run after girls hoping to catch the most popular girl and plant a wet one on the side of her face. Then the tables would turn and the girls would chase us but thinking about it I don't recall the girls excitedly shouting out 'catch the boys kiss the boys'. We were clever though or at least we thought we were. See, you'd run like the 'clappers' away from the girl but you would then slow your pace down when you crossed paths with a girl you either liked or found least ugly!

This took some skill, as you had to have good peripheral vision befitting of top footballers and an awareness of space to avoid the occasional collision with another mate or worse still a girl you didn't fancy. I was no oil painting but one had standards even back then and it wasn't easy trying to actually get caught. Story of my life it seems.

This could go on all play as the packs would heave from one side to the next, take note Mr Attenborough of how the group flowed around the yard and I leant so much about girls on the playground but most of all I learnt how to run bloody fast when needed.

I had several childhood crushes and remember falling big time for a girl called Dawn and I would dream about Dawn till dawn funny enough and me flying around the area on a magic carpet above the rooftops. Not sure why a carpet, I remember watching the Arabian Nights at the time so it might have had something to do with that, but I'm sure any dream

experts out there would say it was linked to me being in a state of early train journey arousal.
In year four Mr Lovelady organised the seating arrangements and to my delight he sat Dawn next to me, Mum was on the school's committee so I guess a pack of twenty came in handy, only kidding Mum he demanded forty! Dawn knew I liked her, I didn't know what to say and if ever a track summed up my feelings it was *'I Cant Stand Loosing You'* by The Police, a track forever remembered partly because of the evocative cover to the single which shows Stuart Copeland hanging from a rope standing on a block of ice melting in front of a three bar electric fire. I remember buying the single with Joey, who was a mate for a few months and examining the cover looking at every detail.
I couldn't keep my eyes off Dawn, I was besotted, I was tongue-tied and I remember Dawn always smelt like soap. The track *'If I had Words'* by Yvonne Keeley seems a fitting song to recall at this point and I eventually plucked up the courage and I gave Dawn my blue pencil case, an offering of love, an ice breaker with an array of multi coloured pencils and a sharpener too, I thought she'd be impressed but sadly her feelings for me were not reciprocated but she kept my case though! I wonder what ever happened to her or my case, I wish you well, wherever you are but you could have had it all Dawn, you could have had it all and we could have flown away on my carpet for an eternity! Oh well, on to pastures new.
Mr Lovelady also introduced me to the traditional folk song *'It's not the leaving of Liverpool'*, he would tinker the ivories on his piano in the classroom and we would sing this song in harmony. Wikipedia alas could not help on this occasion as I can't figure out whose credited with writing this delightful track or when it was first sung but I do know its an old sea shanty song and Irish bands, the 'Dubliners' and the 'Pogues' have both released there own versions. That will be the Irish connection to Liverpool once again.
The lyrics speak to me, they are very poignant and emotional and I remember wondering with awe how people must have felt when they set sail to a new life in a far off distant land never to see my beloved Liverpool again. If you don't believe me then here's a few lines that still evoke emotions in the pit of my belly; *'so fare thee well my own true love, when I return united we will be, it's not the leaving of Liverpool that grieves me, but my darling when I think of thee'*. Simply superb and perhaps being the eternal romantic, those lines echo with pain and sadness and I love them even now after all these years, so thank you very much Mr Lovelady and I think they're over seventy five year old so no copyright

infringement then!

Moving on to other games we played, another favourite was the bionic man, which was on the telly at the time. We boys would run around in slow motion, unless someone other than Dawn was hunting me of course, muttering the noise that went with the slow motion and went something like dddddddddddddd.

Sometimes you had to lift something very heavy but that was no problem for a part robotic all American astronaut superhero with a heavy-duty bionic arm. I remember trying to lift things with just one arm when I was a kid then realising two arms Mother Nature gave us was always better. Sounds like a scene from Animal Farm, two arms better than one Mr Orwell or was that legs?

Sometimes we would use our bionic eye, which basically meant squinting or holding a wink with one eye whilst looking through the other and we would search for objects the other side of the playground imagining they were miles away not a hundred yards.

Then we had superman. We would run around the yard using our coats as capes buttoned around the neck and flapping behind us with one arm outstretched imagining that we were flying above the ground in search of baddies'.

Another craze around this time was karate or Kung Fu, influenced by the brilliant Bruce Lee and his movies, the telly series Kung Fu with the not so very Chinese, David Carradine.

Let's also pay homage to the unrelated but somewhat cheesy soundtrack *'Everybody Was Kung Fu Fighting'* by one hit wonder, 'Carl Douglas'. Here's something you might be interested to know, this track was rated one hundred in the greatest one hit wonders chart and sold over eleven million records world wide making it one of the best selling singles of all time. Kerching Mr Douglas.

Do you recall the 'Water Margin?' This was a subtitled action series based on a novel known in Chinese as Shuihu Zhuan and released in 1973. Thanks again Wiki. The script was a bit bizarre but the action was plentiful and I can still hum the tune in my head. Then we had 'Monkey', similar to the Water Margins but less serious and very funny at times. Monkey, as you may recall was born from an egg on a mountaintop and was, as the track goes, *'the funkiest monkey that ever popped'*. He was cast out of heaven with two former angels, now monsters, Sandy and the annoying Pigsy and this peculiar series first hit our screens in 1979. Pass me the drugs and if you're over forty, I'm guessing you ran around the playground wafting your hand in front of your mouth to summon up a cloud to escape on! Dawn where are you when I needed you?

The country couldn't get enough of all things oriental in the early to mid seventies. I remember watching Bruce Lee at the Classic Cinema on Allerton Road wanting to round house everyone when I came out and being glued to the telly on a Saturday night I think, watching the bald headed grasshopper save the damsel in distress with several accurate kicks! The Kung Fu stories were very samey and were basically about a Shaolin monk called Kwai Chang Caine who was seeking his brother across the American old west.

Cowboys and fighting, pure magic that and always a sure winner for us boy's and the serious ran from 1972 to 1975. We didn't really know what a roundhouse was but this didn't stop us trying to imitate our hero's and kick as high as we could but often with comical effect. When I was about ten I remember drawing a picture of grasshopper and this was the first time I realised I could draw something different than a tent on a hill below a tree, I wonder what ever happened to that picture? Oh well, or is that Orwell? Sorry, I spotted a naff play on word.

On the subject of kicking, one of my fondest memories of school actually took place outside of school. I would walk up the entry at the back of Cranborne Road towards the gate; for those that don't know the area this Road separates the terraced houses and I was kicking a stone thinking I was on Match of the Day.

I found a soggy pound note on the floor then another note and I ran home and gave them to my Mum. Two pound was a lot of money in those days and my bounty was gratefully received. Mum probably said something like 'thanks son now back to school you don't want to be late'. Chuffed with myself I took the same route and kicked the same stone and to my surprise I found a further pound in the dirty puddle, then another. I was beside myself with glee and I ran home again.

Mum was over the moon too, so what if he's late and I left for school for the third time, slightly puffed but pleased as punch. I looked down again and to my astonishment I found the same stone, no only kidding I mean I found four more pound notes. Unbelievable but this time I looked for more ahead of me, I was getting tired by now but that was my lot.

I ran home again then I ran back to school, as I knew Ms Sutton would be on the warpath for stragglers and she would give them a slap on the calves as a punishment for being late. Strangely my memory is disjointed from that point, as I don't recall coming home to a bag of sweats, a cream cake or even a well-done son you shall be honoured and we shall eat like kings tonight! Bring out the steak for your brother!

Come to think of it I should really be feeling a tad sorry for the drunken fool that fell out of St Hugh's social club next to my school as he or she probably lost his or her well earned wages and his or her family probably had jam on toast for days. Me think's I need the confession box again and we really should have spoken to the proprietor. How does confession go again?

Moving on, here are a few words about male aggression and fighting, or more to the point about my handbags at four paces memories. Let me explain. Boys were always shuffling around the pecking order of who could take whom and my mate Oliver was one of the toughest kids in my year. Oliver is his real name and his surname by the way as opposed to the popular fashionable name used today; he was my best mate in junior school. He was tough, always good to have a tough mate and was often getting into fights unlike me. I would just stand there and watch pondering why fight it looks so painful and unnecessary.

I was never a fighter you see, didn't see the point and I would talk myself out of conflict, at least most of the time. Wish at times I had been more assertive in truth and I wish I had inherited my Dad's boxing gene but it simply wasn't in my DNA to raise a fist in retaliation. Still isn't. Oliver on the other hand would rather retort to solving disagreements with his fist than talk and in my eyes he looked and sounded like Nelson from the Simpsons with the barrelled chest 'to boot'.

One day Oliver and me were talking and he said I bet you can't fight Cushion. Cushion, I can't recall his first name, think it was Ian, was a quiet lad, he lived in the next street to me and he also sat at our table. I wonder if he dreamt of flying away with Dawn, I would have gladly boxed him if he had?

We'd never fallen out as I recall, we didn't speak much as he didn't care much for footy but to my horror Cushion got wind of this and said he could take me on. Cushion please be more diplomatic and less confident next time, I wouldn't have thought any less of you.

Oliver was 'shit stirring' which described someone who caused trouble, shouted out during break Cushion's just offered Griff out which meant we had to fight, playground custom dictated we had to take on the challenge, it was the law of the land, similar to throwing the gauntlet down from days of old. What for I don't know other than pecking order bullshit honour I guess or because Oliver yearned to watch a fight rather than be watched.

I thought of all the karate moves I had seen on telly and had rehearsed thousands of times but began to think why was Cushion so keen, had he seen the movies too, has he secretly been taking martial arts lessons? Gulp! Tensions built and the school day ended and word of mouth was used to rally the whole school to the waste ground nearby at the top of my street. Cushion was late and I hoped he had chickened out as I'd never hit anyone in anger before but he turned up and a crowd formed a circle of no escape round Cushion and me. Why Mr Attenborough why? Oliver was the ringmaster and he told the crowd to be quiet and for Cushion and me to prepare ourselves for the pending duel. This meant stand with your fists clenched and ready and Oliver probably wanted to see for himself what it was like to see two boys knock several shades of red out of each other on the floor.

We stood toe to toe and I thought what do I do? Do I hit him, do I do a roundhouse or do I do the honourable thing and embark on a speech of consolidation to the standing crown and concede? Both would leave me feeling lousy, whoa the anguish.

Anyway, the animal in me sprung to life and I ended up punching him in the face and in the style of Bruce Lee I put my hands up expecting him to retaliate with similar veracity. I wasn't proud and I don't confess to it being a hard punch but it was accurate, right to the nose.

Cushion winced and stepped back. He then cried, I could see a trickle of blood peep out of his noise and with that he barged his way through the audience to the sanctuary of Sandhead Street, he ran off home.

The fight was over no sooner as it had started after one tame punch and I felt like an 'arl arse', which translated from scouse means 'I felt really terrible and cruel' and the crowd left disappointed, blood had not been spilt, well maybe a little and wait for it, did they want more please Mr Oliver. Sorry couldn't resist that.

I really wanted to console Cushion to say 'are you okay mate' but he ran off and I don't recall ever speaking to Cushion again. If you're reading this, heavens know how but let's just pretend, Cushion, two simple questions are running through my brain, why did you make me hit you and did you fancy Dawn? So sorry about my lack of control but I had no other option, the playground can be so cruel Mr Attenborough, forget the steamy jungle!

I so hated fighting but every now and then play fighting would get out of hand and someone would have to exert his or her need to be superior I even remember having a fight with Grant and being pinned to the floor by Jeanette, or was that a tactical move on my part? Can't recall the exact details but I got into a fight one day with this kid called Graham. I've no idea what the reason was. Graham was a Black kid who lived on Cranborne Road, smaller than me by some inches but a little powerhouse of energy. He actually turned out to be a mate some months later as it happens and what's that I hear; keep you're friends close but you're enemies even closer.

Graham threw several accurate and expert punches to my head whilst I stood there motionless not knowing what to do, he could smell the taste of victory, the iron in my blood was a dead give away or more likely my sobbing told him I was done and he backed off. Some kids would do that they knew when not to wade in and to back off, victory was sealed but I have seen many fights when male aggression takes over and I have watched some poor kid being stamped on and kicked in the face. Thankfully Graham was an honourable kid, he had clearly won and I ran off home to lick my wounds.

Now maybe things got lost in translation but back home my Dad wasn't at all happy. He dragged me by the collar round to Graham's to confront his Dad. He knocked at the door and said 'your boys just hurt my boy' and with that Graham stepped forward from behind his Dad.

My Dad grew up in Dingle like I said and he was a decent boxer in his time, his broken nose is testament to a lifetime of scrapes. He took one look at Graham, shook his head and walked away in shame and disgust. Had I said 'Dad some big lads just hit me', no I didn't but I could feel his shame and we never spoke of the incident again. Our pink elephant.

I tried to dodge confrontation throughout my childhood. See I was a talker, I'm known for being gifted in the art of verbal diarrhoea and the thought of hitting someone was so alien to me and showed a lack of tolerance and an inability to negotiate a peaceful end! God I deserved a beating, either that or a job in NATO!

Lads can be very cruel, girls too I guess but being popular was normally about wit, looks and physicality but not in any particular order. I was a skinny wimpy street kid able to run fast but that was about it. I don't think I was displeasing to the eye but I never had the striking good looks like Leather or the individuality and sheer brawn like Oliver that set you asides from your mates that made you popular.

I realised as I approached double figures that you had to be funny to survive. It was survival and I got by most of the time, as I was not a threat to any alpha kids out there. I could chat and I loved nothing better than sitting with me mates talking about everything and anything.

I might have craved a big family with older brothers but growing up with two sisters I came to realise that I could talk to girls and sometimes they even talked back! This was a revelation and I soon used this ability to my advantage. You see your slightly Neanderthal lad could hold court in a testosterone-fuelled ecosystem but when girls came on the scene they visibly wilted and became tongue-tied.

Violence wasn't the norm in our house; my parents were rather liberal in their parenting styles, which has had an impact on how I am as an adult and a Dad too. True my Dad would hit me with his belt on occasion but only when I had been really naughty and I know this is wrong but I guess this is how he was brought up and this is how adults disciplined their children in the seventies, at least I think this was the case!

One time I remember goading my Dad into hitting me with the belt, I had relentlessly pushed his I've had enough buttons; I was bored you see, must have been raining outside. He gave in and slapped me with his belt and it didn't half hurt but I deserved it or did I Dad?

Another defining memory of junior school before I move on was an outing to the Liver Buildings, which, you may or may not know, was one hundred years old in 2011. We meandered along corridors and up stairs through boring aptly named 'boardrooms' till we exited onto this windy walled area just below the famous Liver birds feet. Now there's a memory, remember the 'Liver Birds' on the telly from the seventies, a terrific programme with posh Sandra in her sexy hot pants and the common quick witted Polly but less 'pretty'.

Sorry where was I, oh yes it was an amazing sight, not Sandra's hot pants but the view as we could see as far as the Welsh Mountains again and dreams of candy floss and the fair at Rhyll. Before I canter on here's another fact for you I discovered recently, did you know that the Liver Building clock face is bigger than Big Bens in London. Size is very important sometimes! Years later I remember this being a question in a pub quiz machine and winning a tenner, see kids it pays to listen to your teachers?

The only other thing I remember about this trip is getting back to school late for lunch and being miffed because all the bakewell tart had been eaten! I loved bakewell puddings and I was so disappointed and to cheer me up I ended up eating several bowls of custard, nearly made myself sick!

I'm on a memory role here, have you ever been to Colomendy? Tutt, then you were never a scouse kid from the seventies. Let me explain. Liverpool City Council owned this retreat in North Wales, think they still do and this was an opportunity for us scousers to smell fresh air mixed with cow dung for the first time. I later discovered that Dad had been evacuated to Colomendy during the war with his brother Frank and Dad would have been about eighteen months old and Frank was three.

I remember going to this Butlins for kids in 1974, I say that with some confidence as we returned to parents waving flags as the red half of Liverpool had won the FA Cup against Newcastle. I was aged eight. We slept in bunks in dorms, the kind you see in prisoner of war movies like the Great Escape but without the escape tunnel and slightly better grub and we visited castles and market towns with long names with far too many L's and Y's in them.

We would sit and sketch churches and other monuments and one of my favourite memories of North Wales was the canal boat trip we took in Llangollen. I remember these huge orange coloured fish swimming to the top and nearly being able to touch them.

They're certainly a proud nation the Welsh and I have some affinity to my Celtic brethren as my Dad has done some genealogy and discovered that our ancestors lived in North Wales before moving across to Liverpool, not surprising given the Griffith name which originated as Gruffordd.

Anyway back to Colomendy. One day we were bussed to base camp at Mount Moel Famau; more of a big hill in reality but to us kids with fertile imaginations, we had visions of bumping into the yeti which was a popular legend at the time. We all waited at the bottom and Mr Price said as a special treat we would have a chippy dinner as there was a chip shop at the top and I couldn't help wonder if Mr Lee had expanded his franchise once again but did he charge six pence or eighteen?

This was his motivational speech for slackers and lazy sods but dam you Mr Price you were fibbing, why Mr Price, why, we were more than happy with the trek up the hill and I was so looking forward to vinegar drenched chips! The chippy turned out to be a mirage!

We would sing *'On Top of Old Smokey'* as we walked which I've since discovered is a traditional folk track, origin unknown but a song recorded by the Weavers in 1951. The version we sung however was a track but Tom Glazer who had a hit in 1963 titled *'On Top of Spaghetti'* which talks about the loss of a meatball. Although our marching track featured someone sneezing and loosing a meatball under a bush that turned to mush we would sing old Smokey and not spaghetti, which makes me think our version was a hybrid perhaps?

Anyway, I remember the descent from the 'mountain'. Oliver and me challenged each other to a race so we ran and because we were running downhill we couldn't stop ourselves until we crashed into a fence at the bottom. I think Oliver won. Next thing Ms Price is stood at the midpoint and he shouts down telling us we had gone too far! We hade to climb back up, to sneers and laughter from the rest of the group and we were bloody knackered I can tell you.

We also explored caves that seemed to descend for miles! Very spooky, it was so dark as I recall and you couldn't see your hand unless you had a torch. We were convinced that bats would brush our head if we stood tall which most of the time you couldn't do in any case but you were slightly tense with fear. At the bottom we would all crouch down and listen to a scary story about a boy who got lost down the cave. Obviously rehearsed and bettered each year but just as the story ended another teacher would run towards us statuette kids holding a torch in front of his face, you know the scary leprechaun look, that was it and they would scream out loud.

What they did for kicks eh and we almost hit the roof and possibly some bats. We were shaking and utterly traumatised as we quickly ascended to the surface not wanting to be the last one out for fear of being caught and I suspect you couldn't get away with it now but great fun nonetheless.

I recently took a child to Colomendy to rendezvous with his schoolmates as he had missed the bus. Felt sorry for him, I knew what he would miss out on. The place was so different and small and I stood there gazing at this hill that runs down to the entrance to the camp and remember being severely reprimanded by the teachers for running down the hill after being specifically told not to. A night in solitary as I recall and not that I'm a rebel but like I said before if it can be climbed, scaled, or ran down then I was up for it with my mates.

Primary school began blissfully enough but took a left turn for me that coincided with the removal of my appendix when I was ten years old. I remember being rushed to the Children's Hospital in Town with stomach-ache after eating three apples and then waking up with a bandage over my belly to later discover that my appendix had been removed. I have yet another scar to add to the many I have scratched over my body, not the best insertion I can tell you, too high up, I was butchered and from that moment I never had a six pack belly! No Freeman's modelling for me then.

I met a girl whilst in hospital and her name was Sonia, appendix Sonia as I called her for years, she seemed so exotic to me and I remember having these strange feelings for her, oh no back to my carpet again. I talk about Sonia elsewhere when talking about going the baths but the reason for recalling my appendix memory is that the whole experience knocked me back.

Not long after my brush with death, okay a tad over dramatic I know but I had been rushed to hospital, my Mum had her gall stones removed and she too was hospitalised for weeks. Dad had to work shifts at Dunlop's and he simply couldn't care for my sisters and me at the same time so we went to live with my aunty Ann in Speke like I mentioned before.

Speke was not dissimilar to where I grew up except for the houses, which were a mixture of tenement flats and council houses with gardens.

Ann was a single Mum back then and we attended St Christopher's Catholic Primary School, now demolished. My family are eternally grateful to Ann but no matter how hard I tried I couldn't settle in my new environment or school, I missed my home, my mates, singing Crazy Horses and running around the yard reaching high but most of all I missed my street.

After about six weeks we returned home and Mum was back home too; she was recuperating. I went back to my former school and a few weeks later I sat my eleven-plus. Well I failed, I underperformed, whether this was due to the illness that struck my Mum and me and the ensuing disruption to our lives I'm not sure but my teachers were shocked as I was certainly on track to pass. Feeling defeated I was then left with no other option and I had to attend St Thomas A Becket Secondary Modern School in Edge Hill and make no bones about it this school was a tough inner city school and I shall elaborate about this near the end of this book.

Let me talk about how I became a goalkeeper in Primary School. I remember having trials for the school football teams but not everyone made the team and those who didn't had to learn to deal with disappointment. Imagine that getting into the team on merit.

I remember playing at Sandown playing pitches in Wavertree one cold Saturday morning and taking my turn in goal but like my fellow dreamers I saw myself as a budding Johan Cruyff with silky ball skills to match. We had watched the World Cup of 1974 and the final that everyone wanted to see, West Germany against Holland. I yearned to posses the orange Dutch top as that would make me a better player and I remember feeling peeved when the German's won by two goals to one, aided by the likes of Gerd Muller and Franz Beckenbauer.

I wanted to be as good if not better than Leather you see but my future was sealed within minutes as my team conceded a pen. Mr Kirwin and Mr Price were in charge donned with mandatory blue white zipped tracksuits and whistle in hand whilst I stood there in over sized shorts waffling around my skinny legs, fidgeting with my arms out wide.

The ball was kicked to my left and I guessed correctly, usually a fifty-fifty chance, I dived and caught the ball in one slick motion. I made it look simple but this wasn't too hard as I was accustomed to falling over and diving on rough knee scraping ground in our street. Mr Kirwin stood there aghast but impressed as he had stumbled upon a budding star and shouted out, 'you'll do Griffith, and you're the school's goalie'.

I played in goal many a cold frosty Saturday morning and Dad would come and watch me to cheer me on, good old Dad. We played other schools and with the help of Messer's Kirwin and Price we actually became a half decent team. A few months later I remember being introduced to the adult son of the school cleaner who was the sponge man for a local kid's team called 'the Grosvenor'. I think his name was Ray. The Grosvenor was a local pub and they were keen on developing an under eleven's kids team and had heard that I had a safe pair of hands.

I met Ray outside the school and we went searching the area for kids I knew who were good footballers. I know as I write these words, particularly as a social worker, that this sounds very suspect but back then I had no comprehension of paedophilia and I'm not suggesting Ray had an ulterior motive, no, he simply wanted access to the best kids in the area and he enlisted my help and my knowledge.

We drove round Wavertree gathering kids and inviting them for trials at the weekend, the nucleolus being my school team. Back then most kids played out so there was no knocking on doors trying to think of your mate's first name!

Not boasting but we were very good and we ran away with the 'Edge Hill and District' league and cup for several years. Teams feared us as we were very dedicated and professional and we were managed by a lovely old former professional footballer called Frank who lived in McDonald Street round the corner from the Grosvenor Pub, our sponsor. Frank and his team of adult helpers had professional standards and we were kitted out in kits and tracksuits and were made to feel like we were the best. The pub would financially support us and we had coaches and a physio, don't think he was qualified but he had a sponge so that was enough and we would meet at Frank's home address and his wife would make us toast and tea.

Then we would board a hired coach and would travel to Botanic Park to the track *'We are the Champions'* by Queen' ringing in our ears, a track loved by our left back, a kid called Riding who also went to my school. Other teammates included Oliver, who played up front, Heathy, Tarbuck or Dabba as we called him, don't know why and Leather in midfield, Alan; my street mate was on the right wing and Whitehead on the left.

We started off playing in black and white kits like Newcastle's colours but then we changed to an all red kit. Foes would quiver in their three stripe addidas boots I can tell you, we were very good but in truth I would barely touch the ball such was our dominance but when I did I would rise to the occasion and I was a pretty good goalie back then.

Just thought haven't goalie gloves come a long way since the seventies, my first pair were yellow and had table tennis dappled rubber for extra grip unlike the rubber padded kind you get now that make ones hands look bloated! Certainly didn't stop your fingers vibrating with pain when attempting to stop a thunder shot from Heathy!

Our nearest rivals were a team called Ash Celtic, typically named after a pub, the Ash Grove and we would beat them on most occasions. They played in green hoops like Celtic and one year we played them in a cup final at South Liverpool's Ground in Garston, a semi professional football ground, now demolished.

The pitch was huge I can tell you, we could have played fifteen aside, as were the goals and we stuffed them. We were magnificent and triumphant and I remember walking up the steps behind my teammates with the crowd of jubilant parents and friends shouting out well done, to lift the trophy in the air. One of life's proud moments for me!

The next year the final was at Liverpool's Anfield Ground and again we made it all the way to the semi's. We were against our old foes, Celtic and I remember us being two up at half time and our tails were up. After eating half cut oranges we took to the pitch for the second half thinking we were going to stuff them again.

We didn't. Not my fault I might add but they only went and netted three in quick succession, we were knocked out so no Queen for us that day, even Riding was silenced. We'd never tasted defeat like this before and it was such a bitter pill to swallow I can tell you, a lesson in life and we were all duly humbled. Still what doesn't destroy you makes you stronger.

The end of year celebration was a wonderful day for my team. We would meet in a local social club all dressed in our finest Easter clothes as is the Catholic customary thing to do and we would sit patiently with other teams and their parents waiting to be called up to accept our trophies.

We would do this at least twice most years and we felt embarrassed but chuffed to bits as the ceremony was mainly about our team.

My Mum bought me a sweatshirt that had a fictitious university badge that read toodumforuniversity and I wore it one year for my presentation! I knew it was funny and slightly ironic but never quite knew why until I was older. Go on read it again; it's not a misspelt word. I remember shaking hands with Ian St John one year, he played for Liverpool in the sixties and another year shaking hands with Micky Lyons and Davey Jones who played for Everton, that was really cool. I've still got the trophies, some are broken, which I salvaged from Mum and Dad's loft and now they're in my loft hidden away and gathering 'my' dust! I should really build a shelf but my sons amassing his own trophies now and his are much better than mine in size and design. They're either shaped like a bronze coloured footy player about to score or similar to the Jules Rimet World Cup but with a ball instead of the globe.

See, Adam plays football but thankfully not in goal, not yet in any case. He's a tough tackling centre back but still without a good left foot. I attended his end of year presentation recently but unlike in my day there was no ex professional footy player and no one actually played to win the league or a cup, oh no, they awarded a trophy for fair play.

Mind boggles and I know it's all about the playing and taking part and not the winning as things can become very competitive but come on, shouldn't kids taste defeat at some point in their life, I did and surely life is all about ups and downs and there's nothing wrong in a little competition in my view.

Winning teams win trophies based on the behaviour of the parents, how they are turned out and whether they show sportsmanship on the pitch. Adam and his team mates won last year and we laughed about how the league would one day award a trophy for best dressed parent on the touch line, which should go to me I may add, or Adam's favourite, Dad's who think they can coach, again surely awarded to me as I am the annoying dad who challenges the ref who always leaves his glasses at home!

Chapter Six

Knock Three Times on the Ceiling if You Want Me...

You might have worked out for yourself but Dad was a frugal penny pinching kind of guy, always trying to save money and it seems I've inherited this 'tight arse' gene. Okay Neil, there you go, I admit it! What you already knew!
Beryl, who lived at number ten opposite our house for example, would babysit when we were really little but we never had Beryl from when I was about nine. Perhaps Beryl was made redundant like so many back then or resigned over pay and conditions or found true love, who knows but it was around this time that we were left at home to fend for ourselves whilst Mum and Dad went the social club.
I don't think this was an acknowledgement that I was growing in independence but me thinks this was more about Dad saving a few shillings as babysitting can be expensive and needs must. Tina must have been about four or five so thank God social services never came knocking and Mum and Dad must have convinced themselves that we were okay to look after ourselves, heavens knows why, whilst they went to St Hugh's Church Social Club to watch some stand up comedian or a tribute act to Peters and Lee.
Now I'm not having a go at Mum and Dad as this was a safer but this happened every Saturday without fail and Dad would return home during the interval at about ten o'clock as I recall, with bottles of coke and salt and vinegar crisps for me and my sisters, smelling of Brown Ale, to check on us and to make sure we hadn't destroyed the house.
We looked forward to the treat not the smell though and I remember a favoured habit of mine was to squeeze the crisps thinking the crumbs would last longer and I would also sip the coke very slowly to prolong the pleasure. You never wanted to finish first, no that wasn't the done

thing, to finish last meant I could tease my sisters that I still had more to enjoy. God I was an annoying tease.

Going the social club was like a religion to Mum and Dad and the nearest they got to attending Church, if you forget the occasional family Wedding and Christening that is, as the club was attached. The Parish Priests would call in for a half or two to check on the parishioners and my Mum actually ended up cleaning the place for a few years for 'extra pin' money. She virtually lived there so this made sense.

On a Sunday morning Mum would pull back the green concertina metal door, which was the entrance, and we would help Mum stack chairs, replace beer mats and mop up the previous nights spilt beer.

For those of you old enough to remember the 'Wheeltappers and Shunters Club' on telly in the seventies with the sweaty guy in a cap shouting order order as he rang his bell, well, this is how I remember St Hugh's. This show was hosted by the rotund and politically incorrect 'Bernard Manning' and was prime time Saturday night telly as I recall, a chance for millions to settle down for what I now consider to be deeply offensive and discriminatory family entertainment.

You see, attitudes may have changed thankfully but women in the seventies were routinely portrayed as 'play things' on telly programmes like the Benny Hill Show, Miss World and on page three of the Sun Newspaper and were paid less than men even though many women worked. The fight for equality actually began in the seventies with the Sex Discrimination Act in 1975 followed by Equal Pay Act in 1976. Women demanded sweeping changes when it came to take home pay and the campaign at the Trico factory in Brentford epitomised this when dozens of women demanded and won equal pay rights. I saw this in a documentary on telly and I also learnt that women were paid on average thirty five per cent of what men received for the same job.

Comedians thought the way to elicit a laugh was to poke fun at gay men and lesbians, black, Asian people, different religions and other minority groups and for some reason, people from across the water in Ireland. It was acceptable back then even for Marie and Joe and I know some would say this was only a bit of fun to be laughed off but someone, somewhere is being oppressed and subjugated based on them appearing as different and that has to be wrong don't you think. I'm no killjoy but laughter doesn't have to be based on ridicule and mockery due to differences and stereotype.

That aside it may interest you to know that the show wasn't actually filmed on location at some Northern male dominated social club, as it would appear but at Granada Studios in Manchester, replaced years later

by the Jeremy Kyle show. Not really that different then.
Like the show, St Hughes was always full of smoke and you could barely see the acts through the mist; seemingly the dangers of passive smoking were unheard off back in the seventies.
Being the eldest at home I would be in charge when Mum and Dad were out and this wasn't a democratic hand up situation but based on first-born principles! We would watch telly but we only had three channels to amuse ourselves, four if you include HTV Wales when you could actually get a signal, not the nine hundred and ninety nine channels you see on Sky today.
Telly also finished at night, no twenty four hour shows for insomniacs or vampires and for those of a certain age, did you ever sit there looking at the hypnotic white dot in the middle of the screen before the girl with the doll appeared, the test page, telling you to go too bed. I know we were very sad, I wonder if she negotiated a decent redundancy package? Let me just digress a little as all this telly talk has got me thinking about the 'goggle box'.
I do recall with affection watching telly as a family, unlike now I may add, particularly on a Sunday night after us kids had had our usual weekly bath and settled down for the night in preparation for school. There were some gems as I recall and the seventies was certainly a decade of catch phrases and some classic sitcoms.
You had the Generation Game and Bruce Forsyth shouting out 'Good Game, Good Game'. We'd stick out our Brucey chins and we would mimic him and the show was made funnier when the sliding doors got stuck at the end. Such tack would pass along the conveyor belt, except the cuddly toy of course and I remember thinking 'what on earth is a fondue set', I still have no idea, something to do with melted cheese I hear?
A few years later Bruce s crossed over to ITV, to be replaced by Larry Grayson and his catch phrase 'shut that door'. Thinking back Larry was a very effeminate fellow in his speech and mannerism, he would certainly ham it up for the camera as he pouted and turned away but we never thought of him as being a gay man. We didn't know what gay meant other than it normally described someone who was feeling happy and I thought the 'Village People' were just a band that liked wearing costumes for entertainment purposes, it was their gimmick.
We had the show 321, this has to be the stupidest quiz show ever seen on telly, the contestants had to avoid the grinning Dusty Bin wheeled on at the end by working out impossible clues and the host, Ted Rogers, would twirl his fingers round denoting 321. We'd have a go of course

but the best I could do was 312. Oh well jobs safe Ted!
Ted would talk through the answer confusing everyone as he did and the expectant couple would stand there believing they had worked out the clue but often they were left dumfounded and matching Dusty they would grin through gritted teeth as the bin rolled in signifying defeat. Similarly contestants on the popular darts telly show 'Bullseye', hosted by Jim Bowen, would play darts and answer questions, avoiding 'bendy bully' in the hope they would eventually win a car, a caravan but not a speedboat if they lived in Birmingham.
I remember other shows like 'Family Fortunes', 'Mr and Mrs' and Mr Monkhouse's 'Goldenshot'. Whatever happened to shows of such quality where contestants made fools of themselves for crappy prizes whilst being japed by the host?
Then we had competing chat shows like 'Parkinson', Russell Harty and 'Wogan'. I recall celebrities casually smoking whilst answering carefully rehearsed questions me thinks and lets not forget Grace Jones landing one on Russell's head, surely a publicity stunt although she does look very menacing and I wouldn't offer her a fight. Moving into the eighties I liked 'Blankety Blank', Les Dawson's silly jokes and humour tickled me, a comedy legend in my eyes.
'Celebrity Squares' was also funny and unlike 'University Challenge', do you remember the 'Young Ones' parody when Vivian kicks his foot through the floor hitting some toff's head, I think they were actually perched high aloft in boxes or am I just being ridiculous. 'Game for a Laugh' set out to be whacky and had its moment I guess, the candid camera set-ups were funny.
Then we had talent shows like 'New Faces' hosted by the frightfully thin Marty Caine in her swaying brightly coloured chiffon dresses and its rival, 'Opportunity Knocks' hosted by the charismatic Hughie Green. Winning acts on New Faces were decided by a panel of celebrities whereas Opportunity Knocks was the forerunner to modern shows like the X Factor as the viewing public voted, aided by the clap-o-meter which was basically a strip of board with an arrow that someone back stage would shift along to the sound of the audience clapping. Not very scientific but funny.
What about the thrills and spills of 'Show Jumping' on telly and the 'Wall'! Despite the populous mainly living in cities this so called sport was very popular on the telly during the seventies and the name that springs to mind from the show is the Yorkshire man 'Harvey Smith'. He was a miserable git as I recall, so erasable and grumpy but hats off to him as I do remember all the entertaining controversy when he gave the

two fingers to the crowd. A magic moment that.
Thinking of the many kids programs I watched back in the seventies, 'Grange Hill' was a much-loved show for me as it first aired the same year I started at Secondary school in 1977. Tucker Jenkins became a role model to thousands of kids.
It seems most of the kid actors went on to appear in 'Eastenders' after serving their apprenticeship at this school. Phil Redmond, a fellow scouser I may add, wrote the series, which provoked outrage from the public as it controversially portrayed school as tough with kids who were out of control and the story lines read like an agony aunts mailbox. People didn't want to know the truth about comps!
Some other very early gems include the 'Magic Roundabout' just before the six o'clock news, replaced years later by 'Rhubarb and Custard', a show about a badly drawn cartoon of a cat and dog trying to get one over each other. They shook on the screen and I think the appeal of this cartoon was helped by the instantly recognisable theme tune, da da da da, da.. Oh why bother. Both programmes must surely have been conceived in a mist of cannabis smoke if you ask me, as they were zany. I recall watching 'Paddington Bear' also before the news, great concept that, having a bear from Peru appearing with drawn characters. I liked Paddington.
Do you remember 'Captain Pugwash?' I never understood the obvious innuendos when you read the shows character names until I was an adult and how on earth did it ever get past the census that's all I'm saying, someone must have had a huge laugh.
I preferred 'Magpie' to 'Blue Peter' as it was more edgy, more Northern to me. Now I salute magpies and say 'good morning Mr magpie how's the wife and kids' and I do this because this girl I worked with down South did this one day and she said it's bad luck not too. There's a thought, is it just me or are there more magpies in cities these days when compared to the seventies and in contrast are there less pigeons. In fact I can't recall seeing a sparrow in years and they were commonplace around our way when I was a kid.
Now there's an unlocked memory. Dad had left a chimney pot on its side on my bedroom roof and I could touch the pot if I stood on Tracy's bed and leaned through my sister's louvered window. I found a smashed shell in the gutter and wondering where the egg came from and I would watch pigeons, sparrows and the occasional starling land on or near the pot. I was fascinated by their ability to hop around and to suddenly fly away when startled and I would observe many birds come and go for hours at a time.

Have you ever seen a baby pigeon, no, neither have I, so I had this 'birdbrain' idea that I could encourage a pigeon to nest inside the pot, to watch it have baby pigeons and to train it to eat from my hand. This excited me so I went on rummaging mission and I found some straw inside a discarded mattress on the waste ground and I fashioned out a nest inside the snug pot! The next day after school I ran upstairs to have a look at my nest wondering if a bird had spotted the potential to relocate to urban Edge Hill but it was empty. Should have put an add in the Liverpool Eggo. Ouch that hurt!

Not to be outdone I then decided the nest needed food to entice my feathered friends so I ran downstairs for a slice of bread; I then broke the bread into little pieces and made a trail to the nest just in case any birds struggled with the concept that I had built them a home.

I returned the next day but again the nest was empty and the bread had either been eaten or had blown away! Then I saw my cat Tiddle's walking along the wall and it dawned on me that no passing bird would ever nest on my roof for fear of becoming a tasty meal for my ferocious but cuddly toilet trained cat. Dam you Tiddle's.

Another classic programme on telly was 'Runaround' with cockney Mike Read as the host, who also appeared in Eastenders. Then we have the brilliant 'Crack-a Jack' culminating in contestants trying to hold onto prizes to take home hampered by being stuffed with cabbages. A class show.

I'm on a role here, what about 'Jamie and his Magic Torch', surely again written by someone on drugs and another memorable theme tune. Get the tune right and you're half way to having a decent hit it seems.

I liked Zippy, Bungle and George from 'Rainbow', go on bet you know the theme tune, all together now, *'up above the trees and houses'*. Sorry where was I, oh yes, remember 'Finger Mouse', basically some bloke with a white glove on his hand with Velcro eyes and whiskers, very technical I think not.

The 'Clangers' was a terrific show that tapped into kid's fascination with space travel at the time. I wanted Mum to knit me a clanger and I always wanted to live on, or indeed, in the moon and to eat cheese all day, I really like cheese. When I was really young in the swinging sixties we had shows with an array of puppets daggling from visible strings like 'Bill and Ben the Flower Pot Men', 'Andy Pandy' with his sidekick, 'Luby Loo' and how could I forget the loveable 'Pinky and Perky'.

I remember coming home for my lunch from school sometimes and I'd watch Australian soap operas like 'Son's and Daughter', again I can sing the theme tune if you want and its closely related cousin, the 'Sullivan's'.

Before they aired we would watch classic kids programmes like 'Pipkins' with the slightly neurotic and manic Hartley Hair, Octavia the Ostrich and the often lamented Pig and lets not forget pink 'Bagpus' sitting proud in the shop window waiting for night time when it would all 'kick off'.

The 'Muppet Show' was fun on a Sunday night with Kermit the frog hopelessly evading the luscious Miss Piggy. There were so many pigs on telly back then. I felt sorry for Dr Beaker and his whacky experiments as he always ended up with a 'singed' face; I liked Fozzy's silly jokes doing my damdest to remember them for school the next day and the mad drummer, Animal. I also loved the two old gits bemoaning the show from up high wondering why they were there every show if they hated the artists and acts so much.

Talking of American shows, what about the brilliant comedy 'Soap'. The narrator at the end would say 'join us next week when we discover…the actors would then try and stand still like musical statues, a very funny programme if not a bit weird at times.

Remember the Fonze in 'Happy Days'. All the family could sit and watch this show as it was set in the fifties with greased back quiffs and rock and roll themed diners. There's a forgotten memory, my Mum bought me a leather jacket in 1976 like Fonzie's and I would go around saying 'heyyy' with an American accent whilst holding my thumbs up. Don't judge, I was only ten!

Other American shows included the 'Hulk', clearly inspired by 'Dr Jekyll and Mr Hyde' and you'd warn those who annoyed you, usually my sisters, with clenched fists and veins pumping in the neck; 'don't make me angry, you wont like me when I'm angry'.

It seemed Dr David Banner always tried his best to lead a normal life brushing up the school gym and the likes whilst hiding from that annoying reporter, he was very good at tracking people down don't you think, but someone would always push him too hard and he'd turn all green and into the Hulk.

Unlike the films released recently the telly Hulk wasn't blessed with an array of computer generated imagery, no, this was the seventies and Mr Banner would fall behind a stack of boxes or get trapped beneath a truck, to reappear as this beast of a man. His clothes would rip as he metamorphosed into muscle man, Lou Ferrigno, a former Mr Universe, but once back to Banner he would still have the same ripped pair of jeans on. What's the chances' of that happening even as a kid I knew this was wrong and wasn't he so unlucky, as he would end up having a fight every week, did he have a mate called Oliver?

Remember California Highway Patrol aka, 'CHIPS' and their cool aviator sunglasses they wore and the 'A Team'. Mr T' would always croak, I aint getting on no plane', or 'I aint drinking no milk' as the hero's went off to build some amazing machine from throw away pieces of engineering in a disused shed to help some townsfolk beat some nasty gang whilst escaping the military police in their black transit van.
Talking of black vehicles what about 'Knight Rider' and Kit the car, with flashing red lights the car would ask things like, 'okay Michael where to today' and Michael, aka David Hasselhoff, the Hoff, would insist on driving. Why didn't he just sit back and have a doze? That's what I would have done.
The 'Dukes of Hazard' was a good watch because of the car chases and also because I fancied Daisy in her tight denim shorts! Very sexy! I felt so sorry for the girl in the 'Little House on the Prairie' who in spite of having an idyllic home life she lost her sight just like my Nan did.
Back home. I can't decide whether I preferred 'Morecombe and Wise' or the 'Two Ronnie's' as they were both excellent and Christmas wasn't Christmas without their specials. These two programmes were so funny and well written and the 'Phantom Raspberry Blower' from the Messer's Baker and Corbett was hilarious and appealed to us kids for obvious reasons. As for the 'Four Candles' sketch, this scene still makes me laugh no matter how many times I see it.
Eric Morecombe was a genius and Ernie was a decent straight man but funny in his own way. It's amusing how we never thought 'how strange two men sharing a bed together' and I love the dance they did at the end to 'Give me Sunshine'.
I liked 'Swap Shop' for a while, a bit like EBay on telly, with Noel Edmunds and his brightly coloured jumpers but my favourite was 'Tiswas' on ITV. The 'Phantom Flan Flinger', what's with all these phantoms in the seventies; would dress head to toe in black and the show would plunge into mayhem with guests and presenters being splatted with custard flans and I can still recall the Flinger attacking the St Winifred's School Choir.
Come to think of it was that the reason why the little girl who sang 'Grandma' lost her front teeth? The audience played its part to and some unfortunate souls would be trapped in a cage to be soaked at random intervals with buckets of cold water. Now there's a memory, the *Bucket of Water Song*', what a track and I once worked with someone who appeared as a little girl in the video when it was released as a single. There's a thought, do you remember Tiswas spinoff programme 'OTT' that was meant to cater for adults but similar concept of madness and

rehearsed disorder. Why do I easily recall the large breasted Black woman who each week would take her top off at the end as the camera annoyingly panned out till she was a mere dot in the distance! What a tease Mr Producer but funny.

Some favourite cartoons around this time that I can recall with fondness are the likes of 'Scooby Do', 'Wacky Races' and 'Catch the Pigeon' with Dastardly and Mutley who incidentally also appeared in Wacky and Pigeon.

Remember the many characters and their cars in Wacky such as 'Caveman, the glamour puss 'Penelope Pitstop chased by Peter Perfect', the scary 'Gruesome Twosome', 'Sargent Blast shouting out orders at poor 'Private Meekly', and of course the unshaven gangsters known as the Ant Hill Mob. I think the cartoons were made by Hanna Barbera and I shall always remember the line, 'I hate that pigeon' and of course Mutley's infectious laugh.

'Scooby Do' was superb and stands the test of time and each week the 'monster or ghoul' would be revealed to sounds of 'I would have gotten away with it if it wasn't for those pesky kids'. I liked 'Hong Kong Phooey' and intriguingly both Scooby and Phooey were dogs and they would run along a corridor that would go on for hundreds of yards as I recall.

Talking of animals we had the coolest of cats aided by his merry band of cats, yes, we had smooth talking 'Top Cat' who was always trying to outwit poor 'Officer Dibble'. Again the theme tune is embedded in my psyche and I've just seen trailer for the forthcoming movie of Top Cat! Must take Adam to see it.

I must mention 'Yogi Bear' and his hapless pal, Boo-Boo Bear, forever 'smarter than the average bear', a wonderful cartoon although it did encourage stealing, think about it.

Do you remember the 'Banana Splits' and the outrageously funny theme tune, La La La, okay I'll stop now? Hanna Barbera developed this show also; a regular money-maker and we were treated to stupid sketches and silly jokes from Slegal, Drooper, Bingo and Sparky, every Saturday morning. The Splits all wore firemen helmets for some strange reason and they had a very cool six-wheeler dune buggy, a crazy cuckoo clock and a talking moose head on the wall.

The strangest of shows and I always wanted to slide into their world like they did to the La La La tune; I loved the 'Arabian Nights' cartoon that appeared in this show, back to my flying carpet again and the hero would change to whatever animal he wanted to be and he would say something like 'size of an elephant'.

The UK created some classic kids shows and some favourites of mine include the 'Double Decker's', 'Black Beauty' and 'White Horses'. I can still hear the theme tunes in my head and I am transported back in time to a kid sitting crossed legged on the carpet floor gawping up at the telly. I loved 'Vision On', which 'morphed' into 'Take Hart' with plasticine Morph; see the clever link there? Morph was always getting into trouble and causing a mess and I loved the gallery, where kids would send in non-returnable pictures shown to the theme from the *'Deer Hunter'*, a perfect musical piece if you ask me.
I loved 'John Cravens Newsround' and 'Jackanory'. Another wonderful show was 'Mr Ben'. Being the eternal escapist, I would dream of entering the costume shop to be met by the bespectacled owner, to then step out into another world befitting of the costume for an adventure.
Then we had 'Roy Castles Record Breakers' aided and abetted by the knowledgeable McWhirter twins who seemed to know everything and anything and lets not forget 'Michael Bentine's Potty Time' and his no neck little figures, funny voices and his very impressive landscapes. All very peculiar but I would have gladly swapped my toys to play soldiers on his landscapes with real cannon smoke any day!
I must mention 'Skippy' at this point, as this is the zenith of all shows in my mind and was first aired when I was a toddler. Perhaps ripping off Lassie but what a wonderful show from Australia about this very clever kangaroo whose tut's could be translated and each week he would save some poor unfortunate soul from an abandoned quarry or a water well. I don't know why but as soon as the theme tune started, tears would well up in my eyes and I can actually feel the same emotions as I sing the tune in my head as an adult. *'Skippy, Skippy, Skippy the bush kangaroo'*. Oh the memories and please don't tease me or use this to render me defenceless! Now there's a thought pickled onion attack whilst singing Skippy, I think I'd basically collapse to the floor in tears!
I could go on as I am sure there are many other shows waiting to pop into my psyche but before I do it would be remiss of me to not pay reverence to a simple but bloody marvellous cartoon called 'Ivor the Engine' and I say this for two 'palpable' reasons. Ivor is a train who sings in the choir and he has many friends such as Jones the Steam, his driver, so fits in with the title of this book of course but also because it is based in the mountainous region of North Wales and with a surname like mine surly the 'land of my father's'? Besides Ivor my favourite character was Idris the Dragon who lived in an extinct volcano and would heat up the choirs fish and chips with his fiery breath.

Clearly the telly was 'the' source of entertainment for my family and me in the seventies. I wanted too but not having the money to attend the cinema very often, I didn't see classic films from that time like 'Grease', 'Saturday Night Fever', 'Close Encounters of the Third Kind', 'ET' or the very scary 'Jaws,' until I was an adult. I would listen to other kids excitedly chat about films they had seen and I would pretend I had seen them too and would nod in agreement but unable to conceptualise what they were talking about. 'Anyone fancy a kick around?'

I was jealous and the nearest I got to Grease was the chip pan and the album which Mum bought for us at Christmas. Spurious link I know but I do recall a cinema-influenced track that I sang along to as a kid, '*Movie Star*' by the band, Harpo that was out when I was about nine.

On the subject of films I do remember cowering behind a cushion watching the 1930's version of 'King Kong' in the early seventies and being truly petrified when Fay Wraye is 'carefully' released from her shackles by the giant ape with huge but seemingly very delicate hands. Even though the special effects are crap, or 'cack' as scousers would say, when compared to today's blockbusters, they still sent my pulse racing and my hands to the cushion.

Things like that scared me when I was a kid, as did the thought of rabid dogs foaming at the mouth roaming the streets and I made a solemn promise to myself that I would never fly over the '*Bermuda Triangle*' for fear of being eternally lost. I do confess to liking the track however by Barry Manilow and his other catchy hit '*Copacabana*', seemed like a brill place to visit, where all the fun was happening according to Barry and where music and fashion were always the passion!

You wouldn't channel hop either and I guess that's why programmes back then had enormous ratings and a golden era for television lost forever. This was a more innocent and imaginative time before PlayStations, Nintendo Wii's, X-boxes and we didn't have DVD films; catch up television, anything to record on, mobile phones, personal computers, the Internet or Internet chat. How did we cope my kids would ask?

Although we didn't have electronic gizmos or gadgets I do recall my mate Alan having a game console. It was the Comadoor 64 and it would take such a long time to load, I remember loosing interest and when it eventually sparked into expectant life it would invariably and frustratingly crash.

I confess to being a tad jealous of Alan back then as my Mum and Dad couldn't afford such futuristic luxuries and the nearest I got to electronic gaming in the seventies was a hand held Atari space invader game I got one Christmas. Not a patch on games consoles played today but a simple fun game nonetheless and I'd spend hours under my bed covers trying to complete the game in other words nine hundred and ninety nine points, only stopping when the triple A batteries ran out.

I remember getting my first very basic calculator and a craze at school was to see what rude words we could make up by turning a calculator upside-down. I suppose you may need a calculator but it doesn't take a genius to work out what 5318008 means?

Indeed we may not have had electronic gizmos when compared with today's gadgets but what we did have was a fertile imagination and we would think of house games to play rather than immersing ourselves in a cyber world, so let me now devote a few lines to some classic house games that I can recall whilst Mum and Dad were enjoying their weekly night out.

Keep the kettle boiling was a tried and tested favourite and involved making a circuit to clamber over; you'd jump from the couch to the table to a chair to the gramophone for example and the first person to stop or touch the floor was the looser. This could go on for hours and you would urge someone to knock on the door to escape our self-imposed circuit training and I remember the game once ending when I smashed the table! Yes Uncle Tommy's divorce gift to our family!

Then you had 'Murder in the Dark'. The lights would be turned off and someone would be blindfolded with a tea towel or a scarf. The rest of us would spin the person round and round till they were dizzy and then would scarper.

The person who was blindfolded would go searching for the others whilst thumping into the furniture, so that's why my legs were constantly speckled with bruises. Everyone would remain silent and you would try and avoid the outstretched Frankenstein arms otherwise if touched you were on, in other words it was your turn.

Another favourite was 'hide the matchbox'. As the name suggest the object of this game was to hide the box and for players to shut their eyes and to try and guess the whereabouts of said box. No peeking and the hider would shout out 'cold, colder and freezing' if you were way off the mark but as you got closer the hider would shout 'warm, warmer, hot, steaming hot'.

Just thought, what would I have shouted out if I played this game in my fridge bedroom and do people still play this game and if so what do they hide, mobile phones perhaps given the size of them. That said the game would be over quickly; you would simply phone the mobile and follow the latest track ringtone, *'Don't You Think Your Girl friends Hot Like Me'*, not mine by the way, just an example for this book.

Another much-loved game played in our house was 'Boy Girl'. I suspect you've heard of this popular game but if not let me enlighten the uninitiated to the rules. You needed pens and paper, at least two people and quick thinking. Someone would go through the alphabet in their head and when told to stop they would tell you what letter was to be used. On the paper you would draw vertical lines and beginning with boy then girl you would head the other columns with other titles such as countries, food, song, animal, toy, film, that sought of thing.

The minute clock would start on the wall and the object of the game was to write down in each column something beginning with whatever letter you all agreed on. If the answer was the same as someone else then you were both awarded five points each, if no one had the same answer then you all got ten.

Then we had 'Hang the Man', a game Mum and Dad's all over the nation would use to help kids improve their spelling but as you can see from the contents of this book I think I preferred Boy Girl!

When we were small we would make dens around the house to pass the time away. We'd use the seat cushions from the couch and we would stand them upright forming a square. Then we'd use towels or blankets to create a roof, a simple den, not the sturdiest granted as it would often collapse and sometimes we'd drape the towels over the table. As I recall we would squeeze inside the structure but only for a few minutes, you soon got bored, seems the joy was in the making.

Tracy was a budding gymnast, I went to see her represent her school on a couple of occasions and I recall with admiration the agility of the petite Olga Korbet at the 1972 Olympics to then be equally amazed at her successor, Nadia Comaneci in the 1976 games. Tracy was impressed too and like most girls she liked 'tossing over', I did also and I would do handstands against the couch and with practice my balance improved and I could walk on my hands for about six foot across the living room floor. Bring it on Nadia.

In a similar vein I would do headstands on a cushion and would stay in that position for ten to fifteen minutes until the blood had made my face turn beetroot. I could never toss fully over into the crab like Tracy could, not bendy enough but I could do a decent forward roll finishing upright. We would create our own routines and we would give each other marks out of ten.

There's a memory from around this time, the telly show 'Mork and Mindy'. Mork was a lovable alien who would sleep doing a headstand and would communicate using his ears as antenna to his overlord Orson.

Kids would run around the playground saying Nanu Nanu, a terrific show and I've always liked Robin Williams in whatever he does.
I also remember playing the game of 'camels' with Tracy and Tina. We'd take turns of course and if your not familiar with this game, well, basically Tina for example, would stand with her back to me, I'd lean forward and would hold her hands hoping she wouldn't break wind. Tracy would then stand on the couch and would climb on my back and we'd walk around the room. Simple but fun.
Sliding down the stairs on your belly or better still with a cushion was another great game but this was surpassed when Dad stored a rolled up carpet on the stairs, it became a cool slide. Talking of stairs and the landing in particular, I would walk along a two-inch ledge to the highest point of the stairs but to do this you had to lean out and push against the opposite wall so it took a bit of rock climbing courage.
Those stairs were a bit of a death trap actually. Dad remembers me being about two and standing at the top of the stairs and shouting out 'look what I can do' and with that I jumped from the top and thankfully Dad reached out and caught me before I hit the bottom stair.
Another time Mum stumbled down the stairs when I was a teenager and I remember being in bed and Mum shouting for help; she was hurt and unable to move. I spoke to Mum about this recently and she said I helped her to the couch, made her a cup of tea and then went back to bed! See I was a very caring son and always there when needed but a lad's got to have his sleep, sorry Mum!
Another game I liked playing at home was doorframe climbing. You had to wear trainers due to needing a good grip and with your arms and legs you would push against the frame and climb to the very top squeezing into the corner like you were stuck in a web!
So wish I had the agility and strength to do this now, Adam can but with age comes added weight and weaker muscles. This show of strength reminds me of the video to 'The Cure's track *Lullaby*' with Robert Smith trussed up in the corner of the room but he was aided by a spiders web and not his muscles.
There's another game, swinging from the doorframe and hanging on to the door whilst it swung outwards, never inwards, schoolboy error, as you would catch your fingers as the door closed. This is one of the most painful memories I can remember as a kid, trapping my fingers in a door, as well as keeling over after being hit in the goolies by a football.
No list of house games would be complete without 'Eye Spy'. Everyone knows how to play the ever-popular eye spy game and we'd play this when Mum and Dad were out and also as a family. The competitive gene

would always rear its ugly head and I would use really obscure 'something beginning with's' to outwit my sisters. 'C' for 'cloud' in a picture, that kind of annoying brother thing to maintain the lead. Sometimes we'd tire of all this frivolity and we'd think we were being helpful and we would redesign the living room whilst Mum and Dad were at the social club. Not that we would demolish yet another chimney breast but Mum and Dad would come home in a drunken state, to notice that 'Grand Designs' had retouched the house and they would think 'was that really where we left the couch?'

Worst still I'd get my sisters to help me scrub the floor with soapy water in an attempt to bring back the sixties flowery design and I would soak the carpet in sticky suds. I was reminding Mum about our cleaning exploits and she remembers another time when I soaked the carpet. It was during a street party and all the kids in the street would use our house to fill up water balloons and some balloons 'detonated' inside the house, there were puddles everywhere that took days to dry.

Sometimes Mum and Dad would walk in the door with a conga of inebriated men and women in floral maxi skirts to match the carpet and the men wearing flared Farah pants and all wishing to party into the early hours. Very windy and not because of vesta curries I can tell you and certainly no middle class fondue set.

Dad would have a fellow hod carrier with at least two crates of Brown Ale between them. It was going to be a late one but we didn't really mind, as it was to be a night of excitement, a night of Elvis, Perry Como and the Drifters. Mum and Dad liked music and I was brought up on old thirty eights, particularly Elvis who was played at most parties and my favourite Elvis track is *'Suspicious Minds'*.

Bloody hell I've just thought of a track I played over and over again when I was about six, *'My Ding-a-Ling'* by Chuck Berry and this also got a spin at said parties. This was a novelty track and I now get the lyrics and the double entendre meaning with ding-a-ling standing in for a man's dangly bits. Berry beckons the audience to join in with the chorus and to raptures of delight he cautions, 'those of you who will not sing must be playing with their own ding-a-ling. I found that hilarious and I would sing along knowing it was funny but not quite understanding why. Like I said, innocent unknowing times I guess.

Anyway that's enough smut for now, I keep lowering the tone of this book but be warned it ratchets up elsewhere. I learnt to play chess at one such party, can't recall the man who showed me but thanks whoever you are but most of the time I'd designate myself as the DJ on the decks or as we called it, the gramophone, making sure Mum's prized records was kept in mint condition. Take note Tracy, read on?

To this day I can't recall what the women would drink, probably some exotic concoction like Babysham, Cherry B, Martini and lemonade or Pernod and Black but more likely lager and lime. The height of sophistication in the seventies was pineapple and cheese on a stick and a glass of warm Cinzano. What a gem, remember the Joan Collins and Leonard Rossiter in the 'Cinzano' adverts on telly? The drink would always somehow manage to spill down Melissa's, aka Collins, cleavage by the hapless Rossiter, very funny indeed particularly seen through pubescent eyes.

There's a thought did you know Mr Rossiter grew up by my house in Wavertree, in Alderson Road actually, a Road where I bought a house some years later and I never realised this fact until I was an adult. He didn't really sound like us though, must have been a good actor, a good thespian I think.

The comedy, 'Rising Damp' was popular in our house and whenever anyone finished second or had to leave a game early, we'd say 'goodnight Vienna', in homage to the dean of grumpy old men, Rigsby kicking the cat out to woo the luscious Ms Jones and I always thought that Mr Rossiter had a passing resemblance to my Dad if you mix in a bit of Michael Palin from Monty Python, another favourite if not wacky programme and a moustache.

Yes, my Dad had the obligatory seventies Jason King moustache or muzzy as we called it; I'm jealous really as I still can't grow a respectable muzzy like my Dad even though I am in my late forties or a beard for that matter, not that I want to other than to prove I can. It's just a man thing I'd like to do someday.

Now that's just sparked off a couple of memories about late night telly. Tracy and Tina would take the knock and retire to bed to play headlight counting and I remember watching the awesomely funny Monty python; the surreal Salvador Dali influenced animation was strangely compelling viewing for a kid but slightly disturbing at the same time with the squashing and big breasted women muttering to themselves.

I also remember catching a late night film starring Oliver Tobias and the aforementioned Ms Collins and I think it was the late seventies and the film was called the 'Stud'. I was shocked by what I saw on the screen but also intrigued as the film was clearly for adults not for a kid like me and it was the first time I had seen a naked woman. Don't even think I had ever seen Mum naked, I'm very glad to say.

We weren't so enlightened as children are today about nakedness and back in those days if a woman so much as revealed a bare shoulder,

Mum or Dad would jump up and turn the telly over to save their blushes and enquiring 'birds and the bees' questions.
Albeit very tame but girls could find out about boys, kissing, spots, makeup and true-life problems answered by an agony aunt in magazines like Blue Jeans and the Jackie. Nothing really catered for us lads unless you had a peak at your sisters mag's and the nearest we got to having sex education at school was the reproductive system of a rat in Biology in Secondary School.
My sex education evolved through conversation passed from kid to kid and I remember the shock when I was told that I didn't come from Mum's belly button as I thought, I was dumbfounded and very confused.
With growing awareness we'd sometimes come across dirty mag's discarded in the entry and we would dare each other to take a giggly peak at women sitting legs apart thinking what on earth is that, they never show that in the Freemans catalogue? Now there's a superb track and video that's just popped up, *'Centrefold'* by 'The J Geils Band'.
Indeed I read that the seventies was a decade of permissiveness and I'm still tickled when I think of the lothario Lesley Philips and his catch phrase, 'hello' as he relentlessly pursues his next 'catch' whilst twirling his muzzy. The continent had the likes of 'Emanuel' and other arty erotic films; we had 'Confessions of a window cleaner', who would seedily and improperly I might add, spy on schoolgirls in the shower.
I remember Mary Whitehouse being on the news a lot in the seventies and comedians and impersonators lambasting her morality and her crusade to clean Britain of filth and pornography. This became a battle between those with conservative ideals and those who called for a freer society, me I was only a kid without a care in the world so I couldn't care less.
Anyway I was watching the film hoping Mum and Dad were later than usual from the club, hand reached out at the ready just in case, when I realised that one of my Mum's records was the soundtrack to the movie so I sat and sang along to the songs already known to me. I was fascinated with the night club and the life style of Mr Tobias et al and whenever I hear *'Native New Yorker'* by Odyssey, another guilty pleasure of mine, I'm reminded of the film, the glitter ball and not to mention the square tiled floor lights turning yellow, red and green to the beat of the song and no not 'necessarily' Ms Collins swinging on the trapeze showing her sexy bits!
Let me just douse down with cold water and head back to the party. If one of my mates Mum and Dad's came along to the impromptu party

better still as I would run down to their house to return to mine and we'd all congregate on the stairs or in my bedroom.
No sleep for the neighbours but no one ever complained as I recall, in fact, some old dear or two would stop by for a drink and a bit of rock and roll and jiving! Mum and Dad still like to jive at parties as if to prove they were there in the day and that they still have all the moves although Dad's not too keen on launching Mum over his shoulders and threw his short legs but they are good dancers.
Some of the best parties took place around Christmas and particularly on New Years Eve. It was so exciting as a little boy as the party would stop so as we could all congregate at the junction by the Spofforth Pub.
People would appear from different streets to see in the New Year and as if by magic this bloke would turn up in his Scottish attire wearing a kilt and playing the bagpipes to cheers of delight.
The clock would strike midnight and we would all hold hands and sing along to 'Auld Lang Syne' and the circle would flow in and out in time with the music and I remember being lifted off my feet and dropped into the centre of the circle. A halcyon moment but sadly a thing of the past as the wishing of New Year is mainly done outside of someone's house to the sounds of distant fire works in my experience not with neighbours and strangers who descend from all points on the compass!
Oh well, time moves on I guess and I did a bit of research into the origins of Auld Lang Syne and I always knew the song is based on a poem by the Scottish poet Robert Burns but I now know it was penned in 1788 and the phrase was used in similar poems that predate Mr Burns and translates into English as 'old long since'.
People would go around 'saying all the best' and there would be lots of kissing and backslapping in the cold dark night, then it was back to the house for a bit of jiving. If the night went on into the small hours, as it often did, I would beg my Mum to let my mate Alan sleep over? This was before slumber parties of course but she never refused and I knew when to pick my moment usually after handing her another banana coloured drink.
My kids have sleep overs which are organised and agreed by parent's whereas we tended to make our own arrangements by sneaking into each others houses at the weekend when Mum's and Dad's had retired to bed to catch a horror movie or a soft porn film like 'Debbie Does Dallas', granted this was when we were well into our teens. In fact kids today will BBM, use Facebook, tweet and text friends late at night unless caught whereas when I said 'see ye mate' when called in at night, well that was it till the next day unless I sneaked out of course! Kieran has his

fingers permanently glued to his phone and can talk and tap at the same time it seems!

I remember one time when Alan stayed more than any other time at one of the many house parties as he had an asthma attack, ruined the night he did. His Mum was a house-proud person and she would insist on everything being in its place; dust was her mortal enemy you see and Alan hadn't been subjected to dust like ours. Our dust was fierce, our dust was old and he had grown up in sterile 'germfree' house with Poly perhaps, you'll know what I mean by the end of this book and when taken out of his comfort zone Alan was prone to a debilitating coughing attack.

I remember whenever we played in his house we had to take our shoes off and leave the house exactly as we found it down to the tiniest detail. Hyacinth, not his Mum's real name, was nice most of the time, she taught me how to tie my shoe laces actually, funny how I remembered that, but she was a formidable woman and we'd puff up the cushions before leaving the house for fear that she would find out. What had we done wrong other than played in the house?

This is before videophones of course and I'm guessing the CSI team on telly would have struggled to find any evidence of our play I can tell you! If we played today we'd be less stressed out as we'd take a before and after picture with our phone and we'd feel confident that not even the CSI's Grisom could catch us out.

I also suspect Alan, Grant and Francis never offered to scrub their floor, didn't need to actually, although I don't recall his Mum and Dad going out at night very often.

Anyway back to the party. Alan and I slept top and tail and we would talk until we fell asleep. By then our ears were accustomed to shouts of laughter and *'Hey Did You Happen to see the Most Beautiful Girl in the World'* by Charlie Rich; followed by *'Knock Three Times on the Ceiling if you Want Me'*, by Tony Orlando and Dawn. Thanks again Wiki! For fun we'd predictably jump up and down three times but no one ever responded, guess they were all too drunk and jiving but we thought we were funny.

I remember Alan's voice becoming hoarse and it got progressively worse and he was finding it hard to breath. Eventually I had to run down stairs to fight my way through the throngs of rock and roll dancers to find Mum and through the tent like dresses. Alan had to go home much to my dismay for his inhaler and to a clean dust free house and poor Mum looked horrified if not a little mascara running tipsy and full of disdain as she new Alan's Mum would judge her ability to keep a clean house.

See, Alan's Mum would call round most nights for a chat with my Mum when her lads had gone to bed. Although she grew up as a child in the next street, she always had an air of confidence and she sounded so eloquent and posh, the nearest thing to Madame Thatcher in our area stranded in her working class hell. Good on her though for having high expectations and ambition for her family, I mustn't be too critical.

The next morning or should I say the afternoon after the party we would rise with sore eyes and croaky voices. All the adults would have long staggered home; sometimes leaving the door ajar and the place would reek of cigarettes and alcohol. I hear another song forming somewhere in the oasis?

It would take hours to clean up and you'd find empty bottles in all manner of places but you know, they were happy days and everyone always appeared to have a good time, hence the memory recollection. There's a thought I wonder if any one ever copped off with each other in our house, wasn't this a fad in the seventies, keys in the fruit bowl kind a thing, surely not, they were all Mum's and Dad's from the street and certainly not swingers, at least, I hope not. For that matter where does the phrase 'cop off' come from? Replies in writing to…

The adults were a close-knit bunch actually and the street certainly had a collective spirit at its very core. People would look out for each other and doors would remain open in case someone knocked and everyone knew each other.

There's a thought, do people call round to neighbours for a cup of tea and a bit of a chat these days? When I was a kid my mum was always entertaining and various people would knock to interrupt our telly watching and imagine if one of my neighbours were to knock now and said 'just thought I'd call round for a cup of tea', I would think they were mad.

I suppose people don't borrow from each other 'until pay day' anymore or feel the need to chat with someone in person when you have all the modern technologies that have arguably depersonalised verbal communication.

I know my neighbours to say hello too as I jump in and out of my car but I have never really socialised and partied with them or been on days out like we did when I was a kid.

For example I have in my possession this picture with several families posing for the camera, including mine, and standing in a field next to a caravan. Must have been about 1974 if the fashion and the size of me next to my mates is anything to go by and we all went camping for the weekend to some place in Cheshire.

This was a brilliant adventure, seemed so far away but probably about forty miles down the road and I remember us kids sleeping in a large tent all by ourselves and chatting all night, whilst the adults sat outside drinking bottled beer in front of a fire. No coughing attack for Alan this time.

In fact the communal spirit was further epitomised when our street celebrated the Royal Jubilee in 1977 and again in 1981 when Prince Charles married Lady Diana. We had a huge party and it's a bit of a coincidence this, I am writing these words in 2012 when the Queen is about to celebrate her sixtieth Jubilee but I can't see my Road getting out the Union Jacks and bunting like we did in the seventies.

Indeed it tickles me as to why we did this back in the day as I wouldn't have ever described my family or my neighbour's, with the exception of Alan's Mum of course, as Royalist by any stretch of the imagination, we were slightly Cromwellian when it came to the debate about royalty but I guess this was any excuse for a party. Sound like a scene from Shameless!

We did have a good day on both occasions though and the street was decked out in red, white and blue ribbon and there were pictures of the Royals in most windows, even my house!

Cars were parked elsewhere and through the centre you had trestles for us kids to eat jelly and ice cream on with Union Jack napkins to wipe grotty faces.

I have a picture of me sitting on a bench with a wedge haircut and dressed in straight jeans, white T-shirt and blue boating shoes, wish I still have them as they're back in fashion it seems. Just bought myself a brown pair.

Neil S from number twenty nine had an impressive Hi Fi so he played party music of the day, now here's a thought, I wonder if he played the Sex Pistols anti Monarchist track, *'God Save The Queen'*, nah I don't think he did. Bit disrespectful that and rebellious but would have been a cool thing to do!

Chapter Seven

Riding Along on my Pushbike Honey...

So taking in a gulp of some much needed fresh air let me take you outside of my house and let's reminisce some more about my favourite street games from when I was a kid, our adventures and how our fertile imagination was key to developing activities that would keep us occupied for hours at a time.

Adam rarely plays out I've noticed, Kieran never did, he would go to town to hang out with other kids when he was about thirteen. When Adam does play out its usually with his mates next door in their house and my kids expect to be entertained at the weekend whereas we steered clear from family stuff as that was boring. I guess this is because we never had big houses with spare rooms christened dens so in a way we were forced to play out but I am glad we did!

Our houses were very 'compact' and I'm guessing the street had about fifty terraced houses on either side of the street so one hundred or so in total and I would hypothesise most houses were occupied by an elderly person or couple whose children had left home or a young family with children. You certainly never came across single upwardly mobile twenty something's round our way that had decided to invest in property by buying a house in our street.

No, the two up two down houses were built to house families despite the 'cosiness' of the interior and the children ranged from toddlers to teenagers of course and there could be around twenty or so kids playing out or just moping around talking at any one given time.

I have recollections of faces and shadows from my past and I can recall some names but many have evaporated away to a place in my brain that remains locked away but I will always have this sense of other kids playing alongside me from the first time I could sit on the doorstep. Sometimes we would huddle out of the rain in the 'lobb'y' as we called it, a small entrance to our house no bigger than four foot square.

But who was I with back when I was a kid living in Edge Hill, well, lets try and remember some rarely remembered names. There was this girl who was a couple of years older than me called Sandra who lived opposite my house, we were very close when I was little and we would play in each other's houses. A couple of doors up from me you had Sandra's cousins; I think they were called Debbie and Melanie who were friends with my sisters and I vaguely remember another sister and my Mum was good mates with their Mum. They would often borrow stuff off each other as you do when you live in a community.

Opposite Alan and Grants was a family who left the street when I was in primary school and I think one of the kids was called Ian and we would bump into him at the match some years later, he was a staunch Evertonian. At the far end of the street was a large family who's Dad was very stern and I remember this older lad called Harry who would run around with me on his shoulders. I really liked that game and I would pester him to lift me up.

Alan's cousin lived a few doors up from him and his parents gave him the middle name of Kenny Dalgliesh, yes you guessed it, they were Liverpudlians. His Dad was a steward at Liverpool and his Mum had swum the Mersey. Strange remembering things like that.

Next door to Alan and Grants was this kid called Jason, he was okay but tended not to play with us and I think this was because Alan and Grants Mum and Dad never got on with his parents. His Dad was all right actually, I think his name was Derek but I do recall many disputes that went on for years. Then we have Jeanette, Joanna, Neil, Barry, Geoff and other kids I mention elsewhere in this book.

Actually if you take another look at the picture on the cover of this book, it was my first birthday and I am in my good clothes, I have chubby legs, you can see the fat overlapping my knees and I believe the doctor told my Mum that she was overfeeding me!

That aside this picture encapsulates everything that reminds me of my home and my street. There's me of course being held up by Mum in her habitually worn rollers, old looking cars, little houses that disappear into the distance and other kids playing outside gazing at my Dad as he takes the picture and if you look closely between my Mum's right arm someone is playing with a truck! A simple yet revealing picture and I love it, only wish my Dad had not attempted to have cut my Mum's head off, trust me there are many family pictures with people out of focus or not in the centre!

Anyway, you would step out of your door into a relatively safe play area, which had one way in and out from Webster Road and whatever game we played we always injected a level of competition, no harm in that but we were also played cooperatively and kids generally shared their toys in our street and I don't recall many fall outs or perhaps I'm wearing those rose coloured specs again?

One of my earliest and dourest memories is sitting crossed legged eating chewing gum off the pavement floor; I think I must have been around three, so please don't think badly of me. I also recall flicking ants with my finger and ruining spider webs with a lolly ice stick, that also doubled up as a cool 'catapult device' for stones and spit; god I was a horrible child thinking back, a budding Denis the Menace or his descendant Horrid Henry!

Lolly ice sticks could also be fashioned into a convincing miniature dagger and you would do forming a cross using an elastic band to keep it together then you would rub the end on the pavement stone until you created a pointy spikey end for sticking into someone like your sisters. I've just remembered another memory but this time to do with lollipop sticks. If you slowly unravel the stick, taking care not to tear it, then you will find that the stick is actually a piece of tightly rolled paper.

Wouldn't it have been a cool concept if the makers had drawn a coded army message or map showing buried treasure for us kids to fantasise over? They could have called the lollypop something like 'pirates' and the candy could have resembled a gemstone. I think I should paten that idea.

I had many dinky cars and toy soldiers and we would play along the kerb edge imagining you were on a cliff edge or a castle embattlement. I would play army strategy games against other street mates for hours at a time with armies of little men and would invariably lose or gain the odd soldier or car in the process. Didn't really matter, as we were good at sharing and if it had been raining we would use our imagination and our cars would become amphibious vehicles.

I remember this kid who lived in Sandhead Street next to our street and his name was Graham, not Graham the kid who thumped me. He had so many army figures, tanks and things, he was an only child as I recall and I think his Mum and Dad had money.

His Nan lived with him like a lot of families did back then; tradition dictated that grandparents would see out their day's being cared for by the eldest child, not in an impersonal home and usually the daughter. His Nan was a bit of a battle-axe who complained about us being under her feet, see, we would go to his house and play for hours enacting battles between the Nazis and the Allies and we would take the whole front parlour room and on other occasions we would play on this piece of wasteland by his house.

We would set up opposing basecamps and forward facing tanks and we would position infantry army soldiers in neat rows or crouched soldiers in sniper positions ready to do battle but taking care not to tip one over as this would cause a domino reaction like they'd all been shot on mass and I am sure even Mr Bentine's would have been duly impressed.
Alan and I then progressed to Action Man. Action Man was the male equivalent to Barbie played by girls but we never thought of them as 'dolls', no they were boys toys and they had various outfits. My doll, I mean toy-man had a black Velcro head and he wore army greens and Alan had a Navy Officer.
Alan had a tank and I had an armoured vehicle, and both toys were big enough to sit on and ride and we'd hurtle up and down the street crashing into parked cars, walls and the occasional shins of an unexpecting adult as they stepped out of their door!
On the subject of playing on things, when I was a toddler I had a blue metal tricycle, or it might have been Tracy's come to think of it, I cant remember but I would pedal up and down the street whilst Mum watched at the door probably smoking a cigarette.
Then I got an orange spacehopper with pointy antennas and a menacing smiley face and we would have endless hours of fun on what was basically a reinforced rubber ball and I would bounce on and off the kerb and generally arse about using it sometimes as a huge rubber conker. Sadly I'm now starting to resemble said ball minus the ominous grin of course!
We would play 'What's the Time Mr Wolf?' An old favourite when us kids would stand behind the 'wolfs' back waiting for him or her to say in a growly intimidatingly voice befitting of a clawed canine hell bent on savagery, saying one o'clock through to whatever time they then decide to pounce.
The trick was to second-guess the wolf and to stay just far enough back so as not to get caught, otherwise you would surely be torn to shreds! I'd love to know where this game originates from as I think it's popular all over the country, its one of those timeless street games passed down from generation to generation.
Sometimes we would pick partners and we would line up in the street to play 'wheelbarres', scouse for wheelbarrows a game played at every kid's school sports day. You would grab the handles, in other words a mates ankles who on a count of three would walk on their hands like the clappers to an agreed finishing line compressing grit into their palms as they did! Kids would invariably fall over scraping their elbows and I would suggest this game should only be played on a grassy field for

obvious reasons.

Another traditional game we played as kids both at home and at school was 'ring a ring o roses'. I know you probably know this game, another classic but I'll do my best to describe the premise. Kids would hold hands and would shuffle in a circular formation chanting the song and according to urban legend, the song is centuries old and originally described the plague due to participants falling down on top of each other to 'atishoo, atishoo we all fall down'. As if one had caught a debilitating illness.

The Victorian game of Marbles was a very popular street game that we also played as kids but we called the glass marbles that resembled an eye, an 'ollie'. You would play ollies along the kerb gully and if you managed to flick your ollie at an opponent's ollie then you claimed 'keeps' and you would amass or lose a number of ollies in one day. When I was older we would go searching for different size metal ball bearings on industrial estates and garages and we would call these 'steelies'.

Now steelies were very much sought after so rarely used in competition for fear of loosing a favourite steelie and you know I've never queried where the term ollie comes from but again thanks to the internet I now know that ball bearings were referred to as 'ballies' or bollies and the letter 'b' was dropped over the passage of time and I've also learnt that the game of marbles originated in Pakistan. See another fact for you!

If you had an 'ollie' you would play grid football although a stone would do. Water grid covers dotted around the street tended to have two hooks that could double up as goals and you would push the stone along the grid hoping to score. Just like subuteo but using your index finger and the object of the game was to push the stone just hard enough to fall into the goal and as I recall Grant was really good at grid footy, which should never be played in the middle of the road for obvious reasons.

When the sun was out I recollect jumping on my mate's shadow and this turned into a game and your mate would run away trying to avoid being 'stamped'. This game was called 'shadow chasing'.

I'm sure you've heard of shove penny, a game played all over the world including our street and sometimes known as 'pitch and toss' or as I used to think it was called 'pigeon toss', actually now I come to think of it I might be right?

Anyway, standing at an agreed distance you and your mates would throw coins of equal value at the wall and the object of the game was to try and land the coin as close as you could to the wall. The winner took the other coins and if you struck another coin you would shout out 'jingles' and you could then elect to throw again if said coin was too far away and I remember Alan annoyingly being very good at this game. We would play high jump by tying my sisters skipping rope to the drainpipe and someone would hold the other end till the rope was taut. We would all take turns jumping the rope starting at about six inches tall and girls would hitch their 'restrictive' skirts in their knickers. The rope would gradually get higher and higher so smaller kids would fall away and if you barged into the rope you were out.

As I got bigger I could jump higher and higher so I was normally in until the end and I remember scraping my knees on many occasions tripping over the rope determined to beat the record. Jeanette liked to jump and skip and she was a skilled two ball player, she was the one other girls looked up too and I confess to admiring her in so many ways too as you will discover.

Talking of drainpipes but not the trouser kind, you would cup your hand behind the pipe and you would see how far you could shimmy up. Again street records would be broken often. At the entrance to the street you had a lamppost and we would do the same thing but this was harder as you had to pull yourself up without the aid of a wall.

The corner house to Galloway Street had decorative sandstone blocks with little ledges for little hands and little feet and we would see who could climb the highest and I remember jumping off from about six foot which seemed very high and dangerous at the time.

When I was older, I say this because you required longer legs; just like door frame climbing I mentioned before I would use my hands and legs and I would climb up the inside of the entry that we walked through to get to Cranborne Road. This was a dangerous pastime as you could climb quite high, just like Spiderman and you needed strong arms and legs to stop yourself falling from a height.

If we found an old mattress we would cushion our fall when we dropped and on occasions we would use an electricity station, which was a small box shaped building or an old house to jump out of. This was scary but a dares a dare and you would start off by sitting down and easing yourself out over the ledge of the first floor window till gravity took over and you fell to earth.

This could take ages as you would try and fight your natural fear of falling from a high point, then you would work out the difference between sitting down and crouching and before too long you could confidentially leap onto the old mattress sometimes bouncing right off to a standing position and an ovation from your mates! You couldn't go home without doing the dare so you hoped the dares didn't get too dangerous!

If it had been raining we would see who could jump over the puddle and better still if it had iced over as you would break the ice or slip and invariably we would end up soaking wet.

Someone got a Casio digital watch for Christmas one year, can't remember whom but very futuristic, it was silver and the watch could light up in the dark, which was amazing as you could use it at night. We used this watch to time who could run the fastest around the perimeter of the street.

We took this quite seriously like with all the games we played and I remember wearing my footy kit and trainers' thinking this is what they do in the Olympics. Think I must have been about nine and I wasn't the swiftest kid, I think that accolade went to Grant, but when we decided to run ten circuits or more I would often win as I had good stamina and could run for ages. Our very own Chariots of Fire but without the sand and the vests!

I also remember playing Hop Scotch, bit of a girly game, hope that doesn't sound sexist and all you needed was chalk and a stone and an ability to hop without putting your trailing foot down. This is one of the few games I remember playing with my sisters; actually that's not entirely true as I retain this memory of me running down the street racing Tracy with a green hula-hoop rotating round my ankle.

Actually I think Tracy also had a set of 'Klackers' in the seventies, God that sounds rude and I should have said not till the eighties (?), but this simple if not slightly dangerous game involved 'klacking' together two plastic balls tied together with a string and the object was to see if you could get the balls to hit above your wrist.

There was a period of time when you couldn't walk down any given street without hearing the klack as it was a very popular game with kids in the seventies but was soon banned on the playground, as it was not only hazardous but noisy too.

Actually here's another inventive game I haven't thought of for a while, 'cat in the cradle'. You'd tie a length of wool or string together to loop round your fingers several times. You'd then pull your hands inward to create a cradle, don't know where the name came from as it was too small for a kitten never mind a cat. I know this is not my best description thus far and I guess this requires an Ikea type diagram or a YouTube video as I am struggling with the visual concept. There's a thought a book with diagrams?

Then we had kerby as in kerb, not to be confused with Kirkby the spill over town on the outskirts of Liverpool where Uncle Frank lived. With a football or a tennis ball you would stand on opposite sides taking turns to hit your opponent's kerb with the ball. First to ten was the normal rule of engagement, one point for a hit, three points if after you caught the ball on its return back to you and five points if you hit your opponent's kerb then yours with one throw. Sounds impossible but trust me it can be done and on one occasion I actually saw someone, I think it was Neil, win a game in just two shots! In fact Neil S my street mate and Neil Q were both good at Kerby, must be the name.

You had to be a good ball stopper too as the ball would sometimes hit the kerb and would ricochet towards a front room window. Many a good save were done to prevent breaking a window and I guess this is where I first grasped the skills in keeping goal?

On the subject of kerby I can fondly recall another game that we played from when I was about five and this was called 'kerb walking'. You would walk along the kerb, arms outstretched to maintain your balance and the looser would be the kid who fell into the shark-infested waters. We were very creativity in our play, it was always a shark or a crocodile ready to gobble you up and I remember the gas company laying pipe supply lines into various homes leaving a Tarmac strip that ran from one side of the street to the other.

These strips became our walkways, our rope bridge, to jump on to if a gust if wind knocked you off kilter and I know this game sounds daft now but it did require imagination and could last for hours or until Mum called me in for tea.

On the subject of running around the street I remember being slightly OCD at times as I would avoid stepping on a pavement crack and trust me most were cracked, for fear this would bring me eternal condemnation and bad luck. Why, I've no idea, probably a catholic thing to do with falling into the pits of hell and similarly I remember jumping over alternate pavement stones running down the street taking care not to over or under jump as this again was bad luck. Actually there were lots of things that would result in ruining ones luck when I was a kid such as walking under ladders, opening an umbrella indoors and needing to throw salt over my right shoulder to chase Satan away!

I would 'borrow' my sisters balls and throw the ball up on the roof to catch it as it rolled off the slates, perhaps that's why we had the occasional leak, not knowing what angle the ball would fall back to earth. Sometimes the ball would get stuck in the gutter or you would overthrow the ball and it would end up in someone's back yard, lost forever, or mauled by some dog perhaps.

I remember playing 'piggy in the middle' from one side to the other side, which involved two players, sometimes more, throwing a ball to each other while a player in the middle attempts to intercept it but they couldn't mount the kerb and I've discovered that this game is known world wide and goes by other names such as 'keep away', 'monkey in the middle' and 'pickle in the place'.

In contrast to trying to avoid an opponent we'd play ball tick by throwing the ball on the roof to decide who was 'on'. The ball would be thrown up high and if it was my turn to choose I would shout someone else's name and we'd all run away. The kid who was 'on' would catch the ball as quickly as they could and would chase after us other kids hoping to take them out with one throw of the ball. Timing and accuracy was key, if you threw the ball too soon then you knew this could be dodged by someone with a modicum of agility and you would then have to retrieve the ball as it bounced down the street, whilst everyone else ran off in the other direction laughing at your pitiful attempt at throwing.

Alan had a good throw as I recall despite his size and he was an accurate thrower when it came to hitting things like doors, bottles and sometimes my head with stones or wickets with a ball.

The street was the perimeter and if the ball struck you then you were on. If we didn't have a ball we would play 'off ground tick'. As the name suggests you were safe if you were on a windowsill ledge for example, a doorstep or a car bonnet until the owner came out to tell you off but you had a maximum of ten seconds to find another place of sanctuary otherwise, that was it, you were ticked.

You would run away hurtling yourself to something, anything off ground shouting 'barley', why, I don't know just one of those words passed from kid to kid but barley basically meant 'I'm safe so get lost'. Similarly, if close enough you would stealthily tick a mate then you'd run away triumphantly shouting 'last touch'.

We sometimes played our version of street tennis. We'd find old chairs, red road cones, planks and rope and we would erect a makeshift net. We were like the borrowers as we always managed to find the right paraphernalia and I would use Tracy's chalk to chalk out a court and someone would have a couple of old wooden racquets and a ball. We would normally play this game in the next street after the houses had been demolished as the ball could easily smash a window.

We became quite good although I say so myself, the competitive gene in all of us would take over and I think we mainly played tennis when

Wimbledon was on the telly. Before the game we would work out who was Bjorn Borg or Jimmy Connors and I remember accidently smashing some old dears window.

When we were a bit older we would play tennis on a real court, with a real net, granted very saggy in the middle, but a proper net! The court was situated at the back of Sefton General Hospital and we'd refer to playing tennis at 'de ozzie'. We'd sneak past the security staff otherwise they would chase us off and this 'ozzie' holds further significance to me as I was born at Sefton General.

In fact the simple tennis ball could be used for many street games. We also played street cricket as another example, the forever-resourceful Grant, who appears throughout this book, had a bat as his Dad liked cricket. A wall separated each house with a small gas pipe running through the centre and using Tracy's chalk again, I think she had a good stash of chalks; we would draw out cricket stumps.

This game didn't require a wicket keeper for obvious reasons but it did require at least three kids, one to bowl, one to bat and a fielder and I remember playing outside my house and hitting a ball right through Beryl's window opposite. Dad apologised and had to buy a pain of glass to mend the window, sorry Dad but I was never a good at cricket and this memory reminds me of the track *'I Love the Sound of Breaking Glass'* by Nick Lowe.

We did progress to playing cricket on the field at the end of our street. Grant had by then 'acquired' pads, cricket stumps, two bats and a red cricket ball and we would play against other kids from other streets during hot summer days and hazy nights.

I never liked the game in truth, as I was never that good at batting like I alluded to before but at least no windows to smash this time just an open field. I enjoyed bowling a pacey ball but when it was my turn to bat I would end up taking to the crease, finding my centre by asking the bowler to guide me, then preparing myself to whack a ball for a six but habitually being bowelled for a 'bloody duck' and that was after annoyingly spending hours and hours patiently fielding.

Then you had the good batters like Grant who could be at the crease for hours and would smash the ball all over the field, kept you fit though if not a little bit annoyed and hoping he mistimed a bowel! You see the pace of the game was too slow for me and I had little opportunity to shine as it was a team effort and I began to realise that I much preferred solo games.

Just thought of another memory, we would make our way to a field next to Sefton Cricket Club and we would play cricket there seeking inspiration from members and we would sometime break to peer through the fence and watch a Lancashire County cricket match.

Then you had 'spot the ball', although not exclusively this mainly involved a football as you could use a can. Two or three of us would take turns at kicking the ball against the wall of a house at the end of the street.

The house was on a piece of waste ground by Grahams' that we walked over to get to an entry that led to Cranborne Road. We could only play this game when the 'woman' was out as she would often chase us away; I don't blame her really as we must have made a terrible thudding noise that vibrated into her living room. Sorry 'old woman' for any distress we caused you.

You only had one kick at a time so you would be forced to kick the ball from all angles and if you missed the wall you would be on S. Brill way to improve your passing and your spelling for that matter and for each miss you would work through the spelling of 'spot the ball'.

This was street football at its best if you ask me and the winner would be the last one to 'not' spell the game and spoil sports, those who hated loosing and who had a propensity to spit their dummy out, me for example, would add an exclamation mark at the end and an underline to prolong the game!

We would improve our heading by heading the ball to each other in pairs or threes or if I was on my own I would count how many times I could head the ball against a wall. I became quite good at heading actually and I think this is a skill lost on kids today due to lack of practice. I've watched Adam and his friends play many football matches and none of the kids like heading the ball and I can only assume they have not grasped the technique and timing that comes with a good clearance or they perhaps don't like to get the hair messed up!

We would play football in the street using jumpers as goal posts as they say and the game we played most of the time was 'two touch'. This involved two players who would take shots at each other but you were only allowed two touches, which included the block or trap of the ball and return shot.

This was a good way to improve ones ball control and to then shoot as quickly as you could but honestly, I was good at stopping goals but not so good at scoring. Come to think of it we'd only stop playing when the ice cream van turned into our street, even in the depths of winter, to the sound of 'Match of the Day' telling us to run off home children and return with money to buy an lolly ice. The street would suddenly appear more controlled for a few minutes, as kids up and down the street would jostle in front of the hatch for ice cream drenched in raspberry syrup. Another game, or should I say a naughty game but we were kids don't forget, was 'postman's knock'. I'd go mad if someone did this to me so I'm not telling you where I live, but we would pick a door, then we'd knock and run away sniggering behind a parked car or down an entry and thinking how the occupier would complain, *'I Hear you Knocking'* just like the track by 'Dave Edmunds'.

Terrible indiscriminative game as we often knocked at old people's doors and people who were probably not that mobile, never Alan and Grants house as their Mum would be furious. Oh the shame but like I said we were kids and I'm guessing they would have done the same when they were kids as you probably did too and thus the 'circle of life' continues but not round my way?

British Bulldog was also a fun game. A gang of us would decide who was 'on' and they would stand in the middle of the street whilst the rest of us would stand thirty or so meters away. The object of this game was to get past to an agreed safety zone, usually a gas tarmac line in the street and on the shout of Bulldog you had to get past without being grabbed.

The first to be caught would have to take to their turn in the middle next so the defending group would grow stronger with each run. Now there's a memory, when I was about twelve I took up judo for a few weeks at Picton Sports Centre and I would hire the white jacket and bottoms, think the outfits called a Gi. We would play British Bulldog at the end for fun and I remember being the last person to be caught and running head first into a crowd of kids wanting to pin me down on the mats.

I somehow scrambled through the crowd of grabbing arms by wriggling like mad like a captured snake, as if my life depended on it and in the process loosing my bottoms. Blushes spared slightly as I was wearing clean Y fronts this time on account Mum always told me to wear clean underwear in case I got knocked over by a car! What a strange saying, why would I be worried about the state of my undies if I am flat out and probably half dead in the middle of the road and shouldn't have Mum added, 'or just in case you might be disrobed during a game of British Bulldogs', just a thought.

Talking of all things physical let's not forget the way we 'celebrated' birthdays, yes I do emphasise the word celebrated, if ever there was a contradiction, as you had to endure birthday bumps. Remember the track *'Do the Bump'* by Kenny, well, this could have been the song of choice for so-called mates who would hold your legs and arms and depending on how old you where and one for good measure, you would be thrown into the air and as you came down your mates could give you a good kicking to celebrate such a joyous occasion.

This could also be done by a mate grabbing a corner of a blanket to catapult you into the sky but no matter what method used, you would feel kicks to the back in harmony as you came down to earth to sounds of one, two, three....

In a similar vein, the tunnel of death was also used to 'celebrate' ones birthday, I thought birthdays were meant to be fun with cake blowing and prezzies and certainly not a bruising encounter. Mates would stand next to each other leaning against the wall with one hand leaving the other trailing hand to be used as a convenient weapon to give you a slap or a 'dig' as you ran through the tunnel.

Invariably you would have to run through again as someone would shout they weren't ready and I'm ever so sorry if my quick escaping feet evaded your spraying arm. The tunnel would sometimes collapse and that's when the digs really came in but you would have your pay back someday soon and you would threaten 'wait till its your birthday' as you took another blow to the chest.

Sometimes when you fell over playing football or even if you just had a trip you'd hear 'piley on, piley on'. You would try and scramble back to your feet as quickly as possible but time would suddenly turn to slow motion and you could sense lads diving on top of you squashing you into the ground. It was like the Serengeti when you see a lion catch some poor Zebra with its claws and as each lad would land on you, you would feel the vibrations of a thud run through the stack of bodies. Alan was small but quick and he always managed to either escape the piley on or would wriggle out from beneath the mound of bodies.

Unless you had Alana's snake like abilities the rest of us would scream 'submit, submit' smacking the ground imitating the likes of Big Daddy of Giant Haystacks, wrestlers you'd watch on telly on a Saturday afternoon but most of the time you were pinned down until the lad on the summit got bored and jumped off.

I remember my mate Oliver from school finding this huge rubber tyre, the size you find at the back of a tractor. How he unearthed this remains a mystery to me as we lived miles from farmland but we did have hours and hours of fun with this tyre.

There was an element of danger though, the basic principle involved rolling the tyre forward, then you'd sprint at the tyre and mount it and if timed correctly, you would ride over the top as it turned. You'd jump off before being hit, turn round and push the tyre over before it rolled off down the street. Such a thrill and we also discovered that if you sat inside the tyre and held on tightly you could turn dizzily full circle, just like our very own roller coaster ride, who needs the fair eh?

Let me tell you about my party piece, my ability to balance all manner of things. I found a pole that was about twenty foot long; I think it was a discarded banister rail from a demolished house and it was that long, no this isn't a fisherman's story.

Not sure how I discovered my 'circus powers' but after a few tries I was able to walk along the length of the street with the pole balanced on my chin. After mastering this I thought of other ways to keep the pole upright and I was equally adept at balancing the pole on my forehead but this presented greater difficulty as it involved tilting your head further back. I could also balance the pole on my elbow and my ear but my 'piece de resistance' was the discovery that I had the 'Kearns' spongy nose; yes I could balance the pole on my bobble nose! Whenever I come across a stick or even my badminton racquet I always have this uncontrollable urge to balance, why I don't know but it's just what I like to do.

I'm going to jump a few decades ahead here to pay respect to a simple but watchable music video to the track *'One Day Like This'* by 'Elbow'. I love this track, the orchestral sounds are fab and the lyrics are so uplifting and inspirational when feeling down. I mention this because I am also mesmerised by the guy in the vid who's clearly bored so he retorts to tossing and balancing a sign advertising condos for sale. I could see myself doing the same thing and I bet he would be equally adept with my pole?

One year, I think it must have been around 1979; Mum got me the latest fad from America, a skateboard for Christmas, I was over the moon. I had blue and white elbow and kneepads, which did the job, but Mum got me a safety hat straight from some building site, one of Dad's I suspect or from the bingo as with a lot of things Mum acquired.

The skateboard was the thin blue plastic type with red wheels complete with ball bearings to keep the wheels turning; not the wide more stable type you see kids use today with all the fancy skull artwork.

Standing on the board you would lean back to raise the board onto its rear wheels, this is called a wheelie and you would then shuffle the board left to right 'tick tacking' down the street avoiding stones and pot holes. Sometimes you would attempt a full circle turn, Bart Simpsons like, a three sixty as it was called; trying not to fall off but most of the time the best you would achieve was a one eighty or a semi circle, or even worse a painful dismount, yes a painful fall.

We would find smooth stone or crack free surfaces as we would grow weary of falling off albeit with protected knees and elbows and we found Spekeland Road to be the best round our way as it had a steep gradient. Spofforth Road did to come to think of it but more cars cutting through to Toxteth.

The bravest souls would stand up; the less daring would kneel or sit down on the board and off you would go dodging the traffic and any stones at break neck speed. Such an adrenalin rush I can tell you and once at the bottom you'd giggle with wonderment and go back and do it all again.

I also remember catching a 'takey' on the back of a 'bin waggon' as it sped up Spofforth Road to jump off at the top and also mounting a passing milk float hoping the driver hadn't sussed you out.

You would play out in all kinds of weather no matter what Mother Nature threw at us and I often wonder if we are now living in more temperate times. Probably just me but summers seemed hotter and sunnier when I was a kid and the winters colder with snow and ice lasting for days but an opportunity for fantastic near arctic games.

See, puddles would freeze over and black ice would form on the roads, so you would wrap yourself up in your fur rimmed green parker jacket, gloves as well and you would run and hurl yourself feet first or like superman at the ice. Your body would turn over and you would measure who achieved the furthest and most impressive body skid. This was very subjective of course and many an argument would be had but all games usually ended up being a competition. We'd get wet and I remember Alan and Grant panicking and spending hours whacking their socks against the wall to try and dry them out whereas I just went home with squelching feet not worrying what Mum would have to say.

We would have hours of fun skidding on ice till one day Grant discovered how to skid using his bike. I'll come back to 'my bike' in a bit but same theoretical principles applied but as with the evolution of all boyhood games, this would involve more danger.

You would cycle at speed to the ice patch, then you would apply your rear brake, never your front brake as this could result in you going over the handle bars, at the same time you would shove the rear of your bike by turning your hips to the side thus creating a skid. The ice would take the bike from underneath you and you would end up skidding along the ice holding onto your bike just like a scrambler.

So let's talk about my bike but before I do let me tell you about other presents stored somewhere in my psyche. The first game was 'Crossfire' by the makers 'Ideal' with steel ammo and this was a cool game. You fired at this circle encased ball bearing trying to push it into a trough but you had to be fast at reloading otherwise you would loose.

Then we had 'Corgi Rockets' with shooting miniature speed cars that fired down a plastic track doing a loop the loop and I recall having the 'skypark set'.

I also remember my Mum getting me this aircraft carrier and jump jets that attached to a zip wire and the object of the game was to manoeuvre the jets by pulling the wire to land them on the flight deck. This game was my 'big prezzie one year and it lasted all of two hours as I got the wires tangled. I remember being very upset knowing I had a whole year to wait for something as good.

When I say big prezzie by that I mean you were always knew that the stack of carefully wrapped presents waiting on the couch would contain a selection box full of chocolate and the Dandy and Beano Christmas annuals, replaced years later by the Guinness Book of Records. They were more than just stocking fillers and rummaging through my other presents I would always find time to sit and relax with a Curly Wurly flicking through the pages of my annuals in front of the fire.

This has got me reminiscing about the many iconic and wonderfully crafted characters that I had stored elsewhere in my mind such as Denis the Menace, Minnie the Minx, the Bash Street Kids, incidentally I still use the term 'plug' ugly when referring to something displeasing to the eye in honour of 'Plug' a member of the gang, Desperate Dan, if ever I get a large plate of food I still think of Dan and then we have Billy Whizz. If pressed to pick a favourite from both annuals I would go with Billy Whizz and I can remember wishing I could rush around like him finishing chores in super fast time.

Simple delights from a less complicated era and it may interest you to know that both comics were first published in 1938 and crossovers between the two comics occurred occasionally.

Anyway, back to my bike. Christmas would always take eons to come around and I remember one year pleading with my Mum to get me my first proper bike. I think I was about eleven. Boys being boys we were always trying to outdo each other and we would boast that in the New Year we would soon be entering the Tour De France on Eddie Mercs latest sleek creation, a bike with racing handlebars and at least five gears. Some of my mates had 'Choppers' (pardon!), Brad had the closely related 'Budgie' but I never even had its poor relation the 'Chipper' but I do remember my mate Lee having a similar bike from Germany that would stop if you pedalled in reverse. Don't know how he got this bike but it was bloody dangerous but that was Lee for you, danger was his middle name.

The Chopper had its faults but it did look very futuristic in the seventies but it was only good for 'takeys' as it had a long seat big enough for two bums, cycle bums, sorry couldn't resist that. It certainly wasn't a bike for racing, as it was too bulky you see and it only had three gears in the centre of the bike. I still think this is a strange place to position the gears to gain more speed, as you had to hold the bike perilously steady with one hand whilst at the same time trying your best to change gears without hitting a pot hole?

The bike that every kid in the area drooled over at the time was the 'Grifter', a bike that resembled modern mountain bikes as it had thick wheels and a bike made for me given my closely sounding surname. Sadly it was never to be in spite of the similarity and I remember both Grant and Joey having the Grifter and feeling 'dead' jealous.

Anyway, we would dream of leaning over the racing handlebars, racing against your mates expertly shifting through the gears. Everyone begged and begged it seems and by the 25th December we were all convinced that Father Christmas would do the right thing this year, we'd all been good kids, not that many broken windows or complaints from neighbours. Now there's a most stupendous track, 'Kids' by the Pretenders out in 1979 and an even better track by MGMT out recently. Christmas day arrived and I ran downstairs at some ungodly hour as was the custom and to my delight a huge wrapped 'prezzie' caught my sleepy sandblasted eyes, surely a bike, see I told you I must have been very good that year and a better cricketer.

I remember ripping the tree coated Christmas paper away and I could hear adult footsteps descend the stairs taking care not to kick the urine bucket and hoping to see the surprise in my eyes! Again I sound so ungrateful, add that to my character list, but wait for it; yes a bike did form before my bleary eyes but to my dismay the three gear straight handled bar version, with mudguards too that covered half the tyre! An adult's bike, a Morris Minor in a world of Ferraris and I later discovered that my Mum had bought the bike out of the catalogue and it cost a 'pretty packet', a lot of money!

My Mum's lovely but she has carried on this tradition of naff gifts and to this day I will unwrap presents from her jokingly pronouncing that I have yet another top for decorating. Mum, a card will do but if you must insist on buying me gifts, vouchers will do please, trust me I won't be offended. After doing a convincing 'wow' face, followed by thanks Mum and Dad through gritted spacehopper type teeth, I wheeled my bike out of the door exasperatingly in sync with my mates and yes they had shiny five gear racers.

They looked at my bike, Alan and Grant were good friends and no words past but the unsaid word shouted out loudly 'you'll never win a race with that bike', followed by 'and what did you do to deserve that'. I felt their pity but I respected their discretion. Thanks lads.

Anyway once over my indignity we would cycle round as a pack and I would normally keep to the back not to keep the rear guard but because three gears were never going to beat five, no matter how hard I peddled. I really struggled to get up Spekeland Road I can tell you with three gears, did wonders for my stamina and calves but once up I was then an equal for any racer as the gradient was so sheer like I said and on the way back the use of gears wasn't required.

Think of the classic track '*The Pushbike Song*' released by the Mixtures, not Mungo Jerry as I had thought all these years although they did cover the track some years later and the lines 'riding along on my pushbike honey', well that's the image I have in my head that best describes my 'tame' or should I say 'lame' bike.

Did you know it's rumoured that the bicycle vocal sound effect from this track inspired the synth deities, Kraftwerk when they wrote the distant cousin to this track, the sublime '*Tour De France*'. Anyway, in the end I decided to customise my bike otherwise my fledging street cred would have been shattered forever and I acquired cow horn handlebars, I attached better brakes and I took off my old man mudguards. We would look after our bikes and every now and then we would turn our bikes upside down and we'd give them a good clean with soapy suds. I was speaking to Brad about this recently and he remembers cleaning his bike with clumps of soil to clean away rust, how bizarre?

The other day I had to mend Adam's punctured bike. It took me back to the seventies when I would bend Mums spoons, as we would use them to pry off the tyre to get at the inner tube. Once out you would pump the inner tube up whilst it sat in a bowel of water to discover where the puncture hole was as the air would form bubbles.

You would then get the tin puncture repair kit, a useful pencil case as it happens and you would glue a patch over the hole and then you would reassemble the tyre back together again once the glue had dried. Then you were off again. Normally take me about half an hour or so.

I went to Halfords to discover that it's just as cheap to buy a new inner tube, as it would have been to repair it even if I could have found a kit, as they don't appear to sell them anymore. Some tubes even have a protective layer over them to prevent punctures and I just think this is amazing but I am also saddened by the fact that we clearly live in a throw away society!

Probably influenced by stunt men like Eddie Kidd, who I bunked in to see at the Mystery Park when I was about thirteen, or the more famous Evel Knievel, but racing become less popular round our way and in its place came scrambling and stunts using our bikes. Evil was a living legend and I remember him coming off his motorbike in 1975 after failing to clear thirteen buses at Wembley. An ouch moment but we were still impressed though with his courage and determination.

Remember this is before BMX or Mountain Bikes with soft suspensions and we learnt how to ride our bikes using 'no hands' and we would do wheelies and jumps over all manner things. Those kids with racers would turn their handlebars up, me, I had 'cow horns' like I said and we would use our skateboard pads as protection from the unavoidable fall. The trick was to raise your bike onto its rear wheel to then see how far you could travel before either stepping off the bike, a cool trick in itself or landing successfully back onto two wheels. Alan was a natural, I give him credit for that and I remember records tumbling till we were virtually 'wheelying' the length of the street.

Manhunt on bikes was also a good game. Like a lot of games manhunt had followed an evolutionary path that had it's origins in the classic kids games of 'tag', 'kick the can' and 'hide and seek'. These games were contests of strategy involving skill and stealth as the person or team that was 'on' had to close their eyes whilst the others ran or rode away to hide somewhere hoping not to be the first caught otherwise you were 'on' next.

The seeker would defend their position such as a can and they would have a designated jail where those caught would stand but if one of the hiders managed to get back to said position before the seeker, then he or she would touch den or kick the can and shout out 'your free' and we'd all run off. The seeker therefore had to play a game of strategy taking care not to venture too far to the left, as the hiders could be on the right ready to pounce.

It was really horrible being 'on' as the game could be swinging your way with every capture but then someone would free the others and so the balance of power would swing the other way. All sounds so complicated now as I try and fathom how best to describe these classic street games played all over the county, hope my description makes sense.

Anyway back to manhunt. We would agree to a perimeter of about a mile square, our end of Wavertree and one unlucky sod would lose at tick tick tick my blue ship, a rhyme used to make all manner of decisions

and would have to cycle to one end and await an imaginary hooter.
At an agreed time the hunt would begin and all day we would do our
best to avoid the hunter but just like the aforementioned British Bulldog
game, if 'ticked' you then became the hunter and his/her pack would
grow. The key was to hide and maintain a safe distance from your
pending capturer and we'd hide down entries, behind walls and cars
and in deep grass on the wasteland and the game could go on for hours.
Imagine playing manhunt now you couldn't escape down entries as
terraced houses in Liverpool now have gates, called 'ally gates',
accessible with a key.
You'd also cheat and send a text to your mate telling them where to
venture or not and where to catch your prey, back then it was guile and
guess work which prolonged the game but made it so much more fun.
Strategy was a key feature to this game and like most games, knowing
who to chase, who was the slowest, where they would likely hold up
and like a leopard, when to strike.
With the bike came independence to explore worlds unfamiliar to us and
we would go on bike rides during the hot summer holidays. I recall
cycling with Grant and Alan over Runcorn Bridge one day, just because
it was there, which incidentally was miles away from home and it took
ages; when we got back we resembled emperor penguins, as we couldn't
walk properly for hours.
Talking of bridges did you ever make a wish when a train passed over
believing it would come true! Well I did and still do if I am being honest
and this is just one of the many strange childhood superstitions and
oddities that controlled me as a kid.
We sometimes caught the ferry to Seacombe over the water, the place my
Mum and Dad would take me for days out and we would cycle down to
New Brighton. I remember the Perch Rock Battery, which, according to
Wiki, was built in 1829 due to its strategic position at the entrance to the
Mersey Estuary and it looked like a castle, it actually had cool guns.
Can't remember much about the inside other than a room with crazy
mirrors that distorted your image.
I remember Neil and me going the open air baths at near New Brighten
for a day out when I was about fourteen, it was very cold so we didn't
stay long and coincidently my mate Neil now lives around the corner,
get this, he actually lives on the Wirral!
On other occasions Grant, Alan, Brad, Lee, others I cant remember and
me would catch the Liverpool to Southport train and cycle to Freshfields.
We referred to Southport as 'Sou-ey' and just in case you're not from
around these parts 'Sou-ey' is an affluent seaside town in North Sefton

and regrettably famous for being robbed blind during Bank Holidays, a tax haven for older scousers.
Freshfields was a couple of stops before Southport and the walk from the station would take ages and I remember days out with my Mum and Dad and dreading this walk back home. But on a bike it was so much quicker.
Freshfields was an incredible place and is famous for its endangered red squirrel sanctuary but for us it was a cool place to play Manhunt as it had hills and paths through dense pine forests. Lots of opportunity to hide and it also had the largest sand dunes I had ever seen and we would run up and down them looking for the highest peaks to jump off into virgin sand. Sometimes girls would come along and some lucky sods would pair off and go missing for an hour or two for a bout of snogging!
If we had money we would sometimes have a day out at Southport fair. We'd have a go at go karting thinking we were driving some souped up formula one car. I remember Formula One being popular in the seventies mainly because of the rivalry between James Hunt, the fearless playboy Englishman and Niki Lauda, the tactical savvy Austrian and the fight to win the world championship in 1976.
Lauda had a near fatal accident in Germany which allowed 'Hunt the Shunt' to catch up and win! A common joke at the time was, 'did you see the race between James Hunt and Niki, oh what's his name?' A mate would say 'Lauda and with that you would look bemused and repeat the question but 'louder'. Still make me laugh that one!
We would go on various rickety wooden roller coasters, but not the 'House of Horrors' unless you were with a girl to snuggle up too but our favourite was the Fun House as you could spend hours running around for just fifty pence.
I remember the spinning floor and sitting in the centre and seeing who could stay in that position the longest. Spinning force would get the better of you and you would be hurled off the floor into a padded barrier. I also remember clambering through a tube that rotated and mates loosing their balance falling over each other, it was like a scene from the movie Greece. Southport baths was a good day out too as it had slides and a big pool but we didn't do that very often as I recall.
We would sometimes make our way to Botanic Park. I refer to this park elsewhere but this park had a walled garden which acted as a brilliant perimeter for Manhunt. The gardens had shrubs, trees and other cool hiding places and we'd play here for hours taking turns to be first on.

Mates who had a girlfriend would once again use this as an opportunity to hide and smooch hoping never to be caught and we knew when not to catch a mate if you know what I mean.

Not that I am suggesting they were practicing train driving as we were still a bit too young for that kind of thing and the fire hadn't yet been stoked or should I say we never knew where the coal went!

Another cool game was with monkey bars, which were at the far end of Botanic Park. You would cycle up to the bars and reach up and grab. The game was to see how far your bike would travel unaided once you dismantled. Lee was smaller than me, one day he had a go and reached up and missed, his momentum resulted in him doing an impressive somersault but squeamishly he landed on his back, on grit and shards of broken glass.

We looked on shocked but luckily he was dazed but relatively unscathed which is typical of Lee but we had to retreat home as he was shaken up. If Lee fell today on said bars he would land on protective matting or bark and would have no doubt bounced back up to cheers of bravo, bravo and placards of six and five point nine for execution, difficulty and grace.

Chapter Eight

Games Without Frontiers…

I selected the track *'Games Without Frontiers'* released by Peter Gabriele as the title of this chapter because it sort of sums up life for me outside of the safe haven of our street. Like I mentioned before we had left the street behind on our bikes and passed the baton to the next generation of kids, as we wanted to broaden our horizons to seek out new exploits further afield and sometimes they were unsafe and hazardous but fun! Indeed when I think of risky moments I think of Lee as he was always getting into scrapes. See, my mate Lee had this gutsy courageous spirit, he was short in stature and equally short in temper and I can just visualise him with his hands clenched ready to give someone a clout, nearly turning green. He once gave me a punch in anger and was so apologetic afterwards as we mainly got along fine. He was a tough but likeable kid and like a lion he was fearless and I recall one day convincing Lee that if he wanted to be in our gang he had to pass a right of passage, an initiation. More like hells cupids as opposed to hells angels.
By the way we never referred to our collection of mates as a gang as that would have been too territorial for us and would have invited trouble. After all we weren't from New York or Los Angeles, now there's a memory unlocked, do you remember the film the 'Warriors' from the seventies? An atmospheric film about New York gangs, narrated by a female Deejay and a film we simply had to see, one of those videos we watched after sneaking in when Mum's and Dad's had gone to bed.
I must have been about thirteen and I remember the slippery leather wearing creep from a rival gang shooting the ringleader of all the gangs, banging bottles together and screeching out 'Warriors Warriors come out and play'. When out and about someone would break the silence sometimes by copying this phrase for a laugh.

Indeed I watched another classic recently from back in the day, the 'Wanderers'. Similar story line about gangs called the Baldies and the Wanderers battling and outdoing each other but set in the fifties not the seventies. I guess every generation has its subversive youth culture. Let's also pay deference to another adolescent classic while I'm at it, nocturnally watched. Do you recall 'Porkies', bit rude this one but one to watch, the film had some very funny scenes and was bursting with teenage gutter humour. For those of you lucky enough to have seen this film, one word springs to mind and should make you snigger, Lassie! Back in the late seventies in Liverpool we had gangs like the notorious Penny Lane Rebels and the Lawrence Road Lunatics and I remember going out with a girl called Anne when I was about fifteen, who I mention later and she lived the other end of Lawrence Road.

Most nights I would navigate through back streets and entries to avoid bumping into the Lunatics, stupid really as I knew most of them or knew someone that knew them but in my mind I could hear bottles banging begging me to come out to play! Guess I was always a bit paranoid and this has also got me thinking of another guilty pleasurable track, namely, *Avenue and Alleyways* by 'Tony Christie.

Anyway back to Lee. Lee scared the bejesus out of us; he would take 'dares' too far and we were initially wary of him as he had not grown up on our street, he was an outsider, so we made the initiation deliberately difficult hoping he would not pass but Lee wouldn't be outdone and he took the challenge in his stride; he never asked if we had done the same but happily took on whatever we set for him.

On the corner of Lawrence Road and Salisbury Road was and still is an old Church Hall with steep steps. Lee had to cycle down the steps without coming off, this would scare the bravest of us but to our astonishment and admiration if I'm being honest, Lee did this with ease, he was in, he was initiated!

Another Lee moment occurred when we were playing football on the field where Analley Street once stood. Like I said before, the Toxteth riots resulted in the government planting staked trees like that was going to make a difference to the area but we did get goal posts, gone was the need for jumpers and most weekends and we would challenge other streets to matches and forgive the boast but we won most times. All that street footy from an early age had paid off and I was a decent goalie. The team chopped and changed but was mainly Alan, Grant, Derek, Brad, Joey, Lee, me and Scotty who would sometimes play in goal as he was also good at ball stopping. Brad was a decent right back, whereas his brother Joey liked to play in the middle of the park to dictate the game. Grant was also a proficient midfield general and most of the time he was the captain, he was a good tactician. Their Dad who was a good footy player in his day had coached Grant and Alan and Alan had good feet and could skip past most defenders, a superb and sublime dribbler and the only way to stop him was to 'take his legs out'!

Les was a tough no nonsense tackler; he took no prisoners and would go through you to get to the ball believing the philosophy, 'if you go in half hearted for a fifty fifty tackle then you will come off worse'. Shorts were much shorter back in the early eighties and I recall Derek liked to wear his shorts tucked up so as he could show his thighs. Putting aside his modesty Derek was a skilful and tactical player with a strong right foot and I always remember his goal celebrations, he would shake his finger up to the skies whilst running with a beaming face like he'd just scored the winner at Goodison Park.

Everyone was so ultra competitive and we hated losing and we would take it all very seriously. We would work out positions, tactics, whose marking who and even what kits to wear by choosing similar coloured tops which was interesting as some were Blues and some were Reds! We would bicker sometimes on the field about who made 'the mistake' but we mainly encouraged each other realising that a successful team worked well together and no point crying over spilt milk as they say. If our opponents scored then we would score two. It was that simple, defeat was unheard off although I am sure we must have been beaten sometimes but you know what I don't actually recall one time that this actually happened or am I being biased again and forgetful?

We were footy mad and when not playing and thrashing other teams the same crew would practice shooting, volleying, heading and scissor kicking balls into this makeshift net tied between two trees. Typical really but Grant got the net from somewhere, he would never tell you where, a need to know attitude and we would place planks to the side to save us having to chase after the ball down Spekeland Road if we netted. On other times we'd pay Grant and Alan's brother Francis to stand behind the goal to fetch the ball for any wayward shots.

This was called 'head's 'n' volleys' and you needed at least three players, one to cross, and one to head or volley the ball into the net and a goalie of course. If the goalie, which was usually moi, caught the ball mid-air then whoever hit the ball would then take their turn in goal. We would do 'overhead kicks, half and full volleys and diving headers, the muddier the better and we would play for hours until the setting sun would defeat us or cries of 'Alan, Francis, Grant your teas ready' and we would get 'caked' in mood from head to toe!

If you had several players you'd either play 'goalie stick' or 'goalie in and out', stick meant you had to nominate a goalie whereas in and out meant anyone could handle the ball. Similarly we would play 'three and in' which meant the first person to score three goals would take their turn in goal, something most tried to avoid.
Anyway back to Lee. Someone, probably me, volleyed the ball onto the factory roof, which ran opposite the field. The ball was lost forever or so we thought and we were peeved. Lee would never be outdone, he had super powers and he took on the challenge and he shimmied up a lamppost, then he heaved his nimble agile body onto the wall. He balanced himself and shuffled along the wall avoiding the glass cemented to keep any budding burglars away; I'm telling you Tom Cruise would have been impressed and then climbed onto the roof and he must have been at least twenty foot high.
Now this roof had several apexes and from way below we sighted Lee run up one then down another, then again, then he vanished! We heard a crashing noise so we ran to the huge metal doors and peered in through a rust hole but we couldn't see Lee but could hear feint moans in the dark. I ran home and got my Dad and he arrived with his ladders whilst another Dad phoned the firm that owned the warehouse and an ambulance. The number was thankfully painted on the doors.
Anyway my Dad climbed down the ladder through the sunlight hatch Lee had fallen through and opened the door from the inside. It was an amazing sight, Lee had fallen onto a huge oval tanker, which cushioned his fall slightly; he must have then rolled off the tanker and then he fell onto several oil drums below which cushioned his fall. Sure he was dazed, bruised and he had a broken arm as I recall but he could have easily died!
Lee was surely made of rubber and within a matter of weeks he was back on the field playing footy and scaling tall buildings without a care in the World. Now there's a track that I liked, the *'Rubberband Man'* by the Spinners, or the Detroit Spinners as they were called in the United Kingdom so as not to be confused with the Liverpool folk group of the same name.
I can tell you we were careful from there on in to keep the ball in play, as that mission to retrieve the ball would remain impossible, unless rubberband Lee or indeed Mr Cruise was around! This all reminds me of Maincrest, a van hire company that had its main depot on Spofforth Road near to where Lee had his fall and at night and at the weekend we would sometimes climb the perimeter wall for a game of chase.

We would run along the walls and rooftops, slide down the many pipes dotted around the site and we would jump between the water towers. This was our version of street jumping popular with some kids nowadays but this came to an end when the security guards cornered us one night with a pair of fierce looking Alsatian dogs. Lets keep to footy we thought!

I also remember Alan and me exploring this abandoned factory at the top of Spekeland Road. We got into a stone fight with a group of kids, not sure why but we scared them off as we were expert throwers, then this bloke caught us and shouted at us for trespassing.

He grabbed our collars and marched us off on our tiptoes in the direction of the Police Station. He sensed our fear and warned us not to go into the factory again but I'm not convinced he was a security officer, I think he was some criminal who had something to hide in the factory but we were too scared to go searching again.

Memories are flooding back from everywhere as I write these words. I remember sitting on a wall on Spekeland Road by the train station with Alan when these two older girls engaged us in conversation. We must have been around twelve.

They were friendly good-looking girls as I recall but sinisterly they began talking and bragging about drugs and they asked us if we had ever tried cannabis or heroin. We hadn't of course and they asked us to meet them at the same time, the same place the following day and they would bring drugs with them for us to try. Guess they were just being friendly!

I remember Alan and me trying to look unfazed, giving it the 'whatever face' but as soon as we walked away we vowed not to return, as we knew this would be a dangerous liaison, we were young but we also knew there was a line in the sand neither of us wanted to pass.

One day someone dumped tonnes and tonnes of top soil on the waste ground behind my Primary School and this became known as the 'hills'; to this date I've no idea why but legend has it Seb, older brother of Joey and Brad, my medieval family, had wished for hills at the back of his house and his divine wish certainly came true.

There's a memory, sorry about this Seb but you bought the instantly forgettable track *'Ring My Bell'* by 'Anita Ward'. I guess we all have the odd shameful track from our past but I do confess to singing a long whenever I hear it now.

The hills brought with them many opportunities for fun for kids in the area and made even more exciting particularly after a down pore. We would play all day on the hills and we would create muddy cycle circuits, racing around skidding and making jumps, trying to maximise the time spent in the air. I remember coming off my bike on many occasions as you jumped over a hill but my God was it fun despite the scrapes. Needless to say Mum would give me the mother lecture, as I would return all sodden wet and caked in 'dat'll never wash out', mud. I remember one day being in hospital because Mum had been worried that I had contracted meningitis as I suffered terribly with migraines for a while when I was about ten. This woman came to my bedside and began asking me probing questions about home life and was I happy and did my parents ever hit me.

She asked me how I got my bruises on my legs and I told her, in a 'what a daft question to ask way', I got them from playing out and falling over. I realise now that she must have been a social worker and had suspicions that I was being physically abused. Reassuring I guess but way off the mark, my bruises were all self-inflicted and were indeed worn as a badge of honour, a reflection of how dangerous you were; danger was my middle name. Okay it wasn't, that accolade went to Lee like I said but I just wanted to sound momentarily cool!

The hills became firmer with ware and tare and one of the best tricks was to cycle right at the hill to then turn almost horizontal around a bowl shaped hill gathering speed as you descended. Imagine a skateboard park but with mud!

Sometimes you would pass a mate who was at the rim of the bowel whilst you came in from another angle at the bottom. Sometimes we would ride at the bowel shaped part of the hills and would jump straight on top of this plateaux part expertly stopping!

Sometimes we would dig tunnels for no particular reason other than if it can be done then it shall be done. We were oblivious to the dangers but like moles we would fashion out a tunnel through the hills with spades, we were quite ingenious and we would use planks of wood to firm up the walls. Once completed and following the kid's version of health and safety guidelines, this kid called Les would send his Jack Russell dog through on a trial run and we'd all take turns scrambling through as a dare. Invariably the tunnel would collapse later in the day but astonishingly no one was ever hurt.

Les was from a family that had many animals as it happens and his dad and brothers flew homing pigeons as a hobby and we would track them in the skies as they returned to their hatches.

I need to mention some sad news at this point. Les and my Mum worked together as cleaners in Webster Road School and my Mum heard at the bingo last year, the gathering hole for women to gossip, that Les had sadly passed away. He committed suicide, not sure why but you rest in eternal peace Les, you live forever in my memory.

Money was tight and we'd end up customising all manner of things. As I said at the beginning of these memoires, we'd sometimes find or go in search of old prams with intact wheels! We'd dismantle the pram, then we would set about making a go-kart, aka a steerie'. For those of you not in the know you need a plank of wood, two sets of wheels (preferably one set smaller than the other) a fruit box or similar, Dad's nails, some discarded paint, silver or gold preferably and rope.

Still with me, hope so? You would bend several nails over the metal bar that keeps the wheels together nailing them to one end of the plank. You would repeat this but to a piece of wood that would bolt on to the other end of the plank. This is the steering end. You would then make a gap in the box and would nail it to the plank thus creating a cockpit.

You would tie the rope to the steering section, hence the name steery and with the help of your feet you could steer. This is the basic design of course and sometimes we would paint the go-kart, add brakes and flags to the back. The really cool ones looked like our version of American dragster cars and you would find a hill and at the count of three you'd race down the hill in pairs.

Not the safest of games I can tell you and once off there was no stopping unless you hit something, usually a kerb or a wall and our favourite hill to race down was Spofforth Road. If I were to make a steerie now I'd have to include bouncy suspension at the back given all the speed bumps on the way down!

Door dens were another favourite pastime, which fitted in with our desire to run away and sometimes we would sit on the kerb and plot out where we would head off too and what we needed to take with us but we never did. I ask myself, where we that unhappy with our lot or just kids wanting adventures?

I suppose that's because the area itself was an adventure and we had so much to keep us occupied if we used our imagination like I've said throughout this book. The area was scattered with semi-demolished houses sitting abandoned on wasteland and we would find all manner of things to play with. Most families were relocated to places like Skelmersdale or Kirkby under Council inner city regeneration schemes resulting in whole communities being broken up and shifted further out from the bosom and the smell of the Mersey and looking back now I think this was a deliberate attempt to break up communities who were content to live in old houses?

Getting Off At Edge Hill – The Tracks Of My Years

In fact I learnt some time ago that the end of the M62 motorway begins at junction four; did you know the original plan was for a flyover to pass through my area, Edge Hill, right into the City Centre, junction one I presume. Manchester did this with the Mancunian Way and this explains why street after street was demolished to pave the way but why it was never finished is unknown to me but still the demolished streets presented an array of adventures and quests, it became our playground of rubble and bricks.

We would follow the path of the moving JCB's as they cleared away the debris looking for old medicine and clay beer bottles and coins to sell in a local junk shop for a few pennies to spend on sweets. The JCB was very loud and you kind of got used to hearing this metallic moan across the roof tops and when the JCB's had retired for the night like a huge dragon needing to sleep, we would excavate sunken holes with dreams of finding buried treasure but more often than not all you found was more bricks and the occasional smelly sewer.

Sometimes we would find an old telly and we would take it apart looking for the copper wire because rumour had it you could sell the copper for a few shillings. Can't remember if I actually did but I do remember finding these stacked pieces of metal in amongst the telly's workings that looked like a capital 'E'. We would prize them apart and like a 'ninja star' you would throw the E's at pieces of wood or bottles stacked on a wall. Of course we would use stones or catapults sometimes to smash the bottles but the Es' required a bit more skill so more skill involved, they were lightweight and would bend through the air at sonic speed.

Where was I? If you found at least four doors, one with a panel, then you could make a den but trust me this wasn't a re-enactment of Enid Blyton's world and us famous five didn't have sturdy trees to build cool semi permanent tree houses but what we did have was an abundance of wasteland, doors and old carpet. You would first start by finding a smooth patch but not too far from home as you had to keep to your own territory you see for safety and with your mates you would begin to assemble the den.

Someone needed to sneak home to 'borrow' a hammer and lots of six-inch nails if we couldn't find any on the ground, and then you would hammer the doors together forming a square. I recollect the hammer being very heavy as a child and having to hold it with two hands and it really hurt if you caught your finger on the downward swing!

Once the frame was in place you would use other doors or planks and would nail them to the top thereby forming a roof and a sealed unit from the rain. You would use lino or carpet in the interior and we would create separate rooms with curtains or cardboard. Must have been very cramped but I guess we were small back then with a lot thinner waste lines.

This could go on all day and we made the entrance by booting in a panel on one of the doors and there you have it your very own den. Trouble was other kids would watch from afar and would spot what was happening and once you had settled and chatted over pop and sweets you would sometimes hear a big bang or the clanging of bottles, only kidding of course.

Yes we were being bricked and having no windows or any idea what direction your assailant was attacking you from you had to sit tight and play the waiting game otherwise you would run the risk of getting a brick to the head and I've certainly had a few of them in my time. We were under siege but we had camaraderie and rations albeit only until teatime and this actually added to the excitement and we would plot our revenge! The next day if someone hadn't kicked the den over we would do it ourselves, as this was our right and our privilege leaving a mass of wood and debris for someone else to clear away or to make things out of. On the subject of dens, I remember one time when my mates and me went foraging in this abandoned house in our street; we went in every room but decided to make a den in the loft space.

We all went home and came back with butties and drinks and candles used during the power rationing, it became customary for homes in the seventies to have stock piled candles just in case the power was cut off again. We made the place look very homely and there was the usual crowd, me, Alan, Grant, Jeanette, Joanne and Francis. The loft had an empty water tank that was full of disused paper, I remember this because someone perched a candle on the edge and predictably the candle fell in.

We panicked, the paper lit up and the yellow and orange flames got bigger and bigger. The boys did what any respectable boy would do in these circumstances, we all dropped our trousers and peed on the fire but it made no difference so we all ran home and retuned with half buckets of water due to spilling half the bloody contents in our eagerness to get back. The tank was ablaze by this stage so I took the decision to tell my Dad about the loft fire that was taking hold and someone phoned the fire brigade who put it out.

I don't actually remember being punished for this and thinking back someone could have got seriously hurt and seeing as the house was a terraced house it wouldn't have taken too long before the adjacent

houses caught fire. My house was only four doors up the street.
I recall a bleak memory when I think back to the area being demolished. An old house stood on its own on Cadogan Street and we learnt that an old man who lived at the house had refused to leave. This man was a bit eccentric but probably a protagonist against the urban clearance scheme and he was known as the 'cat man' as he had dozens of feral cats that roamed round his house, which smelt of urine.
I was about eight and I remember hearing a commotion and Alan and me went to have a look. Other kids had gathered and a bigger kid had booted this old man's door in, this was all it took for the adrenalin hungry mob to ransack his home whilst he was still there.
We watched not knowing what to do, then this bigger kid 'ordered' us to also go inside and steal from the old man. In my defence we were really scared and we felt cornered, we knew it was wrong but we knew the bully would remember this so Alan and me ran inside and grabbed the smallest ornament we could find thinking the smaller the better, we then ran off home.
I can still visualise the ornament, which was a small glazed ceramic ship, chipped round the edges and I can remember this because I feel utterly ashamed about what I had done as the man was just some old bloke who liked cats and I wish I had shown more courage and stood up to the bully and said no. Again I am very, very sorry about my lack of courage.
Moving on. My Primary School had two sites. One was accessed via Cranborne Road, which I mentioned before and was built in the fifties and was next to the Social Club my Mum, and Dad attended and the Church of the same name. The other site was much older and at the back of our house and it had two long single story buildings that ran side by side, separated by a long playground.
One of our much-loved games was rock climbing around the ledge that ran along the buildings whilst holding on to the grilled covers that protected the windows from being smashed. Three established trees were at the entrance, come to think of it we did have some trees but they were the only trees I can recall in the area until the riots of course.
I think it was around Spring time but one of our favourite pastimes was the gathering of yellow caterpillars and storing them in jam jars with leaves and watching them munch away. Bit cruel actually and I never realised we were preventing nature taking its course as they were destined to grow into magnificent butterflies or probably the boring cabbage white type!
At night or at the weekend we would climb on to the roof of the school and we would run along the schools apex but not if it had been raining

as it was very slippy. I had to be careful though as Mum and Dad could see me from the back kitchen if they stood over the sink doing the dishes. At the other end of the yard was a tin roof shed and you could jump onto the roof from the school building if you had the courage, as it was about five foot away. No problem for Lee! This shed became a goal but if you 'skied' a shot you had to scale the five-foot or so green perimeter steal fence, with pointy spikes, to retrieve the ball. No problem when Lee played?

The other side of the fence was the famous 'Piggy Muck Square', I say famous, as everyone from afar knew of this square. I was never sure why the reference to swine excrement, I think my old school has been a farm, so I used Google to discover that pigs were kept on the square at some point in the past and someone posted an entry to say he remembers an air raid shelter being built under the square. Imagine that and how cool, wish it had been in use when I was a kid.

The square is a little way south of the gas works in Edge Hill and four streets; Cadogan, Carlyle, Cambridge and Chichester streets used to bound it for those of you who may have lived in the area.

Said streets have long since been demolished and the gas works could be seen for miles due to having a microwave tower which was built in 1968 during the space age era. We thought we were getting our very own space rocket as it resembled one and we had dreams of conquering such wonderful feats of engineering but the structure was too well protected behind a huge unassailable wall and barbed wire.

I don't recall anyone ever walking the wall but Brad once boasted he had managed to climb up there on more than one occasion and walked the wall to then drop into the gas works? Come on Brad surely you never really went '*Over the Wall*' as the Bunnymen would sing but he insists on finding a corner of the wall with places to grip and then running across the huge gas tanks when they were compressed down at teatime. Very dangerous Brad, heaven knows how you survived your childhood!

Once upon a time the square had a seesaw, a slide, swings and even a maypole with ringed chains to fly off the ground. I remember the seesaw with affection. Obviously the fun was enhanced when two equally weighted mates sat on the seesaw otherwise one would either be stuck in the air or glued to the ground but I also remember seesaw surfing which involved standing in the middle and maintaining ones balance whilst the seesaw moved up and down. I like to think this is how one later developed rhythm used on many a dance floor some years later?

We would slide down the slide of course but that wasn't daring enough for the likes of us and we soon discovered that we could run or shoe

slide down the slide arms stretched out for balance.
Alternatively we would fireman slide down the poles that supported the slide or we would simply sit on the top, holding on tight and looking out, the highest advantage point in our jungle.
One day the council demolished our swing park, did they ask, no they bloody well didn't and we were gutted I can tell you but we soon forgot as they tarmacked the square and this created new opportunities for growing kids and of course a pretty cool football pitch.
We even painted our very own pitch lines and I can recall many a hard fought match against kids from Cecil Street or the G's, the family that lived in Cranborne Road. We didn't play for ninety minutes though, oh no we played till you literally had no energy left or until night set in or until someone was called in for a bath! Ninety minutes was for wimps.
I remember kissing Brad's cousin on the square when I was about fourteen. Her name was Jane and she was very posh, she came from Little Sutton on the Wirral and she would visit her Liverpool family each weekend to see me but she had to keep this secret from her Dad, as he was very protective of his daughter's reputation.
We had this on, off relationship whenever she came over and some months later I remember walking with Jane, Joey and his girlfriend at the time down Hartington Road to this girl's house and staying till very late. All very confusing but I think the girl was a distant relation of Jane and thereby Joey and Jane was sleeping over at hers.
Anyway back to a more innocent time. I remember someone scaling a telegraph pole and tying a stolen piece of rope from Maincrest Van Hire, to the top. We would swing on the rope until the rope wrapped around the pole causing a crash so best to let go at the end but another cool game, a more dangerous game required the help of several mates. See, you would hold onto the rope and your mates would run back and forth from the pole holding onto the rope and you would be lifted up and down clasping on for your life knowing the how high the fall to earth was. Brad tells me he tried to wrap his legs around the rope one time and he lost his grip, he fell, he turned in the air and landed painfully on his hands and knees!
We mainly hung out on the square and if we weren't playing football we would create other games. I remember playing the Olympics for example and we would create running circuits and agree to run a number of laps whilst someone would count but many an argument would erupt, as someone would accuse the timekeeper of counting too fast!
We would have sprint competitions from one end of the square to the other, standing long jump competitions and the throwing of an 'ousey',

translated as 'house' meaning a house brick, to see who could throw the furthest.

Mum's broomstick was used as a javelin and Brad remembers being hit on the head by a flying broom and he has the scar to prove it and another inch or so and he could have taken a strike to his temple, could have died! We would use planks stacked on 'ousey's' to create steeplechase jump fences, the more bricks the higher the fence of course and we would pick an object to throw stones at such as bottles or a street cone.

We were always throwing stones and getting into stone fights. You'd be playing and next thing a stone would go rushing past your head. Someone would shout 'take cover' and the next thing you know your scampering around for stones to throw back at whoever dared you and your mates to a stone fight. Someone usually took one in the head!

We then used the square as a skateboard park or a place to do stunts on our bikes and we would clear away broken glass with brushes taken from home as glass would get stuck in the wheels or your elbows and we would create circuits and ramps made out of planks and red and white barriers pinched from road blocks. We would kneel on our skateboards and the corner near to the school had a slope and we would see who could knock each other off the board as you took the bend.

We were proud of our area, it didn't amount to much but it was our home and the street felt like a community like I said. Neighbours would look out for you and there was a real collective spirit between families. People would lend money or pass down clothes and many a time someone would knock for a bowel of sugar or some bread for a carry out.

We didn't rely upon the council to clear away rubbish; no we took responsibility for cleaning the entry outside the back door. Word would pass from family to family and we would all chip in and give the entry a good sweep, a scrub with bleach and we would even weed the whole length of the entry. We didn't expect old folk to help out and just like the track by 'Canned Heat', *Lets Work Together* was our mantra; after all, this was our playground, this is where we had hours of fun.

Like I said I lived at number seventeen and Alan and Grant lived at number twenty-nine. We would knock for each other but sometimes we would climb up onto the wall at the back and would walk between the houses. This was a very dangerous activity and you would rest and seek refuge on peoples outside toilets roofs unless they had an extension built. You had to have quick nimble feet and a good head for heights otherwise you would bum shuffle along the wall. I couldn't do this now,

as I would get vertigo where's that list again?
This is before the introduction of various bins for rubbish and gates but I remember the bin man being able to pull out a metal bin that sat in the wall and once out you could clamber in and out of the yard through the hatch rather than the back door. We thought of this as a spaceman's escape pod!
Like I said before Cadogan Street ran parallel behind our Street. If I walked outside my back door I could walk through a snug entry into Cadogan Street then to my school when I attended the Piggy Muck square part of St Hugh's. Street after street came tumbling down and Cadogan Street was demolished when I was about eight and for days the JCB dragon would set about pulling down the houses forming mountains of bricks in its wake.
At night and during the weekend Alan and me would play out with total disregard for our safety and we would explore the changing landscape with keenness, rummaging around in the dirt and between fallen walls. Very dangerous when you think of the potential for bricks to collapse but we didn't care.
We would play hide and seek and we would run up and down the stack of bricks playing chase and army. Mounds and mounds of debris would form and the landscape would change daily as the JCB's cleared the way to leave burst water pipes and an empty patch taking away with them generation of peoples memories and experiences all in the name of inner city regeneration.
My street was thankfully spared the wrecking ball otherwise my family might have relocated to a large council estate on the outskirts of the city, perhaps housed in a flat, some architects dreams of how the future would look when in reality the estates became streets in the sky, concrete jungles, crime and graffiti hotspots, with people stacked together living in fear and wishing to get out.
No I'm glad we remained in our street in spite the fact that the houses were very old and damp and the odd sight of a rat scampering about down the entry chased by some feral cat in search of a meal!
I recall Alan and me challenging each other to a brick fight one day by the gas works, I think we were bored. I thought I was being clever and I claimed the top of the brick hill as I would have an advantage point, any budding army captain knew this of course and in any event it was always easier throwing down than up and I would have enough ammunition at my disposal to last me all day. What I didn't bank on however was Alan getting in their first and throwing a brick hitting me straight on the head as I bent down to pick up my first brick. Battle over!

I had a gash in my forehead, still have but thankfully this is below my hairline; blood streamed down my face and into my eye. We couldn't tell our Mum's that we'd been fighting each other though as that would be senseless so we made a story that we were ambushed by some kids but then the questions came, who where they, where did the injury happen and should we go to the police station on Lawrence Road. I literally dug a big hole but we stuck to the deception.

On the topic of injuries one of the scariest memories I have was when we went on rummaging expedition through houses waiting to be demolished. We'd find all manner of things such as old balls, discarded books and 'girly' magazines and we'd call these houses 'bombies' which meant an empty house desperately in need of repair and the phrase has its roots from the Second World War I think when houses were 'carpet bombed' during the blitz.

Let me pause a moment to impart an interesting fact upon you. At school I leant that Liverpool was targeted because of its strategic role as a port and I read recently at the Liverpool Museum that between August 1940 January 1942, four thousand Merseysider's were killed during the bombing and three thousand five hundred more were seriously injured. What a terrible travesty and beggars belief in this day an age how a country could discriminately attack another country but I know the UK did the same over the likes of Berlin and Hamburg in Germany.

The reason I remember this memory with fear is because one time I walked out the back door of this bombie at the back of my house and a roof slate fell from up above, piercing my left hand. It really hurt and my hand was full of blood and I ran off home to my Mum. I think I was very lucky, as it could have cut my hand clean off or worst still it could have landed in my head if I had been a fraction of a second faster out of the house. Brings a shiver to my spine I can tell you and I have a faded grey scar to match the colour of the slate on my wrist as a constant reminder of my near death experience and this memory has got me thinking of Marshall Hain's catchy track *'Dancing in the City'*, we too ran through many houses.

Anyhow, the Council eventually removed the bricks from the wasteland; they ended their urban slum clearance and no more houses to run through but big patches of land for other games. The council planted random staked trees where Cadogan Street once stood effectively leaving a barren wasteland for fly tippers but soon the weeds and grass took root and the place became overrun with 'bric a brac' and a right eye sore.

Still, not to be deterred we would have hours of fun playing army and Alan and me would stand at opposite ends and then we would drop to the ground taking on the sniper look. It occurred to me whilst writing this book that I mention playing army a few times as this was a popular amongst us kids and probably due to the Second World War still being fresh in adults minds. You don't see kids playing army these days and I suppose it's politically incorrect and at the end of the day we shouldn't really glamorise war and the atrocities that are created as a result of nations taking up arms but in the seventies we were still watching classic war movies on a Sunday afternoon with the likes of David Niven playing the leading part.

Although released in 1981, the film Escape to Victory characterised this and was an instant hit because it had interned prisoners of war plotting to make their escape against the Germans during a football match but it also starred many famous footballers such as Pele, Bobby Moore and Mike Summerby. The scene that sticks out the most for me was when Osvaldo Ardiles flicked the ball over the approaching German footballer and for weeks my mates and me would try and copy this manoeuvre on the field. Adam has since told me this is known as a Rainbow Flick and still memorises kids today.

I remember watching with avid interest the newsreel showing tanks and armed forces pushing forward during the Vietnamese War and I can even recall the North Vietnamese tanks crashing into the gates of the Saigon Palace, which I now know, occurred in 1975!

We also had troubles nearer home and I remember the IRA bombing campaign throughout the seventies and lets not forget Cambodia, Uganda, Cyprus, Israel, Lebanon, Rhodesia, the US embassy in Iran, Angola, Black September, the Red Brigade, Basque Separatist... bloody hell the seventies was a very scary decade thinking back and is it any wonder we played army games as we were spoon fed a diet of mayhem and napalm death.

Anyway, the object of our game, which seemed so innocent at the time, was to see who could crawl from one end of the wasteland to the other without being detected. Trying to avoid the occasional dog muck, you'd crawl through glass and stone to find safety behind a clump of grass growing wild behind a staked tree.

On the subject of dog muck I think there's less of it when I'm out and about these days. Don't get me wrong you sometimes stand in some, which for some reason is meant to be good luck but most owners I think keep their dogs on leads or with them in the home and these days owners are encouraged to pick up any droppings. Outside my house the council has spray-painted a dog pooing with a line across it sign warning owners to pick up the mess.

I remember people being less interested in the whereabouts of their dogs in the seventies but this might have had something to do with most dogs being scruffy mongrels as opposed to trophy dogs of today or even worse those little girly dogs dressed up in twee jackets and bows. People pay huge amounts of money for certain breeds and I heard on the news recently that dog theft is on the increase which is somewhat ironic as dogs were popular as guard dogs when I was a kid not the actual reason why someone would break into the house.

Back in the day dogs would roam in packs or would be locked in someone's back yard howling all night, which was annoying. A few doors up from me this friendly bloke called Fred had a dog-called Major. We'd play out and Major would run after our ball probably thinking he was part of a pack. We couldn't play army with Major in spite of his appropriate name, as he would reveal your whereabouts and sometimes we'd wander off further a field in search of new adventures and Major would follow. We'd end up playing games to try to confuse Major and send him off our scent but this was a fruitless task, as he'd always catch up with us, he could sniff our scent. We'd run in and out of buildings and the little bugger would run around the back, he was a smart dog that Major!

On a sad note I remember Brad having a little Jack Russell, a gifted footy playing dog, good at running through tunnels and nipping at your ankle but it died suddenly after catching a disease from another dogs muck. Brad was devastated.

Back to happier thoughts and being an army recruit. We would think of ways in which we could spice up the game and I'm not sure how it came about but we ended up making crossbows. Now let me tell you how you make a crossbow. You need two pieces of wood and you would nail them together, or better still you would slot them together after making a joint, to form a cross.

You would bang in a nail on each arm of the bow and would attach elastic bands from your Mum's knickers elastic, an old pair I hastily add. You would then nail two nails in the centre of the cross as this would be your sight and you would then chisel out a hole and would create a trigger. You would pull back on the elastic band making it tort and you would fashion a stick into an arrow and place it between the two nails. The elastic band would send the arrow off at distance of about twenty feet, so there you have it, your very own cross bow, dangerous I know but we didn't care, we were boys, we needed weapons and we were in the army!

From the beginning of October we would make a Guy using old clothes and a burst football as a head with a felt tipped drawn face or stacks of the Echo Newspaper compressed together and we would sit outside pubs in the freezing cold. This is when we were being imaginative and bothered as we would sometimes use an old parker and we would stuff the ball into the hood, making claim to it being a Guy.

In fact one year, the smallest of our crew, can't remember whom, sat statuette like on the pub step mimicking a Guy because we needed to improvise in the pursuit of money and we would run up to patrons leaving the premises or people passing to ask them 'penny for de Guy', with an outstretched hand. Most would walk on but some would flick you a ten pence piece but if they actually gave you a penny then you would look at them disdainfully thinking 'I didn't really mean a penny, inflation being what it is.

You know I'd be horrified if my kids did this, as it is basically an acceptable form of 'begging' and although nothing ever happened to us, we were vulnerable to some dodgy adult inviting us to take a look at his little puppies down some dark back entry!

It was customary to then start the gathering of wood for 'bombie night' on the 5th November and I remember Lee being a particularly good grafter, he had stamina and would happily fetch and carry wood all day. Again I think this term 'bombie' derives from the Blitz bombings but I could me mistaken, other people would call this Guy Fawkes Night. On the Wirral they call it Bon Fire night but doesn't that mean 'good' in French. Strange lot them over there but it was good in any event so lets not quibble and we would search high and low for planks, doors, wardrobes and anything else that would burn.

I remember learning how to walk with two doors balanced on my back and I guess you could say we were classic scavengers but we knew we had to have the biggest bomb fire to rival other streets. We would find a yard in a bombie to store our bounty, every street had at least one derelict house and it became a bit of a competition and we took turns on sentry duty most nights to make sure those Spofforth Road and Banerman Street kids didn't steal our wood. Sometimes they did and it became a game of cat and mouse.

When the 5th November finally arrived we would erect this tepee shaped stack of wood built around a tall wardrobe for stability. The process could take all day, which was a bit of a nuisance if it was a school day and sometimes adults would help out. I remember nearly burning asbestos before Jeanette's Dad spotted what we were about to do and he took the poisonous planes away.

The tepee would have a gap just big enough for a thin kid to pack the wardrobe with flammable paper and someone would 'volunteer' to set it alight, usually as the sun was setting. Us pyrotechnic entrepreneurs would then place the Guy effigy used for begging, obviously not the statuette one, pride of place on top of the tepee. Once the bombie was lit it would quickly take hold and we would watch our money making Guy dissolve and the fire would burn majestically against the night sky and families would join us in the crisp cold air.

Kids would make strange delayed patterns with sparklers and some adults would set off fire works like the Catherine wheel, nailed to a stood up plank and rockets of course. All night you would see rockets firing into the sky deploying an array of brightly coloured sparks to be seen for miles. These days rockets fire through the night sky on bombie night but you can hear them for a couple of weeks before and after sometimes, doesn't seem right and takes away the enjoyment a bit if you ask me. Sometimes someone would throw a banger into the fire to liven things up and I can recall gripping my heart as if I had been shot on many occasions.

Across the night sky you could spot other bomb fires dotted around the wasteland and you'd usually go over to compare size and structure with other kids and have a laugh about who stole what from other streets.

The structure would crackle and under its own weight it would collapse inward and we would place potatoes and chestnuts at the edge for a feast for later. We always kept a stack of wood to the side to feed the mighty fire and around midnight we would sit on the remaining planks eating our spuds with charred stained hands and mucky faces.

We would then play chicken and challenge each other to jump across the embers that spat out in defiance as the beating heart of the fire died away and you would stink of smoke for days, your skin would be stained with soot. The following morning you'd inspect the fire and you would find hundreds of nails scorched into the ground, so we were always careful not to have our bombie on a piece of land we played footy or where we rode our bikes on for obvious reasons.

Bombie night was great fun although not for the likes of Major and other poor animals, they must have been terrified with all the banging and shouting that went on into the night and still does but now we mainly attend organised displays, not enough wasteland I'm guessing and no opportunity to bake spuds?

This wasteland was also the first time I played golf. Well, I say golf but not in the strictest sense, as we didn't have any clubs or indeed a golf ball, rudiment requirements I later discovered as an adult. No, we had a stick and a small ball again stolen from my sisters.

We would dig out a hole about ten inches in diameter so more like a bucket and we would then start from an agreed point, our first tee. We would mount the ball on a small mound of dirt and we would count how many hits it took to get the ball into the bucket.

Same principle of the ancient game becoming of a gentleman but this wasn't a par three hole I can tell you as you could take twenty odd hits to sink the ball, more like a par twenty. Good fun though and kept us occupied, with no need for three quarter length trousers.

Near the end of the seventies things were to change and our barren playground was about to go through yet another transformation when several parents, including my Mum and Dad petitioned our local Counsellor. I think it was David Alton, now Sir David, who was and still is a Liberal, to do something about the wasteland as it had become an eyesore, for an adult that is.

Just a pause here, I often wondered how the Liberal Party had such a strong following in Liverpool in the seventies as the city was mainly working class but I guess it was due to the good work the likes of Mr Alton did for the community. He must have taken on board what people were saying; a guaranteed vote or forty and one day a JCB turned over the land and removed our trees and then these big trucks deposited heaps of stinky manure for the parents to work into the land. A few weeks later a gang of men erected a steel fence around the perimeter and we would bring them cups of teas and biscuits like we were monitoring the standard of work they were doing, after all it was our ground.

A committee was formed and each family was asked if they would like an allotment and we got our piece of land outside our back door. Trouble was even though you could see the allotment from our house you had two entry points and you had to walk some distance round the outside to gain access. I told Dad to build a gate but he couldn't, the fence was impenetrable.

Before I tell you more about the allotment I remember foolishly having a 'takey' on the back of a motorbike. Some older kid we knew can't remember who exactly but he persuaded my mates and me to have a go sitting on the back of his bike without a helmet whilst he drove the bike the length of the entry. Unknowns to me Dad was in the allotment watching just as I came off the bike at the end near our house and looking back through adult eyes I could easily have had a nasty accident but thankfully I got up unscathed and promised Dad I wouldn't do something so silly again. He believed me too!

Back to green finger neighbours. It seemed that each family had a need to print their own unique taste on the allotment; it became an extension of their home. Billy and Doreen grew a lawn from seeds and had a plot for growing various vegetables; they had a very nice garden in the end. Alan's Mum and Dad were equally proud gardeners, as was expected and Danny would use top of the range tools and new wood to erect his fence and wanting instant gratification he bought turf and was the first gardener to have a lawn. Both turned out to be very good and keen gardeners, they would have tied first in a 'Galloway in Bloom' competition.

Us kids would watch every now and then and you could see how the adults became competitive, in a friendly way I may add and it was like they had to advertise how well they were doing outside of their home. This old Irish bloke lived next door to me and he was different and wasn't preoccupied with plants, flowers and a lawn to bask during hot months, no he grew rows and rows of potatoes. Bit stereotypical of me but I guess coming from Ireland he was always going too.

My Dad was a scavenger through necessity, he never threw anything away, still doesn't and he would use old yoghurt pots to grow seeds, old timber and scrap metal, everything would have a use. He erected a fence using old planks found somewhere and he built a greenhouse from old windows for example. Dad came to realise that he took after his Dad, as he was able to grow vegetables and flowers from seed, including our small circular lawn. Over time Dad built up his collection of tools and he would read up on planting techniques from a big book and that was his presents sorted for every birthday and Christmas ever since. Thinking back, I'd lost a decent play area but I got a place to sunbathe as I had outgrown playing army by then!

Anyway, Dad was very proud of his allotment, it became his hobby for many years, which was good for him when he was out of work as it kept him busy. Dads should always be busy and my Dad felt like he was doing something for the family, as we would have a crop of potatoes, tomatoes and other vegetables to eat. Most days would be spent digging, rearranging and planting and Dad still does in his house where they live now and I'll sometimes quip to Dad that if he's ever bored there's a garden where I live that could do with a bit of attention!

Chapter Nine

Seasons in The Sun...

Moving on. On the subject of all things green and healthy let me now devote a bit of time talking about the many parks dotted around the area and places we visited that were more leafy and with the onset of spring, warmer weather would arrive, trees would grow leaves and like migrating birds we would go in search of new adventures and escapades.

This was our joy our fun and our *'Seasons in the Sun'* as the track goes and we would be out all day not caring about what time we should be home or what we would eat to replenish our depleting energy levels. One year when I was about fourteen, we decided to take up the hobby of fishing. Why, remains a mystery to me as I loathe fishing, don't see the point but there was a tackle shop on Smithdown Road and several mates and me bought fishing rods and other paraphernalia including maggots! Such horrible creatures and they stank to high heaven and you had to keep them in the fridge to slow the process of them mutating into flies. Mum was not pleased I can tell you and I'm sure Dad nearly took them to work for his lunch on more than one occasion. Perish the thought! Me, Alan, Grant and Brad would make our way to Sefton Park or 'sevvy park' to use the correct colloquialism we would use, at some ungodly hour and would set up our equipment at the edge of the lake. We had rods, lead weights, flies, seats and sandwiches for later and maggots as bait.

I still squirm at the thought of impaling a maggot onto a hook watching all the innards gush out and I believe the keenest of anglers would keep them in their mouth, how disgusting! We would experiment with the correct weights and would cast off hoping to catch a fish but in all honestly I cannot recall one occasion when anyone actually caught a fish. I had more success with Dad with my cheap fishing net attached to a bamboo cane catching 'tiddlers' in Sefton Park. What are the odds and we would sit chatting away for hours until boredom set in; not even the sight of the occasional rat would keep us amused so we would do what any other group of lads would do, we would end up having water fights. I'm sorry if I offend any anglers out there but I just don't get fishing. I remember one time going to Greenbank Lake, which strangely enough is in Greenbank Park in the hope the fish here were more likely to bite despite our obvious ineptitude. Predictably we caught 'nowt', no not a newt I mean nothing and it was a lovely morning as I recall, the sun came up and the park began to fill up as the sun was baking hot. We were enjoying ourselves flicking water and running around oblivious to what was happening around us when these two girls shouted over in unfamiliar accents from the other side of the Lake, beckoning us to swim over.

We initially refused but then one of them said if you swim over you could have a pound. That was a lot of money back then so I jumped in; I was already soaked in any case and I did the 'front crawl' to discover I was the only one who had taken on the challenge. Midway I turned round looking for support from my mates and I kicked the bottom of the Lake! I was treading water as you do to stay afloat but didn't realise that the Victorians had made the Lake and the depth must have been no more than four feet.

I shouted out come in it's not deep but no one followed so I swam on to the girls through clingy weeds whilst thinking about what witty line I could conjure up to impress these fair maidens laden with money, maidens who would run off laughing. They were lovely Irish girls as it happens and as I looked up at them the only words I could muster was; 'where's me pound den!'

They looked at me with eyes that said I didn't really think you would do that and I was gingerly handed a pound note, the paper sort I might add, that's how long ago it was. I put the note in my mouth for safekeeping and swam back; the shame and why didn't I stop for a bit and chat, as they were pleasant enough girls, cant remember why, probably something to do with being a self conscious teenager. I often wondered what they were doing in Liverpool, where they on holiday or students, who cares but this turned out to be a treat as we had chips on the way home but still no fish sadly, not even the battered kind!

Sevvy Park is a very famous park in the South of Liverpool. A bit of a walk for us kids from Edge Hill but filled with so many exciting and noteworthy places to explore. Now I must mention an obvious track we liked at the point that links to all this greenery talk; *'Down in the Park'* by the mysterious Gary Numan.

We basically had two routes to the park. The first was along Hartington Road, a Road that went on and on and on linking Smithdown Road with

Ullet Road. Very boring and to make the route less dreary I would run then walk from one lamppost to the next. I remember one day being with my Dad and sisters at the park, he would sometimes take us there whilst Mum had the job of cooking Sunday roast dinner. I think Dad's mission was to get us out from 'under Mum's feet'. Now there's a memory, 'bubble and squeak' the next day, basically a fry up of whatever food was left over from the roast.

I was being a right grump as I recall, not sure why, probably onset of hormones and I protested that I would rather walk home than get back in the car; it was the Hillman I mentioned before so I was doing a bit of a 'Lisa'. Dad was a very patient man ordinarily but on this occasion and in frustration, he broke and said 'go on then' and with that I trekked the lonesome path back home starving and regretting my stubbornness. I think I actually beat them home to spuds and beef, as the car was not the quickest!

The other route involved going through Sefton cemetery or 'de cem' as we called it. En route we would stop and read the grandiose and gothic Victorian tombs clearly inhabited by some merchant or person of wealth from another time. People, who in death needed to advertise to the world that they had made it and wanted to be remembered for an eternity.

Tales would pass down from kid to kid about Dracula, werewolves, Frankenstein and other creatures straight from the writers of Hammer House of Horror movies that were very popular at the time and we would convince ourselves that creatures of the dead would roam the cem at night looking for us kids to feast upon made even more real as you would spot the occasional rook digging up a worm.

Now I think rooks and crows get a bad press as they are always associated with death and creatures of the night and this reputation is not helped by the fact that a collection of crows is called a 'murder of crows', how stereotypical.

Talking of nocturnal birds did you know a collection of owls is referred to as a 'parliament of owls?' I thank my clever mate Neil for these interesting facts and linking a track with all this, lets pause to remember the Boris Karloff inspired track, *'The Monster Mash'* by Bobby 'Boris' Pickett.

Some tombs had doors on the front and we would dare each other to touch the grave under the threat of being eternally cursed. Stepping forward you would tentatively reach out a hand and it was customarily for someone to then scream out scaring the hell out of you making you jump backwards like a bolt of lightening had hit you. Clenching the place where your beating heart pounds you'd run after your mate to jump all over him in retaliation. 'Piley on piley on'.

The cem was so scary at night as it was dark and eerie and I can remember misjudging the journey home on many occasions and I would leg it through the cem in fear of being bitten by Vlad the Impaler! You weren't as scared when it came to the 'mummy' or 'Frankenstein' with his arms outstretched in front of him, true he would look chilling but with size thirty steel capped boots, come on we all knew he'd be a crap runner.

That used to amuse me actually. Why did the leading lady in those seventies Hammer movies just hitch her skirt up and run like mad instead of standing still like a fool, screaming then fainting to the ground hoping to be rescued by the handsome leading man? Attention seeking behaviour at its worst if you ask me or more likely something to do with societal attitudes towards women viewing them as helpless victims needing to be rescued. We didn't need attention or rescuing and we would literally fall out gasping for breath on to Smithdown Road basking in the streetlights that signalled sanctuary, signalling you're near home, signalling you'd made it alive!

At the other end of the cem was an old creaky revolving door, like a rusty footy turnstile and once through you entered onto Arundel Avenue. You would then walk through a couple of terraced streets and continuing with the ghoulish theme, folk law spoke of witches living in one particular house on the corner but in reality the house was probably inhabited by an old dear with a penchant for cats again but that was enough for our fertile minds and for us to recast granny as a witch from Hansel and Gretel!

Surviving the lure of, 'can I interest you in a sweetie my dear'; you would walk through a swing park for a quick go on the swings and the slides before eventually arriving at Sefton Park. The journey was indeed an adventure and we hadn't even got to the park by this stage!

Our point of entry was usually by the famous caves, on the perimeter of the Park and yet another spooky place with stories of lost kids and ghouls! I went the park recently and I took a picture of a placard that stands outside with an explanation of how the caves came to be.

The caves are actually called a 'grotto' and are described as *'a fine example of a Victorian rockwork cave popular in public parks'*. The grotto was built around 1870 by this Frenchman called M. Combaz who was brought in by the parks designers Andre and Hornblower. The grotto was known in the area as 'Old Nicks Caves', but I don't know who Nick was, do you, probably some hermit who took shelter in the caves?

The cave had two entrance points and went back twenty yards or so and a staircase leading to an opening in the roof now blocked off. I never knew this as a kid but the internal chamber once contained a waterfall that cascaded over the rockwork and flowed into the Mirror Pond that was at the front.

When I was a kid the nearest water feature was over the road in the park and I've since learnt that this is the Lower River Jordan and the Mirror Pond was a borehole that now connects the two. The pond was filled in when we played at the caves, it was just a dusty dirt indentation in the ground but I'm glad to say restoration work has now reinstated the pond to its former glory.

The caves were very dark inside and a pillar with a crack opening that ran right through supported the centre and I now know this is where the waterfall once existed. Being blessed with a twenty four inch waist line back then I could squeeze right through this crack into the deepest and darkest part of the cave. You could barely see your feet and many a fall happened and the place also stank of urine, as it doubled up it seems as a convenient toilet for desperate folk passing by!

We would play tick for hours and we would run and hide in the caves or clamber over the top like mountaineers. Above, you would look down and it seemed so high at the time and the bravest souls would sometimes climb up and rock and climb around the cave. We got to know all the foot and hand holes and we would literally have hours and hours of fun without actually setting foot in the park! For health and safety reasons I guess but the council have erected gates preventing access to the caves, sadly denying local kids the opportunity to play and explore or a passer by in need of the loo!

Using my I Phone again and its clever camera, no I don't have shares in Apple by the way; I took another picture to help with my research. So here goes, I now know that Sefton Park was originally part of the ancient Toxteth Deer Park were the area of Toxteth gets its name. The Earle of Sefton owned the Deer Park and he sold the land to the council and in 1866 the council put up three hundred guineas as a prize in a competition to design the park. The aforementioned Messer's Andre and Hornblower won and his Royal Highness Prince Arthur opened the Park to cheering crowds on the 20th May 1872. Prince who you ask, me too? Ill spare you the history lesson. On other occasions we would walk along the river opposite the caves, the Lower Jordan where my Dad and me used to fish with nets, which meandered through the park like a massive snake to the Lake.

The river disappears under paths to reappear again or through slippy stepping-stones and widens the deeper you get into the Park. When I was a kid a 'Captain Hook Pirate's Ship from Peter Pan' stood in the middle of the river and the Lost Boys had a hut on an island only accessible by the public if you could swim. Now there's a decent film from the eighties and a reminder of a track I like from the soundtrack. The 'Lost Boys' a film about vampires and *'Moondance'* by Van Morrison. Perhaps I do listen to other people's conversations as I overheard this old lady talking to a friend in the Park recently and she said apprenticeship lads built the boat from Camelairds in Birkenhead. Camelairds was and still is a famous shipbuilding firm on the River Mersey that you can see from Dad's old school and I am glad I know that as I had often wondered why. When the weather was warm we would sometimes swim out to the boat and the hut taking care to avoid the park rangers and we didn't even need the lure of a pound note this time as we were talking pirates and skulduggery!

There was also a statue in honour of Peter Pan with rabbits and Tinkerbelle at his feet near the river, which has since been restored and is now situated outside the palm house. A few hundred yards further on from the Captain is a café and opposite is an impressive fountain with Eros on top that's recently been restored too, like Peter, back to its former glory.

By the fountain is the fenced off stream and nearby stands an evergreen tree with branches that reach out from top to bottom. If ever there was a tree designed for climbing then this is it and I would scale this tree to the very top and I recall holding on tightly feeling the tree sway to the beat of any passing breeze.

The tree still stands majestically to this day and it astonishes me to think that it's been thirty five years since nimble me climbed this tree and although tempted to rekindle my youth I doubt the trees apex could support my weight. The word timber springs to mind based on the added timber around my waist!

We would sometimes buy a lolly ice from the cafe in the middle of the park, usually a lime green lolly and would stand admiring the exotic birds in the Avery round the corner. Thankfully this hasn't been restored, as I would worry about the birds shivering in winter thinking what have I done to deserve this. As you approached the Avery you'd hear peacocks screeching, song birds singing in unison and parrots and cockatoos chirping.

As for the impressive Palm House, this is truly a remarkable building, surrounded by statues of famous people and a fitting testament to

Victorian engineering. It was always warm inside as I recall, smelling of exotic fragrances and an utterly fascinating place to visit.

Again the House has been restored but with fewer plants it seems unless my memory has gone haywire. You can get married at the palm house so out with some plants and in with floor space for brides in big 'Gone With The Wind' dresses and although a beautiful place to tie the knot I'm guessing this would cost a pretty fragrant packet.

When I was little I remember the Lake in all its glory. People would go out on the Lake in rowing boats and I remember having a go with my Dad when I was very small. Probably due to some health and safety legislation again the parks recent restorations have not included boats on the lake once more but the many swans, geese and ducks remain. The lake had two of its own rock caves on the edge, one you could walk through and one was a shelter from the rain and both still smell of urine.

I also remember being about four and loosing Mum and Dad at the fair that was on at Sefton Park. I cried thinking I had lost everything and I remember this kind gent selling candyfloss telling me to stay with him whilst he found my parent's. I was so relieved when they came hurrying through the crowds to pick me up and here's me wondering where my attachment difficulties' first began?

Sefton Park has a bandstand perched on an island accessible by a gated bridge. In the early eighties when I was about sixteen during the summer months, I remember watching several bands on a hill that faced the bandstand and this was called 'Larks in the Park' and this was a free concert! I saw Big Country, Nick Heywood, several bottles were hurled at Nick as I recall and Echo and the Bunnymen at Larks in the Park. The splendid *'The Cutter'* and the *'Back of Love'* are tracks that spring to mind when I think of the Bunnymen but like I mention elsewhere I can think of many more.

I also remember seeing a very young Craig Charles recite street poetry from the stand. This was before his Red Dwarf days, the brilliant sci fi comedy that first aired in 1982 with the annoyingly well-informed Kryten, the egocentric Cat, sour faced Holly the hologram, the disgusting but 'sharp as a knife' Lister and let's not forget the insufferable Rimmer. Yes I was and still am a fan and I think the makers should do another series or even a movie.

Back to earth dear reader. As you can see we got to know every inch of the Park and we would roam for hours and hours making up games and generally goofing around. I suppose you would say this was our *'go wild in the country'* period, our taste of freedom from urbanisation, our chance to breathe fresh air. Now there's an unlocked memory; the 'agreeable'

Annabelle Lwin who fronted the New Wave band Bow Wow Wow famed for screeching to the track *Go Wild*. I have to be honest though, for us pubescent lads she was more famous and recognisable for being young and appearing provocatively naked on the cover of the bands album than the actual song.

I took my family to Sefton Park recently and like I said before the place has gone through a major overhaul costing tens of thousands of pounds! Looks really impressive and leaves me with a sense of civic pride and I am reminded that parks were clearly designed as places where the inner city masses could enjoy fresh clean air and long may that tradition continue!

At the risk of sounding a miserly sod though my only gripe is the price of a cuppa in the cafe, its not even Costa fortune, extortionate if you ask me but when your gasping and you have many hectares between you and the nearest watering hole I guess you need to succumb! Someone's got the monopoly on passing trade I think!

Another favourite park was Wavertree Park or the 'Mystery', as it was known in the area and funny enough this park was situated at the far end of, wait for it, Wavertree. I think it was called the Mystery as it had been bequeathed to the Council and no one knew who originally owned it. Or is that just a local myth I grew up believing?

Every summer and at Easter as a recall a travelling fair would pitch up and you'd see posters in the shops telling you what dates the fun started. We would know in any event when the fair started, as you'd hear the likes of the Jackson Five over the terraced houses singing *Can You Feel It*. Yes we could and with fifty pence in your pocket you'd make you're way through terraced streets onto Grosvenor Road, exiting on to Wellington Road, not the Wellington Road school Dad attended by the way, then the gates to the Mystery Park.

Ahead you could smell the fried onions and burgers mixed with candy floss and you would hear exited screams from happy punters, girls and boys as they went up and down whatever exciting and spinny ride was in fashion back then! The sun would be on its heavenly descent and the florescent tubes would light up the night sky making the whole area seem mystical and enchanting to me. I loved it.

Couples, families, gangs and most importantly, girls would amass from all parts of South Liverpool and beyond. Perhaps it was the fun that people were having but you felt safe as you knew most people and as I recall there was never any trouble. We'd steer clear from throwing darts at cards for the chance of winning a cuddly toy from Sesame Street as we knew the odds were stacked against you and even if you did win what

would you do with Kermit unless of course you had a girl you wanted to impress.
We never wasted our time with the slot machines or the arcade games either; we never saw the attraction, well not when until we were about sixteen when Alan and Grant developed a bit of an unhealthy habit for spinning cherries and nudges! I remember many a time standing in a pub and within minutes Alan or Grant and sometimes Manny, would lose a fair amount of money. Sometimes they would win and like all gamblers this would somehow justify the taking part in spite of losing heaps of money beforehand.
My Mum was the same when it came to the bingo. She won sometimes and I remember one time when she came home with a thousand pounds stuck down her knickers that was a substantial wad of money but she must have also spent a fortune over the years but she would say this was her only enjoyment. Now there's a buried track from the psyche, *'Hit Me with Your Rhythm Stick'* by Ian Drury and the Blockheads and the reason I mention this is due to the bingo plagiarised line but again I cant tell you other than to say its about two large persons resembling eighty eight?
I guess that's the draw of gambling and you have to be in it to win like they say in the lottery.
I remember having a spare twenty pence in my pocket one day and I thought what the hell I'd give it a go. Alan was playing next to me and he was transfixed with the spinning wheels. I won to my delight, I think it was about three pounds, a good profit in my book, but Alan leaned over before I could hit the lit up green button to take my money and he gambled my money and I lost. Alan proclaimed that you can't leave it there as you were one step to the big one, to which I annoying replied but I would have been happy with the three pound profit!
Alan and Grant then learnt how to gain credits on the machines using a knitting wire that would be pushed in and out of the money slot! This little device worked on all kinds of devices and I talk about this later when we went on holidays with the Vic.
Then we had the Liverpool Show that came to the Mystery every year in May I think. It also came with a fair but it had all kinds of shows and displays. You'd have this big opening space for marching bands and dog competitions and I remember being transfixed with this army assault course.
One year a section of the show was cornered off for skateboarders and they rolled out this matt that ran for about a hundred yards. It was placed on this incline and we'd take turns sitting on our boards and

rolling down the hill with no stones to send us hurtling. It was even better than Spekeland Road!

The council ended up building a skateboard bowel at the far end of the park by the Bluecoat School but skateboarders never used it as I recall. We would cycle down the hill into the entrance of the bowl and would race around the bowel. This was a thrill but we then discovered an even better 'buzz' as they say, but with added danger. You'd enter the bowl but instead of cycling round you'd hit the steepest part and fly straight out of the bowl at a great height and would land on the grassy incline that the bowel was built into.

This was very dangerous but you didn't care when you're a kid, in fact you had to give it a go otherwise you would be called a chicken and your more heroic mates would cluck away mimicking a chicken until you relented and took up whatever challenge was set.

With each attempt we would cycle faster and faster to maximise the airtime and most of the time fearless rubberband Lee would always win at such competitions. We stopped playing this game when Lee took off at such a speed that he lost control of his bike and as he landed he went flying over his handlebars taking a blow to his 'goolies' but typically he survived.

I entered a bike race at the Mystery and borrowed Grants five-speed racer, his bike was faster than mine. I can't remember where I came in the race, but I didn't come first, that's for sure as I would have remembered.

On hot sunny days a gang of us would go the park to have a picnic. We would raid the cupboard for biscuits and juice and of course a blanket to sit on and a blanket to erect a makeshift tent over our heads.

I played football at the Mystery on the fields and some years later on the Astroturf. The Mystery looks very impressive these days as it has an Athletic Centre with a stadium, a Tennis Centre with indoor and outdoor courts and an Olympic size swimming pool attached to the Sports Centre. My youngest son plays football at the Mystery and most Saturday's you will find me cheering him on the sideline with other proud parents.

Before I move on let me talk about Picton baths. When I was a kid we would spend many a day at the baths, which was an old Victorian rectangle pool. It had a shallow end for novice swimmers and the deep end was six foot. Surrounding the pool was the changing cubicles and the cubicles had wooden doors covered in decades of sky blue paint but without locks and you could peer over the top and talk to your mates through the meshing as you were getting dressed.

You would 'lash' your clothes into a pale blue plastic wash basket and hand them to a member of staff who would give you a coloured rubber wristband with a number on it. I may add girls generally got dressed on the opposite side and there were signs everywhere warning couples that there was strictly 'no petting'. Same signs also warned against running, bombing and jumping on someone's head, all of which we tended to ignore.

We were all competent swimmers as it happens having learnt to swim at Webster Road baths but we never swam lengths or breadths but we would dive and bomb each other unless the lifeguard caught us. I even remember having a smooch in the changing rooms with my appendix friend, Sonia who I bumped into a few years later. We swam together and dived deep and kissed under the water. Oh the innocent fun I had.

I recall doing a superman dive; this involved a one-arm entry, a headfirst dive and deep dives.

We would pretended to be pearl divers in some exotic lagoon and would go looking for treasures at the bottom of the pool but the nearest we got to finding treasure was discarded plasters or the occasional girls hair bobble.

We would try and swim a breadth under water gasping for air as you came to the surface and nearly feinting but a challenge is a challenge! After some hours of fun we would then get a cup of delicious hot chocolate and would take turns playing on the Space Invaders machine but only if someone had a ten pence piece. Picton Baths had a small pool for babies in another part of the building and it was always much warmer but we were only allowed into this pool on the odd occasion.

When I was about eighteen my mate Derek and me would spend an hour or two relaxing in the sauna in an old white tiled Russian steam room, probably built when the baths first opened. You were given white towels on entry and you would lounge on pine sunbeds in between going into the steam room or for a cold shower.

I remember stepping into the shower, which was a round brass pipe contraception that fired cold water from various directions, I hate cold water!

Otterspool was also a good place to idle away hot summer day's and we would mainly go there on our bikes; it was some distance away from home. This was a small park in comparison to the others we went to that opened out at the end and we would reach it by entering from Aigburth Road down a long path. The path ran right through to the Prom by the Mersey where we would play footy and was surrounded by trees and places to hide.

Midway along the path you come across caves and a rocky formation and we would spend hours rock climbing. A railway line crossed over the path and I remember finding some cardboard and my mates and me spending hours sliding down this dirt path.

In the autumn we would go in search of conkers. Most parks and leafier parts of Wavertree had horse chestnut trees and we would 'launch' sticks and anything else we could find into the branches hoping to dislodge a 'bigun!' The outer case of the conker was prickly and inside was a glowing conker befitting of hidden treasure and ready to be pierced. You probably know this but conkers is a traditional children's game played by two players. Each with a conker threaded onto a piece of string you would take turns striking each other's conker until one breaks. If you hit your opponents conker full on you could continue until you missed but if you misdirected and managed to catch the edge of the conker then the first to shout out 'tips' would have the next go.

Most conkers split after a few hits and folklore had it that vinegar made the outer shell very hard and successful conkers would be christened with names in honour of their past glories.

You would have a fiver or an 'eighter' for example, my mate Oliver had a tenner once, no not Pavarotti, but he could have been bluffing, as I never did witness his triumphs. Accidents could happen when playing this game just like with Klackers I mentioned earlier, as the conker would spin round and sometimes catch you on the back of your hand.

So on to my final Park, Wavertree Botanic Garden and Park, which was actually the nearest Park to my house and is another example of a mid nineteenth century public park. I read on Wikipedia that William Roscoe and a group of fellow botanists developed a private garden known as the Botanic Garden, initially located near Mount Pleasant but in the 1830's the garden was relocated to Wavertree Botanic Gardens where we had many adventures.

The park wasn't as impressive as Sefton Park but it had a walled garden and a path that ran through the middle with an obsolete water fountain in the middle. It had a small wood at the far end near the iconic Littlewoods building, a fine example of Art Nuevo and now a listed building although I noticed it's starting to show signs of decay. This building also had a huge clock on the buildings tower facing the Park so you knew when it was time to retreat back home.

My Dad would take my sisters and me to the park to play and I can recall lying at the top of the hill, counting to three and rolling like a log, crashing into Tracy and Tina, until you were nearly sick with dizziness.

By the woods was a dogs home and you would hear dogs barking plans to escape, I wonder if any of them could do the Rainbow Flick like Osvaldo, probably not, too many feet!

The other side of the woods was the perimeter to the tracks that led to Edge Hill Station and the edge had a path and an old wall that ran along it and this became a battlement where I would pretend to play army.

Like I said before we played Manhunt behind the walled garden never fully understanding the history behind its origin and I wonder what Mr Roscoe would have said if he knew what antics we got up to in his carefully planted shrubbery and finery?

Actually this park has extra meaning to me for three reasons. I have an old black and white picture of my Dad holding me in his arms when I was barely six weeks old. I played for Grosvenor under elevens football team at the Botanic winning most matches and also and with a degree of embarrassment, when you came across 'Paula the bunny', then lets just say it was quite apt that this Park should be so near to Edge Hill Station! Tickets please!

Chapter Ten

Everybody's On Top Of Top Of The Pops...

It's high time I dedicate a few pages to some wonderful tracks that I have had the pleasure of hearing a long my life path chronicling my assorted musical tastes and I warn you I do go off on several Tourette like tangents, so be prepared to get dizzy!
Call me biased but Liverpool has always been very proud of its musical heritage and I'm not suggesting other cities are lacking in musical talent but most scouse mothers simply bottle-feed babies on large portions of music and I was no different.
Let me elaborate further. Here's me half way through this book and I've yet to mention that I was born in April 1966, I'm an Aries in case you don't know and the track that was number one when I was born was *'The Sun Ain't Gonna Shine Anymore'* by the Walker Brothers.
This year turned out to be an extraordinary year as it happens, well I would say that being an Arian but truth is it was a marvellous year. England won the World Cup, 'they think its all' over resonated around the county and four lads from Liverpool called the Beatles were changing the face of music forever.
It seems fitting that I therefore devote a few words to the four mop heads before I move on to my 'era', as Liverpool will always be associated with the Beatles. I suppose I took more of an interest in them Beatles with an 'A' after reading this mouldy book that belonged to my Uncle Tommy when I was about fifteen. The Beatles followed one of their tracks and went on their separate *'Long and Winding Road'* and I can vaguely remember Yoko Ono being lambasted by devoted fans on the telly as the reason as to why the fab party came to an end coinciding with the onset of a new decade.
Here's a fact I dare you to challenge. The Beatles are without doubt the best band in the World. If you take away the Beatles then the whole pack of cards tumbles over as the Beatles will forever be known as pioneers and the gateway for all pop music and I would go as far to say that they wrote and threw away the instructions manual still adhered to by

today's artists. In fact it's incredible how many artists site the Beatles as one of their biggest influences regardless of when or where they were born. They are globally recognisable and I am proud of the fact that they come from Liverpool and my childhood was dotted with many wondrous tracks.

John and Paul were superb writers whose competitive edge seemingly drove them on to create many classics, Ringo was creative in his own lesser way and a decent drummer, whilst George, who I have grown to like the best, was seen as the introverted one but he was also a very talented musician and song smith. Music historians would say he was the gel that bound the band together and led his pals into a spiritual trip to new creative horizons epitomised by the creation of *'Sergeant Peppers'*. A little played track called *'Ballard of Sir Frankie Crisp (Let it Roll)* by George is a beautifully hypnotic track and I suggest you listen to it, a favourite of mine.

I can recall singing Beatles tracks at school, *'We All Live in a Yellow Submarine'* for example, due to most teachers in our school graduating from the university of flower power. Personally I wasn't overly impressed when I was in shorts, they didn't speak to me back then not until I became an adult and now I love or should I say 'luv' their music. Perhaps this is due to Mum and Dad as they liked the Beatles but they were into rock and roll and if my Mum were writing her memoires I would guess that she would say her favourite track is *'The House of the Rising Sun'* by the Animals. In fact I grew up knowing that my parents were mainly into American artists such as Buddy Holly, Chuck Berry, Elvis and Fats Domino, they influenced them more, just like the Beatles as it happens and most Sundays Mum would dance around the room cleaning up to one of her old rock and roll LP's.

Mum would say the reason for this was that Liverpool was awash in the fifties with imported sounds that hit these shores because we live in a city built on a river, serviced by a port housing ships from distant lands. Mum told me that someone would know someone who was a sailor or a docker just like my granddad and Liverpool, including Messer's McCartney, Lennon, Harrison, Starr and I suppose you can include Griffith and Kearns too, became hooked on the rhythmic American beat and associated culture and with that teenagers in the UK became beetle crushes be-quiffed leather wearing teddy boys smoking woodbines.

I was very young when the Beatles split up and I can remember knowing that the Beatles were really famous and known worldwide but it felt like no one really cared, a kind of well that was then this is now attitude. In fact I would go as far to say that its only been the last couple of decades that Liverpool and its people have come to embrace the Beatles, driven no doubt by the tourist dollar, the Euro and the Yen and have welcomed them back into its parental bosom.

We now have a museum to honour the Beatles, blaring out music from below the Albert Dock inviting you in but as of yet I haven't succumbed and you often spot the Beatles yellow bus doing it's *Magical Mystery Tour*' with wide eyed fans clicking away on Sony cameras whilst being told, to my right is Penny Lane to my left is the bus station and other famous sites dotted around South Liverpool. We also have the Matthew Street Festival held once a year celebrating all forms of music but particularly the Beatles and people flock to Liverpool to see a plethora of tribute bands from all round the world such is the fascination with the lads.

Indeed Liverpool has finally realised the tourist potential in the fab four and that's a good thing but before it seemed scousers, certainly my generation, felt somewhat uncomfortable and a little embarrassed about the fame whereas other cities would have no doubt honoured the lads with statues, streets named after them, freedom of the city accolades and an array of tacky gift shops.

What other city would have demolished the Cavern, the place where it all began, totally absurd and if anything was to sum up how Liverpool felt about its dearly departed son's, then this is it, short-sighted town planning and a complete shame. Why didn't someone step in and say, 'hold on der, dis is part of ar eritage'.

This might seem odd but Liverpool is a proud city, even in adversity and we consider ourselves to be leaders and trailblazers, a city where everyone has a talent and the Beatles were somehow viewed as lad's who had made it big but then left their spiritual home for pastures new. People wished them good luck of course and I guess they only did what comes natural to us scousers, they 'emigrated' or as we would say, 'dey upt and left' to find their own way in life.

When you talk to people from other parts of the country or the world for that matter they often quip, 'oh yes the Beatles and, annoyingly, Liverpool FC' when they think about my turf and I will hastily reply, 'but what about the city, its buildings, did you know that Liverpool has the most Grade two listed buildings outside of London. The humour, Arthur Askey and the brilliant Ken Dodd spring to mind but least said about Jimmy Tarbuck and Stan Boardman who, particularly Tarbuck, always try too hard to be scouse in his gleaming golfing attire. They're what we call 'professional scousers'.

What about the sense of community and its people during difficult times such as the blitz bombing and the recession hit eighties. Lets not forget the many wonderful bands and artists from these parts, but not Cilla Black, talented yes but again like Tarby she tries too hard.

Did you know Liverpool is famed for being associated with the most records to reach number one in the hit parade, on Matthew Street next to Eric's, I'll tell you more about Eric's in a bit, is a brick wall celebrating the many artists from these parts. Beat that Manchester, London, Glasgow, Sheffield etc. etc. and to think it all started in 1953 when 'Lita Roza' became the first woman to top the charts with a track that has taken on a nursery rhyme feel to it, *'How Much is that Doggy in the Window'*.

What about Everton FC who have had their moment in the sun, not the shitty newspaper as we all hate the Sun and that goes for the blue half too, indeed *'scousers never buy the Sun'* are words taken from Billy Bragg track *'Never Buy the Sun'*, a recent track to my collection and I urge you to give it a listen, hope Billy doesn't mind me quoting his words. I mean Everton have had success, albeit not as much as our 'Red' neighbours but us blues hold the distinction of being one of the founding members of the football league. We will have our day again.

Just thought of a treasured track that reminds me of Everton; *'The Story of the Blues'* by Pete Wylie and his band Wah! It's so perfect, so brilliant, it's very existence makes you want to stand on a chair and applaud. Mr Wylie happens to be a staunch Red but I don't care, this track thrills me and from the moment I hear the first drumbeat my heart skips in time and I actually feel saddened when the song ends. Should have bought the twelve-inch I hear you shout but this song does move me.

Anyway, a common joke in Liverpool is that true scousers support the 'People's Club', Everton, thanks for that Mr Moyes and live 'in' the city, but we know this is just us blues getting back at Liverpool for spreading its wings far afield, even to places like Norway and this is based on them lot winning trophies in the seventies and eighties. Red's will retaliate with 'at least were not from North Wales' like that's some kind of insult, with my name, tut, but it is true that a large amount of Evertonian's do come from places like Rhyll and Prestatyn, you only have to look at the coaches parked outside Goodison on match day.

Liverpool holds the accolade of being a 'World Heritage Site' and the skyline certainly has the wow factor but please Mr Town Planner or more likely some big property mogul, stop building modern angled glass skyscrapers as they are smothering the truly magnificent 'Three Graces'.

That's simply not progress and I've recently head that Liverpool runs the risk of losing this accolade because of the modern feel that's now taken hold of the front.
It may also interest you to know that the Graces originally stood on 'Georges Dock which was transformed from 1907 to 1916 by the construction of monumental new waterfront, the Royal Liver Building, the Cunard Building and the Port of Liverpool Building.
This was indeed befitting of Liverpool as it was and still is a famous port and trade flowed through the city making this nation a world leader and our forefather's rich. But then we have human trade and a blight on Liverpool's past, yes Liverpool was complicit in the promotion of the slave trade that saw Black Africans forcefully uprooted to a life of servitude and wealthy merchants are forever honoured with Streets named after them when all they did was exploit Black African's. Let's hope the newly elected Lord Mayer gets his red pen out and puts things right!
Sorry I'm ranting a bit here but foreigners, people born all points south, north and east of Huyton, will give you that quizzical look, but Liverpool 'is' the Beatles, no it bloody well isn't, they are a mere part of it, a significant part nonetheless but the Beatles outgrew Liverpool and the truth is Liverpool then outgrew them.
In fact I'd watch the Beatles gaffing around on telly when being interviewed and whilst their wit and quick one-liners are certainly steeped in scouse Mr Askey tradition and mimicry, they sounded different than people I knew when I was a kid. They sounded like posh scousers; 'plazzie scousers' as we called them, meaning 'plastic' and usually a derogatory term for folk that live over the water on the Wirral. They'd role their R's; particularly John and even Ringo began to sound like he was born in leafy suburbia like John and not the Dingle where my Dad was born. Paul and George are from more humble beginnings it seems.
I've heard people mention seeing Paul in a local florist buying flowers strangely enough, when visiting kin in Liverpool. I believe he's got a big heart and a big extended family to match and sneaks into Liverpool incognito and fair play to him for managing to retain his links to his past and keeping in touch with his family. Perhaps I'm being too harsh on Messer's Boardman and Tarbuck and Lotta Laughs Cilla. Sorry.
As for John he was clearly attracted by New York, where he ended up living, as it had a famous skyline just like my wonderful city but maybe not as tall, for now that is and this reminds me of a forgotten track by the 'Human League', *Empire State Human*, with Mr Oakey declaring that he

wants to be 'tall' and ironically he is.

Both cities are situated on a river, serviced by large liners and ships from afar with tales from exotic lands. Perhaps the flow of records ebbed back to New York, nah I don't think so but the Yanks, as I recall, were really into the Flock of Seagulls in the eighties, who? Exactly and I blame MTV for this particular export and not a docker from scouseland!

When I was young I remember getting my first ever side part haircut in a barbers on '*Penny Lane*', now doesn't that sounds like a line from the track, '*Eleanor Rigby*'. This was my first proper haircut at a salon; before which I used to get my haircut at 'Mad Millie's' on Picton Road for twenty-five pence and a sweet. Millie was a lovely old dear with a blue rinse but whatever haircut you requested you always left with a 'short back and sides' or a 'crew cut' and she had a reputation for being a bit mad with her scissors hence the name!

I went to the Penny Lane salon with my mate Joey and the irony was I had the mother of all basin Beatles look down to a tee and was getting my hair cut on Penny Lane but I wanted to look grown up! I would stop at every window for weeks to desperately train my hair to remain parted and the part had to be on the right hand side as the law of the street was that a left side part signified that you were gay. Sounds stupid now but I was a kid.

I didn't give it a second thought that Penny Lane was a famous song, a famous place known worldwide, adored by millions when I was sitting in the seat. I must have travelled past Aunt Mimi's house hundreds of times on a bus to visit my Nan and Granddad in Speke without connecting the Beatles story with Menlove Avenue.

I vaguely knew where Paul lived and I now know this is 20 Forthlin Road and when I was older I would visit and sometimes sleep at a house in the same street George was born in, 12 Arnold Grove. Sue's brother lived opposite.

For any Beatles fan, South Liverpool is clearly like a sweet shop is to a child and everywhere you look there is some sort of connection to the iconic band. I now live near and shop at Woolton were the Quarrymen had their famous gig in 1957 at St Peter's Church Summer Fair and this is when Lennon first met McCartney. It may be of interest to know that the churchyard is home to the grave of Eleanor Rigby.

My mate Brad worked at Strawberry Fields children's home before it closed, I've placed children there myself and the disused gates have graffiti from Beatle fans from all over the world wishing to record that they had been there. I often take a stroll around the magnificent Calderstones Park passing the gate to the park on Harthill Road near to

196 David Griffith

Quarrybank School where Lennon attended as a kid.
I read recently that Lennon would meet his mates at the park and McCartney opened up a children's play area at the park in honour of Linda his deceased wife and at the opening ceremony he crept up on the waiting reporters and when asked how he had sneaked in he said 'I know every inch of this park', like we did as kids.
I've sneaked into Dovedale Primary school as a kid to play footy not knowing this was where Lennon went to school also. The Abbey Picture house was a cinema I often went too as a kid, I remember seeing Dr Who versus the Daleks there in the seventies and this was mentioned in the original lyrics to the track '*A Day in the Life*' but the line got left out. I mean the Abbey not the Dr!
This has to be one of the greatest musical scores written and an example of Lennon and McCartney at their best. The song is in segments with Lennon seeking inspiration from contemporary newspaper articles about potholes whilst McCartney drew on his youth.
I don't associate Matthew Street 'where it all began' with the Beatles but with punks hanging out on corners in bondage looking menacing and buying records, not where the Cavern once stood. I could go on but they were just places I now know or knew as a kid but no more significant than lesser known areas or streets round our way.
I asked my Mum if she or Dad ever went to see the Beatles in concert hoping she'd say yes, in a 'of course we did' tone. She hadn't and this is ridiculous; it's like living in Rome and never hearing the Pope preach. Mum said the nearest she got to seeing an actual Beatle was before they became famous. According to Mum, George lived behind her in Speke, at 25 Upton Green and Mum said she would listen to George strumming his guitar whilst it '*gently wept*' in his back garden.
Without doubt I would have seen the Beatles if this was my era but it wasn't and it's only as an adult that I now appreciate all types of music from whatever decade and by whatever artist. Let me explain. In writing this book I realise now that I can associate and attach a track or a band to most memories, so back to the book title again. Music helps frame the memory, it becomes real and the memory becomes more tangible as a result.
It seems to me that kids today are spoilt. If you like music you have catch up TV and a huge amount of music channels to choose from and most people will channel hop in fear of missing something good. We had Top of the Pops, Juke Box Jury, the Old Grey Whistle Test, Something Else and Chegger's Plays Pop when I was a kid and in the early eighties we then got the brilliant Tube.

All six shows were really good, well maybe not Chegger's and everyone, young and old would be glued to the telly on a Thursday night at 7.30pm to see who was this week's number one on TOTP. This was tradition as traditional as families from a bygone age attending church together on a Sunday but instead of leaving with a hymn ringing in your ears we had the number one to mull over.

In fact I have this image, an image I am sure shared by many others, of me sitting in front of the telly, a big Formica encased box rented telly from the Prudential as I recall, with, get this, three buttons and buttons you had to push in with your finger. How bizarre and the more ingenious families would use a big stick or in my case my big toe proved useful as I was usually on the floor 'hugging' the fire. Life before remotes eh, no wonder we've all got large bums and if you stood up to go the loo, someone would say 'turn de telly over would yew!

When I first started watching TOTP I was fascinated with all the glitz and the music was catchy and was harmless enough. This was the era of cheese and on the subject of cheese here's a naff joke, what cheese is made backwards? Edam! Sorry just popped into my head, where was I, oh yes, it's fair to say that my musical tastes have seen both ends of the musical spectrum and let me explain why.

For example we have '*Sugar Sugar*' by the fictional 'Scooby Do like' cartoon characters known as the Archie's. Okay I know this is from the sixties but needless to say that this track effortlessly transports me back to when I was a boy and not only does it vibrate through my creaking bones but also my very soul, a song I shall always remember.

The theme to '*Shaft*' from 1971 was a faultless track as far as I'm concerned; the beginning is remarkable leaving me yearning for it to continue until Isaac Heye's deep growly voice cuts in and seamlessly takes the song up a notch or two. I could listen to it again and again, all-day and everyday its that good. For those that don't know the track was taken from the self titled film, sequels and telly series, bit of a franchise thing going on there and it was done with such style and coolness. Everybody liked John Shaft as he took no messing from anyone and he dressed in cool polar necks, flares and long black leather coats and was probably one of the first Black-leading characters on telly.

I recall the early seventies with fondness and affection and many a good record was made back then. It was a time when men could wear makeup, eyeliner and glitzy ostentatious outfits; yes this was the glam rock era. I was still in shorts but my favourite toe tapping tunes were '*The Ballroom Blitz*' by 'Sweet' and 'Slade's' '*Cum On Feel The Noize*'. Some would say Slade are to be blamed for the atrocious spelling of forty plus

adults like me due to their deliberately misspelt track titles. Think about it, the nemesis for all English teachers.
I was moved to tears for the forsaken girlfriend who lamented '*Billy Don't Be A Hero*' and I loved the gun slinging sounds in '*This Town Aint Big Enough For Both of Us*' by Sparks.
Other notable acts around this time included the trailblazer Marc Boland and T Rex, Gary Glitter, no we no longer want to be in your gang, the androgynous David Bowie of course, fifties throw back Mud and the rather hirsute Gandalf like, Wizard. Such wonderful and colourful characters never to be seen again.
Like I mentioned before we had a gramophone downstairs as did most families, the fake teak kind with an arm that would never sit on the record without the aid of a two pence piece. In fact we kept a spare 'tupence' next to the arm just in case.
Me and my sisters though would play most of our records on this small grey and cream portable record player upstairs and I remember playing Mum and Dad's rock and roll records, Eddie Cochran and Little Richard spring to mind and I also remember singing along to '*Don't Cry For Me Argentina*' by 'Julia Covington' and '*Take A Chance*' by the poptastic 'ABBA'. Come to think of it perhaps I did wear my side part on the left?
I remember buying '*Lay Your Love on Me*' by 'Racy'. I had a ten-pound gift voucher and I was in town with my mate Oliver from school and I had a pound left to spend. Bit of an impulse buy but in my defence you have to remember I was very impressionable or did Oliver bully me into buying the record?
I was just coming out of my centre part long hair, Birmingham Bags era and for those too young to remember BB's, they were very wide nylon trousers famed for having a huge pocket on the side which was handy for keeping your school book in.
I remember listening avidly to BBC1's top forty on a Sunday waiting to be mesmerised by the latest release, to discover new bands. The nearest we got to an illegal download was taping favourite tracks with a cassette recorder, taking care to release the button with the red dot, or the 'rec' button when the DJ had finished talking. How annoying if you mistimed and thank God for the digital age although you cant beat the static noise made by vinyl.
I have many guilty pleasure tracks that I tended not tell my mates about and they included '*Romeo*' by 'Mr Big', '*Yes Sir I Can Boogie*' by those lovely Spanish lasses, 'Baccara' and the catchy '*From New York to LA*' by 'Patsy Gallant'; a magnificent track from the mid seventies for a kid with dreams and aspirations to travel. I must pause here and say thanks once

again to Wikipedia for revealing more about these guilty pleasures.
As for the dancers on TOTP, well that kept Dad interested me thinks, I wasn't interested in seeing the flat chested Leg's and Co prance about on the screen, no I wanted to watch the artists but I was too young to appreciate the 'artistry', I do now!
I recently learnt that the tax income rate for the super rich went up to eighty three per cent in 1974 and subsequently pops royalty took themselves off abroad to avoid the taxman, I wonder if they went to New York or LA and this explains why artists rarely appeared live and were replaced by dancers like 'Pans People'.
Everybody wanted to be on *'Top of the Pops'*, that was the place to be seen, to be gawped at by kids who had seemingly been shipped in from some local seventies comp, probably Grange Hill. They would sway uncomfortably to some naff track disinterested but trying to catch the camera in their three star jumpers hoping to give a big hello to Mum whilst avoiding the searching kamikaze cameraman.
The presenters on TOTP were annoying; they seemed so old and believed in their own hype and thought themselves bigger than the actual acts. The songs got sillier, the presenters were laughable and superficial in my view and TOTP had become a parody of itself.
It had lost its sixties mantra of music and teenage fashion and you can see now how it had become a light entertainment variety show that catered for the whole family jammed packed with novelty acts and not a show for teenagers as it set out to be. You had, for example, artists like Shawadowady and Mud wearing Teddy boy gear similar to what Dad would have worn in the fifties and the all-pervading BBC and its henchmen decided what we should be listening too each week.
Hidden in the shadows though was Punk waiting to take control and it was amusing to see artists like Liverpool Express or Dr Hook but to then hear Paul Weller shout out '...*youth explosion*! My stomach still tingles with excitement thinking about the feelings I had back then, although I was only about ten you could sense a sea change in music was about to happen and it turned out to be a defining juncture in modern rock music. Being a young kid though part of me wanted to remain loyal to all things disco, usually penned by the Brother's Gibb but the youth explosion of 1976 was simply enthralling and in a matter of weeks TOTP 'sluggishly' keeled over under mounting youth pressure and allowed bands that had become huge on the London pub rock scene like the Stranglers, the Clash and the Dammed to perform and eventually the Sex Pistols, edging out the old guard.

200 David Griffith

Looking back I guess this was to be expected in some respects as post war Britain had seen teddy boys, mods and rockers but then we had extremities of punk rock, which and with purposeful menace, put two fingers up at British culture and began to test the morality of the nation. The Pistols appeared live on the Bill Grundy show for example, which was aired nationally and history now tells us that this did more to promote punk as a national phenomena as it appealed to disaffected youths fed up with the state of the nation.

You only have to look at the image. We played army games as kids and war films and telly programmes like 'Dad's Army' reminded us of the huge sacrifice our grandparents had made. Punks however thought differently as they wore safety pins, zips, Nazi and swastika paraphernalia to deliberately inflame the majority of public opinion and the main provocateurs; the Pistols even had a go at the monarchy with the inflammatory but seminal *'God Save the Queen'*, a track that became an alternative national anthem. I remember being a tad scared but also intrigued watching punks walk up and down Matthew Street strutting their individualism like an earing wearing peacock.

I've done a bit of research into punk music and did you know the word 'punk' was not a modern phenomenon but has been around for eons, as far back as Shakespeare I believe and it may interest you to know that a reporter called Caroline Coon first used it in a paper article to describe the Pistols and the name caught on and a musical genre was created.

Actually, this all reminds me of the wonderful Kenny Everett Video Show and the punk caricature that is 'Sid Snott' who would try and flip cigarettes into his mouth. Very funny edgy show with humorous sketches and bands and despite Mr Everett being gay I do think he had an unhealthy fascination with buxom women when you think of his co host Cleo Rocus appearing in nothing more than frilly underwear and high heals, Cupid Stunt and her pneumatic breasts and Hot Gossip who took dancing to another leather clad level!

Not to mention the strangely attractive and voluptuously animated Carla from Captain Kremmen who would try and persuade the world's most fabulous man, the heroic Captain to have casual sex with him. You'd sit feeling uncomfortable if Mum and Dad were in the room, gawping at the telly and thinking this is so brilliant!

Rock music is a medium for social change and it's now obvious that Punk music rescued popular music and became a battle cry spreading out from London to cities up and down the land. You can see that punk music reflected the ugliness of seventies Britain back on itself and certainly challenged the establishment with short thrashing tracks about street life, lack of opportunity and riots and not always about love and romance and when they did they were short and needed to be played very loud.

There's no finer example in my eyes than the first Punk record released by 'Stiff Records', *'New Rose'* by the Dammed. I remember hearing this track for the first time and literally being blown away by the extraordinary guitar rift that cries out loudly throughout the song. True, I still liked tracks like *'Boys Keep Swinging'* by Bowie but punk began to take hold of my mates and me as they were exclusively targeted at young people and that's where we wanted to belong as it had its own unique fashion and language for us to embrace.

Menacing forces of anarchy with spiky dyed Mohican hair wearing tartan drainpipes were unleashed it seems but in the summer of seventy-seven, there was a reprieve when tradition hit back with the Silver Jubilee. I remember the Queen setting out on a nation wide tour captured by the news; parties were held in streets like mine like I said before, kids had a day off school so that was a bonus and people enthusiastically pulled together as one nation; a chance to forget about the many conflicts around the world, the constant strikes that had become commonplace and high inflation.

My clothes began to change, they became more edgy and the more individual the better, unlike kids I see today, so out went *'Racy'*, in came *'Tommy Gun'* by the Clash and the utterly brilliant *'Oliver's Army'* by Elvis Costello.

Here's an interesting fact to part on you, did you know Elvis lived in Liverpool as a youth and he attended my son's old school, SFX in Woolton. I always believed his reference to the 'murder mile' in the Oliver's Army song was due to growing up in Liverpool up knowing the area had gained notoriety in the press as being an area where people got killed but I read Costello penned this song after seeing boys carrying guns when he visited Belfast in 1978.

Still, our area was known as the 'murder mile', not the best of accolades I know but the Cameo picture house on Webster Road near to where I lived was probably the most memorable murder. My Dad told me that two men, Connolly and Kelly had shot dead the manager and his assistant in 1949 after they refused to hand over that nights takings and a huge manhunt was launched.

The two men were arrested following a tip off and Connolly was hung whilst Kelly was incarcerated. Both men protested their innocence and doubts have been raised since with respect to the evidence and the validity of the witnesses who were unreliable prisoners themselves looking to have their sentences reduced.

I also remember this young girl being murdered when I was about ten and Mum's and Dad's being very worried about letting kids play out, she was from a large family and in respect to any surviving family members I shan't write the name.

Here's another pub quiz answer. Did you know that Elvis also appeared in the Arwhites secret lemonade-drinking advert with his Dad? That aside I really like Elvis as an adult as his music has matured, some would say he's become mellow with age like the rest of us I guess, I don't care and I think he's a brilliant singer songwriter and I went to see him in concert at the Empire in May 2012. He appeared for two and a half hours playing non-stop tracks picked after the audience spun this huge wheel.

One-day Oliver's army, sorry couldn't resist that obvious link, I mean Oliver and me had a free afternoon and we went to Matthew Street in town to the club called Eric's; it was the place to be seen and we wanted a quick gander inside to feel like we were part of the growing scene.

I so wish I could meet Oliver again, we lost touch when I was about thirteen and I've no idea what he's up too as it's dawned on me that he's mentioned many times in this book. Best wishes Ollie, may you roll on forever!

Eric's had exploded onto the Liverpool music scene in 1976, everybody spoke about it on the playground and it had become an essential stop on the national tour circuit of punk bands and was opposite the spot where the Cavern once stood. Within four years however the club closed but I am glad to say it has recently reopened in the exact spot it once stood unlike the Cavern and it remains as famous in Liverpool to my generation, as its more famous predecessor is to those who liked the sixties.

We were about twelve as I recall and Punk was at its peak and we walked up to the entrance to be met by this big bloke with outstretched arms who said in a menacing manner, 'sorry lads you're too young'.

We had hoped to have seen a band appearing at the matinee but we ended up sheepishly retreating with a flyer and I so wish I had kept the flyer as the headline act that week was the Clash and later in the year they had a yet to be discovered band called Adam and the Ants performing. Now before you think I was an Ant fan you're mistaken but I do recall thinking 'hey Ollie what a great name' although it was years later when I realised the name was inspired by the word adamant.

I then became mates with Joey around 1978, Brad's older brother who I mention elsewhere. Joey was a good mate and I looked up to him, as he

was a year older than me and all the girls liked Joey. I would save my pennies, usually lose change after going to the shops for Mum and we'd 'pogo' down to this record store called Ali Baber's on Smithdown Road to rummage through the latest punk releases. Now a ladies hair salon! We'd do this every Saturday after listening to TOTP on a Thursday and we'd chat about records in his house playing them on his brother's record player and being blown away.
Some of the groups we'd never heard of but we would buy a record if the cover looked interesting, or because someone had recommended it, or based on the colour of the vinyl. Another good marketing ploy that and I'd buy records that were lilac, green, red and every other colour under the rainbow! *Up above the street*…surely someone should have done a Rainbow punk version with Bungo wearing bondage and Zippy with a safety pin through his mouth!
Here's a buried memory. I ended up falling out with Joey because he wanted me to 'cop off' with Amanda. He'd been seeing her friend Dawn, this is the same Dawn I ended up kissing down the entry I mention later on in this book. Joey wanted to set up a double date but I wasn't keen on Amanda, she was a nice friendly girl, really good at footy and she had a decent left foot as I recall, but she smoked and I didn't like kissing girls that smoked, so I gave Joey a lame excuse and told him I was staying in that night.
Later on Alan and Grant called to my house and they asked me if I wanted to play footy, seemed like a good idea, one never refused a kick around, so we were having a game of 'goalie V' on Webster Road School yard when Joey, Dawn and Amanda walked by the other side of the railing; the upshot was we never spoke for months. Joey felt I'd let him down but Joey I was saving myself and you wouldn't listen to my protests, I did have a choice you know!
Joey had a descent wedge haircut back then but he then shaved his hair, bought a fishtail coat and got into Mod music and with that no more record rummaging, sad really as I enjoyed those days.
Anyway back to my musical tastes from the punk era. One of my favourite tracks was *'The Sound of the Suburbs'* by the Members, I've still got the single somewhere but the cover has seen better days. Joey was really keen on keeping his singles in mint condition and he would place them in plastic covers, rarely taken out and always handled with outmost care.
Then we had the awe-inspiring *'Teenage Kicks'* by 'The Undertones', which epitomized hormonal changes that were rampaging through my body. I needed excitement, in fact I'm with the sadly deceased but

wonderful Radio One DJ, John Peel and I could literally hold this record tight even without the plastic layer Joey and get *teenage kicks right through the night*, it was bloody marvellous.

Talking of changing body parts, I remember having my Sunday bath when I was about twelve and I could see hairs sprouting all over my legs. It was then that I realised that I had a body of 'two half's'. See, if you discount the odd lonesome hair I am pretty much bare chested but I do have 'bushy' legs although my ankles are less hirsute these days! Anyway, 'The Undertones' are for me like 'The Buzzcocks', both influential in their own right, slightly understated, fabulously ordinary and both had a social comment to make that spoke to teenagers up and down the land.

Before Fergal Sharkey went all yuppie with matching shoulder pads in the mid eighties, he would belt out fab tracks in that squeaky distinctive voice of his whilst wearing his mid seventies Parker clearly a hand-me-down from his big brother probably called Jimmy. '*Jimmy Jimmy*', you see, is another cherished track worshipped by Alan and me and let's also pay homage to the jealousy inspired track '*My Perfect Cousin*' which, with an eye on the future it seems, takes a swipe at the merging synthesizer music led by arty types like the Human League.

Pete Shelley was the Buzzcocks vocalist; also famed for his high-pitched, melodic singing that stood in stark contrast to the gruff pub rock vocal styling's of many punk contemporaries. '*Ever Fallen In Love (With Someone You Shouldntve)*' has been covered by many bands, I heard it used on a car advert recently, which is testament to its continued popularity I guess and I loved this track; whereas '*Promises*' and '*What Do I Get*' are equally good, and if ever a track could be held up as a seminal masterpieces, then this was it!

I went to see the Buzzcocks in Manchester recently and they did a great show going back in time and changing the members of the band finishing with a balding Howard Devoto. Devoto left to form the band Magazine and I think '*A Song for Under the Floorboards*' is a magnificent track.

Being locked in seventies music mode I must mention the absolutely gorgeous Deborah Harry, the singer from 'Blondie' as she was living proof that angels do truly exist. Not because of her heavenly behaviour, rumour has it that back in the day she did a rather raunchy set, which actually added to her allure but because she was utterly beautiful and flawless as far as I am concerned.

I do openly confess to having a humongous crush on Blondie, the singer not the band but I also fancied the equally stunning Farah Fawcett

Majors from Charlie's Angels and of course Raquel Welch after she appeared in the film One Millions Years B.C.
Talking of films and sex symbols lets not forget Michael Caine doing a booty call to Britt Ekland and the nude scene in the film 'Get Carter'. I should say this all occurred before I developed hairs under my arms, prior to this my idea of a supermodel in the seventies was an Airfix 1:72 scale Lancaster Bomber hanging from my bedroom ceiling.
Blondie's catchy tracks, aided by Debbie's instantly recognisable voice and that suggestive look to camera she did, sealed the deal as a complete teenage fantasy icon, her image was adorned on many a teenage boys wall. I remember kicking out to '*Sunday Girl*' at a Bishop Eton Church Disco when I was thirteen with Joey, Grant and Alan. The fabulous '*Denis (Denee)*', which I have just discovered is a cover was a really good tune nonetheless, enhanced by Deborah's stunning looks and the clever use of back light, whereas '*Heart of Glass*' appealed to the then suppressed disco gene hidden deep within my dancing toes that was to once again remerge at Dunny's Disco. Read on.
Another classic track I remember from the aforementioned disco was '*Cool For Cats*' by Squeeze. Although they hit the charts when Punk was at its height they were somewhat different insofar as they were clever songwriters and musicians and Chris Dyfford and Glen Tilbrook certainly had a witty take on life. Class record this and I could even cope with the leather-clad ladies oohing and showing their behinds throughout the track in the video. I've caught them live a few times and I'm seeing Squeeze again in December 2012.
Bryan Ferry managed to stay popular during these musically turbulent times having embraced glitz in an earlier incarnation, he was sophistication personified and by the late seventies he had shaken off the glam rock makeup look and he had several good hits including '*Love is the Drug*'. Although clearly well into his thirties by then he always looked suave and debonair and we would try to emulate his attitude and style on the dance floor by rocking side to side slowly kicking out our legs thinking we were equally attractive to girls.
Mr Ferry became our unwitting idol when I was around fourteen and it was around this time that trilbies became a popular fashion accessory. I remember hearing about kids stealing hats from old men as they walked past but hasten to add that I never did.
An often-overlooked band from around the same time was XTC. I added the wonderful '*Making Plans For Nigel*' to my expanding record collection from Ali Baber's, another single defaced by Tracy, I will lambast her later. They weren't punks per se, more like arty college

'musos' but they paradoxically sang about freedom from a life of drudgery and normalisation and I always thought Nigel was written in honour of all those destined to follow in the footsteps of their forefathers but longing for a better life.

In fact my kids don't expect to work in a factory or on a building site whereas I had little aspiration beyond the paintbrush or some other blue-collar trade as a teenager and whilst there's no harm in hard physical graft you knew your place on the class ladder in the seventies.

There were many cheesy punk tracks too as bands jumped on the lucrative money making bandwagon. The self titled *Jilted John's* record sounded effeminately funny and I still chuckle at Jilted as he retaliates at his ex, Julie and her new suitor Gordon; *'she's a slag, he's a creep, she's a bitch, she's a tart'*. Grant had a mate from school called Gordon, which is actually an okay name, but I felt so sorry for him as he was forever known as 'a moron' when he wasn't. We were shocked by the lyrics back in the day and when I think of this track I also think of the closely related screwball track, *'Two Pints of Lager and a Packet of Crisps Please'* by the strangely named Splodgenessabounds! Closely followed by *'Nellie the Elephant'* by the Toy Dolls. Adam loved that track when he was a baby, which is why I remember them with deep fondness.

Mum and Dad would say they liked my music; they had experienced their own explosion with the teddy boy culture, so they understood the magnetism music brings to the soul and they would think back to the time when rock and roll burst onto the scene and not wanting their parents to 'get' their music. Sometimes some band looking for an instant hit would do a cover version of a classic oldie so the likes of my Mum and Dad would, to my dismay, sing along and say 'this is an old one'. For example, *'She's Something Else'* by Sid Vicious was originally done by Eddie Cochran and Mum dug out the album to prove it.

A catchy and somewhat frantic track that caught the energy of youth was the Vapors track, *'Turning Japanese'*. From that day forward I steered clear from Japan, the country not the band, as you will read later; as it was clearly a place where nothing very exciting happened not even sex, drugs wine or women, a dark place according to the Vapours.

My mates and me were mainly loyal to northern punk bands and although we liked the Clash and the Stranglers and I know punk purists out there will tut in dismay at what I am about to reveal but our favourite track was *'Hersham Boys'* by 'Sham 69'. Alan and me played this again and again in his living room kicking out and taking care not to dislodge a cherished ornament or two, so much so we began to hear strange shrieking voices behind Jimmy Percy's cockney warbling. Were we being indoctrinated into some cultish sect I wonder, we even asked other mates to listen t the song as we thought we were going mad! I liked the amusing lyrics contained in the superb track *'Germ Free Adolescent's'* from the self-titled album by X Ray Specs and the equally enthralling *'Identity'* and *'The Day the World Turned Day Glow'*. Yes that kid Oliver again had the album by the Specs, there one and only release I might add, the one with the band in test tubes and I bought it from him for fifty pence. This is still one of my all time favourites and I still have the album in the loft and did you know this is voted the eighth best punk album by the Guinness Encyclopaedia of Popular Music.

Sadly I heard that the lead singer, Polystyrene, her with the brace, died of cancer recently and in spite of the dental scaffold Poly had a paint stripping rock and roll wail never equalled and uniquely intense. Just before we move on did you know her family's heritage is from Somalia; I can't think of another artist with a Somalia connection can you and may she rest in peace, thanks for the many memories Poly?

I'd play singles again and again and I kind of wish I had been so devoted to my schoolwork but the music switch had taken over well and truly by the time the seventies were coming to an end. We'd flip singles over wanting to hear more by the band or artist and we would play the B-side to discover some real gems. Kids can't do that anymore can they, which is a shame really and I remember classics like *'Lucky Number'* by the scary *'Lena Lovich'*, her with a voice that could summon a pack of dogs. On the subject of lucky numbers, when I was eleven I became fascinated with the number seven. I know this is all coincidental but the number seven appeared everywhere in different aspects of my life so naturally it became my lucky number. It was 1977, I lived at number seventeen, Edge Hill is also known as Liverpool seven and I was born on the seventh. Stands to reason don't you think.

'Into the Valley' by the 'Skids' is a track I loved and the B-side was good too, a track called *'TV Stars'* as I recall. The Skids were serious contenders at one point for being voted the best Punk band around for my mates and me. The lyrics to Skids songs were always notoriously incomprehensible, owing to the lead singer, Jobson's dialect but that didn't stop us making up our own words or energetically kick dancing around the disco floor. The Valley and the double single *'Masquerade'* and *'Working for a Yankee Dollar'* were undeniably awesome heart thumping tracks that I've recently been listening too and they still stand the test of time.

In fact you'd listen intently to tracks and sing out loud the words you thought was being sung or shouted, as my Mum would say. I've made some real gaffs over the years I can tell you and my mate Neil still ribs me to this day as I thought '*I Ran*' by the 'Flock of Seagulls' was about the country Iran not about running in sneakers! Neil's got a nerve, an obvious mistake I think and in my defence I didn't have MTV or the record and I find myself actually liking the track a smidgen as it reminds me of a less complicated time in my life and Neil's jibes.

My favourite gaff of all time though was Spandau Ballets overplayed 'last dance' or 'slowy' song, '*True*'. I wasn't a great fan of this track, good to do a slowy dance too but the line with '*my soul*' in it sounded like, now let's not forget my accent thing and that Spandau were cockney lads before you laugh, '*muscle!*' It made sense at the time, wish I could have written the lines to show you but listen to the track and I bet you end up saying oh yes I can see what Dave means. Well at least I hope so to save my blushes. Stop sniggering Neil.

I eventually followed in Joey's footsteps and began to like all things Mod for a while; I must have been about fourteen and a must see film out around this time was the utter brilliant Quadraphinia. I bought '*Time For Action*' by 'The Secret Affair' and the superb re-released instrumental '*Green Onions*' by Booker T & the M.G.s and I wanted a Vespa with lots of mirrors but the biggest Mod influence without doubt, was the 'Mod Father' himself, Paul Weller and the Jam. Weller is a musical genius and he continues to tap into a rich seam of creativity with so many fantastic tracks that span the decades but if I had to pick a couple of favourites back then I'd go back in time to '*Strange Town*' and '*Going Under Ground*'. I had the album 'Setting Sons' by the Jam and I leant it to someone but couldn't remember whom. Then about twenty-five years later I bumped into that someone, his name was Molly and he was from school and he told me he had the album but had lost it! The '*Bitterest Pill*' that, see the track connection Mr Weller, good to know the borrowers hadn't actually pinched it with my favourite torch but why didn't Molly give it back to me, oh well I now have it on I Tunes!

An offshoot from all things Mod was its reggae punk influenced little brother, Ska music, which I also liked and the band that springs to mind as the leader of this movement was 'The Specials'. Britain in the seventies was a culturally diverse nation but with a shared love of music and Ska music was one of the first times we saw black and white musicians playing together in a band. '*Ghost Town*' was intensely depressing but at the same time it was a superb track, '*Gangsters*' was a wonderful track and I also bought my English helping track, '*Too Much Too Young*'. If ever there was a track that could double up as a public information advert then this is it; it spoke of teenager pregnancy and

wearing a cap whatever that was? Surely it wasn't that hot in the UK, although the summer of seventy-six was a scorcher as I recall?
Talking of clothes, a subculture existed whereby someone would knock at our house wishing to sell their ill-gotten 'no questions asked, surely their fake,' gains and said dodgy seller had an expanding *'going underground'* empire and I recall the selling of sweets, meats and tools, pretty much anything and probably to order. The must have fashion in the early eighties round our way was a 'fish tail kaki jacket' with rows of carefully placed little circle badges of the Who, the Jam and the RAF sign pinned to the left breast.
Then we had Fred Perry clothes, I never had the aforementioned jacket but I had several badges and I would pin them to my brown Fred Perry jumper and matching yellow T-shirt that I wore to Christine's wedding thinking I was all Mod. Most people wore Jam shoes with the white top, or Pod or Kicker shoes. I had fake Jam shoes and fake college shoes but I did have a descent pair of blue Pod shoes one year and I remember going on a school trip to London and the teacher in charge of my group congratulated me on choosing sensible shoes.
Yes they were comfy 'Sir' but I chose them because first of all they were the only shoes I possessed at the time, with the exception of my battered trainers used for footy, and secondly because they were all the rage and for once I was up to date! Certainly not because I woke that morning with the predisposition to wear shoes that would shield my tiring feet as I wandered around the Natural History Museum'. As it happens some other kid annoyingly had the same pair of shoes, so much for standing out as an originator!
I was in my thirties when I bought my first pair of Kickers just because I could, when I was a teenager more fortunate kids had red, blue and green Kickers and I was so jealous. I remember a phase when kids would go bowling at an alley to steal the bowling shoes, as they looked Mod like. I guess said fashion thieves must have entered the alley with crappy shoes to exchange and surely this was a give away?
I remember owning a green jockey jacket with a white stripe when I was about thirteen; I thought I looked so cool. I also had a three stripe blue cagoule that eventually fell apart and the stripes became frayed but that didn't stop me wearing it.
I think it was the summer of 1980 but the must have item was a Hawaiian shirt, the more overstated the better and I've no idea how this fashion faux pas crept into the cloudy more temperate streets of Liverpool. Another much-loved fashion statement from distant shores in the early eighties was a ski jumper and this time I had one and I never

had it off my back. I bought it from 'Paddy's Market', or 'Great Homer Street' Market to use its correct term but also known as 'Greaty Market', all very confusing but we understood.

One year I remember haranguing Letitia, Tommy's wife, to knit me an Aaron jumper, as it was fashionable in the early eighties. She gave in but a year later and as we know *'Fashion'* waits for no one, not even David Bowie's 'goon squad', but thanks anyway. Click click!

I loved my blue satin Le Coq Sportif T-shirt bought from Sexy Rexy in town and I really wanted a Harrington jacket and a Fisherman's jacket but sadly they alluded me, too expensive for Mum and Dad. The Fisherman's jacket was reversible, blue for when dry and bright yellow when it was raining and those that had said jacket would wear it off the shoulder long before Madchester did in the nineties.

I'm not implying that my kids are spoilt but they have a wardrobe of clothes to choose from whereas I would wear the same clothes all week and no one 'skitted' you because they did the same.

Shuffling back to music, if in a disco we would mimic the lead singer from Simple Minds who is called Jim Kerr's and his crouching dance to the track *'Glittering Prize'*, great song that came out of nowhere it seems and here's another couple of gems from the early eighties, *'Party Fears Two'* and *'Club Country'* by the 'Associates'. What an image and if ever there was a band made for clubbing, then they were it. The lead singer Billy Mackenzie had a wondrous distinctive high tenor voice and he sadly passed away in 1997 and did you know Morrissey sings about him in the track *'William, It Was Really Nothing'*.

Although a rarity we did have the odd instrumental. In fact it would take about three to four beats of Pigbags track, *'Papas Got a Brand New Pigbag'* and like an involuntary impulse we'd jettison onto the dance floor for some serious kick dancing, if you can call it dancing, reaching all four corners of said floor like spinning tops.

Scene two at Rotter's, played Pigbag most nights and I can recall Grant, Derek, Neil and me fuelled by 'two pints of lager' but spare the crisps, prancing to this track and in total disregard for how we looked. Should you have a desire to witness me strut my stuff then I urge you to play Pigbag but be warned I take no prisoners and need lots of space and probably lots of lager now.

I began to like anything alternative or edgy and musical tastes evolved into another genre when another decade loomed. For a while I liked the B52's especially the bizarre track containing the many nonsensical lyrics, *'Rock Lobster'*. I also enjoyed Devo's *'Whip It'* but less said about the upturned flowerpot hats.

I would say one of the best tracks ever from around this times was '*Echo Beach*' by the wonderfully named 'Martha and the Muffins', I still get a chill down my spine particularly when I hear the opening chords and get this, they were from Canada and I think this was their only hit but what a hit.

In fact Alan and me would discover bands that were on the verge of making it big and I recall ardently reading the music press like the Record Mirror and Smash Hits for reviews and insight into up and coming bands. I would cut out pictures to pin on my wall and snippets from the magazines of bands I liked but once an artist became mainstream, Alan and me would normally drop them and move on. I'll give you few examples.

I bought the debut single, '*Planet Earth*' by Duran Duran released in 1981. I enjoyed this track, I can still hear the slow synthesized electronic rhythm by Nick Rhodes, then John Taylor kicks in with a throbbing bass, followed by Simon Le Bon's unique but dubious lyrics and the track was the first to explicitly acknowledge the fledgling New Romantic fashion movement that I was embracing at the time.

I wonder why dear reader but I did like Duran's other earlier track '*Girls on Film*' though, which created uproar when it was released. The video was raunchy for the time and featured semi-naked women in a wrestling ring and was heavily edited to appear on MTV. This was a must see video for Alan and me and I recall watching the uncut version, in some night club on a big screen and as I recall the Duran's did enjoy and capitalized on the controversy but for me that was their pinnacle.

The Duran's were often compared with their cockney Romantic counterparts Spandau Ballet. What's that I hear, you want me '*To Cut A Long Story Short*', like the track, sorry I must remind you we're already half way through. Alan liked this track and Grant liked the Celtic army look they were wearing and he once donned a kilt. I can still recall the two girls in the video holding hands and this is how girls dressed and danced in nightclubs that we went to in the early eighties.

We liked the band Ultravox when they first emerged and the track '*Sleepwalk*' enthralled Alan and me. This track was an instant like and it raced ahead with a pulsating electric drumbeat matched by the singer 'Midge Ure's' chanting.

Some years later I learnt that Midge had been around for years and fronted the glam boy band 'Slik' before joining Ultravox and I remember the twee track '*Forever and Ever*'. Did you know he'd also played with the band Thin Lizzy so there goes his romantic credentials?

Sleepwalk was Ultrovox's first single, it was released in 1980 and somewhat surprisingly, I'm sure Alan would be shocked too; this defining track peaked at twenty-nine. How ridiculous. Ultravox will always be remembered for their huge hit *'Vienna'*, granted, a wonderfully constructed synth classic but whenever I hear this track I think of the telly advert encouraging businesses to phone Ilene Bilton to talk about relocating to Warrington where Ikea now stands, I wonder if she gets discount on their delicious meatballs?

Alan and me also liked John Foxx who was replaced by Mr Ure when he left Ultravox to go solo and his track *'Underpass'* sticks out as a decent influential track too.

Alan and me were into Depeche Mode big time and other electronic influenced bands. We would play Alan's Depeche album 'Speak and Spell' released in 1981, at his house and the tracks *'New Life'* and *'Just Cant Get Enough'* are exceptionally good tracks from this album. We also liked Visage's *'Fade to Grey'* and did you know Midge Ure co-wrote this track? Okay, credentials restored, but only slightly! I remember Alan and me liking this very peculiar synth track called *'Warm Leatherette'* by Daniel Miller, I bet you've never heard of it, if you have then I am very impressed.

As with most electronic based tracks released in the early eighties, you could hear not so distant echoes from the German four-piece band, Kraftwerk, the forerunners to all synth based music and the track *'The Model'* was earthshattering, a modern masterpiece.

Take Gary Numan for example. The enigmatic Numan unashamedly copied his German counterparts in his fashion sense as far as I'm concerned. His music was similar and he had an air of arrogance with his moody slightly understated gaze, he could have been a fifth member. Numan and his band Tubeway Army, released two ground breaking albums that were constantly played by Alan and me, 'Replicas' and 'The Pleasure Principle' both released in 1979. I loved *'Are Friends Electric'*, an utterly brilliant track that is still able to stimulate special feelings in my stomach and I shall forever be associated with Jeanette, for reasons you will soon discover. Am I teasing you?

In an equally similar vein we must also pay homage to the enigmatically and gruffly voiced 'Siouxsie and the Banshees' with the dazzling tracks *'Hong Kong Garden'* and *'Slide Down the Banister'*.

Like all genres you do get your share of dross and cheese. We've all bought tracks we regret and I bought 'Landscape's track, *'Einstein a Go Go'* for example, a band never to be heard of again although the use of whistling was a neat idea. The track *'Imagination'* by 'Belouise Some' is another example and was relatively pleasing to the ear and I suggest you check out the video, it's far raunchier than Girls on Film.

We keenly followed bands from Liverpool and once again I must thank Joey for this as he discovered the many bands we later began to like. We started to wear camouflage gear and dark jackets and in fact my first ever concert was when I went to watch Echo and the Bunnymen at the Empire Theatre, I think it was around 1980 and I was about fourteen.

I had this green camouflage T-shirt bought from The Army Navy Surplus Store opposite Lewis's in town, never had it off my back. I remember catching the number seventy-nine bus on Picton Road to town and we bought our ticket from the ticket office with no bloody add on fees for admin, how annoying is that.

There was me of course, Alan, Derek and Grant and we were beside ourselves with excitement but to my horror though Mum had washed my 'Fruit of the Loom' jeans and I had idiotically forgotten to take my prized ticket out of my pocket and when I did it was all washed out and crinkly!

Just before I move on, trousers back when I was young were Looms, Lee, Levi or Wrangler, not to mention jumbo and needle cords and then we had Lee Cooper sold based on the coolest of all adverts and the fab line, *'don't be a dummy, Lee Cooper'*.

I can recall being so upset and annoyed with myself and as the day of the concert drew nearer I swung between going and not going, thinking I had ruined my opportunity to see the Bunnymen with my mates. I decided to go in the end and I recall standing outside in the queue praying I'd get in; thankfully I did and we had a brill time. Mac, Ian McCulloch, the lead singer, sang tracks from the album Crocodiles, released in 1980 and we knew every word, every beat and we pogoed in the aisle to every track.

I still have the album on vinyl and also the CD and on I Tunes and it's hard to say which track I would have a particular penchant too but I love *'Villiers Terrace', 'Rescue', 'Pictures on my Wall', 'All that Jazz'*, bloody hell I might as well name every track as they are all sublimely magnificent. We probably looked stupid and gangly at the concert and I remember thinking; what was the point of paying for seats when we never sat down from the moment the band sprang into life. Brilliant night was had by one and all.

Neil and me went to see the Bunnymen in 2010 at the Palace next door to the Grafton Rooms and they played all their early stuff. It was a small close up and personal venue and we got to the front or as my son would call it the mosh pit. We sang and jumped up and down but after three or so tracks we were knackered and we made a dignified middle-aged retreat to a less thumping area of the crowd to stand next to other salt and peppered die hard's with our plastic glass of lager.

We also saw 'The Teardrop Explodes' in the early eighties and I loved the heavily influenced trumpet brass and fast drum-thumping track, 'Reward'. The frontman Julian Cope had everything, the looks, the fighter pilot image, the Scott Walker type voice, how he never became global is beyond me and we simply devoured every track from the groundbreaking and wonderful albums 'Wilder' and 'Kilimanjaro'.

Both albums have certainly stood the test of time and I would still place them in my top twenty all time favourites albums. I simply implore you to listen to 'Sleeping Gas' a track that slowly introduces you to Cope's protestations, the amazing 'Treason (Its Just A Story)', the atmospheric 'Tiny Children', the often over-looked 'Passionate Friend' and the purely wonderful 'When I Dream' that never fails to please my yearning ears!

I also saw Orchestral Manoeuvres in the Dark, OMD for short, at the Empire. I remember Andy McCluscky from OMD playing 'Messages' as the opening track and my mates and me shot up and ran down excitedly to the front keen to copy his every move, forgetting again that we had seats back in the rafters.

Again years later in 2009 Neil and me went to see OMD at Aintree Racecourse and they played all their oldies, tracks like 'Electricity', 'Maid or Orleans' and 'She's Leaving' but the track that has sat comfortably for years in my 'all time top fifty list' is the superb 'Enola Gay'. As a kid I never connected this track to the name of the B52 that dropped a nuclear bomb over Hiroshima, it was just a great track to dance too and they played a snippet of this track at the opening ceremony to the Olympics in 2012! I wonder what the USA and Japan contingent thought of that. Me thinks this was a mistake?

McCluscky played 'Joan of Arc' and for harden OMD fans you knew this would mean he'd kick and swing his arms in random circles whilst gliding sideways across the stage. A dance emulated by my mates and me on many an occasion.

Before doing so McCluscky warned the crowd that he may need a ventilator or a medic in the house but mercifully he got through the track and panted out, 'not bad for an old bloke eh'. We all screamed in admiration truly knowing the effort it takes with or without slippery shoes. You've still got it Andy.

My mates and me then began to follow other alternative music; music that was not in the charts and Neil was particularly good at spotting a good band to follow. This coincided with me going to night-clubs when I was fifteen and we loved bands like Japan, Bauhaus, Heaven Seventeen,

Joy Division and of course the Human League.

You see by the time the eighties came the TOTP audience had become part of the show and although the women looked mighty fine, I appreciated the artistry by then, they were clearly professional dancers and you would see the same faces every week. I think the cameramen must have also had a brief from up above to stop barging into the crowd but to look up the girls Ra Ra skirts, which was easy enough as the hems got shorter and shorter, to make the show appear sexier.

It was around this time when I remember 'the' topic of conversation being, 'was Boy George really a man' and my Mum teaching me a lesson in life should I ever meet 'Lola' drinking cherry cola, look to see if 'she' has an Adams apple, apparently a dead give away!

TOTP ended up becoming very staged, it had become 'variety' again with manufactured acts were popular because of their looks and not because of their music and in the end the Pops was trumped by the instant music appeal in the form of MTV.

I think this is a very sad affair and I for one would welcome a return but using the late seventies format minus ancient presenters and rumour has it my wish may come true as I heard an Internet version of TOTP is being considered. Hope it's on a Thursday, which would make sense don't you think?

Juke Box Jury was watchable but seemed to have been around for years, when my Mum and Dad were kids, it was good to listen to other artists judge or rip into someone else's track though. Chegger's was mainly for kids, fun and innocent but he was annoyingly happy all the time as he pranced about running around the stage.

I appreciate 'The Old Grey Whistle Test' more as an adult, back in the seventies it seemed to be a very serious show with a whispering presenter and watched only by arty prog rock types but that said you would sometimes catch a decent band you liked playing live and they would play more than one track which was a bonus.

Something Else was a legendary music telly programme on BBC2 that featured mainly alternative bands. The programme first aired around the late seventies with young presenters who had undisguised regional accents, I liked this programme and it had a relaxed magazine type format and did you know this programme was the first and last time the brilliant Joy Division appeared on national telly!

Now the Tube on the other hand was a breath of fresh air and an instant hit for us kids. It was up to date, didn't pander to the older generation, wasn't afraid to push the boundaries and the artists played live so you knew what you heard was how they would sound in a concert. Well most of the time that is.

They would feature and highlight up and coming acts, who, for example, can forget the infamous Frankie Goes to Hollywood video to *'Relax'* before it was re-mastered and then banned for being too sexually explicit. Very shocking at the time, but after the ban it became a smash hit all over the world as a result. Youth explosion strikes again.

I remember this lad on holiday in Majorca from somewhere but not my where, telling me that Relax was the best thing to come out of Liverpool. Good track I give him that, but total codswallop and me thinks he was jealous of my town!

Paula Yates was pleasing on the eye with her spiked blond hair and figure hugging leather type dresses; she would flirt terribly and it was a good move to have a performer as a presenter in the shape of Mr Jools Holland. I still enjoy his show on BBC2 as it showcases bands from different genres and I have discovered many a good band and artist after seeing them on Mr Holland's show.

It may be of interest but did you know the Tube was filmed entirely in Newcastle and it started off with the lines, 'welcome to the weekend' as the telly smashed before the string vested Dad on the chair. I guess it rubbed southern Jessie's up the wrong way as the show got canned after a few years; shame really and I've recently been watching the 'Best of the Tube on the Sky Arts Chanel.

My musical tastes became even more eclectic as I moved through my teens and I confess to enjoying a good disco beat from bands like 'Kool and the Gang' and 'Shalamar'. If you look beyond the codpiece and the spandex the funk soul band 'Cameo' were really good. I thought the track '*Single Life*' was, well 'cool' in every sense of the word. I liked '*Just Be Good To Me*' by 'the SOS Band' and I liked other more soulful tracks like '*Let the Music Play*' by 'Shannon' and I guess these songs were blasted out at the various clubs I attended so they became forever entrenched in my sub consciousness.

Thinking back, I was a bit of a chameleon when it came to my music tastes and they alternated over a brief period of time and this has only become apparent to me as I write this book.

Did you know more million selling singles were sold in the seventies than any other decade and for me music from about 1976 through to 1983 was a golden era and many a seminal track was released covering disparaging genres and you hardly had time to catch your breath before the next wave would appear questioning your loyalty! That's my excuse for being so fickle but I have learnt over the years that we should always open our minds and our hearts to new experience otherwise the music world would stop spinning on those decks.

Children have the 'Now' singles collection which began as 'Now That's What I Call Music' that must be close to triple digits by well, 'Now' and I remember the first Now album released in 1983? Throughout the seventies we had an array of combination records and I remember my sisters buying the 'Rock n Roller Disco' album released in 1979 with the picture of someone in roller skates. Now don't be fooled, this album may have disco in the title but it also included a couple of memorable tracks leaning more to New Wave, namely *'Babylon's Burning'* by the 'Ruts', *'Video Killed the Radio Star'* by Buggles and *'Bang Bang'* by B.A Robertson. Come to think of it Video may have killed the radio star but I think video imploded on itself during the eighties and unwittingly killed rock music and related genres for a few years.

Let me explain, with the likes of MTV, a show devoted to screening the latest videos, the producers unashamedly promoted artists based on looks and image and not necessary on talent.

Take Christopher Cross for example, a very talented artists blessed with the voice of an angle and winner of many Grammies but when he appeared on MTV his popularity plummeted as he didn't fit the mould. *'Sailing'* is a lovely transcendental track that inspires you to float away to another place, whereas *'Ride Like The Wind'* is simply wonderful and I only appreciated this track when I became an adult.

We succumbed to artists with a certain look and we're therefore influenced by image but the song and the story behind the artist were more important. Production took over in the eighties whereby it didn't really matter if an artist could sing or write a tune and bands were manufactured as opposed to attending school together as kids.

Svengali's and producers began to dictate once again just like TOTP did in the seventies, influencing what the listening public would buy and you only have to look at the Reynolds Girls as an example. Pete Waterman set out to prove that he could make a pop star out of any Tom, Dick or Reynolds and the annoying thing was they were plucked from the streets of Liverpool, they may even have a mention on that wall on Matthew Street?

Music took a slow and excruciatingly painful death with god-awful compilation tracks around the mid eighties. 'Stars on 45' personified this and was particularly dour so I wont add it to my list, the Chicken song and Jive Bunny were painful and utter dross if you ask me and then we had S Xpress which was just as bad.

Stock, Aiken and the aforementioned Mr Waterman somehow became big and they had a conveyor belt stranglehold on the charts with gushy predictable pop songs that, for some unfathomable reason appealed to teens. I think it had something to do with the hypnotic drum beat that imitated the heart and every song began to sound the bleeden same if you listen closely.

Well that was me done, music had become monotonous and uninspiring, annoyingly perpetuated by good looking soap actors who thought they could muster a tune just because their face had been plastered all over the telly and this has continued through the decades as kids are influenced by wannabes from reality telly shows and the X Factor.

The charts had once more been taken over by variety pumping middle-aged producers.

I'm jumping some years ahead here but I lost faith as the eighties came to a close and found myself starved of musical inspiration and I do confess to living in the musical wilderness for years.

I did stay loyal to my teenage kick arse music in the hope the next big thing would sweep me away but I began to feel old, I never signed up to the Acid house party scene, I just didn't get the constant thumping crap masquerading as original music, for me it was desperate times from bands without a modicum of creativity who were adept at stealing and re-mastering classic old tunes.

I wasn't remotely interested in the Brit scene of the nineties either, I didn't care if Oasis were better than Blur, the publicity hype was so transparent and both bands bored me, although I did like some grunge tracks such as 'Nirvanas' track *'Teen Spirit'* and I've recently took a liking to the Smiths and Morrissey. I liked anything by Ocean Colour Scene though as they gave a backward nod to Mod music, very good in concert I might add and a breath of fresh air at the time.

I like to think I'm more in touch with today's music but whom am I kidding, I'm probably some old fart trying to retain his youth wanting to stay *'forever young'* but I don't care as music is not just for the young but without doubt should be influenced by the young otherwise the musical train will stand still and will begin to repeat itself rather than reinvent. The musical train should be driven by the youth and they should decide what tracks to take and where to disembark.

My eldest son, Kieran gets peeved if I accidently discover new artists that he likes but that's okay as I would have felt the same when I was a teenager and kids needs their own identity and trends, they need their own youth explosion!

Music is often played in our house and I think I have indoctrinated Kieran a bit as he likes some classic punk tracks and I sometimes catch him checking out my I Tunes account for inspiration. He thinks X Ray Specs are wonderful. Come to think of it when I was growing up we had singles and albums stacked in the side compartment of the gramophone, some mine some Mum and Dad's and you had to look after your vinyl to prevent them becoming scratched so no different from when I was a lad. Now I have digitally enhanced playlist with literally thousands upon thousands of tracks findable via a clever search engine and within seconds I can download music from I Tunes but I do miss them scratches and thumbing through records then rushing home from the shop to give the record a spin to then flip it over after a dozen or so plays.

Music has become so instantaneous but this mirrors the must have society we have become and I'm not complaining just stating a point as I see it and a difference from when I was forever young. It does feel like good old-fashioned guitar music played by people who are popular based on talent and not looks have thankfully made a resurgence. I have many guilty pleasures stemming many years but I now prefer folky Americana guitar based music such as the modern day poet, Mr Bob Dylan, the modest but brilliant Billy Bragg and the fantastic 'Felice Brothers' to name but a few and there are many.

I would never ever have admitted to liking acoustic guitars music when I was younger but tastes change with each passing decade and I think that's a good thing and something to celebrate.

Before I end this chapter, sorry its been a long one, I asked my Mum some years after I had left home where had she stored my records and after finding them gathering dust in the loft next to the patched up hole made by Tina when she put her foot through Mum's bedroom ceiling; I discovered to my horror that my sister had written Tracy Griffith all over them.

She had defaced and devalued my prize collection by writing on the middle section of the record but also the cover and she tried to defend the utter indefensible by protesting that she was fearful of them getting mixed up at the penny rec disco which I talk about later. A number of questions spring to mind sis, did you ask if you could borrow them, could you have used labels and did you or your pals even like punk, no you bloody well didn't! I could kill you! Using a scouse colloquialism 'calm down Dave'.

Chapter Eleven

Talk Talk...

'Talk Talk' was and still is a fabulous track by, wait for it, 'Talk Talk' and I chose this track because I want to dedicate a few pages about how we interacted as kids and how we communicated.
There are different forms of language as I see it, body language, sign language and verbal languages for example and whilst I never claim to be a linguistic expert it seems human beings have learnt how to communicate amongst themselves realising the foundation to any society and successful culture is the ability for it's population to *'Come Together'* as Messer's Lennon and McCartney would say in their track and communicate.
Indeed the evolution of civilisations is based on human discourse that allows us to describe, to explain, to request, to barter, to order, to challenge, to debate, to comfort, to appease, I could go on but clearly us humans have learnt to connect with those around us by using commonly agreed speech sounds, the ability to express oneself using words that develop into a language!
I find this to be a fascinating concept actually. Languages develop and mutate and in doing so they then define cultural, social and religious differences across the globe. As people move around in search of new horizons, people learn new languages, some languages then merge and words will mutate and overlap from country to continent and you only have to look at Latin and how the English language is scattered with words used during the Roman Empire as it stretched its marauding muscle and invaded the continent.
Latin digested the native Celtic language and has remained assimilated into the English language ever since and the same could be also said of French.
As you can fathom from this book my English may not be grammatically the best but my language is English, perhaps not in keeping with the 'Queens English' but that's because my speech has been shaped by my cultural vernacular, which is scouse.

I read this interesting fact on a billboard outside the main Library in Liverpool and this goes someway to explain the scouse accent as it's very unique, a fusion of Irish, Welsh, Lancashire, African and Scandinavian dialects and explains the travelling gene inherent in scousers as this city certainly was and still is defined by its multiculturalism. Now there's a cherished track I must pay deference too before I move on, the hauntingly superb *'African White* by the very underestimated 'China Crises' from Liverpool or Kirkby to be precise.

Scouse is therefore a hybrid as I see it and one of many Northern dialects and if someone is born up north you can hear it in his or her voice and using Liverpool as an example, we scousers have an instantly recognisable catarrhal embedded dialect that sets us aside and defines our heritage and where we grew up.

Dialects can change and soften over time I guess, they are also less 'throaty' in some parts of Liverpool, particularly on the Wirral and some people choose to hide or promote their accent depending what they wish to achieve and how they wish to be perceived.

Some, like me, are proud of their accents, some wish to alter how they speak believing their accent will hamper any progress they hope to achieve; some people sound like newsreaders as they have an accent that is undetectable and thereby less regional as that would show bias and serve to alienate sections of society!

Some people move away from their place of origin and they may assimilate into the local dialect over the passage of time as they blend in but somewhere in the persons syntax remains a sound that reveals their true heritage and place or origin and often when returning 'home' the abandoned accent can sometimes reawaken to be heard once more particularly if the return is for a long period of time. I think we tend to act like chameleons when it comes to speech.

Dialect is also steeped in local colloquialisms and this is no different in whatever city or area you find yourself; phrases and customs are passed down through the generations that binds a community together and at the same time roots a person to a particular area.

Take us Liverpudlians for example. It's a common fact that us scousers are notoriously at fault for shortening our words, we speak very quickly so as we can get our point across when hanging around in crowds and we speak *'with an accent exceedingly rare'*, with a throaty resonance befitting of someone recovering from a bad dose of the cold.

If you travel a few miles away from the Mersey to places beyond the likes of Huyton, Kirkby and Speke the accent changes significantly, it becomes more Lancastrian in it's pronouncement and it reveals you're not from these parts are 'yew'? If you listen to a conversation in St Helen's for example you would think you were hundreds of miles away from Liverpool's boarders not a dozen or so and as you move further up the East Lancs the accent becomes more Mancunian.

I remember working in Bootle in the early nineties as a Residential Social Worker and these kids had the nerve to ask me if I came from Liverpool and said I sounded posh to them?

Me, a kid from Edge Hill, an area a stones throw away from the city centre! Now don't get me wrong Bootle is part of scouseland but it's on the outskirts of Liverpool in the socially contrasting area of Sefton so I felt affronted. Were my ears deceiving me, I stood there wondering if my scouseness had become diluted with age and I thought how dare these Marsh Lane kids question my heritage, I'm proud of my scouse roots. They clearly saw me as a 'plazee scouser', someone who adopts a scouse accent and mannerisms in attempt to appear cool and if I were in their shoes I would have called me a 'woolyback' or a 'wool', in other words a person from Runcorn, Wirral, Wigan, Warrington and Southport. I'm surprised they spared me the unfriendly jibe we used as kids, 'there's a woolly over there, over there. There's a woolly over there, over there. With a three star jumper half way up his back. There's a f…ing woolyback, woolyback'.

I must be true to myself though and accept that time has seemingly mellowed my accent, I simply hadn't realised this and the reality is I left Edge Hill when I was in my early twenties so I've spent more of my life away from the place of my birth and I am no longer influenced by what was happening around me when I was a little receptive kid.

I no longer hang out on corners listening and absorbing conversations around me not realising that I would mimic said words to remain on common ground.

For example when I lived in Edge Hill, if I were in a bad mood a mate would say, 'ay soft lad, gorra cob on'. The word 'hey' is shortened to 'ay', scousers tend to drop the letter 'h' and gorra should be 'got a', as for 'cob' I have no idea where this phrase originates from but discovered it's a term used right across the North of England. If I retaliated I might have said, 'yew cudden punch an ole in a wet Echo', which meant you are weak and lame. For any provocateurs that had been rambling on causing trouble you would protest, 'yew'd start a row in an empty house yew'. We would also say 'yew talking to me or chewing a brick', when someone said something you didn't like.

Sometimes you would try and make a mate look at something that wasn't there, why, I don't know but I guess you had to be there and if

they looked you would shout out; 'made you luck made you stare, made the barber cut ye air'. He cut it long he cut it short, cut it with a knife and fork'.
If you touched something or had something that was on you such as a rash a mate would say 'yewv got the mange', mange refers to a skin disease. If you wore tattered and old clothes or smelt odorous you would run the risk of being called a 'meff' or a 'tramp'. Kids today tend to go 'ooooh' when they see something that disagrees with them but in the seventies we went 'eeeeh!'
In fact kids were always 'taking the mickey out of each other', not sure who 'micky was by the way but 'teasing' came natural and you had to be good at dishing out as well as taking it on the chin otherwise names and teases would stick like superglue which was the worst thing ever. You would try and laugh things off but sometimes you would go home in a huff and Mum would say 'sticks and stones will break your bones but names will never hurt you', but sometimes they did Mum.
Scousers struggle to say words beginning with 'th', I'm more accustomed to saying 'the' now instead of 'de', I refer to others as 'you' as opposed to 'yews' and I probably said 'give me a break kids' instead of 'giz a break kidder (or la)', which is what I would have said in the seventies.
When those Bootle kids asked are you sure you're from Liverpool did I exclaim in a broad scouse accent, 'deffo' or was I undone by saying 'definitely'. Had I indeed become the fifth Beatle with an A and is 'dis buck' as opposed to 'this book' lost the plot all together? See scousers use 'u' instead of 'oo' and over exaggerate words ending with 'ck' also. Thinking about it perhaps that's why the Beatles 'didn't' sound like people around me in the seventies as they were influenced by the sounds of the fifties and with this in mind scouse today probably sounds marginally dissimilar to when I was a kid. I walk around and I hear people say 'lad' or 'girl' at the end of every sentence, such as 'ye know what I mean lad'.
We never used this term as a kid; we would use 'la' at the end of most sentences and indeed this makes me wonder if the Liverpool band 'The La's had formed today would they be called 'The Lad's?' Just a thought.
I have the latest I Phone like I said before; it's an impressive little device for many reasons and I upgraded my phone to the 4S version as it also comes with this clever 'friend' called Siri that allows you to ask questions and Siri will do its best to answer. Well that's what it claims to do if you watch the advert on telly, the one where the woman asks how many cups is twelve ounces or what's the weather like today. You see Siri is

designed as an intelligent assistant that's there to help, so Apple claim but I might as well be talking bloody Klingon, as the very helpful Siri is not intuitive enough to understand my scouse dialect, even when I speak very pronounced and slowly. There ought to be a scouse App me thinks! When someone with a strong accent sings they are more understandable than when they speak so on that basis perhaps we scousers should sing when ordering fish and chips at some service station on the M6?

I remember living in Glasgow when I was in my twenties and the girl I was with at the time would have to translate to her parents every word I said. This was a mutual thing as I would sit there nodding away trying to pick up on the facial twitches that suggest I understood, the kind of thing you may do in a noisy night club when appearing polite, when in reality they might have well been speaking Klingon again. After a few weeks I began to understand them and they began to understand me but initially it was very funny and I remember my accent changing slightly as I began to say 'I' befitting of someone born north of the boarder instead of 'yeah when asked questions.

Indeed I think dialects do evolve depending on cultural and social changes and influences or to converse with bloody Siri and I guess every generation uses disguised language as teenagers to hide meaning or to quicken the talking process up and we were no different.

You only have to look at texting and twitter for example and can someone please tell me if LOL means 'lots of love' or 'laugh out loud'; an example of how not knowing can leave you in a bit of a pickle if used in the wrong context, if you don't believe me ask the Prime Minister!

I'm not sure who came up with our 'secret code' and indeed I have since become aware of several city wide variations, but we kids would sometimes converse using 'backslang', a secret language suitable for teenagers and unfathomable to the untrained adult ear.

Good job I'm not in the Magic Circle as I am about to reveal the code that should remain secret, a brave step on my part and I await the hate mail as I might cause a major hullabaloo for those who would read the End Magazine, I fear a fatwa amongst scals and ensuing death threats no doubt. So gulp, here goes, all shall now be revealed.

Simple really and no silly abbreviations, you would place aig before a vowel or a y so single syllable words like 'bus' would become 'baigus', 'cat' would become caigat. If a word had several syllables then the same principle applied. So using my name as an example 'David' would become 'Daigavaigid'. It sounds very complicated and a bit of a tongue twister but that was the point and once understood it was really easy or should I say, 'aigeasaigy!'

I'll give you an example of how this street language could be used in practice should you not have another language up you're 'manche'. Clever eh, great app that 'I Translate', 'manche' means sleeve in French! So picture the scene. You're at the chippy ordering a pie with your mates and this 'stunner' walks in. You want to portray an air of coolness but a rush of hormones would offset your contained aloofness and you would simply have to remark on her alluring beauty to your mates without her knowing.

You would nudge and wink of course when she was ordering her chop suet roll, but you would say something like this, 'laigook aigat thaigat staigunnaiger aigovaiger thaigere'. Times precious so ill help with the translation and I don't think there's an app for this, now there's yet another money spinning thought. Translation; 'look at that stunner over there'. I may add we'd adopt such incomprehensible language when we were in our early teens as we no doubt sounded stupid and sexist so therefore ruining any chances of impressing said beauty. It also assumed ignorance on her part; she may know the code and might have come back with 'aigin yaidour draigeams'! To which I would reply 'yes, do you fancy a ride on my carpet!'

Just remembered a time when I was in North Wales with Alan and Brad on holiday, I'll tell you more about this later but we were using backslang. The girls we were trying to impress in a chippy funny enough, must have thought what part of Wale's did we come from, not recollecting the dialect and here's a thought, did they come back at us in equally undecipherable language known only to those born in places like Llangollen? In any event we never did chat them up.

I feel a tad embarrassed reminiscing about antics like that but I suppose us boy's can be so immature at times, its in our DNA, 'Do Naughty Activities' and we were no exception and I recall playing some slightly menacing games designed to harm and cause maximum humiliation to a mate.

For example we had 'Chinese Burns', a mate would make grab your arm tightly with both hands, then they would turn their hands in the opposite direction causing an instant burn to your arm. I've no idea how this playground favourite started, as it was around when I was in Primary School but suspect this painful pastime had nothing to do with China and any ensuing bruises were worn as a badge of honour to prove you could withstand pain!

Then we had 'bum flicking'. Someone would creep up behind you and with the back of the hand they would flick you on the bum and if your attacker caught you just right then you were left running around with a stinging backside and you soon learnt how to keep a watchful eye over your shoulder. Sounds so homoerotic come to think of it but we just saw this as a bit of harmless fun used to inflict pain to roars of laughter from your mates and not a mating ritual!

Another somewhat masochistic game to inflict on a mate was a carefully timed kick or hand chop to behind the knee joint, this would cause an involuntary reflex response and your mate would capitulate to the ground like he'd lost the will to stand. And as if that wasn't enough we would sneak up and flick a mate on the ear lobe, which was really painful.

'Stamps' was another silly game mainly used when someone had a new pair of shoes or trainers (trabs) to 'Christen' them before they naturally got scuffed playing footy or climbing.

In a similar vein you'd expect a clip around the head to the sound of 'first lick' whenever you got your haircut from Mad Millie's and your mate would spit on their fingers to indicate your first wash, before hitting you. Boys were always spitting as I recall, such a disgusting habit but were not just talking about mucus filled spit to the floor; I mean spit flicking. I almost feel ashamed writing this but you had to amass enough spittle in the canal between your lower set of teeth and your lip and then with your tongue you would fire out rapid spits. This actually turned into a game to see who could spit the furthest; thank God kids now have gizmos to keep themselves occupied!

One of our favourite pastimes was yodelling, I don't mean the Frank Ifield type, do you recall his hit, *'I Remember You'*, good track actually but our yodelling was more reminiscent of a screech than a tune.

I'll give you an example of how this usually worked. You went in for your tea to then discover that your mates had moved on and you hadn't agreed where to meet up. You would yodel and following the reply, should your yodelling be heard, you could work out what direction to head off too. I hasten to add the art of yodelling across rooftops was a pre pubescent pastime on account of the high pitch required. The simplicity, life before texting eh.

I also remember using the name 'Edna' a lot when I was about thirteen. Let me explain. When someone said something that was a bit dubious, a possible lie or perhaps an exaggeration, you would push your lower lip out with your tongue and with your forefinger and thumb you would rub your chin as if you were itching some imaginary stubble, whilst shouting out 'Edna, Edna'.

I've no idea where this odd way to communicate ones disbelief originated from, probably a telly character and Wikipedia was no help

this time, but like most habit forming behaviours, before too long we dropped the phrase Edna and would simply rub our chin protesting doubt.
You would be telling a tale and a mate would slowly lift his hand indicting that his confidence in your tale was vanishing by the minute and then this progressed to just sticking your chin out in silence but speaking volumes. Prior to this chin rubbing disbelieving gesture you'd say 'blagger' when someone was reputedly lying or that's a 'blag' for a lie.
I had an annoying habit when I was about ten. I would constantly twitch my nose like a rabbit from Watership Down and I couldn't stop this annoying habit no matter how hard I concentrated and my Mum would tell me to stop twitching. I guess I was either a bit weird or anxious about something at the time but I also remember other games, if I may I call them that, discovered as a child and to do with my body.
For example and usually accompanied to the nursery rhyme 'Pop Goes the Weasel', placing ones finger into ones gob then flicking the inside of ones cheek would create a popping sound. I've just tried it and yes 'ones' still got it. Similarly, if you puff up your cheeks to the max, like a puffer fish, use the palms of your hand to give yourself a gentle slap; then you've just created a convincing raspberry sound. No I didn't try that!
I hope your still with me on this strange trip around my body, praying you haven't puked yet? The next peculiar body game is a little bit more tricky to describe but here goes. If you pull ones mouth in and smack ones lips together you create a convincing fish sound. Go on I bet you've tried it, not recently perhaps but I guess you did back in the day.
Then we have the 'armpit fart'. Simply place ones palm over ones armpit, what's with all the ones, left or right, it doesn't matter, then quickly drop said arm, or should that be 'ones' arm, to you side and there you have it another believable fart.
I'm on a role here. I remember the first time I leant how to click my fingers but unlike most people I use my ring finger and not my index finger. If you really wanted to annoy someone you would command attention by clicking away as if you wanted to order food.
I could never wolf whistle like my Mum could. She would put her finger and her thumb into her mouth and would easily create this shrill of a noise that could be heard in adjacent streets. How does that happen, all I can muster is a gush of stale breath barely audible if stood next to me.
Dad had a cool trick. He would put his hands together resembling a conch washed up on the beach and he would blow through his thumbs thus creating a horn sound as he wafted his fingers. They were talented

parents my Mum and Dad?

Talking of methods of communication and a slightly more sophisticated one at that, I got a CB and a handy phrase book when I was aged fifteen. CB as you probably know, stands for 'citizen band' radio and it was illegal when I was a child so this made it even more subversive and very cool. My Mum bought it for me from a caretaker at her school who had a moustache who looked like the decathlon athlete Daley Thompson and it came with a six foot Ariel that I attached to a 'Rover' biscuit tin, which I then perched on the extension roof.

The first time I set it up I was so excited but numpty here blew a fuse and I lost my *'Transmission'*. Now there's an inspirational track by 'Joy Division' that must be added to my growing list. I was so upset until my mate 'Scon Head in school gave me a replacement fuse some weeks later and told me what to do, I was mercifully off and running or should I say off and searching and the annoying thing was it was a simple job to fix but I was and still am a novice when it comes to all things electronic. See, I'm colour blind, red and greens can literally 'fuse' into one sometimes and I have always had an innate fear that I will blow something up. I remember taking the test at school and sitting there bemused with the circle of coloured dots that camouflaged the numbers my mates could clearly decipher.

My CB had forty channels, not the mightiest of machines around at the time, some had eighty or even one hundred and twenty but mine was ample enough for me, I wasn't a 'ham geek' like some who took it very seriously. Channel nineteen was where you would talk to your fellow CBers, I don't know why number nineteen but this is where most of the conversations began. Now because it was illegal I figured you needed to read up on the lingo, so I learnt phrases like ten four, which was a code when agreeing with someone or an 'eyeball' when you wanted to physically meet up.

Not as complicated as backslang and I remember watching the 'Convoy' movie on telly to gain an historical perspective as the lingo was steeped in American culture, the craze originated in the States. It was very popular in the seventies, so much so the disc jockey; Dave Lee Travis tapped into the moment with his awful CB track where, dressed as a 'duck', accompanied by female backing singers, he talks about the CB in a scouse voice, why?

You would say 'that's a big ten four let's have an eyeball sometime' when you wanted to meet someone face to face. You would arrange a meeting place but taking care not to be too specific as the authorities could be listening which was silly really as I'm sure there was more important things to eavesdrop on in the World, this was the 'Cold War' era after all. Areas would be described using code names but lets be honest it didn't take a top-secret code breaker to figure out where. Wavertree was known as 'shaky town' for example.

You'd begin a conversation by saying 'nineteen for a copy' in the hope someone would respond and you would say something like; 'take it to the top of the shop', meaning let's talk on channel forty. Other channels could be used of course and this is where knowledge of Mum's bingo lingo, again another subculture language, came in handy. You would say 'take it to Maggie Den', meaning number ten for ten Downing Street, or 'two little ducks' for twenty two.

Over time I developed a network of CB mates and we would have a preferred channel where we would all switch too at night to hear what was happening, nothing most of the time and it was all very secretive. When talking to a QPR, think of Queens Park Rangers and replace Ranger with Stranger, got it? The first question would be 'what's your handle'. This was a 'code name' used only by you, I think kids today refer to this as a 'tag name' or an 'avatar' and it would define your personality, to make you sound interesting and a name to be remembered.

Fellow CB pals had 'handles' like 'Lady Triton', I'll tell you why I remember this particular handle in a minute, 'Mr Universe', Top Dog, me I was called, wait for it, 'Joe Egg'. I can't recall how I came up with this handle but using modern technology again I used Google to discover that Joe was short for Josephine, not so cool then and was about a play made into a film released in 1972 titled 'A Day in the Death of Joe Egg'. I researched more and it was sad story actually, its about this girl called Josephine, who had cerebral palsy and the film was about her struggles and I'm guessing I must have seen an article on the news or something whilst hugging the fire.

Just thought of another memory and a dangerous one at that. Someone somewhere had figured out that you could shrink a packet of crisp to resemble a miniature version of it by holding it over a flame and I remember doing this in front of our gas fire when Mum and Dad were out and burning my fingers.

Very silly I know as I could have seriously disfigured myself or worst still I could have even burnt the house down! Now there's a track I haven't had the pleasure of hearing for a few years from around the same time. *'Burning Down the House'* by Talking Heads.

Anyhow, conversations would go on all night, you would chat about anything and everything and friendships and reputations would flourish or disintegrate depending on popularity! Funny how as a teenager I could talk and talk unlike now it seems and time would accelerate at night much quicker than daylight time and I remember thinking just another fifteen minutes whilst combating the need to shut my eyes but craving to listen in on other conversations for snippets of gossip. Sound so voyeuristic now but you needed to know what was happening in this subversive of all subcultures.

Hormones would rage and for fun you would sometimes marry other CB girls and I'm guessing boys, if that's your preference and you would ask another CBer to preside over the ceremony as an airwave priest.

A very bizarre world in truth but not so unlike Facebook but without the pictures and the need for kids to make up thousands of friends just to prove that they are popular. Again using modern day examples, gamers can lose all track of time as they compete with people across the globe via X Box Live as does my youngest son and the same could be said for people who used the CB.

After talking with someone who you found interesting or if you liked the sound of their voice, you would arrange a rendezvous. This was the funny part, as you would have spoken into the early hours so it felt like you knew the person intimately but you were physical QPR's! You would guess what the person looked like based on the person's description of how they looked, what music they liked, the inflection in the voice I guess or if you were lucky you knew someone who had met the girl and could vouch for her or warn you off her.

Again this was about personal preference and sure you would describe yourself in turn in positive overtures but people exaggerate don't they, it's human nature and the whole experience was like a blind date but without Cilla, you were spared the 'lorra laughs'.

I'm ashamed to say this but there were times when I would walk right past my fellow CBer who I was due to rendezvous with, I know I'm Mr Shallow but some, not many I hope, probably did the same and trotted on by past me. You would joke about wearing a red carnation to make introductions easier and I had several short-term relationships as a result of the CB.

I went out with this girl called Joanne for a few weeks for example and we'd sit in her house on the CB, and then at home curled up under the blankets I would switch on and talk to Joanne throughout the night. How romantic of me and I remember learning the words to *'Only You'* by Yazoo, later covered by the Flying Pickets and singing it to her on our channel and another track I was prone to sing to my CB girlfriend was

'*Souvenir*' by OMD; I must have sounded like a right 'plonker' to others eavesdropping in on our chats.

I may regret telling you this dear reader but the CB was how I came to have my first 'Edge Hill' girlfriend and her handle was Lady Triton but her real name was Paula and she lived for a few months on Salisbury Road. Our first eyeball was a 'steamy encounter' I found myself shovelling that coal like mad down the side of her house and I remember us going the Ice Rink together in Kensington the other side of Botanic Park on a few occasions.

Kenny ice rink was a throwback to the fifties when skating was a popular past time and a place for teenagers to hang out. In fact I think they still used the same boots; they stunk of smelly feet and would invariably leave you with a terrible blister by the end of the session.

I went there a few times throughout my childhood and I remember the first tentative steps onto the ice. You would pluck up the courage and shuffle along the edge trying to avoid the competent skaters who would zip past you and sometimes you would come across a fellow novice and you would do your best to pass them by holding on to each other.

In time your confidence would grow and like a bird taking its first flight into the unknown you would skate from one side to the other grabbing the rail for support with triumphant thoughts 'of I did it'. It was a dead cert you would fall over many times, your legs would either go in different directions or you'd bump into someone. Tick was our favourite game although not allowed and the ice would be cold and wet, naturally and the key was to never leave your hands out in the open as a skater could easily run over your fingers.

Anyway back to Lady Triton. Paula would babysit for a neighbour, this was always a good thing and an amusing thing happened one Saturday night, I know it was a Saturday as I had attended a heavy badminton coaching session earlier in the day.

We were snogging on the couch as you do when all alone babysitting and this is when I discovered I could unclip a girl's bra with one hand. Not the best of boasts I know but a difficult manoeuvre nonetheless. I started to yelp and groan; Paula mistakenly but naturally thought I was getting 'excited' as that train came steaming down the track, I wasn't, I jumped off the couch or should I say track, and hopped around as I had shooting cramp in the instep of my foot because of all the exertion I had done that day.

Oh the memories and I wonder whatever happened to Paula. This relationship only lasted for a few weeks but what a 'steamy' encounter and my mates somewhat disingenuously christened her 'Paula the bunny'; again I think they were jealous.

Back to less steamy matters. The problem with the CB was that other people could listen in to your conversation. Many arguments would erupt and it was basically a free for all with no invite processes like social network sites today where you can delete friends or adults professing to be aged fourteen.

I had male friends to and I remember one time sneaking out to an all night garage around three in the morning, as someone needed milk and suggested we all meet up. After an hour or so talking in the cold, which was daft really as we talked endlessly over the airwaves, I returned home to be met by my Mum sitting in the dark crying. I tried to justify my actions but felt terrible, she was understandably very worried for my welfare as most parents would be and I know I was in the wrong but I was an impressionable teenager seeking excitement. Sorry Mum.

Thinking back the airwaves must have been littered with all kinds of weirdoes and crackpots, present company not included and probably people with paedophile tendencies. Who knows, there was no way of knowing or policing the CB as it was totally uncensored and us kids were very vulnerable but I didn't know it or would have accepted the reasoning behind that at the time as I was hooked.

I guess this is how kids today view social networking sites, as they are brilliant methods of communication but with things uncensored comes vulnerability and potential grooming.

Interesting point to mention but none of my close mates got into the CB, can't recall why but it was my thing and I think I enjoyed the CB because it was rebellious, fulfilled my need to escape again and I could recreate a new persona when at the time I was having a horrid time at school which I will tell you more about later.

The CB was so addictive but also a destructive device too and I can totally understand the allure of social networking but something I have yet to try! The light would spill through the curtains and I would get up and go straight to school all sleepy eyed and barely able to stay awake to talk to Scon Head about the CB and the girls I had spoken with. Regrettably, Aintree, where Scon Head lived was beyond my biscuit tin Ariel range. I would return home to do my paper round which I will talk about later, I would catch forty winks to match the forty channels and would be wide-awake by bedtime and so the cycle of my life back then would begin again.

A dreadful excuse I know but the CB was a contributory factor to me leaving school with a dismal O level grade C in art! Damn you Daley Thompson but there again I did have my Edge Hill encounter with said carrot eater, so perhaps I should say thanks!

Chapter Twelve

Get Down On It…

I've mention numerous mates by now but as I tap away I recognise that what I'm about to divulge may not always show me in a positive light, hasn't so far I hear you say and for that I apologise in advance and I also fear this recollection may be tinged with some happy but also some unhappy memories.

Let me explain. In writing this book I queried why we preserve certain memories and not others and why do some memories gain added credence over time and become more memorable and meaningful than others? Well, not that I'm a psychiatrist but I'm guessing this has something to do with emotional highs and lows and how positive moments of excitement and pleasure and negatives moments of despair and sadness can embed themselves in our psyche because they are situated at opposite ends of the feelings continuum.

I would think about my mates and people I have encountered in my life and I started this process by thinking of a name, then I would brain storm and I would jot down memories on my I Phone note pad specifically to do with that person.

It then struck me that I could recall lots of fond stuff but I would also think about times when I felt a little let down if I'm being honest, when I felt sad and I wondered why I had allowed these memories to remain stored up there in my head. The answer is simple as I see it; it's, like I said before, memories are associated with emotional extremes.

So dear reader read on but please understands that I hold no malice or negativity towards people I refer too throughout this book and I hope they feel the same but I fear not. On the contrary actually as I am who I am because of the shared experiences and like I said before memories are ultimately about perceptions, they are subjective in any event they are by their very nature, personal. Life evolves and I view memory snippets as little terraced houses in need of modernisation like my dear old home, where I can pop in sometime for a brew as I navigate through life to listen to a track or two!

Anyway, enough of the heavy psycho babble. I've made reference to names already in this book, names with no meaning so let me now tell you more about them. My first best mate's, from when I was a toddler were Alan and Grant, not there real names by the way.

Alan's a random pseudonym whereas I used Grant because he who shall remain anonymous modelled himself on Barry Grant in the mid eighties, a character from the soap opera on telly called Brookside. Grant had this impressive curly mullet haircut you see and he was very proud of his curls that reached his shirt collar and a little beyond.

Alan had dark straight hair back in the day but he now has his 'barnet' cut very short and he sometimes has a beard. Actually have you noticed that men who are older than forty tend to have short-cropped hair which is probably due to their hair receding and going grey. Yes, older men with long hair should not be encouraged especially ponytails and mullets if you ask me.

I have kept in touch with Alan over the years but we have drifted apart although we sometimes play golf together but we shall always have a special bond that spans the decades, the unspoken word I guess that connects us to the seventies. He will always have a special place in my heart, the kind of feeling you get when you have seen someone grow up from a toddler to an adult.

I would describe Alan as softly spoken and private, a deep thinking family man who was the best kind of mate you ever wanted as a kid, he was always there to back you up and was good for a laugh. Grant meanwhile was forever resourceful, as I've mentioned elsewhere in this book, more confident than his brother and very competitive which kind of drove us all on and in those early days he was always discovering new things to do or games to play.

I mention this elsewhere in this book but Alan and Grant lived in number twenty-nine a few doors up from me. We were inseparable in those early years; we virtually lived in each other's pockets. Alan was younger than me by two months, he was born in June and Grant was about a year older, he was born in May. Stands to reason therefore that Alan and me would become good childhood mates and we would knock for each other most days after school and at the weekend we would play for hours in our street and beyond the street in places like the Rec which I will come to in a bit.

Whatever games or adventures I refer to in this book then Alan and Grant pretty much shared the same experiences including the bumps, the knocks and the grazes but I think I have more scars and we would bounce ideas off each other and we all had healthy imaginations.

We shared the same musical and fashion tastes like I mention before and without Alan's influence I am guessing I would have missed out on many a seminal track and I thank him for that and I would speculate that this is because we were influenced by the same sounds throughout our childhood that probably began at the 'Penny Rec', if you mix in a bit of rock and roll from our parent's.
So with that let me now tell you about the 'Rec' as this place played a big part in my formative years when not playing out in the street. The Rec was a youth club and Alan and me would make our way to the Rec most nights from when we were about eight, right through to our teenage years and we would hand over our penny at the door. We were a tad apprehensive at first as I recall knowing that we would meet unfamiliar kids from around the neighbourhood but it turned out to be a friendly place to hang out.
Thinking as kids do, I would often ponder how the staff ever made a living; I would do the simple maths and I would work out that thirty or so kids would pay a penny each including me and Alan, but how on earth did the staff make ends meat on such a paltry sum and I thought they were very good working for next to nothing, very philanthropic or so I thought, not realising they were paid youth workers. I actually followed in their footsteps some years later, please read on.
The Rec mainly catered for boys if the various activities were anything to go by. I'm not suggesting girl's can't or shouldn't do woodwork or play table tennis of course but the girls mainly hung out in the disco or the loo if my fading memory serves me well, they probably felt intimidated by the competitive testosterone that gathered in the ether.
I can actually still recall the smell that hit you when you entered the Rec, a dusty, earthy, sweaty smell mixed with dinnertime food and I know this sounds repulsive but like I say elsewhere the smell sense can evoke locked away memories!
But why the food smell, well, when I attended primary school we would march in pairs to the Rec as we had lunch there on long pulled out wooden tables and I remember spuds and cooked meats being served from one end of the 'canteen'. I remember being picked as a table monitor, thinking this felt like an honour but basically meant I was responsible for clearing away the dishes at the end. The irony was my cleaning skills didn't amount to much at home but the adults cleverly instilled responsibility into us kids to make us believe this was an award bestowed on the few.
Anyway, one day, I think it was around Christmas, when I was about nine, I remember attending the Rec in a grey polar neck jumper and

matching grey checked flared trousers with my first stack shoes giving me an extra two inches in height. They were multi coloured and I thought I looked really up to date, cool and hip. I thought I looked 'boss' as scousers say in my Christmas clothes but to my horror this girl from Cecil Street of a similar age walked in with the exact same clothes on that I was wearing minus the colourful shoes.

I didn't know where to put my face and we both looked at each other with the same face of shame and embarrassment. She must have thought, why is a boy wearing girl's clothes whilst, thinking the same but in reverse, I was processing the odds of my Mum and her Mum picking the same clothes from the shop! Seeing as most clothes were ordered from Freemans Catalogue or bought from C&A, my guess is they came from a dodgy bloke in the bingo that both Mum's attended. Moving on from my shame. Once you had paid your penny and signed in at the front door on your left you then entered a large hall, which had four table tennis tables in it, our canteen. I say large but everything seems so much bigger when you're under five foot tall doesn't it even with stacks?

The hall had unpolished dusty floorboards and on one side of the hall was steel framed murky windows encased in protective grills that hadn't seen soapsuds for many a year as you couldn't see out of them. Underneath the windows were old flaky benches to sit on.

We'd play table tennis for hours or until someone stood on the ball, and when that happened it was a dash to the kitchen to submerge the ball in hot water hoping the heat would pop out any imperfections. Remember that tip, might come in handy.

Although I say so myself I was quite good at the game but I was mainly a defensive player if truth were told. Alan, Manny, Neil and Brad, would excel in smashing the living daylights out of the ball whilst I'd scamper around trying my best to return the ball from beneath the table height, capitalising on their errors whilst falling further away from the table and sometimes onto some sods knee.

We sometimes played our version of table tennis at Joey and Brad's house. We'd improvise and use opened books as a makeshift net in the middle of his Mums table and with two other books as bats and a table tennis ball we'd play ping pong for hours at a time.

Funny thing is Neil and I were having a few jars of bitter in Liverpool City Centre at a pub the other month called the Shipping Forecast waiting for this band to come on called 'She Sells Bees' and we spotted a table tennis table in the corner. We were a bit drunk on real ale and Neil looked at me and we challenged each other to a game.

We had to repair the net, which wasn't unusual, and we quickly got into the game. In spite being under the influence of one too many, all the tricks we had learnt in the seventies came flooding back. Neil would serve his specialist sliced serve by standing on his toes creating backspin and the ball would spin to the side of my defending flailing bat but I would then return with a winning topspin serve. Not always but its my story Neil!

Boys will be boys I guess, the gloves came off or should I say we took our jackets off, it was Winter and we became all competitive, playing for about an hour or so stopping for a drink occasionally or to retrieve the ball from beneath several pairs of six inch stilettoes. We played rally after rally not knowing who was actually in the lead but not caring as we had enjoyed ourselves and we both agreed that all pubs should have a table for old heads like me and Neil. Sod darts, dominos and pool! A youth club for old farts, now there's a Dragons Den idea.

Back to the Rec. To the left of the hall you had a hall way and from memory I recall a woodwork shop at the far end. There were lathes, tools and benches and sawdust everywhere and I don't recall making anything but we'd pop in for a look at older boy's being taught how to make joints by an elderly joiner in white overalls and no, not some Rastafarian demonstrating how to role a 'spliff' as they were known. Just a point about drugs, I remember older boys 'slyly' smoking cannabis at the Rec but my mates and me gave drugs a wide berth as we knew how it could get out of hand and the nearest we got to using something to disinhibit ones senses was the odd bottle of woodpecker at a party. No we got our kicks from playing competitive sports.

At the near end of the hall you would turn right and this is where the tuck shop was. The shop had a turntable for the disco and you would submit requests to whatever was in the charts at the time. I remember buying thinly diluted orange juice served in white plastic cups inviting you to nibble the rim and sometimes I'd have a cup of tea out of chipped blue ceramic cups and matching saucers and a 'Nice' biscuit.

The shop would sell crisps, biscuits, sherbet dips, my favourite and all manner of penny sweats and always made a roaring trade. Come to think of it perhaps that's how the adults made their money?

Walking past the tuck shop you entered a large dark room with flickering lights, basically red, yellow and white light bulbs with a faulty fuse. This was the disco and probably the most popular room to hang out in, to be seen in, through the dark that is. Older boys would sit at one end on long benches against the wall, the kind you get in church, eyeing up the girls and I remember a small stage and being younger we'd watch the girls dancing together to the latest disco classic and the boys shuffling about trying to look cool but looking uncomfortable.

I have so many tracks buzzing round my head when I think of these early years at the Rec, mainly classic discos tracks. For example; 'The Real Things', *'You To Me Are Everything'*, 'The Three Degrees', *'When Will I See You Again'*, Yvonne Ellermans', *'If I Can't Have You'*, 'Taste of 'Honey's, *'Boogie Oogie'* and the Jackson's *'Blame it on the Boogie'*.

We were mesmerised by all the shenanigans of the group, the pruning and the showing off and perhaps I had eaten too many KP discos from the tuck shop but it was around this time that I first connected music with dancing, with talking to girls, with getting intimately close to girls, to those carpet flying urges beckoning me to become a train driver.

When the older kids left, probably for a sly smoke behind the sheds, we'd run in and slide on our knees on the polished wooden floor. We thought this was fantastic fun but nothing unusual as kids today instinctively do the same, must be in their genes, pardon the pun and look out next time you're at a wedding or some other event.

As the years unfolded and as we got older we became the dominant kids in the disco but punk had arrived by this stage so no long hair centre parts or disco dancing for us. No, we'd run around pogoing, jumping and running along the bench trying to head butt the red, yellow and white flashing lights to the beat of some band thrashing away and screaming out loud.

I remember pogoing to *'She's Something Else'* by Sid Vicious, pausing a beat, did you know Sid invented pogoing? Story goes he played the saxophone and would jump up and down to music and when he joined the Pistols he carried on this tradition. Sid on sax, who'd have thought! Should have called himself 'saxy Sid!'

At the far end of the table tennis hall was a door that led to another corridor. This corridor gave you access to a large room with a full size snooker table and overhanging lights, just white this time. It felt like a grown ups room and you had to put your name down on a chalkboard to have any chance of playing and sometimes you'd miss your turn because some older boy would muscle in. I remember Grant being good at sinking snooker balls but a few years later Alan became the better player with his brother Francis.

An old bloke who seemed well into his seventies but probably fifty something, would referee matches but was mainly there to ensure no one ripped the precious green blaze or flipped a coin over the table. That was a big no no! The first time I remember having a go, I could barely reach over the table and us smaller kids would have to use the rest for most shots. I also remember the laughs from the side when colour-blind me would pot the brown thinking it was a red ball.

At the end of the corridor was an exit door to a yard that had another hall. This hall was mainly made out of corrugated iron bolted together and had a curved roof. Looked like a huge air raid shelter from the war and very cold in winter, might have been for all I know as it had certainly been erected for decades if the rust was anything to go by. I remember this hall with fondness as this was the first time I played badminton but a very different game to what I play today as we played with very heavy blue rackets with broken strings and crappy plastic shuttles.

We never knew the rules but we'd have fun keeping the shuttle up for as long as possible not realising that the object of the game was to actually hit the floor between the lines.

The whole place had a major makeover some years later and new brick building replaced many of the old worn out structures and I'm guessing the council by then was confident that bombers from distant lands wouldn't go and deploy their carpet-bombing projectiles on our wonderful city?

Alan and his mates got their gambling room; the disco and the table tennis room remained pretty much the same and somewhat predictably, the entrance fee shot up to ten pence. The Rec, which by the way was on Earle Road, forgot to mention that, and I am assuming it stood for 'recreational', again I had never thought of that till now, has been demolished and all that's left is a baron wasteland but heaps of fond and treasured memories of course.

Guess they call this progress but I wonder where kids around those parts play nowadays, where do they get their recreational highs? Probably at home on some console game conversing with mates over the Internet. Doesn't seem right that, serving only to stifle imagination and I pity kids that don't play out, I really do.

When I was about fourteen Dunny's disco started, it felt like a graduation, a right of passage from the Rec's disco to something more mature and akin to clubbing. Dunny's was actually situated on the opposite side of the cobbled street so very familiar and it got its name from St Dunstan's Church Hall, which was the venue surprise, surprise. We would put on our finest garments, word spread and kids would come from all around every Friday and each week the crowds would swell to whatever the DJ was playing.

My Mum realising that I needed to have a good wardrobe to alternate my image, now there's a band 'Altered Images' and the lovely Claire

Grogan squeakily singing '*I Could Be Happy*' and '*Happy Birthday*' after appearing in the superb film, Gregory's Girl'; bought me several pastel coloured canvas trousers from someone at the bingo and I remember once wanting to wear my light blue pair but they were still wet.
Not to be outdone I ironed them dry but they were still damp and I remember walking to the disco across the field like John Wayne, all in the name of fashion. Now there's an image and a reminder of a forgotten track, Hazi Fantazee's '*John Wayne is Big Leggy*'.
I can remember Dunny's like it was yesterday, we would stand opposite each other on the dance floor and we would pogo and kick dance through classic punk tracks of the day just like we did at the Rec and at Bishop Eaton. Come to think of it Alan was probably the best dancer amongst us lads, Brad however could kick dance and pogo like the rest of us but more complicated rhythmic moves were not Brads strongest asset, stick to footy Brad, although I'm sure he'd challenge me to a dance off should he ever read this!
Just pausing a beat. If I could use the Dr's much used Tardis again I would go back in time to when the Northern Soul scene was at its peak in the mid seventies and after a few lessons from those dexterous Wiginers, you would find me strutting my stuff and spinning around in the middle of Wigan Casino with the best of them! What an experience that must have been, so wish I had experienced it first hand but never mind, we had Dunny's!
Anyway back to my disco and less twirls. If the track slowed down you kicked out less, if it had a quick tempo then you'd prance around faster and faster. Occasionally the latest disco track from Kool and the Gang would come on, like '*Get Down On It*', or Michael Jacksons '*Don't Stop Till You Get Enough*'. Difficult moment this! Do I dance or go the loo, as the beat was strangely alluring to someone used to balancing on seesaws with agile feet wanting to dance?
I remember this bruiser of a guy coming up to Alan and me and said 'why yews dancing togeder are yews gay'. We never thought of dancing with a mate as an indication that you were gay, nevertheless we sheepishly retracted into our bruised shells thinking we actually liked dancing but that alpha lad with two left feet it seems had set the discos terms of engagement again. Felt like I was back on the playground with Mr Attenborough watching where bigger lads made all the rules.
This was a dilemma, as we liked dancing, there you go, no shame in that. The only thing for it was to put into practice my aptitude to talk to girls having lived with two sisters. My heart would thump though, the nerves

would flutter and a little voice in my head would say 'go on lad ask her to dance!
Of course I would hone in on a girl who I found attractive but sometimes I would ask a girl to dance because I actually wanted to dance, I wanted to *'Dance Away'* to Brian Ferry's track and this would involve moving my knees in a circular motion and depending on the beat the motion would quicken up till you were kicking out with your feet.
Those dance away moments usually occurred after hearing the first three or four notes, bit like Tom O'Conner but ill dance that song in three Tom and I would jump up and go to the first girl in my line of sight! If I'm being honest though, to approach a girl, most of the time at least, had another agenda which as we all know is can I dance with you but only because I want to get to know you.
I felt sorry for girls as they had their own dilemmas too. Not to be asked to dance during the night was the equivalent of being turned down by the girl of your dreams; it was like a tug of war between the sexes. Some girls would shy away as if you were invisible oblivious to your fragile confidence, you know that glance that says 'get lost', or 'as if'. The worst insult as you could feel your mates' eyes drilling into your back waiting with baited breath to see the outcome. On the rare occasion this happened, it's my story like I said so allow me some poetic licence, you'd come back with a 'she's got a boyfriend' or 'she's just about to leave' excuse. So on to the next girl.
Sometimes girls would say 'yes' but you soon realised they were being kind and sensitive but that was acceptable for me as you didn't lose face in fact you gained respect because you dared to ask. I would get to know which girls were the kind sought, those that would dance but knowing that was all you should expect. In my experience these girl's were the prettiest girls, girls who knew they had something special and girls who were on the look out for an equal match but again this is all about perception and one for the 'eye of the beholder'.
Then we have the girl that actually found you interesting and dare I say it, pleasing on the eye, a possible match. In my day girls never approached boys directly as that was not the done thing, they had to protect their reputation. This sounds so Edwardian and sexist but girls didn't want to develop 'laidback reputations' and once formed the reputation wasn't easy to shake off even if it were not true. A girl who had many partners would develop a 'slag' reputation whilst her male equivalent would get 'slaps on the back' from his mates, so wrong I know but that's how it was in the early eighties round our way.

No, the way girls expressed an interest in you would be for them to send an advance party across the dance floor or in the queue line at the tuc shop, to recci the situation!

Questions would follow along the lines of 'dya fancy me mate' or, in a matter of fact way, 'me mate wants to know if yew would dance wid er later'. Not a full commitment but a strong hint.

Lets assume you've sent the advance party back to its boarders, the perimeter seats, with a positive yes, but not too desperate a comment; you would wait for the first carefully chosen track that you liked.

A word of caution though, never try dancing to *'It's My Party'* by Barbara Gaskin, starts very slow and you invariably miss the moment when it quickens up making you look like a right 'div'. Similarly unless you have a proclivity for sitting on the floor practicing your rowing skills when 'not' inebriated and tapping the floor in rhythm to your fellow floor rowers, then steer clear of the track *'Oops Up Side Your Head'* by the 'Gap Band'. There's a thought, I wonder if the triumphant rowers at the 2012 Olympics did this at the end of night celebrations. Just a thought, probably too young to know the track unless Sir Redgrave was present I guess as he's in his forties?

This was by all accounts a good tune but involved sitting on the floor behind a girl, preferably and moving forward, backward and from side to side but was seen as uncool by my mates and me and should never be attempted in pastel coloured canvas trousers in any event as you end up with a dirty bum and sometimes a wet dirty bum in my case!

Anyway for a few beats of the heart and butterfly flaps you would look at each other deciding your next move. Such a power struggle but most of the time the girl would determine whether you were good enough for a second dance and this would be expressed in their dancing, whether they were enjoying the dance, or the fact they still faced you and looked remotely interested without grimacing, looking to be rescued by a mate. See, loyal friends would look across at their mate or mates' who were hopefully dancing with your mate and you hoped your mate hadn't bored her mate by trying to explain the off side rule thinking this was an interesting topic of conversation. This sounds very complicated, just like the off side rule actually.

Some boys and girls hunted as lone wolves but most mainly hunted in packs, it was a safety in numbers thing! The second track was the start of better things as it opened more doors and would allow you to ask three important and well rehearsed questions taught on the street corner; what's your name, what's your star sign and what school do you attend.

Folk law past down from lad to lad had spoke of such questions, origins unknown but the first question was needed as you needed to know her name of course, always helps and once said do not forget or worse still, inadvertently say another name, a girl you were perhaps chatting to the week before.
The second injected a bit of fun, as you would remark that you always liked Leos but never Gemini's as my sisters were Gemini's and they literally had two moods, bad and intolerable! Sorry sisters but it's the truth and I've just thought of an astrological link to a fabulous track called *'Float On'* by the Floaters. If I was a 'floater I'd sing, 'Aries and my name is Dave and I like all kinds of women…' followed by the cool choreographed dance that complemented such wonderful soul songs released in the seventies.
So then we have the third question, which allowed you to work out whether you knew other girls in her school and thereby determine whether you were on safe ground. Word of mouth was key you see, as we never had Facebook to expand reputations be they good or bad!
It was certainly in the stars that she was probably from Notre Dame School in my case! Most girls I spoke too wore the petrol blue uniform with pride and they certainly didn't swing from the rafters shouting the bells are making me deaf! No most girls from this school were pretty according to my mates and me and in fact some years later I married an old Dame girl, as did Neil and Brad, told you it was destiny.
If you got to the third track you knew you were on to something potentially good, she by then had laughed or pretended to laugh at your jokes, didn't really matter, she found you interesting and liked the way you shuffled your feet. You had passed several tests of the verbal, shuffling and looks kind by this stage and I may be wrong but I think girls have a thing for guy who can shake his hips in pendulum time to a record as it alludes to good rhythm and dreams of Edge Hill Station. My *'Station Approach'* so to speak, a marvellous track by Elbow that's accompanied and enhanced by a rhythmic mantra that I simply adore! Or is this my perverted brain kicking in again, sorry about that?
Then the slowies would start. If you timed your move just right you would ask the girl to dance just as the night was ending but you would have to guard against one of your mates asking the girl you had your eye on, so timing was always crucial!
I came to realise that you never asked a girl to dance at the beginning of the night, why you may ask, well let me explain the theory us lads had. Firstly, the girl of your dreams is always with her mates, never on her own, stands to reason she would attend the disco with 'a pack', a

collection of girls and she would have to decide whether to dance the night away with you, thereby 'binning her mates' in the process to do girly things, whatever that may be! If you asked too early then the odds were definitely stacked against you and rejection like I said was a bitter pill.

Secondly, the girl might find you dull and boring once you had gone beyond your scripted three questions. You certainly had to be a skilled conversationalist with many quips and jokes in your back pocket, as the girl would, nine times out of ten, simply lose interest unless she liked footy of course and could tell 'you' the offside rule!

Thirdly and the most important part of this theory, you never ever wanted to appear desperate, a classic school boy error made by many a mate and me sometimes; you practically stank of 'please talk to me as I'm lonely'.

Actually I think I'll throw in a fourth reason, perhaps even more important than the last three, well certainly for me that is! Times were hard and fifty pence pocket money had a limited shelf life even back then when stuff was cheaper and it wouldn't stretch beyond two orange juices! If the girl you wanted to impress was thirsty and you had no money, well the shame but being a modern kind of guy moulded by my dear old Dad I would have expected her to put her hand in her pocket or purse or wherever she kept her pennies to buy me a drink back!

So a late approach was always better as it increased the chance that you would stay on the floor till the end as neither you nor the girl wanted to sit on the side on their lonesome, enviously watching the crowd sway to Peaches and Herb's track, *'Reunited'* or some other slowie, both thinking, well, any ship in a port.

As for tracks, my favourite and a classic slowie track, was *'Always and Forever'* by Heatwave and if this track came on; then all ones birthdays and Christmas's had come together at the same time, you'd be 'made up' as we would say. Unlike other tracks from this era you see, this track had a twelve-inch version and stands to reason this would increase the chances that she would succumb to your wit and charm as it went on for ages.

Whilst I've got Heatwave on my brain did you know they were a UK based disco band and I saw them on telly recently singing the splendid *'Boogie Nights'*. The three black guys look comfortable in their glitzy figure hugging cat suits, but what's with the head towel, as for the drummer and the guy on the piano who I think wrote the track, I'm sure they must have had second thoughts and now squirm in embarrassment. Look on YouTube if you don't believe me.

Moving or should I say smooching on. You would submerge your head into the girls neck and your bodies would fuse together as you both shuffled clockwise, never anti clockwise, something to do with most people being right handed, trying to avoid stepping on each other's college shoes or whatever was fashionable at the time.

I also leant to never sing out loud either, you think you sound in tune but most of the time you don't and this is another schoolboy error and as for humming, no really don't do that either. It was always very funny when the music stopped and you would hear someone mid sentence shouting out because a few beats earlier they couldn't be heard.

Then, as if by some celestial defined moment you would turn and face each other, you would lean forward slightly feeling her breath swathe across your face, hopefully smelling of mint and not cigarettes, her breath would pass your nostrils and if you were really lucky your lips would touch in unison for the first time.

That was it, she liked you, you liked her and you would kiss or 'snog' away oblivious to who was around you lost in the moment willing the DJ to play an encore and then another, the twelve inch version again please! Sorry I'm loosing it here and I'm not suggesting this happened every week of course; not for the want of trying but when it did it was a wondrous teenage event and from it came many fond memories, memories of meeting girls, growing up and once and for all leaving street games behind.

Alan, Brad and me also hung out with these girls from Cranborne Road for a year or two when we were around fourteen, Cranborne is a Road that ran like the top of a capital T to our street. Sara and Amy were twin sisters and Kayleigh was a friend of theirs who lived over the road. Kayleigh had an older sister who was into punk music and Alan borrowed several singles from her and I remember being totally blown away by *'Tommy Gun'* by the Clash. We'd pogo on Alan's pristine carpet floor in his house, playing this track again and again.

We'd sometimes loiter on the twin's doorstep and chat but I can never remember what we talked about and most weekends we would babysit with them. These were amusing times as we weren't meant to babysit at some stranger's house but we would sneak in once the unknowing parents had gone out for a pint or two in the local boozer.

Babysitting you see was 'the' leisure activity for most girls when I was a kid and we'd wait in the entry for the call, usually a wolf whistle inviting us to *'Estienne a go go'*, we would scale the wall like it was the 'Krypton Factor' when the coast was clear and being hormonal adolescent's things would get frisky once inside.

We'd play slightly illicit games with one eye on the clock of course, such as spin the bottle and other true, dare, kiss, command games in an attempt to sneak a kiss and a fondle. Snogging techniques were refined during babysitting but I never got many kisses in truth, I think the bottle was 'loaded' as it evaded me more times than mathematically possible and when it came to true, dare, command I'd be told to put my shoes on the wrong feet or something stupid like that.

Sara and Amy had, now how do I put this, oh what the heck, they had womanly bodies with pointy bits comparable to Kremmen's Carla, they were nice girls but the pointy bits were the main attraction if I am being honest. Such wonderments and I remember sitting next to Sara or Amy and using the daft chat up line whilst pointing to some distant point, 'nice wallpaper eh', then leaving ones arm perched on the neck. If said arm was allowed to stay then that was a good sign if not, oh well worth a try. All sounds so seedy and predatorily, it was I suppose but that's what life was like when I was a teenager in Edge Hill and most nights it would turn into a game of cat and mouse. I certainly remember Brad and Alan being more successful than uglier me!

I did have this brief liaison with this girl called Mandy who lived on Earle Road and she was also friendly with the twins, they all went to the same school as Tina, St Margaret Clitherow's. She had the house to herself most nights and as I recall Brad, Neil and Derek saw her at different times some months later.

I had a huge crush on this girl called Sam and her sister was a friend of Alan's. Our paths rarely crossed, she lived on Cecil Street and I remember having this strong need to express my feelings so I knocked on her door to tell her that I liked her. Sam was a year older than me, she invited me in for a cup of tea but nothing more happened, her feelings for me weren't reciprocal sadly and she let me down gently. I still left feeling over the moon though having spent the night with her!

The Look of Love', a track by ABC, in its truest form, eluded me, which I'm glad about actually as I was just a horny teenager but for Alan on the other hand it did, he fell for Kayleigh and they ended up marrying each other. Some years later when we were about sixteen I think, Alan told me in the middle of playing a badminton match in Waterloo, why oh why do I remember so much detail, that he was going to become a Dad and months later Paula was born. This was a shock; Alan was the first of the gang to become a Dad.

I also remember Alan saying that the baby wasn't planned but when Paula, his daughter, was eighteen he could then go to clubs and pubs as he would be free from the responsibility by then and I remember thinking, 'but Alan shouldn't you do your clubbing bit now and not when you're all grown up'. Guess Alan was justifying his Edge Hill actions in some way and as it happens Paula's a nice kid, I say kid, she must be in her late twenties by now and she's just qualified as a social worker. I wonder if Alan ever did go clubbing?

I also remember how Alan stepped up to the mark once he knew Kayliegh was 'up the duff' and took on his responsibilities by getting a job at Tesco's where he still works actually. I am proud of Alan for doing that as he could easily have sponged off the welfare state like some lads did or worst still walked away from being a Dad. Well done Alan.

Cranborne Road features a lot in my childhood now I come to think of it. We played footy against the twins brothers and their mates, we usually won, we were also friendly with other kids such as Adele, who had a brother called Dave, her mate Paula with long blonde hair and Jane. Jane also had twin brothers must have had something to do with the water up that Road and an annoying little brother called Ian.

I hung out with this kid called Andy sometimes and he lived opposite Paula and I remember playing footy with Andy and his Dad in Sefton Park. Andy loved anything to do with Gary Numan and we would sit on his step playing records.

A few doors up from Andy you had Clint, Paula and Craig who some years later emigrated to America and I remember thinking how amazing and adventurous. I believe there still there.

Alan looked younger than me as I was always taller than him and when we were about sixteen he started knocking around with mates who were mainly younger than him by a year or so and I would sometimes cross paths with them in the Rec. I'd pop over sometimes for old times sake for a game of table tennis but I had discovered that I could get into pubs and clubs and I started to hang around more with Grant, Derek and Neil by this stage.

My defining memory of this motley crew was that they all liked to gamble for money, particularly the card game Black Jack and they all smoked. Alan became addicted actually and some years later he had a major operation caused by years of heavy smoking and he eventually gave up but before his scare he was a serious chain smoker.

I'm about to recall a bleak memory at this point. This being the ying and yang that memories evoke eh. My sister Tracy was on the field opposite our street with Alan and his mates and she recalls losing her front door key in the grass. Some days later the 'lecy man' or to use the correct term, the electricity man came to our house to empty the meter of its fifty pence booty but the meter was short by a few pounds.

We then worked out what had happened, we had been robbed and because there was no sign of a forced entry we surmised that someone must have had a key to gain access to our house to get to the meter. I never had absolute proof but Tracy had a gut feeling that the key was found or should I say had been acquired on the field.
The key didn't have an address pinned to it, as that would have been stupid so this added to our suspicions and I remember feeling devastated and talking to Ray the Vicar about my feelings and what to do.
Now this has got me thinking about Ray and I'll talk about him soon but Ray was very helpful and supportive and I decided to do nothing believing if Alan and his mates had broken into my house then they must live with their own guilt, which was punishment enough and I always hoped Alan had nothing to do with this dishonourable deed. I'm probably way of the mark but I knew Alan's mates were obsessed with making money and I knew they were well into stealing stuff to feed their gambling addictions. All the evidence pointed at Paul and James.
I remember Alan offering me a Moor cigarette once, a thin brown Clint Eastwood kind of cigarette and to my shame I liked the taste and the head buzz and I remember smoking several over the next few days but then thinking hang on this is getting out of hand as I could feel myself liking them too much. I had seen my Mum smoke for years and it just wasn't for me, bad for your health of course and probably, more to the point, too bloody expensive. Brad, still boasts that he has never tried smoking and casts a disparaging look at me for my lack of control back then.
Truth is I wasn't that rebellious and I always thought kids who smoked deliberately encouraged other kids to join in as it then increased the chances that someone would have a 'biffter' as we called them, to share when gasping. To me it was a sub culture within a sub culture and typical teenage behaviour as it defined rebellion within certain youths in spite knowing the health dangers as a consequence of smoking. Otherwise why do people smoke, can't they read the bloody label?
I recall having this 'special' relationship with Jeannette, who I mentioned earlier, she had long straight mousy coloured hair and she lived at the far end of our street. Jeannette was the same age as me and I think Alan had a brief encounter with her younger sister, Joanne.
We grew up with each other and we had many an adventure, she was part of our gang, we joked about running away and I recall having these 'strange feelings' for Jeanette when I was about eleven and she felt the same too. I would never describe our relationship as 'girlfriend and

boyfriend' in the strictest sense but I do remember going to the park with Jeanette and kissing her under a blanket whilst sharing pop and jammy dodgers. Probably the first time I had kissed a girl and I liked it, the touch lips kind of kiss, not a proper kiss.
When Jeannette started senior school she found new friends and she moved on to pastures new, Netherley I think. Then, in June 1979, Jeanette came knocking at my door. My mates and me hung around the street with her talking about music and fashion and what she had been up too these past few months. I say this with a degree of certainty as I recall my mates then heading off home to watch Gary Numan sing his number one hit *'Are Friends Electric'* on TOTP. Again I have Wikipedia to thank for this factual date.
Jeannette stopped me when no one was looking and suggested I stay out with her. I was really torn, as I so wanted to catch the track, I thought this better be good Jeanette are we going for a game of manhunt. The street would empty whenever the Pops was on telly you see, this was the norm for us seventies kids as we never knew how a band looked like until they appeared on the Pops. I also knew my mates would come out afterwards with sounds of 'did ye see im' but I was intrigued also and those 'special feelings' were overhauling my desire to sit in front of the telly for half an hour.
So Jeannette and me wandered up to the gas works, a more discrete place and I remember sitting on this ledge in front of the boiler house, kissing Jeanette with her standing between my legs thinking, good choice this is better than chasing after my mates and heaps better than watching Mr Numan.
I then stopped as I spotted in the corner of my eye, Dad's Vauxhall Viva driving down Spofforth Road right past me with my Mum and sisters returning from my Nan's. I saw them rubbernecking me, one of those oh no caught in the act memories but a proper kiss I may add and we retreated to the back entry and oh boy what a moment!
Now here's a link worthy of mentioning. Although my mates and me used the term 'entry' to describe the back passage between houses we would sometimes call the entry a 'jigger', which is a traditional scouse term. We would say 'up de jigger' meaning a place to canoodle hence the link and it may be of interest to know that the words origin comes from 'jigjig', which I've since learnt is an African sailors terminology for having sex.
No choo choo train journey with Jeanette I may add but a fond memory though and I lost touch with Jeannette shortly after our 'gas work' encounter, it was if she had learnt so much on her travels away from our

street but had to return for one last time to show the gang that she was growing up.
Her Dad was made redundant from Dunlop's like my Dad and her family then moved out of the street in the early eighties; they bought a greengrocer shop in Bootle I think and I have never seen her since! I wish her well and I hope she's doing fine.
I remember one time knocking for Alan and Grant and this lad I had met a couple of times around the area but not from our Street stepped out and punched me in the face, lets call him Richard because he was a 'dickhead' but I guess I could be accused of being a tad biased. This was an unprovoked assault albeit an accurate punch and I stumbled back several steps and banged my head on the kerb, I almost gave myself three 'kerby' points it was an accurate hit.
Seriously though, I must have been about fifteen, I had blood streaming from my nose, I was dazed and in slow motion the double questions of why had I been hit and why had Alan and Grant allowed this to happen ran through my mind but either way I was livid and absolutely enraged with everyone in my sights!
Grant could see that, I could see it in his eyes and he quickly shut the door. Instinct then took over and I sprang to my feet and I banged and banged at their oak varnished but very secure door, they wouldn't come out and they certainly weren't going to let me in, god this is sounding more and more like the three little pigs nursery rhyme I should have huffed a little!
As it happens I was puffing with anger and I shouted through the letterbox using several expletives but not caring who was listening to my protestations and indeed Doreen was on her doorstep, she must have heard the commotion and came out to have a look at what was happening outside her door.
This gave me an idea, I ran through my house to get to the back entry because I knew from years of running between our houses that I could climb Doreen's wall to drop into Grants back yard but they had worked out my plan, the door was locked.
I kept wondering why Alan and Grant had not let me in or why they had not thrown the lad out but I don't blame them now as the red mist had smothered the common sense section of my brain, I was out of control and I suspect they were very wary of this lad as he was a 'nutter', a bit of a wanderer with an older brother who had an equal reputation and dressed like Saxy Sid Vicious. They were scared of him.
Darkness then set in and I kept a vigilant guard on Grants door until I had to go in for my tea. Mum and Dad could see I was charged and

ready for action but I never told them why I was fuming but Dad knew I had been in a fight as I had blood on my top. He knew any advice would fall on deaf ears.

The lad then had the audacity to knock on my door 'offering me out' as we would say, on the wasteland by the 'hills'. How dare he do that? I remember feeling nervous as I never expected him to bring the fight to me especially after witnessing my rage, this was unexpected but I was still pumped up with adrenalin and I had to accept and I told him to be there in ten minutes. Why ten I've no idea but I needed time to gather my thoughts.

Ten minutes later I arrived as planned, it was dark and cold, no one was around and I could still taste the iron in my mouth from my bloody nose encouraging me to be brave and not to lose no matter what and my hands were clenched fist shaped in anticipation.

I waited and waited but he never showed up and after a further ten minutes I went home and I remember feeling aggrieved, as I wanted my revenge but slightly relieved as with each passing minute my anger had begun to subside replaced by logic sensible thoughts.

I never did see Richard again and I wasn't normally so inflamed but something inside me snapped that day, pent up anger having walked away from fights for years revealing my demonic side but looking back I'm glad I was denied vengeance as I would have hurt him badly and I don't think I have ever lost it like that since and that emotion was a very frightening encounter.

I naturally felt let down by Alan and Grant as we had been friends all of our lives and I was bemused as to why he had hit me but later discovered that another lad had told this lad that I had said something derogatory about him, I hadn't, a serious case of 'shit steering' again. A few days later Grant said the lad had been 'bad mouthing' me and when I knocked he just ran out and Grant said he was equally shocked but didn't know what to do as I was in a rage and I'm guessing Grant discouraged this lad from ever calling again.

Strange how I can effortlessly recall this incident and I feel slightly miffed because there must be many lovely memories throughout my childhood that have faded away lost forever whereas this memory remains lodged in my head and I know this is based on trauma retention and remembering feelings when I felt infuriated and hurt.

Moving on. Let me tell you more about Neil S who lived next door to Alan and Grant with his older brothers, Barry and Geoff. Geoff joined the RAF, which was an achievement for a kid from Edge Hill and Barry was a cook in the Merchant Navy.

Doreen and Billy were rightly very proud parents. I remember Barry being away at sea for months at a time and he would return with all manner of fancy gifts from far off exotic places, probably the Isle of Man sometimes but I was impressed nevertheless and remember telling myself that I would travel to the four corners of the world when I was older. I remember Neil having this onyx paperweight for example and a marble table with gold-gilled legs, so sophisticated and elegant.

Neil tended to play with older kids when I was really young and he out grew us, as he was a few years older than me. Our paths would pass from time to time and I remember telling Neil in the chippy that one day I would be bigger than him and I'd take him in a fight. We got on really well in truth, this was just innocent banter between lads; Neil was a top bloke you see and years later he would look out for us in pubs when out and about with his mates.

Now this is an extremely sad moment and this memory haunts me still. I think Neil got into a fight as a young adult, he wasn't a fighter but I guess he was in the wrong place at the wrong time as he banged his head and then developed life-changing epilepsy. He managed his epilepsy through medication so I'm told but Neil was tragically found dead behind the wheel of his car after having a fit some years later, leaving a young wife and young kids.

Doreen, his Mum, my messenger when in a jam, has never gotten over her loss, how could she and whenever I see Doreen I can see the grief in her eyes and she lost her husband Billy a few years back. Please know Doreen should you be reading this that I think you're a marvellous individual and you were a significant and caring adult when I was a child and a very good friend to my Mum and my family. I remember you buying me the game 'battleships' for my tenth birthday, which I played with for days, so heaps of thanks to you for many reasons.

I was friend's with Manny who was a Chinese kid who lived in the chippy on Earle Road next to Parkers sweetshop. I see Manny from time to time as he still plays badminton; in March 2012 I played against him in this over forty tournament and coincidently Manny played with Dave B who I refer to later.

I could never beat Manny at table tennis though, he was a genius with a bat, he would serve using the Chinese way of holding his bat and the ball would back spin away from you and back over to his side of the table. He was even more accomplished at spin serving than Neil.

There were many other kids who you would 'know' out and about and I remember large families dotted around the area shoehorned into small terraced houses.

I was working as a social worker some years back and I sat in a meeting with a family and this bloke said; 'do you have a sister called Tracy?' He was from one such large family from when I was a kid and I asked him if he was happy with me working with his family given the connection and he said 'yes'. This actually helped; as the family knew I was from the area and we developed a good working relationship for the betterment of the children.

I met Jean and Sue when I was about thirteen. They lived by Picton Clock and they would visit their sister from time to time in Cranborne Road. We thought they were posh as they had a garden but years later I discovered that they were from a large family and times were very tough for them as their father had passed away as did their mother a few years later. I know this because my mate Brad ended up marrying Jean and Sue became my wife and the mother of my children.

I asked Sue if she remembers the first time we met and she recalls me standing outside her sister's house in a stripy T shirt looking all shy and uncomfortable and she thought I looked cute but seemingly not cute enough to tell me at the time!

We had a night out in 1991 and this is when I first started going out with Sue when she learnt I was not that much of a 'toy boy'. Back when I wore my stripy T shirt you see, she thought I was the same age as Brad which would have made me four years younger than Sue, a big gap when you're a teenager, so she said this is why she never revealed her feelings to me.

Sue's a keen astrologer, I think she liked the Floaters too, so she studied my star sign and using all these logarithmic type equations based on the exact time and location I was born she worked out that we were a compatible match whereas I thought it was down to my dancing feet and those three important questions!

Chapter Thirteen

Summer The First Time...

Alan got me into playing badminton, a sport I still play to this day when my backs not sore and I have since become a qualified coach. Alan had heard a radio advertisement on Radio City inviting new members to the Liverpool Squash and Badminton Club on Picton Road and me, Alan, Grant, Neil and Derek soon joined.
I had played badminton at the Penny Rec like I said but not seriously and the sport was considered to be a sport for rich kids and not competitive or mucky enough for us rough street urchins.
I was so wrong and I recall attending very strenuous coaching lessons with this bloke called Mike at the club when I think I was about fourteen and I loved the sport, the athleticism, the social aspect, the winning and we all started playing the game and we took it very seriously.
Our game improved as the weeks unfolded and we would challenge each other to games and I would play in tournaments at the club and around Liverpool. I remember Mum scraping together enough money to buy me my first racquet; made by Kennex I think and kit, up until then I had used my footy gear.
I would dress in white, not a good luck as I soon discovered that I suffered with a sweaty bum and I constantly had to lick my hand to stick my fringe to my forehead, should have used a clip and I'll tell you more about my growing hair later.
We would attend coaching every Saturday morning at the club, remember the bunny and we became pally with Dave B from Childwall and I can recall many a good night out with Dave and his mates in town who had this cool choreographed dance to *The Look Of Love* by ABC.
Like I said before I see Dave from time to time and he hasn't changed much over the years, same size, same haircut that sought of thing.
I have very fond memories from this time and looking back badminton served a purpose as it fulfilled our need to compete at everything and anything and it kept us off the streets; from scally wag temptation and a life of debauchery, although, come to think of it, that concepts

increasingly debateable after proof reading this warts and all book. After the coaching we would retreat to the changing rooms and this was the first time I had used a sauna. So exotic and continental, I had dreams of gorgeous Swedish girls from Abba urging me to *'Take A Chance on Me'* offering to wipe my brow and we would sit on the wooden sweat stained benches taking bets to see who could sustain the killer heat the longest whilst beads of burning sweat would pore from every sinew. Someone would succumb and would burst out to the sanctuary of the cold shower, followed by the rest of us slipping on the floor, most of the time I was the first.

There's another bet, like I said everything was a competition, we would see who could sit in a chair under the freezing water for the longest, then back to the sauna but again I was usually the first to concede. Oh the fun we had eh and it was around this time that I learnt that I loathe temperature extremities be that icy cold or scorching hot!

That aside we would stay in and out of the sauna, intermittently running to the shower, for hours and we got to know other older blokes like this stout tough looking bloke called Gerry. My memory of Gerry is that he was a powerful ex army type, think he had actually been in the marines in Northern Ireland and he would shave in the sauna, clearing his discarded bristles into a white plastic cup. This wasn't very hygienic I know but I was never going to tell him, 'eh Gerry do you have to'. Gerry was good bloke to know and he was a fanatical Evertonian and his family lived above the Belle Vue pub opposite the badminton club.

Now there's a memory unlocked. Many a weekend from when I was about sixteen to seventeen, we would have a lock in at the Belle Vue and I remember Derek and me falling out at dawn bleary eyed and drunk after listening to the Juke Box which was be free all night. Gerry's family were always celebrating something or other and a few years on I remember the bar staff laughing when I told her I was eighteen, knowing I'd been a regular for a few years!

I also remember taking this girl called Pauline to the Belle Vue one time on a date, it wasn't exactly what one would call a chic joint, a place to impress but I didn't fancy being knocked back at another pub. I drank a pint of lager and Pauline had lime and soda, I probably remember this because it was the cheapest drink served if you discount water of course, which should be free and on this occasion it didn't seem appropriate of me to ask Pauline to get a round in; I know I'm such a gent.

I went out with Pauline for a few weeks, we met at badminton but hit it off at a party at the Huyton Suites and I remember dancing to Paul Young's track, *'Wherever I Lay My Hat (That's My Home)'* with her, yes,

another slowie memory. Pauline was an attractive red head, my first and only red headed girlfriend, not that I was put off by the flaming haired type, no, on the contrary, this is just a fact.
I also remember Pauline as being a determined girl, she lived in Tuebrook and I would visit her at her house most evenings, which is something I tended to do with most girlfriends when I was a teenager. See I never took girls back to my home as we only had one big through room and someone was always home and my bedroom, not that I ever imagined saying to Mum and Dad, 'don't mind me I'm just popping upstairs for a snog', was too cold in any event and usually untidy with yesterdays clothes, undies and socks on the floor.
I had a cheap Formica wardrobe with drawers and a mirror panel but most of the time I would use my 'floordrobe' to store my clothes because putting away clothes was seemingly too arduous and a time consuming task, I was a lazy bugger!
I remember Derek going out with Pauline's friend, a girl called Kate from the club but he admitted to fancying Pauline in the sauna one day and he asked me if I wanted to swap girlfriends. Don't get me wrong Kate was nice too but I was happy seeing Pauline and in any case Derek should have thought about Kate's feelings so I told him to get lost.
After the sauna we would make our way to the bar upstairs for a bitter shandy or a pint of orange and lemonade with ice, as we would be gasping for a drink and we would play pool for a few hours whilst listening to the jukebox.
A few years later the owner of the badminton club expanded his business empire and he opened a nightclub next door to the badminton club called Winston's. The theme was John Lennon as Winston was his middle name and the place had brooding and smiling pictures of Lennon on every wall. Mike, the coach, managed the place for a while, he lived above the club with his girlfriend and we'd play badminton on a Sunday night then we would all pop over to Winston's.
These were halcyon days as far as I'm concerned and the track that springs to mind when I think of these times is *'West End Girls'* by the 'Pet Shop Boys'. Winston's has a significant place in my heart equal to the Rec and Dunny's and most weekends we would attend the club and I have lots of memories cascading round my head about Winston's and I shall return to this later when I talk more about Brad.
I also played badminton for St Dunstan's Church in the church hall, yes where Dunny's disco took place, with huge pillars that ran down the outside of the court. Ray, the local vicar, or the Vic as we called him, the person I spoke too after we were robbed, started the club when he

moved in and he was a good player, a lefty, one of life's gems.

I must pause again at this point, sorry about my wavering prose but I need to talk about the Vic but before I do, do you remember the track '*Is Vic There*'. Whenever I think of the Vic for transparent reasons I think of this track and remaining true to my tendency to research everything at the moment, it might be of interest to know that this track was by the New Wave band Department S. So there you go, now you know.

If you're lucky you sometimes come across people in life who are that significant that they have shaped who you later become, they are supportive, understanding and they unconditionally instil ambition and drive. Well the Vic holds that distinction for me.

Unlike most members of the clergy that I came across as a kid, be them Catholic or Protestant, the Vic did so much for the community and for us kids, wishing to enhance our dour lives with opportunity to see life away from Edge Hill. Edge Hill may not have been suffering from famine or shot to pieces through the rigours of war but the Vic was seemingly on a mission to enrich our inner city lives and the only bad thing about him was he supported Manchester United but he tended to keep that to himself.

As well as playing badminton with the Vic and promoting sport and a healthy lifestyle, he would often take a gang of us on various holidays and weekends away. The Vic would hire a mini bus and would organise everything from where we would stay to the food we would eat and he was always raising money.

He wouldn't charge us either, he knew most of us would have struggled to pay and I remember going on several fun packed trips to Cornwall, Devon and North Wales. The Vic always knew someone who had a house to rent and on other occasions we would stay in Youth Hostels and would walk from town to town in our hiking boots that Vic also acquired for us.

Once we walked the North Cornish coast from Boscastle, later made famous for being flooded, to Lands End. We had such fun walking in the summer heat singing songs, learning to read maps but mostly larking around but a bit of a shameful one this. See, Grant and Alan had figured out how to 'wire' slot machines for free credits using a knitting wire and I remember them doing this a lot in Cornwall.

The Vic had gotten wind of this and he would cast a disapproving look at Alan and Grant but one day he came into our room and asked for their help. He wanted a shower but to do so he needed a ten pence piece for the machine, this was hostelling after all and the Vic didn't have any change. The Vic turned away and said 'I'd really appreciate it if someone could put a ten pence piece in the machine', Grant understood the hidden meaning and he 'wired' the shower with enough credit to shower all night long! Actually there's a track *'All Night Long'* by Lionel Richie that was probably out around the same time.

We stayed in this Youth Hostel in Newquay and the games room had a sit down space invader game. Alan wired the game and left dozens of credits for us to entertain ourselves and I would picture the proprietor thinking, as he emptied the machine, hang on those scouse kids were never off this, where's the bloody money? The proprietor had been 'ad off', I know this is shameful and is it any wonder why we get such a bad name and I went to Newquay some years later with the family and I was half tempted to apologise to the current owner but we are talking decades later. Dear Father please forgive me for I have sinned....

Seeking penance after saying three Hail Mary's and four Our Father's let me tell you about Devon and Cheddar Gauge. This is such a breathtakingly beautiful part of the county leaving one in awe and a sore neck as you peer out of the window at the sheer rock face on either side of the road that meanders through this natural masterpiece. I remember having cream scones and tea in this small town built into the hillside, felt very cultured, then we went for a walk through an assortment of deep caverns admiring the incredible stalagmites and stalactites on the way. The Vic then spotted an advertisement inviting any budding explorers to travel deeper into the cave system with a guide and before too long we were all dressed in overalls and boots, wearing safety helmets with lights on the front like my bike light!

This was an amazing experience and I remember descending further and further into the dark and damp caves believing we were below ground to be told we had moved upwards into the mountain. At one point we walked to this end of this cavern stopping at a 'thin end of the wedge' shaped corner and the guide asked if anyone could fathom the way out of this cavern. We had no idea then he pointed to the floor to a small hole barely wide enough for me let alone the Vic and with some trepidation we all took turns and squeezed through head first.

This was not a place for anyone who dislikes closed spaces and it felt like the cave had actually given birth to you as you slid down this slimy six-foot hole popping out into the arms of another guide. Half expected someone to cut the umbilicus cord and thankfully the Vic managed to get through his birthing experience but with the help of forceps me thinks!

On the same trip I remember staying in the popular resort of Minehead and I got talking to this older woman in a pub, can't recall how or her

name to my shame, read on but she was with her boyfriend and he was a manager at Butlins.
I must have told her that I would be interested in working at Butlins during the summer months, remember I had been to Butlins with my Mum and Dad and she took my name and address to send me an application form but then she began writing to me.
I must have been about sixteen and we became pen pals, do kids still do that? The letters became progressively saucier, she'd split up from her boyfriend by then and I would talk to her on a phone at Paddington Comp, which I'll talk about in a bit but one Wednesday night she suggested I visit her for the weekend.
I was always doing mad things without much thought so I jumped a National Express Coach again on the Saturday and made my way south to exotic Devon arriving teatime.
This is about a year after I had met her and my memory of her was feint, we never sent each other photographs, so when she met me at the bus station I was pleasantly surprised, she looked very attractive but clearly older than me by some years. I stayed with her for the weekend, I had ten pounds spending money, she liked Phil Collins, *'In the Air Tonight'* was her favourite track, we ate fish and chips, played pool, walked along the beach, all good fun despite the music she played.
I returned home on the Sunday and went in search of my mates on the High Street and we never wrote or talked to each other again which is strange really as I had a fantastic time but I shan't divulge why but lets just say I should have caught the train home and not the coach! I can recollect what meal I had, her musical tastes but not her name.
I can't recall the places we visited, probably because I couldn't pronounce most of them but we also stayed in holiday homes dotted around North Wales.
The Vic would spread the word that he was organizing a weekend trip away and we'd put our names down. There were lots of different kids and adults who attended these trips so sometimes we would have the use of two min buses but the regular participants would be me, Alan, Grant, Brad, Derek, Sharon and June. Alan's Dad attended sometimes as he helped out at St Dunstan's and I remember Don having a good old laugh at my expense but no hard feelings, as this is a funny if not embarrassing story.
See we stayed in this house in the middle of nowhere, your quintessential Welsh village with a dozen or so stone cottages, a post office, a Spar supermarket, always a Spar, a Church or course and an old man boozer.

This was your classic North Wales pub where everyone reverts to Welsh as soon as a stranger enters the establishment and all enquiring eyes stare at you trying to work out why you had stumbled into this particular pub and should we let you leave unharmed or sober.

Let me explain further. The soundtrack to this trip was Heaven 17's album *'Penthouse and Pavement'*, a very underestimated album in my view and we prised every track particularly *'the Height of the Fighting'* and the brilliant *'We Play to Win'*. Grant and me were regular club devotees by then. Play to Win would be played in scene two and we would act all mysterious and enigmatic when truth is, we probably looked pubescent, spotty and odd!

Someone had copied the album to a cassette and we insisted on the Vic playing it in the minibus on the way, he obliged, and on the way home, must have driven him nuts but I guess that's what kids are like, they can play tracks repeatedly until every word and note is memorized and can still be recalled decades later. Strange that, but ask me to do long division and I simply can't remember and as for my grammar, well enough said.

So scene duly set. Grant and me decided to put on our finery to wow the locals with our contemporary New Romantic look. I walked in thinking I looked sensational in my white frilly shirt and matching white canvas trousers, I had black suede tukka 'elf like' boots but the piece de resistance was my purple scarf fastened loosely around my neck.

I had accessorised my outfit, I had a crush on Sharon and I really wanted to impress her with my sophistication and maturity. She must have thought I looked a right twerp!

Thankfully Sharon and June were running late that night but Don and the Vic were already at the pub supping a pint of Guinness. The door opens, Don looks up, white froth on his top lip, he took one look at me and exclaimed, 'look who's just walked in, it's Tom Mix.' I'd never heard of Tom but the regulars had it seems and I later learned that this was a cowboy from the black and white big screen era, when cowboys wore pristine white hats and scarfs!

I felt mortified, I was ambushed by a group of strangers who sounded equally strange, I looked around for an escape route and everyone, to a man and his Welsh-barking dog stared and laughed. I spun round on the heels of my elfin boots as if I had an urgent appointment somewhere, probably needed to saddle my horse, I was ready to shoot from the hip, to come back at Don with a pistol firing and equally funny quip to win people over, but sadly I was left feeling mute, I fired blanks.

Grant was behind me, he had been spared this verbal assault, he also had a scarf and I barged past him to sounds of laughter, to sit in the cottage with the other kids and the cassette. Still if I can make people laugh then no harm done, all's happy in my world.
Another memorable trip was when Alan, Brad, the Vic and me went on a charity walk in the Yorkshire Dales. We stayed in a house in Kirby Lonsdale and I remember Brad and me trying hopelessly to chat up some local girls in the square. Brad used the classic line, 'eh girl what time is it' to strike up a conversation, surly she'd fancy one with such wit. Sadly this wasn't the case, she said nothing but raised her hand like Danny does from the film Grease and pointed high above Brad's head to this huge clock tower behind him.
So funny, I creased with laughter and I've been to Kirby Lonsdale recently and I couldn't help but smile to myself as the clock tower still stands tall and proud informing its townsfolk the time and warning fair maidens from talking to strange scousers. A lesson learnt Brad but God loves a 'tryer' as they say, you weren't alone?
Putting asides Brad's antics, we did the three peaks a few miles away over twelve hours clocking in and off at the end at some café. I think we covered about twenty-six miles in total and I remember Alan tip-toeing over this wet bog mid way with a sheep's skeleton immersed in it! Remember Alan was smaller than me and also Brad so together we thought of a strategy and decided to give it a good run and jump but we fell and sank into the bog.
We sank deeper and deeper and just like Lady Godiva, Brad reached out with his camera shouting save the pictures, its proof we did the walk. There's a thought, kids today can take instant pictures on their phone that they can email, edit and delete there and then whereas we had a wind on camera with twenty four or thirty six snaps not knowing what you had taken until processed.
Our instamatic camera was thankfully saved, Alan and the Vic had to pull us out and we were covered in mud from head to toe. In fact Brad did the rest of the walk in his long johns as I recall. The walk was so tiring but we were spritely teenagers and I remember running the last leg to finish first at the café.
I told Neil about this walk a few times over the years and the fun we had so we decided to do it again in the late nineties over a few pints of bitter. Brad wasn't up for it but Alan was, with two of his friends from work. We met at the Salisbury Pub on Lawrence Road and we planned the trip, the Vic had sadly moved to another Parish by this stage and we had no way of knowing how to contact him.

I found us a reasonable bed and breakfast near the walk and on the second night, the eve of our walk we downed one too many pints and Alan and his mates were truly hung-over, they baled out. Neil and me would not be outdone by mere alcohol so we made our way to the café and clocked in, we were made of sterner things. The owner gave us a look of 'I really hope you guys know what you're doing' as it was wet and cloudy and people were retuning to the café muttering to themselves that it was far too rainy and dangerous.

We did the walk in spite of this and what an adventure was had. We tried to follow a map but got lost and veered off the walk by some miles. Neil's fault I might add as he was convinced he knew how to read a compass. Then we lost the map in a gust of wind only for it to be handed in at the bed and breakfast, trusting folk those Yorkshire lot.

We buddied up with this group of athletic looking policemen on a charity walk that had caught us up after the second peak by this viaduct where we had a much-needed burger and a cuppa from this van in the middle of nowhere!

The weather was awful and night was setting in as we approached the final hill, Wernside I think. We all looked at each other and made a unanimous decision to plough ahead as we had come this far and up we climbed. This was a bad idea, the wind was very strong and the policemen lost their map to a fierce gust at the top. It was blowing a gale and visibility was about ten yards, I'm not exaggerating and we walked around the top of the hill trying to figure out which way was down as there was no obvious path signalling our escape route.

Now I was the only one who had actually done the walk, granted it was some years later and I told everyone to follow my homing pigeon instinct but my reasoning fell on deaf ears, maybe they couldn't hear me over the wind or understand my accent and everyone walked the opposite way. Although I knew this was wrong, Neil and me decided to stick with our new mates for safety in numbers reasons; we were simply exhausted by this stage.

We kept walking or in my case stumbling down as my weak ankles caused by twisting on the badminton court, had gone, hoping to find a house to ask for directions. We did in the end and I remember knocking at this farm house door in the middle of nowhere trying not to sound too scouse thinking I'd scare the living daylights out of them as it was nearly dark. The owner wasn't at all put out as it happens, probably used to hikers but probably not scousers who had lost their way and he said follow the track lad and you will find a small town.

I shouted ahead and they all followed me this time and we eventually stumbled into this pub.
Neil bought me a double whiskey, straight of course and straight to the head and when we had composed ourselves we phoned Alan after first finding out the number of the bed and breakfast and what town we were actually in. This in itself was a mission and a half and oh to have the 'I phone' back then.
Alan had a map thankfully and he drove out to rescue us, it took him well over an hour, that's how far we had veered off the walk and Alan said he thought we had died and had already began to think of a fitting eulogy.
Alan had a shiny new escort car and I sat in the back on my own. I was probably suffering from shock but not being a very good traveller like I have alluded too throughout this book and suffering for years with motion sickness, I felt really sick, not helped by all the bends the car was taking as it wormed its way round hill after hill.
I tried to open Alan's window, honest, but it only went half way down, a child safety thing, he was on to his second child by then with Kayleigh, Mark, my godson and I was sick everywhere. Next day I got up early, I felt terrible and ashamed and with my Swiss Army penknife I did my best to clean up my mess and sprayed a whole bottle of deodorant around the interior. Sorry but thanks Alan for coming to our rescue.
In a way I have the Vic to thank for all this, not the sick bit of course, as he gave us kids an opportunity to experience life away from the city but what really impressed me about the Vic was that he never preached or used this as an opportunity to convert the likes of me to become an Anglican. The Vic was just a kind altruistic man and I really respected Ray and all he did for the community, a legend as far as I'm concerned. Really hope he's doing okay and in good health.
I did attend Christmas Mass one year at St Dunstan's, sorry Father whatever your name was, based on my respect for the Vic and I was very drunk as I had been out up the High Street.
I was with Brad and I knew most of the people including the alter servers when the Vicar, as is the custom in the Catholic Mass too, invited the Anglican congregation to shake hands with the people around you to the words 'peace be with you'. Well, I took this a bit further and decided to walk onto the alter and I insisted on shaking hands with everyone much to the amusement of the Vic who was grinning from ear to ear probably thinking 'you soft drunken apeth'.
At the same Mass I went up for Holy Communion and unlike in the Catholic Church at the time I took the 'blood of Christ' in the form of

wine. Now I really didn't need any more alcohol but the reason why I remember all this was to be revealed when I returned to my pew. When I knelt down I revealed to the congregation that my shoes cost £19.99 as I had left the tag on the soles and Joey and his family were laughing and ribbed me about how good value my shoes were.

Once again back to badminton and other teammates who played for Dunny's. They included Alan, Gary with the moustache, the aforementioned Sharon, Elaine, who smoked, June and Jimmy a Chinese bloke who always seemed to have top racquets from Hong Kong. We'd practice on a Sunday and Thursday evening; playing matches all over Liverpool in other cramped church halls, where the court line would sometimes run along the radiator.

Sharon would pick me and Alan up which was a thrill because we could sit and talk on the way. I remember playing twenty-four hours of badminton with the team for charity on a few occasions, taking turns to catch some shuteye in sleeping bags on the side on the parquetted floor. Not sure if we raised a lot of money or got much sleep as I'd talk to Sharon and June most of the night but good fun.

This bloke called Danny came to our club and he was a decent badminton player, he played in the top division. He wore tattered and torn jumpers and shirts, he was famed for them and he coached Alan and me and taught me so much about the game. Years later Danny became a support worker in a team I managed and I thanked him for being a person who had been significant in those early days; I embarrassed him but that's the truth Danny, you were a good mentor.

Like I said before I had a huge teenage hormone induced crush on Sharon who was about five years older than me, a dark haired petite but fully developed busty woman if you catch my drift. She came on the trips with the Vic I mentioned before and she knew I was mad about her and she would flirt with me but looking back I think she actually loved the adulation and she certainly flirted back. Whenever I hear the track '*See You*' by Depeche Mode I think of Sharon and my teenage crush.

I was about sixteen and we developed a close friendship and I would follow her round 'gooey eyed' in my teenage uncomfortable way wanting to strike up a conversation.

Sharon and I would sometimes go to Huyton baths together, she had a yellow mini metro and she'd pick me up from my house and I would hope the neighbours were twitching behind their curtains! I wanted them to all talk about me.

I think Sharon preferred Huyton as it was away from enquiring eyes but I didn't care as it was like a day out for me, she was probably just going for the exercise. I would run into the changing rooms but no matter how fast I got undressed Sharon always managed to get into the pool before me; she knew my jaw would drop at the mere sight of her in her costume so she was sparing my blushes. We'd splash and frolic around in the shallow end and then we'd have hot chocolate, a drink surly designed for the baths, in the café and with dripping hair.

We'd sometimes bump into Sharon and June on nights out, although thinking back was this coincidental, who knows but one thing's for certain they were both terrible teases. Me, Grant, Neil and Derek would be eyeing up other girls, girls of a similar age or slightly older, sometimes a lot older in my case, planning how or when to make a move, using all our techniques polished at Dunny's disco, but often Sharon and June would grab one of us by the hand dragging us onto the dance floor.

Perhaps they were starved of attention, not sure why as they were good looking, but they would dance closer and closer and I would feel them gyrate their hips in tune to the music against my groin area, I nearly blew the train hooter on a few occasions I can tell you! All planned me thinks but hey we never complained, as that would have been rude!

I was so into Sharon and I would tell her one day we would kiss and fall madly in love with each other, it was only a matter of time so why resist and she'd play along with my pubescent fantasy. June was in on the fantasy too and she knew I loved this track called '*Summer the First Time*' by Bobby Goldsborough, a track I first heard on the radio. I would talk on my CB and listen to this DJ called Johnny Jason on Radio City's Peaceful Hour under my blanket when I went to bed and into the early hours, hoping someone out there would declare her unyielding love for me by making a request. This was our Radio Atlantic, our Luxemburg, but no one ever did or perhaps I was asleep!

For those of you who have never heard this track, tut, as it is such a classic, as was the very tearful '*Honey*' also by Bobby. It was about this young lad who was willingly seduced by an older more experienced woman and the track builds to a crescendo and the youngster shakes off his teenager angst and watches the sun rise as a man, cue seagulls, violins and waves crashing against the shore for added poignancy. This track told a story that resonated with most adolescent boys as far as I was concerned and it became our song, our tune. June found it in some junk shop and bought it for me signed from Sharon and June with a kiss but later Tracy took it to the Rec disco and defaced it.

My infatuation was all good fun and when I was about seventeen I bumped into Sharon on New Years Eve, she was very drunk and with

Elaine. I was blown away, she actually leant forward and asked me for a kiss right there on this wasteland, now there's a track title and as our lips met I was thinking yes finally after all these years of playing badminton, stooping into her mini metro and racing into the swimming baths I would get my chance but then my sensible 'this cant be right' conscience took over.

See, I so wanted to kiss Sharon, make no bones about that but it didn't feel right kissing the woman of my nocturnal *'Sweat Dreams'* as Annie would say but not when Sharon was so drunk or maybe it was because I was sober, who knows but I did the honourable thing and I pulled away and gave her a big sensible hug, the three second kind befitting of a good friend and not a possible lover. Why oh why I would question many a time for years later as I wasn't normally so restrained or chivalrous!

I keep drifting away from badminton, oh yes where was I up too? Ready for a boast. I won the Liverpool Youth Association cup in singles on two occasions and I twice represented Liverpool at Nottingham University. Happy days and for years I would tell people that I was Liverpool's champion when in reality the competition wasn't that prestigious but I dined out on that story many a time.

Before I go any further I need to say a humungous thank you to two teachers from Paddington Comp, aka Paddy Comp, namely Geoff and Glynn. They ran a badminton club out of Paddy without fuss for many years and we started going on a Wednesday and a Friday night. There was me, Derek, Neil, Brad sometimes, Brad's brother Seb, Alan, Grant, the aforementioned Sharon and June and many others who wanted to try out this sport.

Geoff and Glynn were fantastic and affable men, always happy to help out and they would take us to tournaments and matches across the city. They became significant adults in my life just like the Vic, Geoff lived by Carmill Dam and when I was a painter some years later I decorated his gutters. The last time I saw Glynn was a few years back at Don's funeral, he wasn't a well man and said he was moving to North Wales and I suspect he may not be alive as I write these words. Eternal peace to you Glynn and thanks.

At Paddy we became friends with older lads who attended or should I say survived Paddy Comp as kids and these include Paul, Lynn, Geoff, Tony, Sandra and Peter. Paddy was a very rough school and stories were spoken of teachers being bullied by the kids and kids having their heads flushed down the loos. It sounded very tribal and made my school sound like a kindergarten.

Paul was a very funny and an intelligent man who had a degree in something or other but was unemployed when we first met him. He'd proudly wear ripped shirts and battered converse baseball boots as a working class badge of honour and was a profound socialist at heart. Some years later he ended up working in insurance and he ended up wearing suits, never lost his wit though. The crew moved to the Royal Liver Insurance building where Paul worked to play badminton and they still play together till this day and for a few years I played with them too.

Both Paul and Geoff were into Karate as they needed to survive at Paddy and they would show us various moves in the changing rooms where all the banter took place. You wouldn't think so to look at them but they had all the moves particularly Paul, his hands were like lightening speed and he was 'fit as a fiddle'.

Take Geoff for example, he was and still is a quiet unassuming down to earth bloke but one memory I have of Geoff is bumping into him on Cranborne Road one winter night. Geoff didn't live by us you see but he was searching for this lad who had made offensive remarks aimed at his girlfriend Liz, he bided his time, revenge being a dish best served cold and that dark cold night someone leant a valuable lesson in life and good on you Geoff, very chivalrous of you.

I still see Geoff most weeks as he plays at the same club I play at, he brings his son along and his name is Neil, makes one feel so old. Geoff eventually married Liz, a tall woman but not very good at badminton no matter how hard she tried, poor thing, she had no coordination, something ones born with me thinks but a very nice woman.

I don't see Paul these days but Geoff told me recently that Paul has a brain tumour and he's been undergoing treatment but typical of Paul he is being very upbeat about it and told everyone to stay away from the hospital. Hope you get better Paul; you're a top bloke and I looked up to you in a strange way because you were an interesting and entertaining chap but tactically you were left wanting on the court, ha!

Perhaps it's my age but Geoff also told me about this other lad who played footy at Paddy, he was also called Paul and he bumped into him recently in a wheelchair. Apparently in 1989 Paul had a car accident and is now paralysed from the neck down; he was the life and soul of the changing rooms and very active, what an absolutely horrible, horrible situation that one can never imagine such a thing ever happening. Puts life into perspective doesn't it?

Tony was a bit of a 'geezer' he became a Deejay some years later and I remember going to this nightclub called Flintlocks with him on a few occasions. Tony was a black lad and back then Flintlocks had a reputation of being a place for black kids and I remember loving the soul music being played and the atmosphere was electric, we had a great time. I met Tony recently in Morrison's of all places and after giving each other the 'do I know you stare', he thought I had attended Paddy school; we stopped and had a chat about Paddy and what people were up too. He looked well and it was lovely 'catching up' with Tony and he remembered our nights out on the town!

Pausing a beat, I have yet another gem in my shameful back catalogue of bright light music and although this track appeared in the sixties it reminds me of wanting to go out to Town to bars and clubs like Flintlocks, *'Downtown'* by Petula Clarke. I swear I can see the neon lights and hear the traffic when Ms Clarke sings and this track always makes me feel good and melts away any lingering sadness! The best of guilty pleasures so a certain addition to my list!

Peter was a British Pakistani bloke and he married Sandra who was Chinese, if ever there was an amazing mix of cultures and heritage then there you have it. I remember going to Peter's family business, a wholesaler that sold all manner of things, before Christmas 1983 and leaving with 'discounted' presents for my family. He was a really funny bloke Peter with a dry sense of humour and very proud of his heritage; I wonder how he's doing? Lynn was a lovely kind hearted woman and I remember Derek having the hot's for her but we all did in truth. Kieran still has a teddy bought by my mates from Paddy when he was born and he calls it 'Bo Bo's' because he looks like he's sleeping.

Now all this talk about Paddy has got me thinking about a girl I met at Rotters and the track *'Inside Out'* by 'Odyssey'. I was aged sixteen and I had danced to this track with this girl and we ended up 'snogging' on the dance floor. Seemingly my trio of questions worked that night!

The following week the girl turns up at Paddy to play a match against my team. She told me she played badminton but this was a coincidental encounter but a welcome sight.

My partner and I played her and her partner and after the match it is customary to shake hands at the end with your opponent but for some reason I kissed the girl on the lips. The rest of the club was watching the match and I could feel their enquiring eyes as I left the court thinking, 'eh Dave that's a bit familiar of you' and not keeping to the rules on etiquette! I didn't care, it was quite amusing actually and the girl took it all in good fun and we retreated to have a drink of orange squash at the side.

Now back to my boast. The first time I represented Liverpool in Nottingham I met this girl called Kerry, who was also playing for Liverpool. She was a pretty girl with flowing strawberry blonde locks; way out of my league I thought and her accent was less abrasive than girls I knew. She was of the posh type.
At night I put on my finest clothes and I attended a disco for all the participants and I stood on my lonesome watching the crowd wishing I had my mates nearby to help me.
I remember these black kids from London or somewhere down south if their accents were anything to go by, making a move on Kerry. She looked like she needed rescuing but I held back, then the track *'Hello'* by Lionel Richie came on, she politely barged past them grabbed my hand and said dance with me, so together we swayed and I still think of her whenever I hear Hello, I wonder whatever happened to her but what a naff video?
We started seeing each other but the relationship never really blossomed. Let me explain why. Kerry was from Maghull in North Merseyside, a smart area for those not acquainted with Merseyside, hence the accent and a zillion miles away as far as I was concerned. Her Dad was a bank manager so they had cash, not that I'm implying that he stole from the safe; no, but the house was huge with an immaculate garden on three sides and they had two cars, yes two cars! In contrast I lived in a two bed terraced house squashed into a street of similar houses, some with fake stone cladding. It was never going to work!
Our phone was cut off so I would talk to Kerry by payphone most nights pushing ten pence pieces into the hungry machine and we'd arrange to meet at the weekend. Where's Alan's wire when you needed it?
I remember bussing it to town to catch a train with a saveaway ticket, a ticket that allowed you to jump on and off public transport. I was always thinking about saving money so I would try and avoid scraping off the silver box to activate the saveaway, unless a sneaky conductor confronted me. I did this for weeks at a time as money was always tight but once a scally always a scally.
Kerry's Mum was very nice, as were her sisters and she would welcome me into her home and make me sandwiches and cakes, she'd put on a bit of a spread! Seb, Joey and Brad's older brother, had a mate, can't recall his name but he had bad acne and a car and the three of us would drive out to Maghull to play badminton at Kerry's club in Deyes High School. We'd play mixed doubles together, her in her short skirt, me in my sweaty white shorts, really, what did she see in me?

One sunny Saturday her Dad suggested we went to Southport Fair, I looked embarrassed, as I knew I was skint but he took me aside and gave me a five-pound note. I was always happy to return home on the train, never did though as her Dad would give me a lift, some miles I may add, so he knew the area I lived in but he never judged me or discouraged Kerry from seeing me. This was a real kind insightful gesture and he understood that I didn't have the cash to treat his daughter to the fair and I guess he was saving my blushes.

Just thinking why didn't he give the money to Kerry, guess it was a different age when men, or should I say boys, were expected to pay for everything. I never agreed with this concept and always respected girls who at the very least got the last drink at the end of the night like I said before but rumour has it I'm a tight so and so.

Anyhow, five pounds may not sound like a lot of money but it was in 1983 and I remember it being very hot and sunny and me and Kerry going on ride after ride and then sharing salt and vinegar drenched fish and chips on a riverbank. How very romantic again eh, no shorts this time, but it was lovely and I've come to realise that I have a thing for fish and chips, seems to pop up when I think of certain memories of people and here are some interesting facts that I read on 'fake' newspaper would you believe whilst eating fish and chips at a Harry Ramsden's restaurant recently.

In the novel Oliver Twist released in 1838 Charles Dickens refers to fried fish warehouses but the first fish and chip shop appeared in Oldham in 1863. Fish and chips was also the only take away food not to be rationed during the Second World War as it provided affordable ways of adding protein and vitamins to the populous daily diet and you may also wish to know that twenty per cent of takeaway meals served on a Friday are fish and chips. How cool is that, thanks Harry?

Anyway, the utterly brilliant 'Roddy Frame' and his band 'Aztec Camera' were out when I was seeing Kerry and I bought her the album 'Hard Land, Hard Rain' for her sixteenth birthday on the back of her telling me that she liked the track *'Oblivious'* which peaked at a paltry number eighteen.

I wonder if Kerry's still got the album, I suspect not but it was an excellent album and being forever frugal I remember taping it on my cassette player before passing it on to Kerry in silver wrapping paper. Seemed daft not too.

While I think on, I also like *'We Could Send Letters'* and *'Walk Out to Winter'* by Mr Frame et al and recently I went to see him at this small intimate concert in Liverpool. He's really good live should you ever get the chance to see him and a very talented artist with an impressive back catalogue, why he was never huge still baffles me. Keep gigging Roddy, one day your time will come again?

Anyway let's go back in time. One night Kerry and I went for a walk down a long county lane to a pub at the top a hill; my mate in work who lived in Maghull as a child, worked out this may have been the Red House. His name is Ste and he knew Kerry and he told me he nearly went out with her before me!

Anyhow, I bought a pint and half of lager and lime, it felt rural, it had a real wood fire and it felt like a different world, which it was and I felt very self-conscious and out of place. Why was I so self-conscious with image back then, simple really, I was a teenager and I remember thinking one-day lad, one day!

As a result of all my working class insecurities I eventually drifted away from Kerry, as I was mindful to the fact that we were poles apart with respect to our different cultures and social class. Not that she was snooty or that I was ever made to feel unwelcomed by her family, on the contrary like I said, but one day me and Kerry were walking along the canal, it was a lovely sunny day again, it was always sunny in Maghull and she pointed at this house and said my Granddad lives there.

Then she commented on how small the house was; I squirmed inside as the house was certainly smaller than its bespoke peers but was way larger than my house.

I was never ashamed of my roots before you say anything and I know this was an innocent throw away comment by Kerry but our fate was sealed from that point as I could never imagine taking Kerry to meet my folks, to discover that my Dad was working on the side to make ends meat, to see my dusty grimy area, terraced house after terraced house and certainly no canals or country pubs, but most of all to see how cramped and cold our house was. Shame really but there you have it.

We would speak on the phone sometimes for weeks later as we parted on good terms and she told me she was into heavy metal music, so that was the end of that, I couldn't stand long hair and rock music!

Didn't stop me trying again a year later back in Nottingham mind you but Kerry was standoffish this time, I hope I hadn't hurt her feelings but I felt ashamed, I never returned a book she leant me. See, not being on the phone had one and only one advantage, if ever I wanted a relationship to end I would simply let time pass without calling and I realise this is a terrible thing to do but I hated ending relationships, I still do and I was a coward.

'*There She Goes*' is a great track by 'The La's' or is that the 'Lads' and Kerry did, so feeling rejected I consoled myself by chatting up this girl from Devon, I never thought to ask if she's squeezed through any cavernous holes, well what else was I suppose to do, the music, the lights but no Richie this time, that would have been too weird?

Chapter Fourteen

Billy The Mountain...

So now lets think of some defining memories about Q. Neil Q, his real name and as you might have guessed he's still my best mate, the lad famed around our way for having blond streaks above his ears.
Yes Neil was and has always been an individual both in personality and his political ideology, he leans more to the right than me and does not tolerate idleness or scroungers believing if him and his Mum can carve out a good life through adversity and hardship then anyone can.
We are politically poles apart with disparaging ideological views that seem to be converging as we get older strangely enough but he's my forever mate and always around when I need him and I thank him for that and I hope he thinks the same of me even though I sometimes say the wrong thing, its just my way.
So when did we first meet. I think I must have been about twelve when Neil moved into our area and he would sometimes hang out with my mates and me on the corner of the Spofforth Pub and we become 'bezzie' mates along the way.
Strange memory this but Neil introduced me to small circle pizzas, basically a tomato sauce coated pizza bed sprinkled with thinly grated cheese. Very tasty and full of E's no doubt but back then we didn't care or know in any case!
One day I was at Neil's house, must have been lunchtime as he made me a quick snack, he threw these small pizzas into the oven and they were delicious like I said and Neil told me recently that he recalls his Mum shouting at him as we had only gone and eaten that nights dinner. Sorry Freda.
Neil had this big dog, a big brown coloured dog, a cross breed with a Great Dane and its name was Bruno. His Mum worked at Plessey's on Edge Lane and we'd hang out at Neil's sometimes as he didn't have any annoying sisters and we'd listen to music on his impressive futuristic hi fi system. I remember it having various stacks stood on small silver

pillars; bright flashing equalizer lights, still can't fathom out what they did and an array of fancy knobs.

I always thought Neil was lucky but truth was his Mum was a proud hard working single parent who ensured that her and her son had a good life. Her attitude and resilience in the face of adversity certainly rubbed off on Neil.

Neil was into Japan, the band that is although we did embrace all things oriental somewhere down the line, I'll let you work that one out for yourself. Neil would model himself on David Sylvian from Japan hence the blonde streaks and he also liked the gothic band Bauhaus but the really nuttiest track in his collection of obscure records was *'Billy the Mountain'* by Frank Zappa, with this tree called *'Ethel'* on the mountains shoulder! Neil would play this track over and over and we thought the lyrics were hilarious and like all tracks that touched a nerve I can still recall some of the words.

Then we have whiskey and how it should be drunk. Neil took me to his Granddads on a few occasions, he lived off Wavertree Road where his family originated from and we went to this local boozer, a real rough place and probably shut down now.

Neil ordered a whiskey but said in a 'now listen lad's I have a lesson in life that needs to pass from generation to generation' voice, 'never add water or ice or even worse, lemonade, to whiskey especially a good old malt, as that would ruin the drink, a terrible sacrilegious act he would say!' Neil, know that to this day I drink whiskey straight because of you and the only thing I put in my whiskey is more whiskey, which links to a great track by the wonderful Felice Brothers, although lemonade with Southern Comfort is tasty but some would say that's not really whiskey is it?

Neil didn't get football like the rest of us, not until he was older that is, a sign of his individualism again and I don't think it was physical enough for him. He played team sports but football was the wrong shape ball as Neil's sport of choice before discovering badminton of course, was rugby or rugger and I think this was on account that he attended the Collegiate and that he had a barrel chest.

Trust Neil to play rugby, even back then he had his sights on moving up the social ladder, I sometimes have to remind him that he comes from Edge Hill originally to bring him down to earth now and again. In fact Neil was actually born closer to the station than me!

Neil lived with his Mum in Bannerman Street, which was about a hundred and fifty yards from my house, a street painted red and white by its residents to celebrate Liverpool getting to the 1974 FA Cup final.

At the far end by Neil's house was the Maincrest perimeter wall with Shankly painted in six-foot letters, he was the manager and every kerbstone was painted alternate red and white, as were the lampposts. How they got away with this beggars belief and I often wondered if any Evertonian's lived in the street and if so was this a democratic decision and how did they bloody cope walking out of their door each morning to be greeted by such abomination and graffiti? Surly the street had some blue noses living there after all we are talking about the inner city of Liverpool?

At the weekend from when I was about fifteen and a half Neil, Grant and me would dress for the occasion and hit town. We were into the New Romantic scene but not the make up that most people think of when they think of New Romantics although I do recall Grant once wearing nail varnish and eyeliner. Think Neil did too, sorry mate and if it's any consolation I confess to using my sister's crimpers and having my hair crimped sadly believing this looked cool!

No, our look leaned more towards alternative individualism with a touch of flamboyant northern city angst. We certainly never looked like Boy George, too flamboyant or Pete Burns, who was actually from Liverpool but we did take inspiration from bands like the Human League and Japan, bands that dressed differently but above all smart. Indeed Grant acquired a kilt from somewhere after watching Spandau Ballet in their early days but being an Englishman he never braved going bare commando as I recall.

While I think on, we once attended this party in Garston, a friend of Alan's I think from school. I was about fourteen and I remember fancying this girl that looked really contemporary for the time. She was dressed as a punk with hair that looked like she hadn't combed it in days in honour of Robert Smith from the Cure, her name was Donna and I wanted to get to know her. I wasn't so hip in my Pepe jeans and Le Coq Sportif T shirt and my stomach turned, but I was brave and after minutes of should I or shouldn't I inner talk, beads forming on my brow, I asked her for a slow dance to '*Reunited*' by Peaches and Herb.

I know her a punk too. My mates just stared aghast at me but jealous me thinks and I proudly swayed along to the music with my face buried in her neck, chewing on her hair thinking is this what they call necking? Never went anywhere though, think we kissed, one of life's encounters but two things remind me of this girl, firstly Grant ended up seeing her for a few weeks after my brief encounter and the fact that she worked on a Saturday at the Probe Music shop on Matthew Street in town.

Now this was such a cool thing at the time as it was in the seventies when punk was at his peak, the place to be seen, and the place to buy records and to check out the latest fashion. The person who stood out the most was none other than Pete Burns before his spin me round fame, he always looked ahead of his time, although I do think he's overdone the individualism thing, have you seen the state of him now. What's with the lips?

Oh another memory, at the end of the party we decided to catch the bus home but missed the last bus, but thankfully Dad had a Vauxhall Viva car and he came and picked us up. I had to find a phone box and I phoned Doreen who ran down to my house to get my Mum. This was how I communicated home for years whenever in a jam or staying out all night, if I bothered at all as the phone was switched off. How times have changed.

On the subject of parties, some would say the '*Art of Parties*', I remember Grant's sixteenth birthday party at his house. The usual crowd bopped away and I remember it being a really good night, 'bring a bottle' was the norm and the Woodpecker Cider flowed to the sounds of Depeche Mode, Japan and the Human League. Neil will always remember this party as he stumbled and fell backwards and put his elbow through Grants glass panelled kitchen door. There was blood everywhere. Still, Lesley and Anne, who ill come to in a bit, nursed Neil in the bathroom, I still think Q did this for attention and all that was missing was a couple of nurse's uniforms but that was Q for you, always the opportunist! Grant was less impressed I have to say as he was in a right panic; he knew he was in for the high jump when his Mum and Dad came home.

This has got me thinking about my sixteenth birthday party. Mum and Dad let me celebrate by having a party at home, it wasn't as good as Grants party and I got predictably drunk as I recall and my puerile behaviour resulted in me head butting the bathroom door mid pogo causing an indentation. It was high up so had to be me as I was probably the tallest and thankfully it wasn't a solid door. I ended up polyfilling the damage some months later.

Neil and I would go round junk shops such as 69A on Renshaw Street, looking for weird gear to wear at the weekend. My favourite outfit of all time began with a musty black tuxedo jacket! I was copying Neil to be honest, as he had the same getup and I accessorized with big baggy black trousers, Dad's waistcoat from his black suit. I bought a dickey bow and a turned up white shirt, the kind Dracula would wear and the look was rounded off with Chinese slippers, the kind you see in Kung Fu movies. I bought them from China Town, very painful if you stood on a stone and no good to play footy in but conversely the best shoes ever to dance in. I thought I was the dog's bollocks in my attire, so wished I'd taken a picture!

On the subject of Chinese slippers another unexpected memory has just popped into my head. One hot summer day Neil, my Mum, my sisters and me went to Alton Towers Theme Park near Stoke. Mum made sandwiches and we had beef Monster Munch and we caught a coach from Picton Clock. Can't imagine how this happened or how I remember the crisps as I wasn't accustomed to going anywhere with my family by this age but we ended up having a good day. Neil and me went off on our own and I remember talking to these girls on the boating lake and said girls taking the mickey out of Neil and me for wearing the slippers. No sense of style, them not me!

I also remember queuing for rides. At the time the 'Corkscrew' had just opened and kids at school would speak of this amazing spinning ride that turned you upside down in your seat. This was the next generation when it comes to roller coaster rides and we just had to have a go. I remember standing in the queue with Neil next to signs informing you that you had one hour and thirty minutes to wait and we thought this was surly a mistake.

One hour thirty numbingly boring minutes later we fastened ourselves into our seats taking care to turn our toes up so as our slippers would stay on, we were off for a breath-taking thirty odd seconds ride. Was it really worth it other than to boast you'd survived?

Having been to Florida on several occasions I can see that roller coasters have evolved and the Corkscrew seems so tame in comparison. I wonder if they still have the signs, probably not and I'm guessing this is now viewed as a kiddies ride and people can jump on and off with no queuing?

Now before I tell you more about some of our exploits let me describe my hair. Now I've had many haircuts that can now be found in humorous birthday cards in card shops, I even had a perm once, I know typical scouser but I wanted to look like the lead singer from this group called Blancmange but it looked awful. My Mum's mate's daughter cut it, her name was Rita and she was nice looking, she looked like Susan Ann Sulley from The Human League, so I guess this is why I never paid much attention to what she was doing to my hair and why I was such a willing participant.

I regretted the perm as soon as I got home and I tried to straighten it but it ended up looking like a curly side part befitting of a poet laureate. In contrast to this disaster my all time favourite hairstyle was my Phil Oakey cut. See Mr Oakey headed The Human League and I remember when he first appeared on TOTP, no Jeanette this time to distract me; he was very charismatic, he had a certain presence and looked amazing. He had this very distinctive look and I realized I had similar facial features, although younger of course so I modelled myself on him and I grew this fringe that covered my face past my chin.

I would tell the barber to cut my hair into a wedge cut but to leave my fringe and he would look at me dismayed and I often thought should I suggest I only pay half given the barber only cut half of my hair!

This lad called Curly, don't know why he was called Curly as he had straight red hair but I guess that might be the point! Anyway Curly was obsessed with Mr Oakey and his room was adorned with posters and he must have had every one of their records. Curly would say, 'Griff, I want your nose and hair', sounds very gay looking back now but I think it was just jealousy?

We would bump into Curly and his mate Carl when out and about in Wavertree, by the bridge on Picton Road. I remember taking a short cut across the railway tracks over this bridge many times and taking care not to touch the lines as I knew they had thousand of electrical volts running through them.

I can't ever imagine my kids doing something so idiotic and dangerous and the daft thing is after scaling the fence you would have shaved a few seconds off your time but it was the deviant thrill that drove you to take risks not necessary the inner sat nav telling you to cut corners.

I remember attending parties at Carl's house and the place would be heaving and the defining track from said parties was *'Love Plus One'* by 'Haircut One Hundred'. The guitar and brass elements to this track make it a bloody marvellous tune to sing along too with visions of hot sunny days dipping ones toe in the water off some pier, sorry where was I, oh yes this is yet another lyrical gaff of mine. Smiling Mr Heywood sings a line I am forbidden to repeat but all I'm saying is have a listen, my deceiving half covered wedge haircut ears take in, 'its down to the lay café.

Sorry about this but again another memory of a girl. Neil was with this girl called Pam; one of my ex's I may add and Grant also went out with her for a few months. She had a sister called Jane and about a year ago I sat in the waiting room at Childwall College on Queens Drive and you know when you look at someone's eyes and they look familiar. Well Pam and Jane were sat there with this kid who I assume was one of their son's. I didn't let on though; they last saw me when I had a fringe.

So were at this party and this girl with long blonde hair from Garston, asked me for a dance, no not Donna, she wasn't a punk, so I obliged and we were hitting it off and she told me she was into heavy music! Another dilemma. Neil was in the yard with Pam kissing away and we had this arrangement whereby we would take ten-minute time slots for a spot of discrete smooching. Neil would cough 'times up mate' and he would take his turn. I never possessed a watch so who knows whether Neil was being impatient as I would be lost in the moment, could have been five minutes for all I knew! Neil's always been an impatient chap. I also remember this girl's friend being very drunk and being taken advantage off in a bedroom upstairs by a group of Wavertree lads. This wasn't on so I went upstairs and mindful that this could get out of hand; I pretended that she was with me and I rescued her. They never objected thankfully and for the rest of the night I had two girls on my arm. Nothing happened but it didn't half fit in with a fantasy held by my mates and me; I had to shove my fringe up as I was smiling ear to ear. We got friendly with these two girls we called Donna the punk, not Donna the punk from Garston or the heavy metal girl either, God this is confusing and Lisa the weirdo, I think we met them through Carl. Lisa was younger than Neil and me but she dressed differently and was very eccentric, which really appealed to us and I think she later ended up in a career to do with design and fashion and got a job in Paris, which doesn't surprise me and I'm reminded of the track *'She's Strange'* by Cameo, she unequivocally was in many ways.

Another shameful memory to add to the ever increasing list but you had to be there to understand how we thought, so please consider that when judging us.

Neil and me were reminiscing about Donna the other year and we couldn't work out how we ended up seeing her at the same time. Back then you either went out with a girl or you were 'seeing her', which described a more casual relationship.

See, Donna would babysit and Neil and me would work out what days of the week we would 'see' Donna. I think I would see her Tuesday and Thursday, Neil was Monday and Wednesday and this went on for weeks before we both moved on and Grant typically ended up going out with her for about a year I think.

Here's a funny memory of these two girls. We were on Picton Road and Neil and me were chatting to Donna and Lisa. Neil suggested we go to the cemetery by Picton clock and they agreed. We said goodbye to Curly and Carl and off we went, I was paired with Donna and Neil was with Lisa. So picture the scene, its dark and were walking through the

cemetery looking for a place to sit off, when Curly and Carl jump out from behind a gravestone.
Well, I literally jumped out of my skin. They had run ahead and had well and truly pranked us. When we had finished cursing them to the sound of my thumping heart, they left and I remember smooching on this pyramid shaped gravestone out of sight of Neil of course. I could hear him on another tombstone; I was still spooked but no Casey Jones steam engines and Neil we really should have let that dead guy sleep!
All this took place when I must have been around fifteen. We were obviously too young to legally drink but this didn't stop us trying and Grant, Neil and me certainly had many knock backs from various hostelries I can tell you.
One night we went for a drink at the Sandown Pub, the old man end of the High Street. This pub was usually a sure bet and was famed round our way for selling condoms. We walked in and the manager took one look at us and said 'you've got to be joking lads' so we turned, tail between our black baggy trousers and we skedaddled out in our Chinese slippers.
Sometimes we'd jump the number 78 bus to Woolton Village stopping off at the Half Way House on Woolton Road for a pint and eventually having a pint in the Baby Elephant in the Village. It felt so different to Edge Hill and I longed to live in leafier parts with less grime and in particular there are a group of houses opposite the Black Woods that I would pass on the 78 bus called Cabbot Green and I would dream of living in such luxury believing this is where people who had 'made it' lived.
One of the most famous pubs round our way that we sometimes attended as anyone could get served at this pub and in complete contrast to the fashionable Elephant; was the Dead House on the corner of Earle Road and Webster Road by the murderous Cameo cinema strangely enough.
The pub was actually called the Earle Marshall but became known as the Dead House because many a patron had reputedly died whilst supping their pint in this pub. I think the owner did too. It had several rooms including a bar and a pool table and you could press a bell on the wall and the bar staff would come to take your order.
Then we had the Botanic Pub; funny enough this pub faced the Botanic Park that I talked about before. We would play pool at this pub and I remember some guy challenging Neil to a match on a Sunday night but he was all spent up and was left with his bus fare to work the next day. Seeing as we had attended the Rec for years we were really good at pool

and Neil accepted the challenge, thankfully for him he won so he didn't have to phone in sick the next day.

Like a lot of pubs round our way including the Dead House, the Botanic was demolished a few years ago and as you drive around the area you can see that most pubs are now boarded up.

There are several reasons in my view as to why local pubs have closed for business and I know this is the case in most cities. Some would say the smoking ban is the main contributor to landlords calling time due to punters being forced to smoke outside, a ring of fire as it is known these days. I'm not convinced, as I think the rot had set in some years before. See, in the mid eighties we would start our night out around 8pm by popping into a local boozer. We'd either stay up the High Street until last orders was called around 11pm or we'd catch a taxi into town to attend a club or we'd attend Winston's if we wanted the night to last.

Trends have changed and more and more people head to town and usually on pay day, by passing local pubs and with the advent of the rave scene in the late eighties young people were more interested in attending a club than moving from pub to pub as we did.

The price of alcohol has also influenced people's drinking habits and people often drink at home, supping cheaper alcohol until gone 10pm to then attend some late bar or club in town.

People simply can't afford to drink as often as they would have done in the mid eighties due to the mark up price on pints, bottles and shorts, so less popular pubs situated in areas where only old men with whippets drink, have been forced to close. I also believe most people are more concerned with health and diet and whilst some people enjoy the occasional night out they are more picky about when they go out and more likely to pursue other interests in the pursuit of happiness such as the gym, the cinema, concerts and the theatre.

Just a theory of mine but drinking in a local boozer particularly during the week is a dying pastime confined to the last century, all very sad.

Talking of pubs and like I said before, most nights my mate's and me would congregate outside the Spoffy on the steps outside come rain or shine just in case you missed out on something.

This is another pub that has called last orders some years ago but back when I was a teenager the landlord had two daughters and we became friendly with one of them, her name was Dawn, a pretty blonde girl, the girl Joey was with when he wanted me to cop off with Amanda.

It seems most girls we knew babysat and Dawn was no exception. I remember her babysitting in Neil's street and she would invite us round once she had finished reading the likes of Snow White to some toddler.

When I was thirteen Dawn asked me if I would like to have a Christmas kiss in the entry, I was really nervous as I wasn't as confident with my technique but I remember thinking oh well, one has to learn on the job. I remember passionately kissing Dawn for a few minutes when Grant suddenly appeared in the shadows. He shouted out 'quick Dave ye Mum's coming', she wasn't, I thought how odd we live the other side of the road and Mum's at the Bongo, he was jealous and he eventually went out with Dawn, yet another girl to add to the list.
So lets talk about another ex girlfriend. Sorry about this Q but I need to mention Anne, something we never talk about, a mutual skeleton locked in a cupboard somewhere in the recess of both our minds, a pink elephant. I met Anne at Dunny's disco and we started going out with each other, I was about fifteen and I think it was around autumn time. Anne was a smart attractive girl from Wavertree, near to where Lesley lived, who I later mention in the chapter about school.
I would go to Anne's most nights and I would walk the length of Lawrence Road past this graffiti, not that I promote wanting vandalism I doth protest but it was actually a good poem and I'd mutter the words to myself like a religious mantra to make the walk less arduous.
As an adult I've often wondered where the words came from, where they conceived inspirationally and original, where they taken from some obscure protest track, from the NME perhaps, who knows but I would hazard a guess they were written by a disgruntled punk worried about the future of music. What junk remains in your head but the first two sprayed lines went like this: *'someone told me punk was dead, was it a mod or was it a ted'*.
So wish I could recall the rest but sadly the poem was erased when the owner white washed his gable end. I know, I think I was a very strange kid indeed.
Talking of Lawrence Road and before I return to Anne, I remember these two louts stopping me one night to ask if I had a spare ciggy. I explained to them that I didn't smoke but they got a knife out and menacingly asked 'what would yew do if we tuck ye money off ye'. I was penniless actually but they weren't to know and I summed up my options. I had seen them around and I knew they knew lads I knew so I decided to laugh off their threat but all the time feeling very scared and I ended up talking to them as if I had just bumped into two long lost friends.
Not sure why but they mellowed and we chatted and I remember choosing the right time to say 'anyway lad's I'd best be off', as I was worried it could still turn out ugly at any time. I left not wishing to look back and I can't help wondering if they mugged other kids and perhaps

some old dear or two. I hope not of course but I somehow didn't see them repenting their sins or giving a toss about the feelings of others. No they were destined for a life of crime and drugs me thinks.

Perhaps I need to prove I have some guts as I mention being a bit of a wimp throughout this book so let me tell you how I have apprehended a mugger on more than one occasion. One day Alan and me were walking through town on our way to play a football match. I was in my early twenties and we were on Matthew Street and this woman screamed out loud. I spotted this man running away and I ran after him and eventually caught him in British Home Stores with her handbag and I handed him over to the security guards.

On another occasion I was on holiday with my wife and her family. This is my James Bond dry martini moment. Earlier that day I was the only one in the party who had a go at paragliding, everyone else was scared and later we had a pool competition and this night I won. On my way back to the apartments there was I thinking what a god day I was having, when I spotted Sue and her sister and they were pointing to a man in the shadows and they whispered that he had just burgled next doors apartment.

I had been learning karate for a few months taking inspiration form Paul and Geoff so I mentally rehearsed some moves as I approached the man. He tried to escape so in a split second I decided to throw him into the pool and when he tried to get out I pushed him back with my foot until the police arrived. Once apprehended, I then topped the night off by diving into the pool to retrieve his bounty from the bottom of the pool, a cheap watch. Everyone needs to be a hero sometimes and I was 'shaken but not stirred'. Ouch!

Anyway back to my story of Anne, just building the suspense Q. She had a younger sister and her Mum and Dad were nice and after getting the aforementioned poem out of my head, we'd sit in the back parlour listening to records and would play board games. She had the album 'Dare' by the 'Human League', the one with the boxed faces, an electronic masterpiece released in 1981 to critical acclaim.

I thought it was amazing how The Human League had quickly evolved from an avant-garde electronic group from Sheffield singing about *'Being Boiled'*, another cool track by the way about silk worms of all things, into a commercial pop group. Tracks from the album included classics trailblazers such as *'Open Your Heart'*, *'The Sound of the Crowd'*, *'Love Action (I Believe in Love)* and the defining, *'Don't You Want Me Baby'*. Little did I know at the time but this turned out to be a prophetic question I was soon to ask Anne! Read on.

I also remember watching Tenko on telly every Thursday with Anne, I think this was when her Mum and Dad went out, but my favourite night was Friday night though, as I'd meet Anne at Dunny's disco.
I'd mainly be with my mates acting cool but at the end we'd pair up and slow dance, then I would walk Anne home afterwards. We were a couple and everyone knew that. I think the relationship lasted about three months, not long I know but we saw each other pretty much every night so the relationship was a bit intense and we packed a lot into the short time we were together. I should have played it cooler but I was like that with most relationships.
I remember buying Anne an 'Earth Wind and Fire' Album for Christmas, she bought me a grey Slazenger jumper but it shrank after one wash. Good old Mum! Now here's were Wikipedia helps with more memory recollection. See, I now know that the album was called 'Raise' and the track *'Let's Groove Tonight'* was a big hit from the album, which is why I bought it as I think we must have danced to this track at Dunny's.
I'm still building this up Q for added drama so bare with me! Anne would have suitors; this was only natural as she was attractive. I remember a mate of Neil's from his school, his name was Johno, he was a decent lad actually but he turned up at Anne's house one night whilst I was there. He was obviously trying to muscle in, I think he was a *'Jealous Guy'*, which by the way is an impressive cover by Bryan Ferry released shortly after the original singer, John Lennon, died and to me this is a complete gemstone of a track.
Johno was liked by most girls, he had a blonde 'wedge haircut' so he probably thought Anne would have a thing for lads with fringes but she sent him on his way.
Anyway all this was to change one memorable night at Dunny's hence the ability to recall this memory. I was sat with my mates doing the usual stuff but from the corner of my eye I could see Neil chatting to Anne through the swaying crowds. I thought nothing of it at first; Anne and Neil had often spoken as we all hung out together but next thing they were dancing. Again I'm thinking this is fine, what's in a friendly dance and I told myself to remain cool about it.
But then the music changed to 'copping off' music and they stood closer together and then they slow danced! Looking back the relationship was fizzling out but I was heart broken, I walked out, went home and closed the door to my cold bedroom for a night of, teeth shattering why and what had I done to deserve this, self-questioning and self-loathing. The track *'Is She Really Going Out with Him'* by Joe Jackson resonated through my broken heart.

Life goes on and a few days later I bumped into Neil outside of Grant's. I had heard that Neil had walked Anne home that night so I guessed by then that they were an item. I walked up to Neil and I remember saying something like 'as far as I'm concerned you can have her', like I owned her but I do remember the need to feel in control, I needed to be mature but truth was I was cross with Neil and linking 'ABC' track to this moment, I had given Anne *'All of My Heart'*, knowing that Anne's lipstick and lip gloss had sealed my fate.

Some months later I'm at Rotter's with Neil and Grant, we all got in this time. We're in scene two, which was upstairs and catered for the type of music we liked, edgy, alternative and New Romantic. Anne was there with Paula, her mate and sister of Lesley and I asked her for a dance. Just before I reveal more, nearly there Q, another breath-taking track that reminds me of this time in my life is *'Love Will Tear Us Apart'* by the awesome Joy Division.

One can only imagine what wondrous songs Ian Curtis would have penned if he had managed to fight off his demons before his death; he had an instantly recognizable voice, unique dance moves and I'd literally salivate to every beat of this song matched by words of alienation and desolation. This was 'the' track of the moment and will forever hold a place in the stratosphere of all time pivotal great's that I revere.

Now before you call me a charlatan I knew Neil and Anne had *'Tear-ed Apart'* a few weeks after that night so don't make a disapproving look my way; I'd heard that her parent's didn't take to Neil like they had taken to me. Anne and I danced and we were getting along just fine when Neil does the Gentleman's excuse me trick, yes he patted me on the shoulder and asked if he could dance with Anne. I was lost for words and I retreated from the dance floor feeling wounded again. Now before you go saying I'm a first class wimp again, I hope I had quelled that rumour, we often did the tap on the shoulder trick so this was quite normal behaviour between us lads and all part of the chase.

I decided to console myself and I went to scene one, the disco part of the club, to lick my wounds. I bumped into June and Sharon who was dancing to some track by Shalamar, so I danced with them and tried not to think of Anne and this all happened before my wasteland kiss with Sharon.

Then I felt this tap on my shoulder, surly not Neil, no it was none other than Anne! She then said, 'just because I danced with Neil doesn't mean I want to be with him'. I remember every last word she said and we then danced the rest of the night, we were oblivious to what was happening around us, yes we kissed like at Dunny's and at the end of the night she went home with her mates and I trotted off with Neil and Grant trying not to gloat.

The next day Paula came to my house on a mission, a recci trip again, to pass on a message, as was the custom! She told me that Anne wanted me to call round to her house and that she really regretted what she had done and how she had treated me! What did I do, well I decided not to rekindle our relationship and I told Paula that I had really enjoyed our night but I had moved on. I suppose I kind of told Paula to '*Say Hello and Wave Goodbye*', a track by Soft Cell and let's be honest there aren't enough superlatives to describe this track and I shall forever connect it with the bright lights of nightclubbing in 1982.

Anyway I think my stubborn wounded pride came to the forefront, who knows and shortly after that I heard that she was going out with someone we didn't know, they got married eventually.

Life goes on I guess and I totally forgive Q, we were young and reckless and all is 'fair in love and war' and as I see it, this was part of growing up so absolutely no hard feelings Q and if I hadn't had '*waved goodbye*' I might have lost a really good mate.

Like I said Neil attended the Collegiate near town and some months later whilst on a sixth form school holiday at Colomendy, he met Janet. Neil and Janet are still together and guess what school she went to, yes you guessed right, Notre Dame in Woolton.

Janet had a close friend and her name was Sandra, they were inseparable, they looked similar and I have this memory of Neil walking along this corridor at Paddy Comp towards the badminton halls with Sandra and Janet both linking him. Sandra was a bit weird to be honest whereas Janet is lovely, one of life's gems and one of the most generous and kind-hearted people I have ever met. Anyway, they were going on a night out and Neil was proud as punch and he new everyone was gaping in awe, the Ping-Pong sound suddenly stopped!

We still went out most weekends but Neil's relationship with Janet became serious. One weekend Neil told me he had to go to Norwich for some mad reason and I think he must have been around eighteen. Janet had a secured place studying Art at Norwich University and in one weekend Neil found a flat and a job in a photographic shop, he was set and soon after he left to live in Alan Partridge country.

I'd lost a good mate, a wingman and someone I admired and looked up too but this was typical of Neil, full of drive and determination and he was scarcely an adult. We lost touch around this point, like I said this was before mobiles and social networking but thankfully Neil managed to track me down working in Surry when I was about twenty one and I'll tell you more about that later.

I really missed Neil, we are different in so many ways but we share this Edge Hill brotherly bond that now spans the decades and pay bands I may add! I love the fella and over Neil's expensive malt whiskey, with no ice of course, I've often teased him about settling down too soon when in his prime, but truth is Neil has no regrets and I admire him for taking such a huge step. Takes guts and fortitude that, but that's Q for you and at the end of the day Janet is right for him and he is right for her.

Janet is very impressed that I have taken time to write this book and she can recall similar memories as we both went to the same primary school. I think I will give Janet a copy for her to read and I pray you're feeling stronger Janet!

Before I move on to the next chapter here's one last embarrassing memory of Neil to make his cheeks go crimsoned red without the aid of a good red vino. He once declared, now wait for it, to liking to the track *'Zoom'* by 'Fat Larry's Band'.

I liked it too but Neil was less eclectic than me back in the day and he was always 'alternative' and certainly never disco unless dancing in his enigmatic understated way with a girl that is.

Had he developed a suppressed sentimental streak, was he drunk I would ask myself, as this confession certainly raised Roger Moore like eyebrows, Neil liking smooch soul music, with his Monte Carlo 'I think ill just pop into the casino after taking a spin in my Aston Martin whilst wearing my silk cravat' reputation! No surely not, but he did and I wonder if he still does?

Chapter Fifteen

Singing The Blues ...

My favourite clubs when I was fifteen to sixteen was Cagney's off London Road, Tuxedo Junction on Duke Street and Rotter's, the club I have mentioned elsewhere and this club sat on top of St John's market. I remember being in Cagney's one-night and Fred the owner of Major the dog, was serving food out of a hatch, how weird was that? I also remember these black kids checking out the moves made by Jeffrey Daniel from Shalamar as he popped and slid across the TTOTP stage to *'A Night to Remember'* on this big screen. They were in awe and I must confess to being impressed myself wishing I had the same moves. Anyway, gaining entry to said clubs was a hit and miss affair for me and my mates but that's not surprising as we must have all looked very young and not mature men about town as we thought we were. I remember this one night queuing up outside Rotter's and getting in to the club but Grant got knocked back so Neil followed him back out, could have happened to any one of us.

But this time I was in, my mission had been achieved, I waited and waited and in the end I decided to stay in as I was torn. How I wished I had a mobile as I had left it too long by then, you see I had no idea if Neil and Grant were outside or strutting their stuff in another club.

So not to ruin a good night I got friendly with this girl from Bootle in scene two, she never questioned my scouse credentials and I remember dancing to *'Rip it Up'* by the wonderful Mr Edwin Collins when he was in the band 'Orange Juice' and being drunk on water downed lager. It didn't take many pints despite that and to my shame I had to do a quick retreat off the dance floor mid song and in my wake I left a trail of vomit showing my path to the bog.

I stumbled into the toilet to freshen up and on my return I got reacquainted with my Bootle lass to the track *'In the Name of Love'* as I recall, by 'The Thompson Twins' and I must have stunk and I think I even had vomit down my double breasted Dr Kildare shirt! Not a pretty sight I am sure.

The same night I was wearing a khaki coloured cord jacket that was fashionable at the time and I had to wait until the very end of the night because I had lost my ticket and the cloak woman wouldn't give me it back until everyone had left. I loved that jacket, it had an attached belt that you pulled in at the waist and I wore it most nights for a few months. I also had the formulaic scouse sheepskin but mine was the light coloured version, very warm in winter but very heavy too and I wore it so often that the part that covered my bum had a worn patch after sitting on walls talking to my mates in the cold.

On another night out occasion Grant and me had been to a church charity night at St Dunstan's, another one of the Vic's fund raising affairs. I wore this shirt that fastened on the shoulder and I remember this DJ shouting out as I made my way to the loo; 'look here comes Dr Kildare', yes I had the same shirt on but what's with people skitting my look back then, it was fashionable, honest. He was actually a decent DJ and perhaps influenced by my slightly flamboyant attire he played Japan's *'Quiet Life'*, which by the way has to have one of the best synthesiser introductions tracks in music, then surpassed by the 'I have to dance' snare drum beat.

Not sure where Neil was on this occasion, probably with Janet at her house but Grant and me were up for partying so at the end of the night we wandered up to this club called the Dallas on Tunnel Road, as it was still early. We got chatting to these two older women on the road who had also left Dunny's with the same idea, a need for brighter lights and we then paired off. I went in first and I could hear Grant bickering with the bouncer as he had been stopped again. We weren't very loyal when it came to chasing girls I guess so again I stayed in and ended up dancing with both girls. Sorry Grant should you be reading this.

I remember having a thing with one of them at the end of the night down an entry and as she got into her taxi, not the train, I just had to tell her that I was only sixteen and not twenty like I had claimed to be.

Grant was a good mate but he had developed this reputation of being someone with whom you couldn't trust when it came to money. Many a time I would sub Grant just so as we could go out clubbing, were only talking a few pounds for a couple of drinks but he never paid me back. So, if you're reading this Grant, donations gratefully received and with interest too and no ozzy dollars!

One thing sticks in my throat a little; Grant and me went to pick some records from the record shop on Lodge Lane, Mum's record club that I mentioned before. I think I actually owed him a pound on this occasion so in exchange he persuaded me to give him the fabulous single

'*Messages*' by OMD. See Grant I always pay my debts and at the time. Typical of most teenagers I wanted to beef up so my Mum bought me this 'Strong Man' chest expander device for my birthday. Can't think of the name but it had three tight springs and at each end it had red handles for pulling. You'd stretch your arms out wide, your muscles would ache, you'd count to three before returning back but definitely taking care not to catch your nipple in the process, very painful. I lent it to Grant one night but, you guessed, I never did see it again.

Then I had this suit I bought for interviews when I was sixteen, I think I bought it off my mate Derek from Izzy Crown, so a decent suit. Well, I lent it to Grant and the next time I saw it he had hemmed the sleeves to fit his shorter arms and the bottom but that was Grant for you, he'd make excuses and change the subject when you asked for your items; he just acquired stuff, possession being nine tenths of the law and we just got used to that part of his character.

Here are a few lines about my eighteenth birthday celebration, not a great memory granted but a lesson in life that I learnt. Neil had emigrated by then, Grant, Derek, Scotty and me and I think a couple of others, went on a pub crawl round town. I say went but we never made it too far as I got totally wasted in Yates Wine Bar by Lewis's opposite the now closed Blackler's, we listened to UB40 on the Juke Box.

I was never a big drinker but I would normally last the night, this night someone suggested we have Aussie Wight Chasers with our pints of Tetley's Bitter. Why I don't know but this was a lethal combination and four or five rounds later I was seeing double and coincidently slurring my words to '*Red Red Wine*'. Great track by the way.

I have this fuzzy memory of my mates and me somehow making it out of Yate's and we made our way to the Harrington Bar to the sounds of the track '*Ain't Nobody*' by the big thighed but strangely captivating 'Chaka Khan. A couple of drinks later I staggered to the toilet, I felt really sick again and I decided to take refuge on the floor of this cubicle. Using Mr Elvis Costello track, '*I Can't Stand up for Falling Down*'; I was literally legless like someone had shot me down and I couldn't physically move, I was paralysed from the neck down and all I could do was lie there in all the piss and whatever else was on the floor. I know totally disgusting, I'm ashamed and I actually hoped that the owner would lock up for the night and leave me there; I was in such a bad state, I needed sleep, I needed rescuing or better still to be left on my own. My so-called mates would come in and check on me when they were emptying their bowels and I remember Scotty saying 'Dave it's ye round, where's ye money'.

I knew Scotty was just fleecing me for money, my taxi fare home, so I mustered all my energy and rolled over to make it difficult for him to retract the last twenty pounds I had in my pocket, as I needed to get home and it was hands off as far as I was concerned. Funny how one manages to find the energy when it comes to money. He gave up in the end and what seemed like hours later I staggered out of the toilet, barged past people on the dance floor and like a deep sea diver taking his or her first gulp of fresh air, I stood there taking in the cool fresh air of the night, expanding my lungs wishing I could sober up.
I had one thing on my mind, bed, and God knows how I made it home that night but I did. I had to sit down on several occasions though after taking 'two steps forward' and 'one step back' and I must have looked a right state and I remember this kind couple asking me if I was okay as I sat in a doorway catching my breath?
I was sick all night and I slept for a whole day afterwards and I made *'A Promise'* to myself, a great track by the Bunnymen by the way, broken many times since, that I would never get so drunk again. Did someone spike my drink I don't know but I can tell you one thing, I've never hugged a toilet since. A lesson well and truly learnt!
I don't mean to be too down on Grant as I also have many a good memory of him too, he was actually a good mate and good company, he would lend stuff off you but would also be very generous and I remember him borrowing me clothes when I went on holiday with Derek.
So let me tell you more about Grant and with that it would be poignant to talk about football due to Grant and his family being passionate Evertonian's, true blues and proud. Whereas my family never really followed football, except for uncle Tommy who went the match, but if they had to choose, it would be Liverpool Football Club.
Seeing as I am being honest in my memory recollection I confess to watching Liverpool a few times when I was about nine. Neil S and his family went the match every home game and they took me with them sometimes in Billy's green van and I would stand in the Boy's Pen, which was a corner section of the Kop for kids.
I wasn't that interested in the game as I recall but I remember being utterly mesmerised by older kids whose mission was to scale the steal frames like little monkeys and to drop into the Kop unscathed and without being caught by the stewards.
When I was about thirteen I really got the bug for watching footy and I decided that I wanted to get into supporting a team and Everton were seen as the underdogs so I decided this was the team for me. I went the

match on my own for a few months and I kept this a secret, as I knew I'd be ridiculed and called a 'turncoat' which I was I guess. Sorry Adam I sense your disappointment as you read this.

Not sure how my secret was revealed but I started going the match with Grant, Alan, their Dad Don and his younger brother Francis. We'd catch the twenty-six bus on Tunnel Road and from when I was about sixteen we'd have a pint at the Hermitage Pub or the Blue House in plastic glasses before and after the game. I have many fond memories of supping beer and singing tracks like *'Singing the Blues'* by 'Guy Mitchell' in said pubs and we got to know lots of likeminded lads. Derek would come sometimes when not working and we would watch the match from the Enclosure.

Everton had a good team back then, a good manager in Howard Kendal and we became the team to beat and I attended many a memorable match. You'd get swept away with the excitement, I even appeared on Match of the Day once, well, when I say appeared I mean you could spot me in the crowd after Andy Gray had scored. I was pushed up against the bars screaming with the rest of the crowd and some lads up the High Street said they had seen me on telly.

We'd go to away games sometimes and semi finals and the occasional final. I remember going to Old Trafford with Grant and Derek and Derek's crazy mate called Kevin, a mad lad as I later found out from Norris Green. We got Man U in this bizarre competition called the Super Cup, the crowd was small, and we only took a few coaches. We never wore hats or scarfs, Liverpool supporters tended to do that, that wasn't for us but you had to wear a small badge to signify whom you supported. A badge of honour and I had a cherished badge that I lent Grant and yes you can guess the rest!

I'm not suggesting I was a fully fledge 'scally' as the term goes, short for scallywag but I would wear Addidas three stripe trainees, my 'trabs' as we called them, my slightly flared faded jeans with slits at the bottom and my favourite look was a beige lambs wool jumper. Real scally's would wear named tennis gear such as Lacoste, Fila and Ellesse, probably stolen from abroad or counterfeit.

I would try and copy this fashion and I remember Derek taking me to this industrial estate on the outskirts of Maghull one year to meet with a lad who had cheap Lacoste gear. Someone had a car and we met in the dark. The lad opened his boot and began to rummage for my size but all he could find was a lemon Lacoste Cardigan. I didn't really want it but I had come this far so I bought it, big mistake, not only was it very bright but it turned out to be counterfeit.

I did buy an authentic Lacoste T-shirt some months later and I have had several since, it was white with green and red stripes round the cuffs and collar and I wore it daily. I ended up passing it on to Dad when it began to look washed out and he wore it for work, the trendiest Dad on the building site me thinks.

When I attended Everton Matches there was often a menacing air created by football hooliganism that first crept into the game in the seventies. Railway stations, high streets and service stations come Saturday afternoons became the realms of footballs boot boys and every football team had its gang or 'firm', it had become an epidemic and an exhibition of tribal aggression and one firm I remember in particular was West Ham's 'Inter City Firm'.

We never played West Ham that often because they were in the second tier of football but talk would spread about respectful city gents travelling to away matches in first class train carriages to avoid the police and leaving call cards after a brawl.

I also remember listening to Birmingham's away supporters; I think they were called the Zulu Warriors, chanting and stamping menacingly in the Park End throughout the match, thinking it was going to kick off at any time.

The football sometimes became secondary as you would watch and see the crowd jostle for a better place to intimidate the home supporters and Everton had its own crew and other teams feared the 'Blues'. I remember hearing about a Millwall supporter dying in the Gwladys Street in the sixties and we knew of graffiti written on a wall in London that read, 'please God give us Everton in the cup'. Not sure if this was ever true or folk law but I remember being genuinely scared of the prospect of our two balls being drawn together from the silk bag in the early rounds of the FA Cup.

Word of mouth would pass along the terraces like a wave about past skirmishes with rival supporters and where it was likely to kick off later that day and although I was never part of this scene in truth, more of an observer, what struck me back then was that your typical Everton scally was generally discrete and non descript, they would never appear 'hard' but when the tensions boiled over scals would appear with spraying arms hoping to land a punch.

I remember singing out loud with the rest of the ground and there were some very funny mimic taking jibes, which was all part of the fun, but I hated the overtly racist chants that came from some sections of the terraces aimed at the supporters and the opposing team. This sickened me and looking back I really regret the fact that I kept supporting

Everton but I told myself the chants were made by a minority section of the crowd and not my mates and me.
Of all places I remember Old Trafford as being a very scary place to visit. The police would march you to the ground in a long line of chants about how much we hated Manchester, then they would disappear at the entrance as if to say 'down to you now scousers', each one for himself and you feared a stab in the back so you would hide your badge with your hand as if you had an annoying scratch on your chest.
Once in the ground you were relatively safe amongst the crowd, that is most of the time. On the night of the Super Cup we were in the stands, which is stupid really as you sat down? Could never work that one out. We sat there chanting and cheering and we noticed the seats around us had started to fill up. We scored a goal, and then it all kicked off.
I recall Derek and Kevin launching themselves at these two blokes and Grant and me just stood there bracing for a fight. Never happened as the police quickly waded in, it was all over in seconds and Derek and Kevin were evicted from the ground, Kevin got arrested as I recall.
Back at the coach a funny thing happened. We boarded and Grant charmed this pretty girl who we sometimes bumped into at the match and he suggested she sit next to him on the coach. He said 'best sit on the inside as we might get bricked', which she did, he was very chivalrous our Grant.
I was sat behind her when suddenly this brick comes crashing through the window the opposite side of where Grant was sitting, his right and it landed in the girls lap, as did the many shards of glass that followed. She wasn't hurt thankfully but Grant wasn't touched at all. We laughed at that back at the pub.
Here's one of the fondest memories I have of following Everton, trust me there's been many sad ones to. I had saved up a couple of hundred pounds as I had applied to become a helper with Camp America and I was told to have money in reserve as you worked all summer, food and lodgings included, then you had a month to explore the states, hence the money.
I must have been about eighteen and I had attended this interview in Manchester and I eagerly waited for the envelope to land on the doormat. Sure I was really nervous about leaving home especially as my plans involved travelling to a far off distant land but I wanted the adventure and I knew of other lads who had done the same.
I watched Everton win round after round in the Cup Winners Cup, we'd won the FA Cup in 1984 and it looked like we would make it to the final. Ask any Evertonian over forty what game sticks out in their memory and

I would guess most would mention the semi final at Goodison Park against the mighty Bayern Munich.
We were one nil down and we needed to score twice as they had an away goal advantage. The place was rocking and the whole ground sang in unison spurring the team on and I remember promising my mates that the drinks were on me if we won the match. Well the gods were on our side that day, granted my wallet took a knock but against the odds we won.
Having already clinched the league, our first league championship in fifteen years, we had to face the tough tackling Austrians, Rapid Vienna. I had a dilemma. Grant and Derek had booked a coach and had got tickets for the final, which was in Rotterdam in Holland. Should I use my Camp America money not knowing if I had been successful at the interview or go the match.
Grant, you're a star as he convinced me with the slightly prophetic words; 'Dave we may never get to a European Final again, you've got to come'. He was right and I thought sod it and the day before our coach was due to depart I went over to the Wirral with Derek and did a deal with this travel firm. I was in!
What an experience we had. There was Derek, Grant, Scotty, me, and this tall lad we knew called Brian. The journey down South was one of drinking and singing footy chants till your throat hurt and we got to know our fellow supporters on the coach.
We caught the ferry over from Dover; I have a funny memory of trying to keep my balance with a tray of pints as the boat tilted and talking to these French girls. I also remember saying in my thickest scouse accent that American's are always loud as we looked on at these college types and this old dear saying 'were not all loud son' with a New York twang.
Driving through France along the coast I remember someone asking the driver to stop the coach for a pee, too much lager and we stepped out and I then realised we were on the French, Belgium boarder. This is the first and only time I have ever peed at the same time in two countries at once! Now go and add that to your bucket list.
We stayed in Ostend in Belgium and the place was teaming with Evertonian's. The place was very picturesque from what I can recall, must go back sometime and we checked into our hotel, then quickly changed into our scally gear for a night of drinking. Great night, we turned a corner and bumped into Gerry from the sauna, yes and he was clean-shaven.
He joined us and our crew grew bigger and I remember a fight against local youths in the dock area of the city and being very scared. I saw

scals wade in with stools from a local bar and I remember the ebb and flow that comes with gangs goading each other. One minute you're standing there transfixed feeling very uncomfortable, next thing you're running away like mad worrying you were either going to get hit over the head or 'nicked' by the police. I remember telling Derek who was always up for a fight that this wasn't what I wanted to do and we all left the area and went on a night of lager drinking.
The bars were amazing, the beer was cheap and I remember this guy giving me a pinch of snuff. I'd never heard of it before but it didn't half clear my head. Realise now but we were in the red light area of Ostend by the port and I remember this big brute of an Evertonian kicking this brothel door protesting that he hadn't got what he wanted for the money he had spent. We laughed till we cried; he was not pleased I could tell you.
We ended up at this bar and it was about four in the morning. We got talking to the bar lady who offered to show us her breasts if we handed over some money and we laughed, me part with money, I don't think so. Behind the bar was an array of Kodak pictures of punters from the past and our 'new found friend' asked if she could take our picture, we obliged but we decided on the following, why I've no idea seemed a good thing at the time and we didn't even charge her any money. Read on.
We all dropped our jeans you see, we turned round and with a felt tip pen we asked her to write Everton on our backsides. She then took a picture, wafted it as you do to dry it, then she pinned it pride of place on the wall and I've often thought of that picture showing my tanned hairy arse in the centre of my mates white cheeks and wondering if it was still there? I know highly unlikely but funny thought.
I think I had the letter R on my arse. Soon after our bum showing antics we made our way back to the hotel to freshen up for the journey over the boarder to Holland, but no peeing this time. I shared a room with Derek and he decided to get a refreshing bath. Next thing I hear Derek screaming out loud about the colour of the water, as it had turned blue. I barged in thinking he was hurt but then realising what had happened, I told him to relax, as it was the blue ink from the pen.
It was the 15th May 1985 and we all boarded the coach to Rotterdam, still drunk from the night before. We arrived to swoons of blue and green in every street, on every square and at every bar. It was relaxed and it felt like a festival of football and we went for a few beers. I exchanged a hat with this Austrian bloke sitting outside drinking larger in a bar; wearing a hat was deemed appropriate when playing abroad and I still have the

green hat in the loft, bit tight round my head though, I'm guessing Austrians must have small heads.

Four days later we had to walk out at Wembley in a bid to retain the FA Cup against Man U so we were on for the treble. It was a memorable evening, the stadium was open air and there were Evertonian's to my left and right stretching almost round the whole ground. This was our night and I remember sitting in front of the camera high up in the stands behind the goal.

I remember it being a tough nervy game and we broke the deadlock in the fifty-seventh minute when Sharpy raced in to a poor back pass, he chipped over to Andy Gray and he fired home. I ran at the camera like a raving lunatic and yes again I was spotted on telly back home.

The place erupted and it seemed like our victory was sealed in the seventy-second minute when Trevor Steven thumped the ball into the back of the net. The Austrians clawed themselves back however; Hans Krankl beat Southall from close range. We were nervous, we couldn't be denied our moment and is it happened it was a temporary setback as Kevin Sheedy hammered home a third goal straight from the kick off. Kevin Ratcliffe went up to collect his second cup in the space of few weeks; the reception was awe-inspiring as he lifted the cup to sounds of 'Everton, Everton, Everton'.

Everyone knew we were the best side in Europe at that time, we were unstoppable and we were only denied further glory after English teams were kicked out of Europe following the Heysal disaster. Now I'm not blaming Liverpool as this was a terrible tragedy and many Italians lost their lives in this fated final but how ironic that our arch rivals would thwart our predicted march into the annals of famous European teams. NEC sponsored us at the time and the joke from Liverpool supporters was that this stood for 'No European Cup'. How true that became!

Anyway what a night we had and we got back to Ostend early in the morning and went back to our bum-revealing bar for a couple more beers but no pictures this time and certainly no bear breasts.

Later that morning Grant, Derek and me went to this seaside café and we ordered fresh orange, we decided we must be a bit civil and cultured. Grant was not amused; he might have been still drunk as he shouted at the waiter 'eh this glass is dirty'. Derek pointed out, to fits of laughter, that the glass had been dipped into sugar, as is the custom in posh gaffs.

The coach returned us back home and the driver dropped off at various points in Liverpool. We had got friendly with this bloke who we had christened stinky as he farted a lot. He ran a pub in the Dingle, we got back about midnight and he persuaded us to come in for a lock in. What

the hell we thought so we did and he wouldn't allow us to pay for our beer and we had chasers seeing as it was a free bar. God knows how I survived on a diet of alcohol and hot dogs.
I eventually got home just as the postman arrived. In his hand he had a letter addressed to me, the envelope had red white and blue stripes across one corer. This was it, my letter from the United States; I was skint and in that moment I thought of schemes in which I could raise some money for my adventure but to my horror I had not been successful! I didn't know whether to laugh or cry but you know Grant; I have you to thank for such a wonderful memory, as I would have missed out if I had taken the sensible route.
I was naturally disappointed with loosing out on an adventure but a gamble that paid off as Everton have never made it to a European Cup Final again but our time will come. Keep the faith Adam.
I now had nothing to loose so I managed to scrape together enough money to attend the FA Cup final, probably through the bank of Mum and Dad, an IOU but this time tickets were like gold dust.
The same crew assembled on the morning and we went to the match in the back of this white builders transit van. I have no idea who owned the van, which had no windows and it had had an array of cushions scattered around to sit on and smelt of cement. We stopped off at an off licence in Netherley and bought several crates of Budweiser, God I must have supped some beer that week I can tell you.
I didn't have a ticket so I approached a cockney tout, a real 'geezer'. For twenty pound he promised to get me into Wembley, as he knew someone on the turnstile. I remember one of his helpers taking me to the correct point of entry but as I walked in this undercover cop spotted me and in one move I was evicted.
I ran down the steps to the tout, he told me to take off my beige lambs wool jumper and to tie it round my waist. I did, I had a pale blue Ben Sherman shirt on and again I tried the same manoeuvre but this time I was successful. Once passed the turnstile the next gate was easy as someone would throw you a ticket stub to get past the steward. All very dangerous as the official attendance was clearly a lot lower than the actual amount of people who crammed into the ground as I know I wasn't the only one without a ticket.
After the highs of Rotterdam this final seemed a bit subdued, a damp squid as they say, the players looked tired and leggy and I guess we were all knackered too. One memorable moment in the game occurred when Peter Reid was hacked down when through on goal by this Man U

player called Kevin Moran but to our dismay the referee bottled it and he only received a yellow card.
Man U were in the ascendency and Norman Whiteside cut in from the right wing and as if in slow motion I can recall him, with his left foot, bending the ball round Southall into the back of the net. We were gutted and dumb struck. The treble had evaded us.
Some years later I went to an Amnesty International concert at Wembley, I was working down in Surrey at the time and I watched Bruce Springsteen, Peter Gabriel, Tracy Chapman and Sting. I was one of the first in and I remember purposefully sitting on the hallowed turf, I say turf but the pitch was covered with this blue plastic layer, at the spot where Mr Whiteside had scored, or should I say shiteside, as we called him, at least we did before he actually joined Everton in 1989.
Continuing with the theme of footy, for a while I played centre forward for a team mainly made up of players from Grant's work. He was a support worker with adults who had learning difficulties and he worked for the Brothers of Charity out of a place called Thingwall Hall.
This was a large imposing institution first opened I'm guessing when Queen Victoria sat on the throne, the kind of building you find on a hill and the kind of place Mum would threaten to send you too if you didn't buck your ideas up. I went out with this girl called Pam that I met through Grant and with her help I applied for a job at Thingwall but was unsuccessful; I was miffed at the time, no one likes to be rebuffed but fate was on my side as I ended up with a much better job in Surrey some months later.
Also, I didn't like the way some of the staff treated the men they were allegedly looking after as care workers. Many of the men had lived in institutions for decades; they were vulnerable adults, obviously someone's son, brother or uncle but it seemed they had no one to advocate on their behalf and certainly no voice.
A culture of bullying existed and I like to think I would have challenged poor practice from within if I had got to the interview stage and beyond. I would have been a whistle-blower without doubt as I was sickened with what I had observed. Some of the adults seemed to irritate some of the staff, I won't mention their name but I hope they hang their heads in shame and look back and realise what they did and are duly apologetic.
I remember this time when Brad and me were making our way to one of the units for a shower after a match. This elderly man ran up to one of the players, he seemed happy to see this member of staff and he wanted to show him a fuzzy felt picture he had made; he said look at this. The nameless care worker knocked the picture out of his hand scattering the

pieces and told him to, well let's just say it rhymes with 'buck' and ends with 'off'.
Brad and me were appalled and we told the staff he was out of order and in an attempt to justify his actions, he said he does that all the time and is annoying and in any case he was on his day off! He was in good mood too as we had won our match!
This moron was missing the point, the person had a learning difficulty, you were there to care for him and he should have been showed dignity and respect and the annoying thing is the worker was a paid employee. Total tosser, I should have told him to 'f--k' off, wish I had now!
I remember all this because my mind wandered all over the place and Thingwall reminds me of a time when Grant and me embarked on a crazy weekend of footy, drinking and travelling. Let me explain, Grant had this mate who worked with him and he drove a white Ford Capri Ghia, he also played for the team but was a decent bloke unlike the aforementioned tosser.
After our match, I scored the winner, which is why I'm probably remembering this bit; Grant asked Mr Capri to drive us to Old Trafford. After some negotiation we gave him a tenner and the next thing I know were hurtling down the East Lancs, aka the A580 that separated scouse land from Manchester as we had one hour to get to the match. We left our muddy kit at Thingwall and we had an overnight bag!
We made it, just, but we didn't watch Everton with our fellow blues, no we were in the lion's den, the Stretford End. Felt strange supporting your team through gritted teeth and having to restrain ones excitement with every attack or near miss.
We did despite our urges to jump up and shout 'come on you blues' and the strange thing was we spotted other restrained blue noses standing by us! You could tell by the clothes they were wearing and this certain look us scousers have, no not curly perms and muzzy's. It was a league game and we drew one one as I recall.
Not sure how we got in with our bag past the turnstile but after the game we met up with a mate of Grant's who supported Man U but lived in Leeds. Can't remember his name, I think I'm loosing my memory but they met on holiday the year before and this lad would sometimes visit Liverpool for a night out. We caught a train to Leeds to stay the night at his Mum's with his fellow Man U Yorkshire men and women.
We had no idea what to expect in Leeds, we knew Leeds was in Yorkshire so we naturally thought the place would resemble the set from Emerdale from the telly. We never realised just how big Yorkshire is! We had crammed a suit into our bags, believing we'd look really smart and

men about town but sadly we looked more like door to door salesmen having a quick one after work but forgot when to stop.
Anyway you can't always get it right so 'suited and booted' as they say, we hit the town. We thought Liverpool was the place to be but Leeds was in a higher league, every pub had a theme and the throngs of people we encountered were so trendy and the music was up to the minute.
We looked awkward in our suits, we didn't see any sheep, and no rolling hills and the woolpack was a million miles away, more probably fifty.
We had a brilliant night though and the next day we caught the National Express back home promising that we'd go there again but we never did! What would I have done without the National Express, should charge them advertisement rights the amount of times they crop up in this book?
Before I move on, here's one more memory of Grant. We had been invited to this fancy dress party in Wavertree. The rendezvous was the Town Hall on the High Street but Neither Grant or me had a clue what to wear. We scratched our heads and suddenly a light switched on; let's ask the Vic. We knocked at St Dunstan's Rectory and we asked the Vic if he could help us out with any costume ideas. Like I said the Vic was a superb human being and without a moments hesitation he lent Grant and me two cloaks. He knew we would be out drinking but he trusted us not to spill too much beer on his treasured garments and secretly I think he was jealous and would have loved to join us.
Grant became a convincing Vampire, he had a dark suit and he found some comedy fangs. I became, well, the Vic but with dark hair. I wore my Dad's black waistcoat again, by black trousers, I had a black shirt and I made a dog collar out of white paper. I had a bible and Doreen from up the street let me use her recently deceased fathers gold glasses, the kind that are cut in half and his crucifix necklace.
The look was very convincing, punters up the High Street thought I was selling bibles or other religious stuff, all that was missing was a charity box. We had a great night and yes we managed to return all the aforementioned items back to their rightful owners and with no lasting damage.
Grant now lives in Australia. He's a qualified psychiatric nurse and he emigrated with his 'younger' girlfriend after separating from Joanne in the nineties. He has two kids to Joanne and the last time I saw Grant was at his Dad's funeral in 2010. We were all there except Brad as he was on holiday, Alan was there of course as it was his Dad too, Derek, had heard of Don's death so he was there, I had told Neil and Cliffy came too, as he was Joanne's brother, I'll talk about him later.

We all promised to keep in touch and to get together for a drink but we never did, so if any of you guys are reading this it's such a shame how we have all drifted apart as we share so many memories together, let's not get together just because of funerals and let's keep in touch eh, that's if I haven't offended you? And you know Grant you had your faults but your good points outweighed them and I guess I miss my mate and one day I must search on my son's Facebook account to post a message to say hi. After all keeping in touch or finding someone has become a lot easier when compared to when I was a kid with the advancement of modern technologies, there's no excuse unless someone lives life under the cyber radar.

Chapter Sixteen

Just Be Good To Me...

Moving on. Let me tell you more about my mate Derek who I've mentioned more than a few times already. Derek lived the posh end of Wavertree and I met him through Alan as they went to New Hey's School together, so this must have been when I was about twelve. Derek isn't his real name but I chose this name due to Del Boy from Only Fools and Horses.

Derek was always scheming you see and I became close friends with Derek but he was pally with everyone, the kind of lad who had fingers in various pies, probably still does knowing Derek, a good lad nonetheless and a mate who would always go the extra mile for you when needed. In fact Derek could 'charm the birds from the trees', he was a funny confident and self-assured kid with a glint in his eye and a cheeky freckled face and it was no surprise that he got into sales as a career. Derek would sometimes come down to Edge Hill with Scotty for a kick around, but we'd mainly wander up to Wavertree, the other end of Lawrence Road.

Derek had this other mate and I can't remember his name which is a blessing really as he was a racist. He lived a few doors along from Derek; he looked like Dave Stewart from the Eurythmics and he was a couple of years older but he had this unconditional negative attitude towards Black people.

I tried to steer clear of him whenever he appeared as I didn't like his attitude but I remember enough was enough and getting into this philosophical debate with him about racism and how he needed to change his attitude as he was totally irrational and absurd.

Like most people with racist attitudes however he rationalised that black people had created 'all' of societies problems and he would proclaim that 'they' should return to the country of their birth even when confronted with the fact that this is nonsense as most black people where born in this country.

We talked about The UK being invaded by various nations over the centuries and if he did a bit of genetic DNA testing then he would discover that we are all mixed race with ancestral origins from all over the world. I felt particularly offended because I had been racially abused myself as a child and at the time I believed my paternal ancestors were Native American.

He was an intelligent bloke actually, which frustrated me but so engrained was his opinions he wouldn't accept that we live in a multicultural society or accept that the counties problems, high inflation and unemployment, were manly to do with right wing politics that drove a wedge between neighbours spurred on by an individualism agenda promoted by the Tories. I accept that this in itself is an opinion but an opinion that could be backed up by research, that isn't offensive and not based on bigotry ideologies.

In fact he argued that the Tories hadn't done enough to promote Britishness, whatever that means and he told me he allied himself to the National Front. Perhaps he just felt like winding me up but his right wing narrow-mindedness pissed me off so I decided to walk away from him and Derek and decided not to waste my breath anymore and I don't recall ever seeing him again, thankfully.

Derek's Mum was called Joan, she was very sociable and friendly and he lived with his Mum, his step Dad, Les, his brother, Gary and his Nan. They lived in a terraced house like we did but the double bay windowed type with bigger rooms and a morning room we'd call round and hang out in Derek's with his Mum sometimes and we'd chat about all sorts of stuff for hours, like how Derek's family originated from Scotty Road, whilst his Nan sat in the corner shouting out instructions. She was a bit absent-minded.

Les was a decent fellow and he had a descent job to match and his Mum worked in a launderette on Smithdown Road. I wasn't exactly Nick Kayman, you know the model on the telly who advertised Levi's in the eighties to the sound of *'I Heard it Through the Grapevine'* by Marvin Gaye, superb track by the way, but this worked out well for me as I would sometime call in out of the cold for a brew during the cold winter months, the launderette was always warm of course and Joan would give me a good deal on any clothes I needed dry cleaning.

I collected coins as a hobby for a few years, not obsessively but every now and then someone would pass me 'shrapnel' from various parts of Europe and the World including Uncle Joe visiting Liverpool and I would organise my collection of coins into neat stacks. I had over a three hundred coins including old pennies, Farthings and Shillings found or bought from a local junk shop and given to me by Granddad like I said earlier on.

I vaguely remember old pennies as a toddler and it may interest you to know that they went out of circulation on the 15th February 1971 when we all switched over to decimalisation. Thanks again Wiki.

Derek had this mate who also collected coins and I am at a loss as to whether I lent them to Derek's mate to compare with his or if I just gave them to him in a moment of madness, either way my journey into all things currency ended then and I really regret my indifferent attitude, I think I was about fifteen at the time.

When I was seventeen, I saved my dole money whilst working on the side as a painter and decorator so as I could go on my first foreign holiday abroad, to Majorca with Les, Gary and Derek and I would give Joan thirty-five pounds a week as a kind of tontine. I discussed this with a bloke I worked with called Ste and he persuaded me to loan him my weeks wage, as he knew it would sit in Joan's hands and he needed money to pay his car insurance. Being both gullible and trusting in equal measures I did but he never paid me back and from that day forth I rarely lend money unless you are a close friend and although I could afford the loss the thought of someone stealing from me was repugnant and left me sick and when I confronted him he threatened me and I knew I was no match for him physically so I had to put that down to experience.

A lesson in life and this still makes me angry when I think back about this so lets move on but before I delve into my holiday memory here's a few words about the expansive of all bands, UB40 as they took their name from the UB40 card used to sign on, to get your dole money every two weeks.

UB40 were a British Reggie band from the Midlands and Derek and me went to see them live at the 'Royal Court', this was a terrific concert, we watched a short film about the band with their hits playing in the background and then they appeared and sang hit after hit.

I had the 'Labour of Love' album from 1983 and I would sit back and absorb the excellent, *'Please Don't Make Me Cry',* particularly the trumpet segment as it eases into the song. *'Cherry Oh Baby'* and *'Many Rivers to Cross,* were superb and I could go on and on but every track was a hit in my view and my favoured track was *'Red Red Wine'.* I never realised this at the time but the whole album is an album of cover tracks and oddly, Neil Diamond wrote Red Red Wine. I believe Mr Diamond has incorporated UB40's version into his stage show including the rap section at the end. How surreal is that?

UB40 also released a politically charged track called *'One in Ten'* on account that a tenth of the population was unemployed, this was certainly a one in ten period and looks like the 40's need to rerelease a 2012 version as the unemployment figures are on the rise again.
Anyway back to the holiday. Joan never went anywhere with Les, which I thought was very strange and so unlike my Mum and Dad. In fact I remember Joan being somewhat relieved to be on her own and she'd quip about getting a bit of peace.
The excitement built as the holiday got closer, Derek was a seasoned traveller so we would sit and talk about the guaranteed hot weather, the warm sea and of course the topless women on the beach. The day finally arrived, Les had arranged for a taxi to take us to Manchester Airport and after being all confused about how we proceeded through passport control we boarded the plane after first buying the obligatory Kouros aftershave from the duty free shop. I also bought Pac Robane for an alternative spray, how very chic of me and I probably wore a shell suit for comfort, a travelling must back in the eighties but one of life's big fashion no no's and very dangerous when stood before a hot fire!
I remember the plane climbing higher and higher into the heavenly clouds as we looked down on the many houses and car's as they shrank into the distance thinking how amazing it was to be on a plane, how did it stay up but also praying for a smooth and safe flight, especially the outward journey as at least I would have had a holiday. I'm sure others have had this slightly perverted thought?
We arrived at the airport and we caught a bus with other holiday revellers to a place called Alcudia, travelling overland through deserted dusty towns. We turned into the port and Derek said quick look out of the window. Our Noses were pushed against the window, yes, there was a glorious hot golden beach overlapped by wave upon wave of turquoise sea that met the cloudless blue sky on the horizon, but no, whilst this sight was a beautiful sight to behold, we were more interested in other attractive delights, fallen angles as far as we were concerned, yes topless, foreign and bronzed women in skimpy G strings! It was the eighties after all.
Oh my God, know that I typed that slowly for extra drama and sorry about the blasphemy but I had surly died and gone to heaven whilst singling the brilliant track *'Peaches'* by the 'Stranglers' and thinking I too could miss the 'charabang' back home if beaches were like this in the UK. For two weeks I would lie there in my skimpy speedos borrowed from Grant who always seemed to have clothes and from every corner of my eye I could see bare breast after bare breast. Now I know I'm coming

across as a right perv but I was a hormonal teenager after all, in search of holiday romance and this was all too much for me, I had never seen so many boobs! I ended up getting a real good tan being of the olive type but lets just say my back was several shades darker as I had to, (cough) hide my (cough) growing embarrassment on occasion. Sorry kids, unrefined I know and I nearly bought a single train ticket.

It's funny how we use high factor sun tan lotion these days recognising the increased chances of catching cancer from the harmful effects of the sun but back when I was a pimply youth you simply had to get an all over tan to zap away those spots, the deeper the better and I remember using oil with no protection and coming back several shades darker and proudly showing my 'skimpy white bits'.

In fact going abroad was still seen as being very extravagant round our way in the early eighties and you would walk around like a peacock using large amounts of after sun lotion hoping to prolong the tan that would fade within days and not being used to moisturiser I remember being on holiday with Derek and feeling my body, God that sounds rude but I was amazed just how smooth my skin felt!

Being a modern man I now use Nivea cream to fight the onset of aging, another example of how trends have changed over the decades, seventies men wore brute and Denim aftershave and that was about the only thing sold in the cosmetic side of the department store that catered for men except for Gillette razor blades of course.

Anyway you simply had to knock for your pasty mates to show them your white bits and it was the one time I didn't mind going the shop for mum, in fact I was positively willing knowing the stares I would get. Not that I am accustomed to 'showing off' as we'd say but a bit of harmless pruning both under the sun I guess and holding ones head up high was acceptable and indeed encouraged and you wanted to shout out 'hey I've been abroad on my hols'.

All seems so different when I compare then to now with the onset of sun beds in the eighties and all the tanning shops you see up and down the high street called 'tan city' or 'tantastic' or something 'tanningly' similar. In fact young people are driven to imitate celebrities in their quest to have a permanent glow enhanced by stuff from a bottle so no one stands out anymore or needs to say 'hey I've been on my hols'. The Costas have become less costly like I said before!

I remember using a girlfriends sun bed before I went on holiday wearing little protective glasses and speedos, my first and only time under a bed and I did this so as I could have a head start, didn't want to burn myself the first day.

My mates were no different and I remember Derek seriously burning himself under a heat lamp, he'd only spent a couple of minutes under the lamp but he was quite fair. It wasn't funny at the time but tickles me now, he walked into the Town Hall pub wearing 'shady' Roy Orbison like shades and looking like he'd been slapped around by someone who'd spent the day kneading beet root with their hands! Should have stayed at home but it was the weekend, I'd have done the same!
When I go abroad now I still sun bathe but not so intensely, no more teeny weeny white bits on this ageing body but I do confess to liking the glow the sun makes on my skin, makes me feel healthy and evokes memories of sun, sand, sangria and stares! In fact I remember all this because I am tapping away these words from under a palm tree in sunny Menorca drinking a cold beer smeared with factor ten on my last day of my annual holiday in 2012 but minus the skimpy speedos, a bad look for a middle aged man no matter what decade and I guess old habits are hard to shake off.
From one Balearic Island to another and memories of Derek and Majorca. I remember going to this open air night club and tasting Bacardi and coke for the first time, a drink I always associate with foreign holidays, a drink I still get in for Christmas for old times sake and memories of burnt backs.
The place was heaving with girls from all over Europe, Germany, Dutch and French girls, I thought the place was so exotic and the DJ would play thumping twelve inch tracks from Europe into the early hours like '*Rock Me Amadeus*' by the sadly departed 'Falco'.
Think about it, a disco outside under the stars, how amazing was that, beat Dunny's and Rotters hands down and the atmosphere was electric and this rubbed off on us and we oozed with confidence in our pastel coloured shirts. Derek fell head over heals in love with this girl from Stockport, near Manchester of all places, that was unheard off when I was young, a relationship with a Man United supporter, bad enough seeing a Red Nose! He kept this relationship going back in Blighty and I think this red devil temptress eventually broke his heart but Derek I did warn you this was too far to travel.
Not to be outdone, me, with my reputation. I met this drop dead gorgeous, blonde cockney girl, well I would say that wouldn't I, my story after all, but she was, I've certainly copped off with a few not so good looking girls in my time, for the dance that is, to compare her with. Told you I'd be an honest writer and before you tut about my shallowness, taste is a personal thing and she probably thought any ship in a port as I was certainly punching above my weight. One person's

terrorist is another's freedom fighter. Where is this going?
Okay back to my romantic encounter if you can call it that. The girl was staying in the same hotel and I remember walking back, hand in hand to the sound of crickets, no not Buddy Holly's mates, the insect kind and under a smiling crescent moon. Perhaps I was humming the track *'Moonlight Feels Right'*, a guilty pleasure by this seventies band called 'Starbuck', a mere consonant away from being a coffee franchise but once again I was in heaven and I remember kissing my cockney lass good night at her door wanting more and she said 'I'll see you later'. This is where I find ascents to be a fascinating subject like I alluded to before as I heard; 'you must come to my room later' not realising this was how people down south said goodbye. Sounds like a real poor excuse, something I wanted to hear perhaps but truthfully I was confused, it seemed to make sense at the time and an open invite. In fact I've just recalled a guilty pleasure of mine that exemplifies how I felt at the time, *'Invitation'* by the jazz funk band Shakatak and I can still hear the sound of her clicking stilettos in my head?
Anyway I was probably drunk on Bacardi and Sangria but plucking up the necessary courage, that stomach turning feeling again, I knocked on her door and fibbed that Derek was in the room with his Stockport girl and I didn't want to 'play gooseberry' all night, where does that saying come from.
Anyway, she let me in and we laid on her bed chatting and laughing the night away as she too expected her friend to walk in at any moment. Magic moment this, which is why I can remember so much detail and for years I would tell my mates that I was wearing my lucky boxing shorts, the pair I wore on that memorable but innocent night and annoyingly she implied the next morning that I could have stayed 'properly' if she had known that her friend was staying out all night!
Sorry lads for the embezzlement of this memory; the truth finally comes out as I never even got to buy a ticket to board the train or more appropriately a plane back to Edge Hill! There's a thought, I wonder if she celebrated and revered her lucky nickers, nah, I doubt it somehow.
Now here's an embarrassing memory. Some years later, I was taken in 'hook line and bloody sinker' by this girl from London who I got talking to on the High Street. I had my doubts, I'm not that gullible but she read me like a book, I was wearing my lucky boxers and she persuaded me that she knew my dream cockney lass; she was her best mate she claimed and she gave me an address.
Being a right Rodney plonker, I guess Derek if writing his memoirs would have called me Rodney, I wrote a letter, get ready Elvis in the

wings, but it was *'Return(ed) to Sender'*, great track played often by Mum. I felt ashamed and cross with myself for being such a fool; made worse by the fact that it had been read by some post office employee as he or she had returned it to my address which was written on the first page in the hope she would respond.
What a job eh and I bet he or she had right good laugh at my expense. Still, serves me right for being so gullible with dreams of open aired discos. Glad I brightened someone's day though.
Just before I return to Liverpool on that successful inward flight, phew, I wouldn't be here writing this story would I; another two memories have just popped into my head about this holiday. About a mile to the back of the hotel was this big hill and Derek and I decided to climb it for a laugh and we did this on a whim and without any preparation. We had our skimpy speedos on and flip-flops and we climbed the hill around the time when most had retreated for a mid afternoon nap, the heat was blistering just like Derek's back.
Never to be outdone we did climb the hill and on the way back all puffed out and thirsty, we fell into this ditch trying to take a much needed short cut back to the hotel and we got covered in all sorts of crap and leaches. We were 'minging' as we would say, so we found the nearest hotel and jumped into the pool for relief and a good clean. We didn't care about other punters; we were hot and very bothered.
We also went on this 'all you can eat and drink western themed night', the kind they sell you on the first day with offers of a free cocktail. You know the sort, sangria and cheap vino flowing like a river and you would put an empty bottle on your head indicating to Manuel that you needed more. Not to mention the obligatory sombrero hat plonked on your head so as some guy could sell you a picture at a good profit I might add, which I still have somewhere, must have seen me coming. Anyway the reason why I am recounting this story is because the coach driver had warned everyone through the translator, not get too drunk even though the drinks were free, or should I say paid for in advance. Be warned, anyone found to be too drunk would have to get a taxi back to the hotel and I'm guessing this had happened many times before. Derek and I decided to get our monies worth in spite of this warning and we consumed copious amounts of vino and we were literally legless. The affable disco track *'Dolce Vita'* by Ryan Paris was ringing in my ear, Derek and me were up for a party and a bit of girl chasing.
We staggered through to the disco and I spotted some girl dancing in a tree so I decided what the heck, I think ill join her, probably had a need to demonstrate my masculinity and prowess as I was good tree climber. I

fancied her; I hoped she'd fancy a bloke with such agility and a bit of a guilty pleasure of mine; I lost my *'Self Control'*, a cool track by Laura Brannigan.
Contact was made, she liked me, or at least I think she did and as I jumped out of the tree all *'Tarzan Boy'* like, another guilty pleasure by Baltimora, to show her I was also good at swinging, as in swinging from the tress, one girl at a time! I wasn't though, I landed awkwardly and I went over on my ankle, the same ankle that I broke some months previously, please bare with me. I was in agony and I writhed on the floor surrounded by staring tanned faces.
The night was ruined. Derek was annoyed and we were ushered to a waiting taxi, there was always someone too drunk waiting to be exploited. We or should I say I, caused a right commotion I can tell you and this continued back at the hotel after I had fallen out of the taxi. I wailed in pain, cursing everything believing I had ruined my holiday as this was the first week and Derek asked if there was a doctor in the house.
I know sounds so corny but there actually was a doctor in the house, an Asian doctor from the UK holidaying with his family. I was put to bed and the doctor told me to rest my ankle in a bag of ice and no more climbing trees, which I did and being very drunk I fell asleep and woke up to the sun glaring through the curtains in a pool of water. I thought I had peed myself, so I jumped out of bed and I went to the loo all confused. With that Derek shot up and noticed that I was walking unaided, definitely not in pain, I hadn't been crippled, I could stand up unassisted and although slightly tender I was by all accounts fit and healthy although I had a banging headache.
Derek and later his Dad and Gary, looked at me and warned me to limp when I was out of the room as I had caused such a stink and for the rest of the holiday I would lean against Derek for mock support as we entered the restaurant for our meals. I'd forget sometimes and Derek would give me a kick where the pain should have been, still cheesed off I'm guessing but very funny though. I did deserve a good kicking.
Anyway safely home. Derek was fashion mad and he became renowned for looking you up and down checking out the cut of your clothes whenever he met you. Derek followed his aspirational calling by getting a job as a sales assistant at a clothing boutique called Izzy Crown in St John's Market in the city centre. He started to amass a decent wardrobe as a result and began to hang out with lads who fancied themselves rotten and he would tell us stories of girls coming into the shop and being given their telephone number.

He worked with this lad who was in the group 'Are Kid' who had a hit in 1976 with a track called '*You Just Might See Me Cry*'; can't remember his name but sometimes girls would approach him and ask if he had been in the group ten years or so before.

Derek would sometimes grow weary of certain shirts or trousers moving on to the next must have clothes and he would either pass me his cast offs or sell them to me for a couple of quid. He was a good mate like that so in turn I also began to dress well, although not quite as up to date as Derek and I soon got to know some of his mates in the shop but I always felt like I didn't quite fit in as I was a painter and decorator by this stage. He had a good mate called Tony from the Orrel Park area of Liverpool and I got to know Tony's mates but my memory can't recall their names other than this older lad called Carlos, Marty who was a hairdresser and Mark who joined the Navy. We attended Marks leaving of Liverpool party in Bootle and I remember swaying to Rod Stuarts track '*We Are Sailing*', an apt track for the moment.

Derek was your archetypal salesman, still is, he's worked as a car salesman and now works for the energy company Eon selling door-to-door electricity and gas packages trying to convince punters to switch over, I bumped into him in McDonalds recently.

Derek was good at his job and he was promoted by Izzy and became the manager of a market stall in Birkenhead market. Derek needed help so he asked me if I wanted to earn some extra cash so I worked there too on a Saturday selling clothes to punters. I remember Derek being very driven to beat the previous weeks takings and excitedly phoning Izzy with the result as if he was trying to impress his father.

The pressure was on and I followed Derek's lead and I remember convincing many a punter that the shirt really was in fashion and the jeans fitted perfectly sir, when in truth all I was interested in was securing a sale. I'm not proud of this but the fifteen pounds I received for selling my soul to the devil was my supping money for that night but sometimes I'd forfeit this and would pick a top as my reward knowing that the extortionate mark up price far exceeded my wage.

Most weekends when I was around seventeen, I'd get together with Derek and his fellow poses and we'd go to clubs such as Tuxedo Junction, the Harrington Bar where I hugged the loo, Hollywood's or the Continental in town. Before going the club the place to be seen at, where all the good-looking people amassed in whatever was fashionable at the time, was Plumbers on Hardman Street and sometimes you'd see a local celeb or a footballer.

You felt famous by association but it was all so false and full of shallow people it seems and we would just stand at the side trying to look hip and cool. Many a night I would walk home on my own thinking why did these shop folk make such an effort when it seems all they were interested in was trying to outdo each other in the looks and clothes department and they didn't seem that bothered about chatting girls up? So alien to an ex Dunny's attendee!

A tradition of the shopping fraternity worthy of a mention at this juncture, was attending this bar below the market called Quinn's, Christmas Eve being a particularly good night. We would get there at 5pm as it opened and we would mingle with all the other sales assistants wanting to let their hair down after being on their feet all day and we had many a brilliant night there. Christmas Eve sought of gave you the courage to ask girls for a festive kiss just like New Years Eve and later we would trot off up the High Street in Wavertree.

One year I was in Tony's and he told me he and his mates were going to Torquay for the week. I had to square a few days off with my boss so Tony said why don't you follow us down at the weekend. I did, that weekend and on a National Express bus once again stopping off at town after town and having to change on two occasions. I was always doing impulsive things like this and I was only seventeen and actually my escapism antics reminds me of a terrific book I read a year or so ago, 'On The Road' by Jack Kerouac. An autobiographical book based on the spontaneous road trips of Kerouac and his friends across America. Haven't read it, you should.

Not that I am comparing the M6 to Route 66 and I never hitchhiked but I had the time of my life and I was put up on this camp bed in Tony's room in some cheap bed and breakfast joint. Torquay had a good nightlife as I recall and I remember dancing in this club with this Welsh girl to U2's *'Sunday Bloody Sunday'* and the Cults *'She Sells Sanctuary'*. I really like this track as it builds in momentum then explodes around the senses and Ian Astbury, the lead singer, has a phenomenal voice.

Let me pause a moment to talk about U2's thought provoking track. I've been to both Northern and Southern Ireland recently, the people are very friendly and hospitable and the rolling landscape is inspiring and is as strikingly beautiful as anything you would find in the Lake District. Back in the seventies however things were very different, Ireland was a place you feared and as a child I remember watching the newscaster report the latest atrocities, which seemed to happen every night.

The IRA was determined to extend its campaign of terror at home and in the UK in the name of freedom and as a kid I couldn't fathom out why people who lived so near would want to kill and harm neighbours based on religious indifference as I had many friends who were protestant. That said the Bloody Sunday massacre in 1972 when British paratroopers indiscriminately opened fire and killed thirteen civilians would surely make you choose which side you were on if you had to live through the troubles I guess. Thankfully Mr Bono et al can now protest about evils further afield.

When I was eighteen, Derek, Tony, Marty, Carlos, Scotty and me went on holiday to the party Island of Ibiza. It was just before it became bonkers on drugs and the acid house scene a few years later and we stayed just outside San Antonio in this apartment with a pool. Most days were spent 'recovering' by the pool;

You might have caught the Inbetweeners on telly, great series if you haven't yet seen it, very funny and a reminder of what life was like as a teenager, the antics they get up to are all too familiar to stuff we did, lads trying to impress the girls and running around playing immature games. I look back and think how different I was then and many a time I would find myself having to jump over a wall to retrieve my discarded trunks or being 'lashed' into the pool to the count of three. Once again boys will be boys I guess.

At night we would have chicken in a basket then off to a local club. We got friendly with this band from Liverpool and we became their dancers, we even got on stage and sang a couple of numbers with them, mainly classic soul numbers. It all got a bit boring in the end as we went there most nights and I had itchy feet to try out new places.

The first night of the holiday was memorable, we attending this party where the organisers made you sit boy girl, boy girl, I half expected them to hand out pens and paper but what a seating plan and I recall dancing to the terrific track '*Slippery People*' by 'Talking Head', a band I introduced Tina to and she followed them for a few years.

What a night we had and we all got lucky, even Carlos who was, lets just say, a complete stranger to taking train journeys. Derek and me danced to '*Don't You Forget About Me*' by Simply Minds with these girls from Bolton and we ended up going back to an apartment on the other side of the bay and I had to remind Derek of the post code theory.

I'll try and be discrete but this is a funny memory. The girl I was with insisted on a late night swim, a bit of a fantasy of hers, it would have been rude to refuse so we got in the pool and I took my onyx ring off, the type with a Centurions face on it, very eighties.

For some incomprehensible reason I placed the only ring I have ever possessed with the exception of my wedding ring that is, on the side and that was the last time I saw it. Now this ring was a Christmas gift from my Mum and Dad, not sure how much it cost, probably inexpensive but that's not the point and Mum was convinced that I had sold the ring, as she knew we ran out of money. Probably why I can remember all this, I hadn't Mum; I simply couldn't confess my skinny-dipping drunken train journey antics to you at the time. Sorry Mum.

Oh yes before I finish this sordid memory I remember then having to go into the bedroom where Derek had ended up, for a towel to dry off. I was naked and I ran in with my hands strategically placed like I was standing in a wall about to defend a free kick during a footy match, to sounds of Derek giggling and shouting 'bit to the left, no right', only kidding, he shouted from over some girls shoulder, 'dya mind mate, get out'. We walked home the next day and slept the rest of the day on a sun bed nursing a hangover.

We also went on a boat trip and I have a picture of us all on this secluded beach after playing alcohol 'make a fool out of us' games, you know the sought were someone falls over after spinning round a pole.

I'm at the back of the picture and everyone including me is barely dressed except for my mates as they had burnt themselves and were reduced to wearing hoodies in the scorching heat and buying yoghurt to soothe their blistered pain.

Good memories these of partying with my mates in sunny climes but teenage antics resigned to the past.

Chapter Seventeen

Live It Up...

The above-mentioned mates were decent enough lads but it was around this time that I started to drift away from them as I had become pallier with Brad when I was about eighteen. I'd known Brad since, well, since I can remember and like I said before I was mates with his brother Joey for a few months before Amanda came between us.
Brad's not his real name by the way but he often joked about using a pseudonym, namely a professional tennis coach called Brad, so this name kind of fits his self imposed image.
Brad was my best mate for a few years and I'll talk about our antics in a minute. He was always there for me whenever I needed an ear, in fact there was nothing Brad wouldn't do for you, he's a funny, generous and reliable lad and basically an all round top bloke. Brad and I drifted apart sadly when I went to work down south and I often regret moving away for that reason but I had to find work.
Brad's married to my wife's sister and we work in the same office so we do see each other but the relationship has never been the same if I am being honest and I remember Brad telling me once when he was very drunk that it felt like he had lost his left arm when I left and I think he never forgave me for that.
Could be wrong Brad and all I can say is I am really sorry mate and we should go for a pint one day and put all this nonsense to one side but the fact is we're both stubborn bastards!
Anyway, Brad was a 'lucky bugger' as we'd say, as he thankfully, by the 'Grace of God' evaded death on more than one occasion. Brad you see, attended the Heysel Final in 1985 when the wall crushed thirty-three Juventus and six Liverpool fans and I remember listening to the commentary unfold at St Dunstan's on the radio as we had a badminton match and worrying abut Brad and his brothers as they were staunch Liverpool supporters.
Some years later Brad attended the Hillsborough semi finals in 1989 and en route his 'new' white Ford Escort car puzzlingly broke down which resulted in him and his brothers getting to the match late, otherwise he

might have been one of the first in to the Lepping Lane end where ninety six fans died.

I vividly remember both disasters like they were yesterday, the whole city was in a state of shock and mourning and I can recall Liverpool supporters, including Brad's brother's, ferrying the injured across the pitch on advertising boards. I cried and cried watching this on telly and feared I knew someone had been killed.

It resembled a disaster movie, a surreal scene before my eyes and I knew how it felt to be penned into a stadium like cattle behind high steel fences, I had experienced the bottleneck crush of fans eager to get in to watch the match, I had been pressed against barriers in the stands being lifted off my feet and it was only then that I realised just how dangerous it was.

Questions were asked of the policing policy and could the disaster have been avoided and I can recall the shitty Sun newspaper falsely reporting that Liverpool fans had pick pocketed dying fans as they lay on the turf, there recent apology was not accepted. Indeed its some comfort to now know that Liverpool fans have been cleared of any wrongdoings following the release of all papers relating to the disaster trawled through by the Hillsborough Independent Panel but it's equally alarming to hear about the authorities attempts to conceal what had happened by falsifying police statements.

I see Sir Norman Bettisson has announced his early retirement following the release of the report in September 2012 but one cant help but feel that he jumped before being pushed to salvage his right to a full and hefty pension? Call me a cynic?

I can also recall feeling very humbled by the outpouring of emotions after the disaster watching the field of red and blue scarfs at Anfield expand daily eventually taking up the whole of the Kop. Like most Evertonian's we dislike the song 'Walk On' as it will always be associated with Liverpool FC so not included in my list but I do remember being moved to tears when I heard the song after the disaster. In fact the city was united and I still get a lump in my throat when I think of the disaster and I can only imagine how Brad and his brothers felt at the time and how they feel now. Brad's older brother Seb has not attended a football match since, prior to the disaster he had been a season ticket holder for years and attended home and away matches. He was a fanatical red.

A year or so after the disaster Brad was working on a building site on Bold Street in Town. Brad told me later that night that he was having a 'brew' with the site foreman over a table, he then walked away and suddenly the floors above collapsed on top of themselves like a deck of cards instantly killing the poor bloke below. Brad escaped unhurt mercifully but obviously shook up.

When we were very young I remember Brad knocking round with kids from Spofforth Road and we would stop and talk with them sometimes but we knew you had to be loyal to your street. Sometimes though we would have huge games of manhunt and other times we would have brick fights between streets with kids taking up positions on opposite sides of the wasteland.

An early memory of Brad was when a gang of us went to town just before Christmas; we were all in our early teens. Someone decided to steal a pen from a shop as a gift for his Dad and the next thing I know everyone was stealing from shops and boasting about what they had acquired, reminds me of the track *'Shoplifters of the World Unite'* by 'the Smiths'.

Being a Catholic with all the associated guilt I was torn and I refused to get involved and I would stand and watch, the burden of guilt was very weighty! Peer pressure then took over and to prove I had guts, as this had become a game of dare by this stage I stole a Yorkie Bar from Boots knowing I'd have to recite several Hail Mary's in confession.

My mates laughed at my bounty, sorry I meant Yorkie Bar. Now Yorkie bars were the 'Daddy' of all bars as they were big and chunky and have you noticed how small chocolate bars are nowadays compared to bars in the seventies and when you open the wrapper, which has shrunk too, the bar is barely enough for any hungry kid, never mind his mate.

On the topic of chocolate bars my bar of choice, followed closely by 'Curley Wurley' would be a 'Topic'. So delicious and the advert went *'what has a hazelnut in every bite, Topic*! We and I guess thousands of kids up and down the land would of course come back with 'squirrel shit!' Anyway returning to my 'Faganesque' past, I ran out of the shop, I think it was Boots on Church Street, as I was so frightened and I feared the wrath of God. I asked Alan where Brad was and he said the security guard had stopped him and worst was to come as they contacted his Mum and Dad and he deservedly got a right roasting.

I'm glad to say that was our first and only time we went shoplifting unless you count the occasional penny sweet when the shopkeeper turned away to get a jar form the shelves, oh yes, and the occasional bottle of pop from Minsters.

Most weekends I'd go clubbing with Derek and the other shop assistance like I said trying to act all grown up supping lager and flirting and sometimes 'copping off' with girls but during the week I would hang out

on corners like I'd done for years before my growth spurt.
See, growing up in a small terraced house with a through room and two annoying sisters meant I would have to go out most nights, the thought of staying in was abhorrent.
Telly had become tedious at times and tended to cater for older people and I had nowhere to escape too with people who understood me, a temperamental teenager. I see traits of me in my seventeen year old son, he'd never want me to say that but teens are from the planet 'why me, I know best', whilst Mum and Dad come from the distant sister planet, 'what's wrong with him, what did I say'. A constant cosmic catastrophic battlefield, try saying that when your drunk!
Whatever the weather I would hang out, an alien notion now, you had to be 'there' to know 'what' was happening and 'who' was with 'whom', this was us social networking I guess.
I'd surpassed the Rec and Dunny's disco had closed due to the trouble caused by tracksuit and bling wearing gangs, they were break dancers and tensions sometimes ran high and many a skirmish took place. I never got into body popping or the music, I liked some of the beats, some rapping tracks were likable such as *the Message*' by 'Grand Master Flash and the Furious Five', but truth was the scene wasn't for me so we found new places to loiter in.
Before closing I remember Neil rallying a few rugger friends of his from school and I asked my schoolmate Cunny to come down to Dunny's one Friday night. The previous week this gang of lads had threatened to take over the disco and all week plans were made to counteract this threat with a bit of muscle. It worked, I remember the gang walking in to be confronted by our crew and after a few punches it all ended, they had no chance and they new they were no match for good old *Eton Rifles*! I stood at the back!
I felt too old for youth clubs having had moments on many a club dance floor so the Spoffy pub became our favourite meeting place during the week as it was central, we'd laugh at the drunks falling over themselves, we'd listen to the Juke box when someone opened the door and we could stand in the doorway if it started to rain. But most importantly of all it was a pub and we wanted to know what was going on behind the door, our Narnia if you like, and this became our gathering point for a few years; we did this most nights unless, that is, we got wind of someone babysitting, a party or it was the weekend.
I was trying to jot down the type of conversations we had stepping foot to foot in the cold trying to keep warm but they are, sadly, lost forever as my mind now draws a blank. What do teenagers talk about, probably the

usual drivel so immediately forgettable but it feels like a switch has been turned off in my head.

Perhaps ones defence mechanism kicking in or is this Mother Nature's way, after all we are talking of a secret sect with secret languages and mannerisms like I said before that should not be remembered past ones teens.

Fair to say though we must have talked about girls, snogging and techniques for those of us who had 'developed' beyond kissing; we probably spoke about footy and certainly about music, who was in the charts, who was about to release a must have album, who was on TOTP. Never about school, politics or religion, too boring!

I can't even remember who was there either; it was like a meeting place for fellow Inbetweeners, the place to find out what was happening on our turf. I remember Alan and Grant, Neil before he emigrated, Brad and sometimes Derek but there were lots of other people whose names escape me.

Brad knew I had been clubbing and I would tell him all about my adventures, the girls, the music and like me, he wanted to grow up quickly so as could experience going out to town. Brad had grown wary of his mates who were into gambling and smoking, he was about sixteen so his right of passage had come and I was eighteen months older.

In time Brad and me needed to spread our wings further a field and we'd go on long walks; we'd talk and walk for miles and we'd cover most of Wavertree. Our usual walk took us up Lawrence Road, by then the Lawrence Road Lunatics had disbanded, I'd still mutter the punk poem in my head for old times sake and we'd end up on Penny Lane. We'd make our way round the Mystery Park returning home down the High Street and we'd sometimes meet girls along the way, some were past friends, some knew acquaintances. We were pally with lads in other areas, we never felt threatened as we knew most people either by name or 'the nod' and in any case Brad was part of a big family with older brothers so no one dared challenge us!

Brad, should you be reading this book remember the track *'D.I.S.C.O'*, by 'Ottowan' and singing as we walked and lets not forget you're favourite track, sorry mate, I must tell, *'Feels Like I'm in Love'* by Kelly Marie.

Brad and me had talked about going 'up the High Street' so not long after my eighteenth birthday Brad and me took the plunge and soon we became regulars, part of the furniture.

Brad looked younger, obviously, so I would usually go the bar and I would drink 'brown mild', in other words half a mild and a bottle of brown. I didn't really like the taste but you got a little bit more than a pint and you couldn't stand there without a drink or worst still, a glass of coke. Brad liked brown bitter.

Truth was though it wasn't about getting drunk, although a little bit of Dutch courage would help, it was about opportunity and being in places where older girls hung out. I had drank lager, the drink choice for most of my peers, as did Brad, but I remember a brewery strike in the eighties which resulted in lager running dry and then trying my Dad's favourite tipple, brown mild.

I'd call for Brad and spend half an hour or so talking with his Mum and Dad, as he was always late and they would offer me a bite to eat. I'd try and outwit Brad and would occasionally arrange to meet him at 8pm but would arrive at 8.15 pm to be greeted by him ironing his shirt in his undies. Not a pretty sight and I am sure Brad would hold off getting dressed until he spotted me walking past his window. We became mates with this lad called Cliffy, he lived with his sister Joanne and she went out with Grant like I said before.

I've just thought of an amusing memory to do with knocking for Brad. I decided to wear my black trousers but with a pastel pink lambs wool jumper I'd bought from Derek some months before. Your probably grimacing at the mental picture but you had to be there to understand, pastel colours were all the rage in the mid eighties, honest!

To my surprise Brad was actually ready this time, he answered the door fully dressed but to my dismay he was wearing the same clothes as me, yes he wore a pink jumper with matching black trousers. We took one look at each other and we both thought the same thing. 'Listen Brad, (listen Dave) you need to go in and change'. Trouble was we were late and we'd arranged to meet Cliffy in the Town Hall so we couldn't faff around for too long, decision made, we left for the High Street looking like twins!

Maybe we were being too self-conscious but the whole journey was spent thinking of answers to quizzical questions about our mutual appreciation for pink lambs wool jumpers. What would Cliffy say? In the end we decided honesty was the best response and as we walked up the steps to the Town Hall we both admitted to feeling nervous. Cliffy was stood at the bar, I think you know what I'm about to say, wait for it, yes he too was dressed in a pastel pink lambs wool jumper with matching black trousers.

After the initial 'I don't believe it' shock we looked at each other and we laughed. We didn't care what others thought and it actually turned out to be a really funny night trying to explain to people that this was all coincidental and not staged. Looking at this from a contemporary position perhaps we'd get away with it today as you often see groups of lads on stag do's wearing the same T shirt proclaiming to be something there not. There again I can't quite imagine saying to, let's just say for arguments sake, the local rugby team, 'hey lads were celebrating his last night as a single man, who's up for wearing a pink jumper!' What a memory though.

Me, Brad and Cliffy then found out about pubs in the Old Swan area and we decided to add this to our tour of duty. I know we sound so predictable but we developed a circuit and we'd start off in the Swan pub then over to the First Avenue, which had a really good atmosphere. I recall a night when Brad bought the first round, which was unusual, confidence evaded him back then and he used a ten-pound note but the bar staff gave him change from a fiver.

Now Brad and me were certainly no mugs and we were sober as well, so we demanded to speak to the manager who thought we had scammed him. We hadn't but he wouldn't budge, he wouldn't check his till and Brad had to go back the next day after the manager had worked out his takings and ended up giving Brad his money back.

We guessed many young punters wouldn't have bothered going back so we figured he or his staff were on the make and I think we never went back to the Swan as a result. A protest vote.

The one thing I remember about the First Ave, which has since reverted to 'an old man boozer', is that the place had futuristic strobe lighting enticing regulars, like flies to part with their hard earned cash. Brad and me used hair gel to grease our hair backwards; I know one of my many faux pas and under the ultra violet light it looked like someone had sprinkled talcum powder over our hair and our shoulders. I also remember the track by 'Swing Out Sister' called *'Break Out'* being played most nights and swaying on the steps by the dance floor.

Anyway After the Ave we'd sometimes have one more pint in the Masons if not to late, before heading off to the Gardeners, which is by the start of the M62, should have been called 'Junction Four'. Just a thought but this place was very popular and even had bouncers on the doors. The other year Brad and me went on a reminiscent pub-crawl and we went the Ave then the Gardeners, though twenty five years later we still hadn't forgiven the Swan. It was a Friday night, the Ave had lost its ambience and its fancy lighting or maybe we had just got old. In the Gardeners we were the only people in the pub, so no need for bouncers sadly, this was such a shame and I noticed the place eventually closed months later like so many pubs in the city.

Oh well back to the more distant past. After the Gardeners we'd jump a taxi back to the High Street and we would start off at the Town Hall to embark on our second circuit. The High Street today is a shadow of its former self; most of the action is now on Allerton Road, which had no pubs on it in the seventies. It was known as a 'dry area'.
Back then you had pub after pub full of people having fun, the Street was heaving? We'd always start off at the Town Hall, then the 'dick and glass', or to use its correct term, the 'Cock and Bottle'. We'd move on to the Lamb, then the Coffee House and we would finish off at the 'Thatched House' as the manager would take his time at 'kick out time'. The Thatched was the first pub to have music videos pumping out from small telly's perched on high, playing tracks of the day. The *'Final Countdown'* by 'Europe' and *'Living on Prayer'* by 'Bon Jovi' we're always on. Yes this was the year of big hair and spandex.
We had our own circuit, as did others and you got to meet regulars at similar times of the night, it became uncanny at times and if someone wasn't there at a particular time or did another circuit, anticlockwise for example, then we'd question what was going on, where had they gone? We'd flirt with girls and older women, Brad would sometimes buy a packet of pork scratching's, hairy bite size snacks that looked disgusting but somehow tasted nice and we'd talk to other lads about footy. I would watch Everton and if they weren't playing at home then Brad would watch Liverpool; so we'd spend time analysing the game, who scored, who played better, that kind of stuff.
I remember this one fanatical red and no matter how poorly Liverpool had played he always had a positive spin. When not looking Brad would give me the look as if to say 'we obviously weren't at the same game'. Brad was honest in his critique.
At the end of the night Brad and me would part from Cliffy as he didn't live near us and we'd walk home chatting about girls and footy. On the way home we would buy 'pasty, chips and beans' from a chippy by Picton Library. Sometimes though I'd leave a little until I got home to make a chip buttie and Brad could never understand how I had the will power. Brad liked his food you see. Sometimes we would dare a plate of chicken fried rice from the Green Spot restaurant. This was a right shit hole, you'd sit down and before you could finish your sentence the plate would appear before your fuzzy eyes! Beat that McDonalds?
I wouldn't exactly describe myself as a Michael Jackson fan although there's no doubting he was a talented performer, but I do remember the buzz in 1983 around the track and video to *'Thriller'*. It had been seriously hyped up, a mini dance horror story with the creepy Vincent

Price for added effect and we knew it was the most expensive video made at the time with must see special effects. It went on to be one of the most influential videos in pop music and I remember it being the weekend as I recall and the pubs emptying out on the High Street as there was a special screening on the telly appropriately at midnight.
Slightly inebriated I remember watching the video with my chips and credit to John Landis, the director and co-writer with Jackson, it was very good but it did unashamedly rip off the film the 'American Werewolf in London'.
Now there's a superb film, caught it recently on Channel Four and I love the track *'Bad Moon Rising'* by 'Credence Clearwater Revival'. One of those gems you discover when your older. To this day I still feel slightly perturbed when I walk from platform to platform whenever I'm on the tube in London, not because of any terrorist on a fatwa but fearing that my head will be ripped from my neck by this huge Yankee dog. Tell me why didn't the guy just run away up the escalator, he had the time? There's another track I simply must pay tribute too, a track that forever warns one not to carry a take away curry home to ones wife; the Jam's *'Down in the Tube Station at Midnight'*.
Where on earth did we get the money from, I've often contemplated that, as we'd go up the High Street and then Winston's, which I'll come to in a minute, each and every Friday, Saturday and Sunday night? I'm guessing I harangued Mum and Dad for a few quid every now and then, I had my painting and decorating money which I will tell you about a bit later and if I was short Brad would pay, he knew I would repay the favour when he was skint.
I do remember one time when I was paid twenty pound for a days work, our weekend night out money. Brad got us an 'extra' part in a film from his sister in law who worked at the Job Centre and the film was about the life story of the Russian composer Shostakovich and the respectable Ben Kingsley played him.
We were told to meet at St Georges Hall in Town, this Hall apparently resembles a building in Moscow and we knew we would be part of a crowd scene and we were asked to dress up as Russian's from the thirties. What do Russian's look like we thought, we asked our Dad's and both decided on Black Donkey Jackets. The same jacket that kept me warm at night under my covers.
The Hall had rows upon rows of chairs and for no particular reason we took our seats near the middle. People were faffing around, we could see cables, cameras and lightening equipment, it was really busy. We just sat and watched. Then, to our astonishment, Mr Kingsley arrives and sits

four seats to our left; we both looked at each other and had the same dream of being up there on the big screen. The make up artist arrived and it was rather comical. Brad and me had gelled our hair back to look older, we looked the part but some of the lads who sat by us with similar dreams, had long mullets. They were told to sit elsewhere or they could have a free haircut. Perhaps star stricken, they chose the chop and it was funny seeing these lads having the quickest of snips for their moment of fame.

In spite being herded about like cattle we had a good day; the filming took all day, we got paid and we had a free lunch. Some years later I was channel hopping and later that night, at some ungodly hour, BBC2 were showing my film. I set the video to record that's how long ago it was, as I'd never seen the film and I also watched it. Wish I hadn't. It was a very dreary black and white film and my moment of fame, my scene, appeared near the end. I say appear, the Hall was all smoky and I could make out Mr Kinglsey but everybody else was a blur, a mere three second smudge in the background. Did make me giggle though reminiscing about how the former mullets would probably have wished they had sat at the back if they only knew how it would all end after the editing.

Our favourite haunt on a Sunday was upstairs at the Town Hall as it had a disco and a slightly later bar but it was a killer getting up the next day for work. We'd follow the usual circuit, minus the Old Swan but we had to be careful not to leave it to late as the bouncer in the Town Hall took some persuading to let you in despite getting to know him, as it would get packed. Not quite Studio 54 but a risk.

The bar would be at least three deep and as it happens I would order three pints of lager. This would actually become a bit of game to see who could get served first and my strategy was to muscle in gradually and to ask for just one pint. The bar staff thinking 'oh he just wants one pint', would begin to pour, as I would be one less punter but I would then say 'and another five pints please'. Worked most nights.

The tune I most associate with the Town Hall is '*Misfit*' by Curiosity Killed the Cat. In the video the beret wearing singer, Ben Volpeliere-Pierrot, danced gangly down a New York side street whilst Alan Warhol's referenced Bob Dylan's '*Subterranean Homesick Blues*' by dropping pieces of white card in time to the music.

The Town Hall was a good venue actually and I remember talking to this woman who was a few years older than me and she was staying at her sisters who lived in my street. Coincidently she worked as a secretary in a factory with the brother of a mate of mine, I think this is how we got talking. She was nice and I cheekily suggested she pop over to my house for a coffee, I know a terrible chat up line, seemed to work on the Goldblend advert.

Anyway I got home after having my obligatory pasty, chips and beans and I was about to retire to bed when someone knocks on the door. She had taken my invite seriously, I was a bit dumbstruck, she stayed for an hour or so, we did indeed have coffee and yes we kissed but that was that, the train never left the station.

The next day I called round to her sister's house and we became mates for a few days, nothing more and truth was we just didn't connect at a romantic level. This was all to end however, she knocked on my door some days later, she was clearly troubled and probed me as to why I had told my mates brother that we went all the way during our coffee encounter, an alleged train journey encounter.

I naturally defended myself and told her I hadn't but she wouldn't believe me. Why my mate's brother, who shall remain anonymous, was this shop floor banter? Regardless of the motive I totally understood her anger, as it must have tarnished her reputation, especially in a male dominated environment, who knows perhaps he fancied her and wanted to sully any relationship that might have blossomed?

Anyway lets get back to something more positive, lets talk about Winston's. I talk more about this club elsewhere in this book when I refer to badminton; when it opened we couldn't believe our luck as it turned out to be a great club, it prolonged our night and it was on our way home. The only downside was that we had to change our 'end of night culinary tastes' as our pasty, chips and beans chippy was back up the High Street, so we would stop off at this take away and mainly eat pizzas or kebabs.

We got to know the bouncers at Winston's; we became regulars and most nights the same people we'd bump into earlier on up the High Street would be there to, it was like home from home. The place had a dance floor and a DJ of course, this was the mid eighties, so you had your share of crap music.

Brad's other guilty pleasures, sorry again Brad, was *'Live It Up*, a catchy track I admit, by this Australian band called 'Mental as Anything!' I actually have this image of the singer in my head and Brad looks a smidgen like the singer, same hair colouring you see!

Brad and me were at Winston's and the night was drawing to an end. I looked over at this group of women and one of them rolled her eyes at me. I'll spare you the punch line this time and I mouthed across the throngs of people, 'dya fancy a dance'? I turned to Brad and said 'I've

just been 'knocked back', this means being shunned, 'by dis woman over der'. Brad said 'ye haven't mate', next thing I turn round and she's standing next to me.
We walked to the dance floor and as we did the DJ softened the music and next thing I know she has her arms round me, I beckoned her to '*Move Closer*' a rather decent 'one hit wonder' track by Phyllis Nelson. This all happened in a matter of minutes, I barley knew her name let alone her star sign and she was certainly too old to still be attending school, I wonder if she went to Notre Dame but she then said 'do you fancy coming back to mine?'
This was all very dreamlike to me, the kind of thing that only ever happens in movies, she was very attractive, older and she had her own place, and how could I say no, she was in charge. Perhaps influenced by my dear old frugal Dad I hesitated slightly, I asked her where she lived and I did the maths while fiddling with my money in my black and white chequered trouser pockets. That postcode theory again like I said before. This time the maths did stack up so I said goodbye to Brad and Cliffy to enjoy pizza on their own, they understood, we hailed a taxi and well, that's enough of this memory but let's just say I never caught a taxi home, no I got the cheaper option, I got the bus to Edge Hill after steaming down the track!
One hot summer night I remember returning from a Charity Shield footy match at Wembley. I was with my boss Jimmy, I'll mention him later, on a coach singing '*American Pie*' by Don McLean and I had a dilemma. I still went out with Derek and his mates to Town sometimes and I was undecided as to whether to go out with Derek when we got back to Liverpool or to catch up with Brad and Cliffy. I asked Jimmy what he thought and to pass the time as we drove up the M6 we had a long chat about how late it would be and the fact I would be wearing the clothes I'd had on all day. My favourite it jeans and jumper.
Jimmy said I'd go up the High Street if I were you. Not possessing a mobile of course I knew I would have more success finding Brad and Cliffy as I would correlate the time with where they would normally be on the High Street circuit. See, a bit anal but good planning or what. The theory worked as it happened and I found them and after a quick pint to get me in the mood we made our way to Winston's.
I mention this night because we met these three girls and after dancing the night away we arranged to meet them next week. The chance of all three of us finding romance on the same night was a rare phenomenon and relationships blossomed.
It was a memorable night for all three of us. Cliffy ended up marrying

Mandy as it happens and he's still with her, she came to Alan and Grant's Dad's funeral with Cliffy; Brad and me went out with Julia and Wendy. I was with Julia for a year or so and she ended up being my first serious girlfriend and this became a memorable part of my life not just because of Julia but it was around this time that I began to change from a young person to an adult.

I was growing up and I say this as it was the first time I remember seriously thinking about what career I was interested in and where I wanted to be in the future, I developed ambition and drive and you can find out more about this in the sequel to this book.

Chapter Eighteen

Eton Rifles...

Do you like the picture then? Me neither, I was in school and I was told to make my way to the hall so as I could have my picture taken and I think I was about fourteen at the time. I look bloody awful and a number of questions spring to mind. Why didn't the photographer stop and suggest I take a look in the mirror so as I could at least straighten my tie? Why did my Mum buy the photo seeing as I look greasy with a huge pimple sticking out like a beacon and what's with all the stains on the photo?

It's not very flattering but you know I actually treasure this photo as it reminds me of my school of course and the struggles my family went through at the time so this is why I have decided to include it because this is how I looked, this was me, a spotty teenager smiling at the lens but feeling very sad inside.

See, I've yet to cover my secondary education as it is a topic that I'm not too keen on talking about as I eventually came to hate school which is probably why I haven't talked about it till now.

You see I have some bittersweet memories but I guess I have to recall all my memories regardless of whether they are good, bad or indifferent, so here goes. Gulp!

After the relative safe haven of St. Hughes I attended St. Thomas A Becket Secondary Modern on Spekeland Road. It's demolished now but back then it was within walking distance of my street, just on from the factory that nearly caused the death of Lee. I also attended the nursery like I said before at the far end of the school.

The school was also famous round our way for 'shaggers' as we called them, sorry about my crassness but 'lovers' looking for dark secluded place to park their cars would sometimes be spotted in the dark. The side of the school had this dirt track you see, that went nowhere and at night-time we'd spot car lights in the distance inviting us to sneak up and have a peak. Very dangerous I know but life was dangerous and I must assert that we weren't burgeoning 'doggers' just curious kids.

I vividly remember my first day in big school. Mum had rigged me out in a black blazer and 'warm' full-length trousers instead of grey shorts as I was used too. Thank God, as I hated the winters and the pervading drafts around by skinny legs, legs that was still hairless, at least for a couple of more years.

Alan came to my house, we were the same age like I said and he had a different uniform than me as he was a Protestant and had attended Earle Road and was moving up to New Heys Comprehensive in Garston.

I walked to school and he got the bus. I was jealous of that as I to wanted to escape the area and some of my other mates were either going the same school, as Alan or they would catch the same bus to their school. Seemed so unfair and it felt like I had been cast aside.

I'll give you an example. Bishop Eaton Church had a weekly disco; it was popular, so much so it became a ticket event. Grant, Alan, Joey and Derek got the bus together and I can now visualise the conversation upstairs at the back of the bus where it was customary for kids to sit, the furthest point from prying adult eyes and ears.

Someone seemingly had acquired four tickets to the disco and they must have talked about who was going and then realising I would be left out, at least I hoped they gave me at least a passing thought, they conspiratorially plotted the night out, where to meet and what to say, that kind of thing?

Anyway, blissfully unaware I knocked at Alan and Grants house on the night of the Disco as per usual to be told by their Mum that they were up by the station train spotting! Was this code for watching 'shaggers'?

It was Friday night, I remember thinking why hadn't they knocked for me but then thinking, train spotting, come on this sounded very suspicious, train spotting was for old blokes in macs! Indeed this was a year or so before I discovered the attraction of getting off at Edge Hill when opinions changed, we certainly tried to spot as many trains as we could and sometimes numbers were exchanged in the hope you'd catch that train again! Ouch all this not so secret code is making me woozy.

Where was I, oh yes the deceit. Why involve a Mum and I told my Mum and she said 'it sounds like they've let you down son' and the annoying thing is they carried on with the pretence the following day digging a large hole as they did. I could sense the uneasiness and I remember playing along, as it felt good to see them fall into traps forgetting I wasn't actually there dancing alongside them!

Hindsight is truly a wonderful thing as they say but I like to think I'd have been honest if the tables were turned, I'd probably still have gone because I was on the bus, I'm not that honourable but I would have talked with my mate hoping he'd say 'go, I understand, no point wasting a good night out' and it's times like that when mates need to say 'it's cool, really'. I'm also guessing this must have really upset me seeing as I am able to recall the night and the string of lies but no hard feelings chaps, time and people move on and this is all part of growing up.

So back to big school. I was so nervous, I knew some of my friends from my old school would be with me including my footy pals like Oliver, Leather and Whitehead but I also knew I'd meet other boys too. I knew kids would attend this school from Toxteth and further afield and I knew this meant tougher and rougher schools.

I knew the first few weeks would be about who was the toughest and meanest and in contrast who was the geekest, the meekest, the one to be bullied. You'd have the 'cock'; the top kid at school, wanting to take their rightful place as the cock of our year but knowing other cocks would be thinking the same. Forgive my use of the word cock as this sounds so not right but them were the terms we used, think its to do with poultry or something like that.

Friendships would be formed, I knew that but I was an insecure child who took things to heart rather than laugh things off and like I alluded to before I certainly wasn't a cock by any stretch of the imagination.

I walked into my classroom and this huge black kid called Madge, sat alone and I thought he was a prefect from year five sent to chaperone us first years kids until the teacher arrived. He was actually the same age and he must have been over six foot and the same weight as I am now, he was a giant of a kid in kid's clothes!

I was very cautious of Madge to begin with, he looked menacing but he was actually a decent lad and he sometimes stood up for me and helped me out of a jam or two! I guess being so big made him a loner at times and I guess we shared that trait in common and I could sense that he felt sorry for me.

Madge was also a good runner but with legs taller the size of an averagely adult it wasn't surprising. Sometimes, PE or physical education to use its correct term, would involve running a circuit of three or so miles for an hour up Spekeland Road, along Tunnel Road, onto Wavertree Road, down Spofforth Road and back up Spekeland.

I was a pretty decent cross-country runner after having practiced running round our street for years and up ad down the aforementioned Roads and I ran for the school on a few occasions.

I had a good engine, I wasn't fast but I could run for miles without stopping, I had good stamina, still have I think and I had an inner determination to win at all things I tried! I couldn't or wouldn't fail, that

wasn't an option for a chariot of fire runner like me!
The race would start and the teachers would then retreat to the staff room once the last straggler had turned the corner for a brew to later show their face at the finishing line to shout at the kids as we staggered back!
Some would set off at a pace up Spekeland hill but would soon run out of steam, stopping and choking for breath with hands on hips and a killer stich. Others, usually the rotund type, those carrying too much timber around their waist, never even tried and just walked the whole way knowing there was really no point to this exertion so walk and accept ones fate and use the opportunity to chat.
Me, well, I'd pace myself keeping Madge in my sight, as he would sprint off. It would become a race of tactics. Madge would look back hoping to shake me off and I could tell when he was struggling but I annoyingly just kept on going and going and sometimes I'd catch him up and leave him in my wake to win. He was a decent pacemaker but I mustn't credit myself with winning all the time, as Madge would take the honour when I was having a bad day stitch.
We'd also do circuit training in the gym. This involved passing a heavy medicine ball from mate to mate, jumping over vaults, climbing up and down rope ladders and the dreaded greasy rope climb. There's a thought, why was this heavy suede ball linked to prescriptions, something to do with the onset of pain me thinks as you take one in the belly.
The teachers name was Mr Day from Wales and he would scream at us to climb till we touched the roof some twenty feet or so off the ground. So tiring, your arms would ache with pain and you would slip down the rope burning your hands and the inside of your thighs to collapse on the floor to Welsh shouts of 'get up you lazy sod and now give me ten press ups'. I sensed Mr Day liked rugby.
Was this really necessary Mr Day, it felt like we were new recruits in the army being put through our paces, a throwback to fifties preparing us louts for army conscription in case Blighty went to war again?
In fact Mr Day thought he was a Sergeant Major and he ran a very tight ship where strict discipline was a given. When we got changed boys being boys we'd chat and shout about stuff and he'd come in with an old battered plimsoll, a predecessor to Converse, in his hand looking to dish out his form of punishment. He'd make random choices to show he could slap anyone as he was in power, he held the plimsoll, a demonstration to maintain order.

He honed in on me once and hit me across the calves before I could protest, didn't half hurt and I hadn't done anything wrong. Thinking back though he never chose my running mate Madge, I wonder why short arse power crazy Day. Oh no I'm becoming twisted and embittered again, where's that list, another addition?

Metal work was another memory I have of this school. We'd line up in our white overalls and this teacher with pock holes in his face from a lifetime of acne I guess; can't remember his name, would warn us about safety and the dangers in his workshop.

Don't know why this memory has stuck in my mind but I remember him warning us not to buy a tin of beans with a dent in it as it may have been contaminated in some way and to this day I can see his acne face as I fiddle around with a can of beans in Tesco's checking if it's in perfect shape. You never know he might have been right.

We made all sorts of useless stuff like metal plum line levels for decorating and shoehorns; I still have the shoehorn as I gave it to my Granddad before he died, so not so useless I guess but I haven't used it for years, if at all now I come to mention it.

I also have a creosol stained fruit bowl made from wooden slats dovetailed and pinned together in the loft that I made in woodwork. I did use this and for years it stood proud in the middle of our table at home and sometime it even contained fruit!

I always considered myself to be a bright kid but I realised that I liked working with my hands too but when the teachers sneaked off for a fag the place became very dangerous. Again Mr Attenborough you should take a look sometimes, see boys and chisels is a very bad combination when left on their own and you had to tie your laces one too many times to avoid missiles!

Within a matter of weeks I soon discovered that most of my peers were only interested in mucking about and cock fighting, this was a Comp after all and they were only concerned with who could take whom.

I simply didn't fit in, I really regretted failing my 11+ and I decided to knuckle down and concentrate on my learning, as I wanted to learn stuff. I soon became the studious sort and although I came top in most subjects this had its downside as it left me vulnerable to the class bully. I would do my best not to publicise what I had got but the teachers would let slip not realising that they were sealing my fate and I leant quickly that kids generally don't like a smart arse and I think I had become a smart arse by then trying to avoid trouble.

It became a game of cat and mouse and I would hate unstructured playtime, as I had to stand on the yard and try and mix. Sometimes it would be tolerable and I'd mix and chat and take my turn in goal, then other times someone would randomly offer you out for no reason other than to move up the cock ladder! I'd refuse which made things worse as I couldn't see the sense and I am guessing the provocateur knew that.

I realise now that I should have said yes just to prove that I had it in me to fight back, my Dad would tell me 'one punch and they wont do it again'. I would give myself motivational speeches as I walked into the yard, I'd feel the inner anger in me boil up but I couldn't sustain my confidence and I would cower away to avoid trouble.

I hated my inability to fight back and it was like the archetypical American prison movies were the good guy, if I may be so bold to refer to myself as the good guy, has to watch his back, a guy who chooses his friends carefully, then that's how it felt for me.

I don't think I'm over dramatizing things and its no coincidence that this school was later demolished because of its school of hard knocks reputation despite being less than thirty years old, a sixties monstrosity built to house inner city kids with little hope or aspiration beyond the trenches, be that cannon fodder on the battlefield or diffing some drains as a labourer.

I became quite depressed thinking back and I just kept on applying myself more and more to my studies but this made things worse for me. I was in a no win situation as this was a tough inner city school; good at containment but not the nurturing, rewarding, learning type of school I come across today in my work.

In fact the head teacher, a good old geezer called Mr Gill spotted my potential and he knew how unhappy I was, probably something that was mentioned in the staff room but he probably spotted me sitting against the fence at break times through his window.

Mr Gill couldn't understand how I had not made it to Grammar School, should have showed him my appendix scar and by the third year he seemingly pulled some strings and helped me move out of the hell hole I was living in.

My Mum and Dad were subsequently invited to attend a meeting with Mr Gill and he asked if I wanted to attend Cardinal Allen Grammar School in West Derby? I was so chuffed, a chance for early parole, to escape and to raise the bar of expectation, all my hard work had not been in vein or so I thought. I was certainly keen and I had ambition in droves so we said yes of course.

I've just thought of another memory to do with Mr Gill that fits in with this. I attended this public meeting with Alan and his mum at Earle Road Primary School to talk about improvements and plans to the area.

Whoever was in charge, probably some counsellor but not David Alton, had plans to improve St Dunstan's and surrounding area, making it into a sports centre and to turn our field into a proper football pitch.
I must have been about thirteen and I sat in the crowd and although my stomach was in knots I wanted to contribute to the debate and to offer up a young person's perspective believing I had good ideas to bestow on the people listening to drivel about what adults thought kids wanted. This was my first salvo into public speaking and I raised my hand and once acknowledged I stood up and talked about tennis courts, a running track and properly maintained footy pitches, all the games we had played in our street but games that only occurred because we had improvised not having the right equipment or facilities.
I was on a roll and afterwards the main speaker pulled me aside and asked if I would like to join the committee, I never did though but I did leave with a huge roll of paper with the proposed designs and I was asked to show them to my head teacher.
The next day I knocked on Mr Gills door with the plans and he was very impressed and who knows whether it was because of this sense of civic pride but a few weeks later he invited my parents and me into his office for that chat about moving school so in a strange way I have Alan's Mum to thank for that?
Anyway, we then attended another meeting with Father Cheetham, the head at Cardinal Allen Grammar School, in his musty old world office full of dusty books. I was mid way through third year, kids today call this year nine and my family had high hopes of me attending university, will he become a doctor, a lawyer, an architect, the world was at my feet it seems with aspirations that I'd end up with a career and not just a job and a career that would be safe and secure.
Before I left the Comp the English teacher treated the class to the brilliant thought provoking black and white movie, 'Lord of the Flies', based on William Golding's book. For those who don't know the story, this is about a group of school kids marooned on a tropical island who become increasingly paranoid about the mysterious beast and after a while, chaos ensues when Jack and his followers lose it, choosing to ignore the voice of reason which is Ralph. I felt an affinity for Piggy, a sensitive and sensible kid in glasses, as I knew how it felt to be bullied although I would never have admitted it at the time.
Kids at St Thomas A Becket weren't quite like the choir boys in this acclaimed book but they knew I was moving on so I decided to bunk off school the afternoon of my final day to avoid a goodbye thrashing. Word had passed around that I had to walk the tunnel of death so bunking off

seemed the logical thing to do and this was alien to me, in spite being so unhappy at school I never bunked off or called a sickie.

I vividly remembered my first day at Cardinal Allen. It was January, the start of a new decade, it was 1980 and I left my Secondary Modern School with echoes of *'Another Brick in the Wall'* still ringing in my ear, I was nearly fourteen. Annoyingly I caught the wrong bus but still managed to get to school on time in a panic and I nervously presented myself to the receptionist at Cardinal Allen. Again I was full of trepidation but with dreams of bigger things and pastures new having escaped Alcatraz to what would surely be a better life. I sat outside the heads office fidgeting and watching throngs of children pass me by trying to work out who I was.

After what seemed like an eternity I was taken to my form teacher, a big burly and imposing man with collie-flower ears and bulbous nose. His name was Mr Daley and he, like so many of his fellow teachers were fanatical about rugby as was the school. I soon realised one simple rule, if you liked rugby you were made and I'll come back to this honourable if not violent sport a bit later.

I was introduced to the class and our form class was in a biology lab on the third floor and we sat behind large desks on stools surrounded by pickled animals in glass jars, Belfast sinks and Bunsen burners.

I was in Barlow, which I was to learn was an important thing to know as you had to honour the bullshit old school tie network. I was introduced to the class as the new kid and everyone gave me glancing looks checking me out as they did, was I a genius, was I hard as nails, was I a threat, was I into rugby? A second past and Barlow quickly knew I was none of these.

I buddied up with this lad who looked like Ringo from the Beatles, his name was John and he came from Melling, an area near Aintree Racecourse. I mentioned him earlier when I was talking about my CB. He had a decent Romanesque nose, sorry John and his nickname was scon head, can't remember why, probably decided in year one and we became good mates, he was from working class roots like me.

I soon come to realise that most of my peers were from nice parts of Liverpool like Woolton and Gateacre and some were even fee-paying students shipped in from miles away from places like Runcorn and St Helen's. You might think I have a personality complex but being from Edge Hill was a clear disadvantage as it defined your social class and again determined what pecking order you were in. I decided to do my best to keep this a secret.

True, like John, other kids came from town, Wavertree and other less leafy parts of Liverpool but they had learnt to hide it and people moved on, their story became old as it was told in year one, unlike mine as I was the new kid in town.

Also when a group of kids embark on a journey through school together they separate into friendship groups based on appearance, values and social class. I realise that now and kids instinctively become tribal.

Me, I arrived in year three, clearly from a family with little money if my uniform was anything to go by and try, as I must, I struggled to settle at my new school or make 'real' friends. I was on the outside once more and I soon discovered that I wasn't the cleverest kid; I knew I wasn't the toughest and I came from Edge Hill.

This wasn't an issue at St Thomas A Becket of course, as we were all poor and from the same area. I had to wear a uniform but in my new school looks was everything and some of the kids dressed immaculately unlike me with clean shirts on everyday, how odd is that? Take a look at pimply me and see what I mean!

We had a kit for PE, indoor and outdoor and the uniform was very posh and had yellow, red and black braid sowed around the blazer cuffs and at the top of our pockets. My Mum couldn't sew to save her life, sorry Mum but true and the braid would hang down as if to signify that life was tough for me. The track *'Baggy Trousers'* by Madness, which was out when I started at Cardinal Allen kind of sums up school for me at that time but my peers trousers in contrast were straight with a pristine crease sharp enough to cut bread!

This has got me thinking of other tracks by Madness that I haven't thought of for years, for example I had the album *'One Step Beyond'* and I would lose myself by drawing the silhouetted 'Nutty boy' image in art. I liked the title track but I also liked *'The Prince'* and *'My Girl'* but I went off Madness when they gained in popularity, I preferred their earlier stuff.

I also learnt that the boy I replaced had been hounded out of school as he to was from a poor area and although I never met Churchy, this kids name, I could connect with his plight and indeed some of the lads would mock that I was just like him! It felt like I had been sent to the school to replace poor Churchy, new fodder to prod and skit, I had moved from Alcatraz to San Quentin but hoping to catch the brilliant Johnny Cash.

I only possessed one pair of shoes that became increasingly scuffed and one shirt that became dirty round the collar by the end of the week.

It wasn't that my Mum purposely sent me to school looking scruffy; she just couldn't afford to match my peer's Mums, Dad was out of work by

then and we would sometimes wash our clothes in last night's bath water as the washing machine was often broken.
My kid's shower daily whereas I had a bath once maybe twice a week and my kids use deodorant whereas I probably whiffed sometimes. I remember the chemistry teacher doing an experiment to do with the chemical reaction of soap. His eye caught mine and he was about to say 'you, come here and wash your hands in this glass container' when this kid called Macca put his hand up and offered himself and thereby saved my pending humiliation as the water would have turned a dirtier shade of grey. Not sure if Macca did this through kindness but he was a really nice kid, a really good sportsman as I recall, but I like to think he took a bullet for me.
As a father acutely aware of how cruel kids can be and worrying about how they appear in school, I make sure my lads have a shirt for every day and new shoes when they need them. This is the benefit of having a job I guess and I've just thought of something, I hope they don't bully those less fortunate? No not my two, I've brought them up better and I just wouldn't allow them to either be a bully or to be a bullied but as parents do we really know what goes on when our kids are out of sight. Thinking back to my school years I have often wondered if Mum and Dad knew how unhappy I had become, surely my demeanour and attitude wreaked of sadness but I don't recall them asking me how I was doing but there again if they did I probably would have just told them I was fine.
Teenagers rarely reveal their true feelings using words in my experience but perhaps in their disposition and one would never own up to being bullied in any event but would rather suffer in silence blaming oneself like I did for being so crap at fending off ridicule.
Dad would have wanted me to hit back being an ex boxer, whereas Mum would have told me to laugh it off as she was the sociable sort but all I can remember that first year at the Grammar school was a strong sense of feeling lonely. Indeed I had left a school full of testosterone and wannabe cocks to a school full of old boy testosterone and posh La cocks! Different type of bully but just as cruel and once again I speculated why I never quite fitted in, was it me, it probably was?
I remember sitting in rows of desks in French class, this is ironic as I'm actually holidaying in France as I write this on my I phone drinking a nice red vino, when the teacher started conversing in French to the class and to my horror they answered him back in fluent French. I could count to twenty but the nearest I got to understanding French was singing along to the Manhattan Transfer's love track, *'Chanson De Amore'*. I

remember singing ra da da da da, or rat a tat a tat as I thought it went. Yet another lyrical gaff to add to the list.

My French vocabulary did expand slightly following the weird Gallic punk track by 'Plastic Bertrand', *'Ca Plane Pour Moir'*, which I've discovered means, *'this works for me'*.

My peers understood nouns and tenses, I was out of my depth and I remember choking back the tears, I know I'm a wimp, I whispered to the teacher that I didn't understand and good enough he was very sympathetic, he was considerate, he took me to one side and gave me a year one book to help me try and catch up. So when my peers practiced more complicated French words and sentences, I would sit at the back learning how to say hello and goodbye and I would also take this book into Latin, you see Latin was well out of my league and I was spared this lesson as it was taught from year one!

I never did catch up though and the long established school mould had to be broken some six months later to accommodate me and several other 'dunces'; we were allowed the earth shattering decision to take art instead of a language. This I am told had never happened before as the teaching of a language was compulsory at my school and this must have caused a right commotion in the staff room.

The strangest thing happened recently. I was shopping with Sue and Adam saving a few quid in Home Bargain store and behind me stood a teacher from my old school and his name was Mr Gower. Unlike me on account that this was thirty odd years later, he looked no different from when I last saw him save a few extra pounds in weight and he still had a baldy head and beard. Funny how I can remember his name and that he was a kind hearted teacher but I can't recall what he taught but I think it was French.

I wish I had said 'hello Sir' and I should have asked Adam if he knew how to ask for directions to the toilet in French and who knows, he might have intersected with the knowledge bestowed to a retired teacher versed in the Gallic mother tongue with 'orientations pour la toilette'. Thanks once again to I Translate, who needs French lessons eh?.

Another thing that set you out as different and poor was free school meals. Good intentioned I know, allowing kids from unemployed families to have at least one good meal a day but the school might as well have tattooed, 'hear thee hear thee, here stands the poor kid waiting to be fed! Now tuck in lads and rib him some more!' Glad to see kids today are spared this humiliation and they have cards to use for lunch and no one knows who's on free meals and whose not.

Getting Off At Edge Hill – The Tracks Of My Years

On the topic of freebies, I would get to school with my free bus pass that was pink in colour with my carefully pencilled time table on the inside and I'd not only have to catch a bus to school but I had to catch two busses.
Before attending this school the only bus I had caught was to my grandparents or to town and I'd certainly never caught the bus to school and no one ever told me what to do if I was late so rather than ask which makes sense of course, I decided to never be late that first year.
The school was a very strict and scary to me and I would leave in a panic arriving earlier and earlier and before 8am on some occasions. I would sit on my own watching others arrive kicking at this tree stump in my pointy black imitation Jam shoes to pass the time. I tell you that stump became my stump; something to absorb my anger on and I feverishly reshaped it over months and in the process ruining my shoes!
For a good year and some I would stand alone not knowing what to do with myself as I had lost all confidence by then. I hated secondary school, I hated my old school and I hated this school and I longed for home, my mates and my street.
At break I would get myself a ten pence hot chocolate from a vending machine and I would sip slowly pretending I needed to be by myself. The thoughtful kid and I guess if this happened now I'd tap away at my phone looking like I was texting an important message to my mate or updating my Facebook account or telling someone on my twitter page that I was loving this chocolate?
Did you know the actor Ian Hart went to my school, as did the McGann brothers? Stephen Gerard did too but by then the school had lost its Grammar School status and changed its name to Cardinal Heenen.
I remember seeing Ian around the school, I'm guessing he was known as 'Harty' to his mates and the staff, he was a year above me and years later he would play a very convincing John Lennon in a film about his life and Professor Quirrell in the Harry Potter movie the 'the Philosophers Stone'. Isn't it funny how you never forget a face to then see the same face years later on the big screen? It's all in the eyes they never change.
I was in the new Liverpool Museum the other day looking at Liverpool life exhibits mainly about the Smithdown Road area where I grew up, its worth a visit should you be passing this way and I took a glancing look to a bloke to my right as you do and it was Paul McGann, standing there examining the same set of pictures.
I love Dr Who like I said earlier and I thought how amazing to be standing next to one of the doctors. I winked at Adam and said under my breath, 'it's the Dr'. Adam looked quizzical and said 'who', oh no not

that sad joke again and I later explained 'who' the man next to me was. This got me thinking, famous people must see all kinds of funny face twitches and growly whispers from people trying discretely nudge a companion to say 'look whose over there', taking a don't look straight at them kind of glance.

One day an older lad came up to me at the vending machine, he randomly picked me out and said, 'tell him these are the words to '*Eton Rifles*' by 'The Jam' as he shoved a piece of paper under my nose. I was secretly pleased as I thought this must have meant that I looked like the kind of person that would know, perhaps he had taken a look at my battered fake Jam shoes. Truth is I didn't know but I pretended I did so the lad then sold the lyrics to a mate for ten pence. Hope I was right.

As it happens the track was a classic and went straight to number one and if ever there was a track that summed up the school this was it as it was all about class war and the establishment! I had been jettisoned into an Eton type school, I was overflowing with pent up frustration having had years of knock, Fuck the lot that's all I wanted to shout!

At the start of year four, year ten, I had chosen my options, mainly the arts I might add as I had started to accept I was no boy genius. My form teacher was a kind priest called Father McNamara, a name I shall never forget unlike when I was a nervous fourteen year old. Father Mc was at least fifty, he left mid school term as he had fallen in love with a woman and this caused a right scandal at the time. The school tried to hush it all up but we all knew and you could hear the echoes of shame pulsate around the corridors.

Mr Wainwright, who was to be my art teacher, was patrolling the corridor by the hall one day, always a busy spot and there was I keeping my head down minding my own business probably on my way to my date with a vending machine hot chocolate. He shouted at me, 'come here, what's your name boy and who is your form teacher'.

I became all tongue-tied and just stood there looking like a fool in front of what seemed to be the whole school. He mocked me; he belittled me and once again I was innocent of any wrongdoings just like when My Day went for me with his slipper. Indeed was he an acquaintance of Mr Day I ask myself, same university perhaps?

I hated Mr Wainwright for demeaning me on some power trip of his but I had my revenge some years later. I'll talk more about work in the penultimate chapter to this book but one sunny day I was up a ladder in Childwall painting the outside of some semi detached house singing some naff song and I remember asking the boss who was the owner of the house? He said his name was Wainwright and just as I was about to

tell him about my former teacher, old Wainwright appeared.
Well, I clambered down with purpose and gusto and I gave him a piece of my mind and finally got to ask him why he had picked on me. He looked scared, he remembered me, hadn't been too long since I had left school and I guess he could see years of pent up anger in my eyes but he couldn't recall the incident, one of many such incidents I suspect. I went on to tell him that he made me feel like crap at a time when I was struggling to be accepted by my peers to also find that some teachers were as bad and came across as older bullies. He apologised profusely and I actually felt sorry for him.
Just thinking out loud, being an artist why didn't he paint his own house, lazy sod but I actually took my time painting his outside, as I felt obligated to show him that I was a decent painter! He was all right all things considered and as I said before he taught my fellow dunces and me and was a funny if not a somewhat inappropriate teacher at times. See, there were two art classes and two art teachers; Wainwright and Ms Schofield had a class each. Those that chose art as an option went to her and took art very seriously, they learnt more complicated and intricate artistic methods and the history of art from Cezanne to Giotto.
Good old Wainwright in contrast would sit at his desk passing the time by chatting about world affairs and the news. He appeared bored and I remember him telling us all that we'd be officers if the war in the Falklands escalated, he was quite convinced that good old boys like us wouldn't end up as cannon fodder, no we would be leaders of men. All bullshit of course but believable at the time!
I'm sure he made up subject matters as he walked the corridor and as he entered the room with his cup of tea in his hand. He would say arbitrary things like, 'draw a harbour scene', 'life in a valley' or 'my favourite pastime' and you could pretty much draw or paint what you wanted, whatever inspired you.
One day I remember drawing an ink picture of John Lennon who had sadly died that week, I drew him in his signature round specs and with a bright red rose across his face. It was very good even if I say so myself and I convinced myself the late John had inspired me from above as I knew he was a decent artist, a gift we had in common!
At home we had what was to be his final swansong album 'Double Fantasy'. Such creativity lost forever and I loved and still cherish the tracks *Beautiful Boy* and *'(Just Like) Starting Over'* and how ironic as John was about to reinvent himself with the aid of Yoko after being in the music wilderness for a few years.

Wainwright had an inclining to be one of the boys, as he knew us pubescent boys fancied Ms Schofield or 'big tits Schofield' as she was known. Again sorry for my abject vulgarity but that's what she was called and I even remember Mr Wainwright holding his chest mimicking Ms Schofield's rather large features and we knew there was no love lost between the two of them. Perhaps he'd tried it on at the end of term booze up in the staff room, or perhaps more likely he'd drawn the short straw in teaching us and he may have held some resentment over her because of this. Who knows?

One day we had a student teacher and with Wainwright we went on a field trip to Calderstones Park to sketch various plants and flowers in the green house. We worked hard without any hassle as this was a treat and Wainwright let us go around 1pm. We were delighted of course and we all went our merry way only to find out that the student teacher had grassed to the head the next day and he got old Wainwright into trouble. He let it be known to us that he disliked this guy from that point and said the Head had seriously reprimanded him. We were outraged. How dare this upstart do such a dishonourable thing to our Wainwright and he never taught us again.

By year five I had began to carve out a niche for myself. I had given up on my studies, my grades had plummeted like shares in Betamax videos and I began to take on the role of being the class clown.

I used humour as a defence mechanism and I was able to fend off trouble by acting silly as it meant more to me to feel like I belonged than to work hard and leave with qualifications. I realise the need to feel accepted is a typical psychological concept with most teenagers but by then I had accepted my lot; I really did wear the todumforuniversity shirt given to me as a boy and I accepted my place on the blue-collar conveyer belt into mind numbing labour intensive employment, if indeed I was lucky enough to get a job as the country was in deep recession and unemployment was rising by the week.

If we needed to annoy a teacher then I was up for it and I would sit with other like-minded brethren ready to disrupt lessons. I would sit with Cunny, short for Constable, Wally, short for Walsh and Mossey, short for Moss and I remember Geography lessons being particularly funny and intimidating at the same time.

We'd sit with our heads down with one arm strategically placed to guard the sniggering and pretending to work but as soon as the teacher went into a room at the back where he kept his maps and stuff, we'd get up to high jinks, poking, prodding and throwing stuff. The teachers name escapes me but he had a handle bar moustache like an Army Sergeant, or

someone out of the Village People and true to his image he'd come storming out of said room bellowing in a deep growly baritone voice with a huge ruler. He'd rush down the aisle and would whack the ruler on the desk and accuse my mates and me of talking and would scream, 'were you talking just then'. 'Me sir, no sir, I've been working, honest', would be my reply but I had been talking!
We suspected he had a peephole but to admit that he saw us would mean that he'd have to own up to spying on us, therefore his eye in the back of his head reputation would have been foiled unless we stupidly copped for it, which we never did.
I respected that teacher as he was fun but I didn't learn much sadly other than a river meanders and as it does it form levies. When Don McLean sings *'American Pie'* I think of the duelling we had with him as this track mentions taking a car to the levy for a bevvy me thinks or is that my scouse lyrical interpretation of a classic? It's amusing how situations, songs or smells can transport you back in time don't you think.
I remember being in history and the World Cup was being played in Spain. We had test papers marked by Mr Duffy, a short stout fellow who said he liked Dexy's Midnight Runners? I liked some of their songs too but I found Kevin Roland words to be unintelligible most of the time but I do confess to trembling with delight wanting to kick out in uncontrollable convulsion when I hear the opening trumpets to 'Geno' followed by the football inspired chants that takes you on an inspirational journey into Geno Washington's life. A magical track!
Anyway when Duffy left the room we ripped the test papers up and threw them from the window as they did at the stadium before a match. We were on the third floor and it just seemed like a good thing to do, we didn't care but Mr Duffy, who was normally a good guy, someone who you could have a laugh with, well he cared and he was fuming, as he must have spotted the paper drifting away on the wind as he descended the stairs. How did we think we'd get away with it and for break for two weeks we had to pick up litter from the yard until we filled the stainless steel bin as our punishment?
On the subject of breaks we had to stay on the school grounds during lunchtime, it was a written rule that no boy should step off the grounds during the day unless on a school trip. There's a memory catching the bus to Shropshire and visiting Brunel's Iron Bridge and other museums. It was a good day out, I learnt who Isambard Kingdom Brunel was and it was good to get away from school for the day.
One day we concocted a plan to escape during lunch, we wanted to play space invaders in this local café and I was a tad unsure as this would

mean forfeiting my free lunch but peer pressure was more important so I relented and we plotted our escape.

As it happens we never made it to the shop, some teachers who had also escaped, probably to the boozer for a quick de-stressing half, had caught us. We spotted them walking our way but we were trapped in a pincer movement and we hid behind the wall at Alder Hey Hospital but the teacher walked along the wall and said 'you, you and you' to the sound of him whacking us on the head, 'straight to Father Hingham's office'.

Now Father H was a notorious disciplinarian, the Deputy Head and I have this image of him dressed in a long black cape like he was some dark overlord and his favourite weapon of choice was a leather strap with a whalebone through the middle.

We were petrified, well I was and we stood outside his room but you dare not show your mate, as this was a sign of weakness and feebleness. Not all of us got caught, some had hidden behind another wall and Father H had worked that out and we were told to either rat on a mate or face the consequences, in other words the strap!

Now as much as I didn't relish getting a whack from Father H we all knew that you must never ever 'grass' or 'clat tale' on a mate as that was against our law! I figured this was indeed a test and secretly the school would have been disappointed and saddened if you had ratted, as that was not the stuff of future officer types and leaders of men. Our fate was sealed; we had to take a bullet for our mates as we had been caught.

Anyway, Father H kept us hanging for days, not literally, punishment in our school wasn't that severe and we would stand outside of his room during breaks thinking this was the day we'd feel his wrath. We did this for a week and he then ushered us in to his room, told us to stand in line and said 'let that be a lesson and don't bunk off again'. Maybe he didn't have the swing anymore, he was getting on a bit, I don't know but like I said I think he admired our loyalty and resilience in a strange way. As for us we were relieved but this never stopped us escaping on other occasions!

Like I said before the school was obsessed with rugby and beating our rivals, St Edward's, another Grammar school up the road. Me, I'd never held a squashed ball before let alone knew the rules of rugger and to my dismay the school didn't encourage footy, or have any teams unless you played for the sixth form team, which ironically was always making it to the Liverpool schools final as I recall.

Back when I was at the school I guess footy was for the unruly masses, too working class and this had to be thrashed out of us Grammar boys in the mud, sweat and blood on the field. I avoided the game like the

plague, many a time I had forgotten my kit and the subsequent detention was worth it in my view as it all looked so 'barbarian' to me.
In year five however I relented, the four classes in our year would compete against each other for bragging rights and I had to play, Barlow was short on fit players and I remember it being a wet and cold spring morning. I didn't posses any boots so I ended up playing in my beige 'addidas trabs'. I ruined them, they were made of suede.
The ref blue to start the game and this kid from Arrowsmith dropkicked the ball into our half and I asked a teammate whilst the ball floated my way; 'what do I do if the ball comes to me'. His name was Dunny, short for Dunne, he played for the school team, a regular, a brute of a kid and he just smiled at me with a knowing grin and said 'run like mad' pointing at the opposition.
Well needleless to say fate played its part and yes the ball dropped from the heavens into my 'goalie' arms. I ran with one arm outstretched as I'd seen my team mates take on this stance before, with the muddy ball under my arm towards what can only be described as an oncoming onslaught! I was brought down too easily, I blame the shoes and all I could feel as my face sank deeper into the mud was a thud on my back, then another thud, as different kids took turn to crush me into the ground and I half expected my own team mates to jump on my back shouting 'piley on'. I never did catch that ball again, call it luck or strategic standing behind Dunny and co; I'll let you work that one out. I know once a wimp always a wimp.
During the same match Livo, short for Livingston and Macca, my chemistry saviour, challenged me to kick the ball over the letter H shaped post after our team had scored a try. In case you don't know this is called a conversion, they kept goading me and goading me and I kept avoiding the pending embarrassment, don't forget it was wet, I had trainers on and the ball was the wrong shape.
Anyway, near the end I yielded and thought I'll show them just how good I am with this trusted left foot. We scored a 'try' but right in the corner and on the side that suited a right footer. Still, I had said the next one is mine so I had to accept the challenge. By this time other kids were watching as was a few teachers including Mr Daley and other chisel chinned teacher. I placed the ball on a muddy mound for elevation, took three steps back to match my three striped ruined trabs, then shot forward and gave it an almighty toe end kick, which means a kick using the toe obviously and not the inside or outside of the foot.
The ball sailed off spinning majestically into the grey sky towards the post and to my astonishment; it passed cleanly through the capital H! I

didn't think I had done anything out of the ordinary but I was told this was extremely difficult given the angle, the distance the ball had to travel, the six foot target and that I was a left footer, not to mention the mud and my ruined trainers.

After the game several teachers asked if I wanted to take the game up and have a trial at becoming the teams 'fly half' as I seemingly had a gift for kicking but I declined as I valued my looks and my waistline. See, most ex rugger lads have tell tale rugger marks such as broken noses, an array of scars, occasional torn ears and broken bones and they all carry beer bellies such is the need for alcohol celebration after the game.

On the topic of drinking and years later whilst out with Brad up the High Street, I would sometimes bump into my battle weary schoolmates and every time they would retell my famous kick story as it had become etched in folklore! Told you Livo and Macca I could kick!

Here's a few more lines about the boy giant Livo. He was a character and someone you were glad to have on ones side. The school had been having skirmishes with West Derby Comp, Eton Rifles again and during assembly we were all warned not to enter into tribal warfare but then Father H tells a story of Livo practicing his rugby kicking on the field on his own, probably trying to emulate me, when some lads from the comp appeared.

Single handily Livo sent them on their way and gave them a good kicking and I swear Father H looked pleased as punch. I'm guessing Livo was probably frustrated because he couldn't emulate me, get over it Dave, I did, straight through the posts!

Livo looks so different now, a bulk of a man, he's lost all his hair, one of his ears has a piece bitten off and he told me he has bolts in his leg keeping him together. Should have played badminton my friend, less physical although one day I was rushed to hospital after being hit on the brace of my nose by some kid with a badminton racquet.

We had PE and to my delight the teacher decided to let us play badminton. I took my turn on court and the shuttle flew over my head. I turned and being adept at the sport I knew I could get to the shuttle before it hit the floor. I accept this was a tricky manoeuvre but this kid saw the shuttle and thinking I had no chance he hit out and caught me square in the face. Thankfully my nose remained straight otherwise I might have turned to rugby.

Back to Livo. I sat in front of him in class on occasion and he was mocking my greasy hair telling me to get a wash, yes have a look at that picture again. I probably did need a wash but I'd had enough by this time, blame it on years of taking all the crap I had endured from bully after bully but I unwisely shouted out 'Livo your a leper' as he had bad acne.

No one and I mean no one ever mentioned his spots and abruptly the classroom went silent. The silence was then broken; I felt an enormous whack to the back of my head smashing my forehead on the desk lid, making a loud thud followed by gasps from the others who had turned to see who had dared to skit Livo.

To this day I have a lump at the back of my head the size of a small pea as a result of this whack and years later during a chance encounter at the pub I told Livo and jokingly offered him out. He knew I didn't mean it and took it in jest, he said sorry and in any event I am no match for a man with chewed ears. Hope I never go bald though, as I don't relish explaining why I have a lump on my head.

There was another kid in my class who like me had to duck and dive and his name was Paul. Paul left my school by year five as he'd had enough of the bullies; Paul was from Netherley which is a large housing estate made up of mainly council tenants so I always felt we had something in common.

Years later I met Paul; unknown to me he was a good work friend of Alan, my mate from home. I played golf with Paul on many occasions and although we both acknowledged we attended the same school we never spoke of the joint humiliation we had endured as kids and indeed we both played down our shared ordeal as to truly admit it would have been an acceptance that we were somehow weak.

So annoying as an adult because we weren't weak and in fact it took guts and courage to go through what we both went through but I guess some memories are too painful and best kept locked away. You know what Paul to do so means they have won and sometimes its best to talk as it might help as this book has helped me. Invitation remains open mate!

Getting away from school at the end of the day was literally a nightmare and I would want to return to my area, my mates and to feel safe. As you came out the gate you had to turn left unless you had a pass to show the prefects indicating that you lived in West Derby.

To the right of the school was Broughton Hall Grammar School for girls and whilst this provided some needed eye candy them girls would get on the bus before us lot and it would take ages before the number sixty-one would stop. Sometimes it was quicker to run or walk home as the crow flies through Old Swan.

The solution to my problem was a bike. I got myself a job delivering papers in the evening so I managed to convince my Mum to get me a racer this time, from the catalogue, as my old beloved bike had had its

day after years of wheelies and mud racing. I got a red five-gear racer at last and I would cycle too and from school in the same time, if not a bit faster, than the two buses I would catch.
True I had to then deliver papers but it was well worth it as I got fitter and I could also sleep in a little bit later in the morning. Happy days as far as I was concerned!
In year five I had discovered girls and the CB as I discussed before and so began the complete and utter demise of my education. Every cloud has a silver lining though as the upshot was I suddenly found that I was popular and I felt accepted for the first time since my primary school days and school suddenly felt like a tolerable place to be!
Let me explain. I began to lead a double life. In school I was this scruffy kid from a place no one respected but out of school I had girlfriends and 'encounters', forgive my modesty and I had started going to nightclubs. I liked clothes and fashion and with my paper round money I would add to my wardrobe and would mix and match.
I let my fringe grow down over my face like I said and I had a pretty decent wedge haircut in year five. Bit greasy admittedly given the burst of hormones I was going through and I then got the nickname egghead as the back stuck out like an egg. The irony being I was Joe Egg on the CB, I'm sure there's a yoke there somewhere! Oh no I'm cracking up again. Ok I'll stop now!
I'd tell everyone in school that I had been clubbing at the weekend but no one believed me, they would try and catch me out and I could hear them saying 'no not Griff he looks so scruffy, how could he get in'. Well I did get in, I was tall, I was with Neil and Grant who were a year older than me and the fringe over the face not only helped hide my zits but my genuine age.
Kids at school thought I was 'blagging', in other words they thought I was lying but this all changed when Cogsy, short for Corrigan spotted me at Rotters or should I say I spotted him and with determination I made my way over to him to say hello. Rotters would stop for twenty or so minutes to allow the bar staff to collect the glasses and you were ushered out into this open space and Cogsy was standing opposite me. He was surprised and I acted all cool like, 'oh hi fancy seeing you here'. When really I was thinking 'its me, its me, told you I came here, now go spread the word'.
Cogsy was a bit mad but a decent enough lad and a few years ago whilst at church the priest mentioned him, telling the congregation that he'd died. The Catholic guilt had gotten the better of me and I attended

Church for a few years when by lad's started Catholic School, I didn't wish to be seen as a hypocrite.

This saddened me as he would have been in his thirties and I looked up to the heavens and gave old Cogsy a big thank you as he had told everyone at school that I had been out clubbing and so my elevation up the hierarchy began. Thanks Cogsy.

Then we had the lovely Lesley. When I was just fifteen my mates and me got friendly with Lesley's sister Paula, who knew the twins I mentioned before as they attended school together. Lesley and Paula were half Chinese, their Dad owned a chippy on Lawrence Road that we frequented on occasion, please don't tell Manny and her Dad would be out every night. Lots of opportunities presented themselves, as this was a place to hang out without any fear of being caught but before I tell you more, the captivating Lesley reminds me of another favourite track of mine, '*Visions of China*' by Japan for obvious reasons.

I was expected to 'cop off' with Paula at the end of the night, to kiss her and she invited my mates and me to her house. We got talking and I met Lesley who was actually in my year and therefore a better if not unlikely match. Little did I know but she saw potential in me, she fancied me it seems and she said my hair looked really greasy, fair cop as it often did, I wasn't offended. She asked if she could wash and blow-dry my hair for me and I thought that sounded reasonable, as you do and before you know it I was in her bedroom.

Her room was girly pink and I acted all coy, I was nervous, I hadn't been in many girls bedrooms but I had been in several entries by then. She spent ages on my hair, we goofed around and me not taking the bait she gave up and said 'are you queer?' Even I knew this translated as 'bloody hell slow coach why haven't you kissed me yet'. On this occasion I didn't require the help of I Translate; I was in and we kissed for ages.

I remember lion heart Lee getting jealous as we had been missing in action for over an hour and he shouted up the stairs 'for God sake how long does it take to dry your hair'. I came out of the bedroom and proudly stood at the top of the stairs arm in arm with Lesley with a decent haircut and Lee was literally blown away. Yes that hairdryer was very strong!

Fair to point out that I felt sorry for Paula but she later told me she was 'cool' with me seeing her sister and I went out with Lesley for a while and we always ended up in her bedroom, she'd wash my hair sometimes but no train journeys although I do confess to nearly embarking on a few a racing train on occasions!

One night we were kissing and her front door opened, to my horror it was her Dad. He never came home from the Chippy and I was petrified, I had heard from someone that knew someone that her Dad had once chased a boy from the house with a machete! I hid trembling behind a couch in Lesley's bedroom in fear of my life and to my relief he was just popping home; imagine if he had stayed the night, how would I have sneaked out? I probably remember all this because I was trembling.
Now forgive my modesty but Lesley was seen as a catch round our way and I just had to tell my mates at school to gain kudos amongst the rank and file but once again my assertion was met with disbelief as some of the lads at school who lived around Wavertree had heard of Lesley and thought 'no way', not Griff'.
This became a bit of a joke between Lesley and me for the three or so months that I was seeing her, Lesley would leave bite marks all over my body particularly when she knew I had swimming the next day. Now I detest love bites, the branding mark of teenagers and before you ask they were made innocently but back then they made me feel good about myself, like a peacock strutting his feathers again and as I undressed and entered the pool with marks around my neck and my arms all eyes would be on me.
The shame but everyone could see that I had a girlfriend as some of the bites could not have been self inflicted by a vacuum cleaner and word even got round the teachers that I was seeing Lesley. I'd get winks and back slapping from some of the staff as I walked round for my hot chocolate at break.
Months later our relationship fizzled out and Cunny asked me to set up a date with Lesley. By then I was seeing Lesley's friend from school a pretty girl called Debbie, she was from Old Swan and she dressed very smart with matching hats and scarfs.
I would go to Dunny's disco with Debbie and I really liked her but she wanted to see me every night and even for me that was too much so taking counsel from the Clash, I asked myself, 'Should I Stay or Should I Go', well I did 'go' in the end. Debbie remains 'the' only girl I ever took upstairs to my bedroom during my teenage years and I remember Tracy barging in on me on once occasion and by the way did I mention both Lesley and Debbie attended Notre Dame.
Not that Debbie will ever read these lines but I wish to apologise to her, as I never ended our relationship and I've often regretted this. That phone excuse again, yes it was still unconnected so she couldn't contact me, days past, then a week and I never phoned her. Sorry about that!

Lesley and me had remained on talking terms, we'd bump into each other out and about so I became a matchmaker; Cunny went out with her for a while and thus once and for all convinced the doubters at school that I had been seeing Lesley and that I had really been leading a double life.

One night when I was about sixteen I was walking back from Larks in the Parks after watching Big Country in concert and I bumped into Lesley. I had lost Neil and Derek in the crowd, which was heaving. We ended up kissing in an entry by her house and we arranged to meet at Derek's the following night. I got to Derek's late and it was clear to me that she had a thing for Derek and they ended up having a fling and then she went missing for about nine months and we would tease Derek about him possibly being a father but he was adamant that he got off at Edge Hill.

Neil also had a brief fling with Lesley, again this all sounds so unscrupulous and promiscuous of me and my mates, it wasn't it was part of growing up in an area where someone knew someone who knew someone else and relationships were usually very fleeting.

In May and June of 1982 I took my exams knowing I'd fail and I even missed my Religious Studies O'Level as I had been on the CB all night and I'm guessing I must have still been angry with father let me have your side burns?

I knew my potential and regrettably I had by then accepted my low expectation, my prophecy came true and in fact the only qualification I left school with was a grade C in art like I said before. Good old Wainwright, you were a bully sometimes but you came through in the end and so began my decorating story which ill talk about in the next chapter.

Before I move on to work and the end of my education memories, I must return to badminton at this point. As I said before I had played this sport from about thirteen and one day I decided to take on the school champ at a club run at lunchtime.

I know this is becoming a reoccurring theme but no one believed me again when I told my mates that I had played competitively in tournaments so again I needed to prove a point. What is it with people not believing me back then?

Anyway, I won convincingly. Not boasting but I was good and the teacher could see that and enquired if I was staying on at six form? I knew this meant six form for kids who were not likely to pass many if any O'levels, they called it 'sixth form removed', but basically this was an additional year for kids who could represent the school at sport and thus uphold the school honour and reputation at not only being a school for bright gifted officer types but also able to win at sports too.

Perhaps I shouldn't have chopped my nose off to spite my spotty face but I told the teacher 'no' and inside I remember feeling affronted and peeved as I had attended this school for two and a half years by then and at times it had been absolute hellish and not one teacher had taken any interest in me or in the early days taken me aside to ask if I was settling in, had I made friends and did I need someone to talk too.

The lyrics to Tears For Fears track *'Mad World'* ring ever so true for me as teachers did look right through me and only now after thrashing the school champ at badminton did someone finally care to ask!

Coincidental I think not?

Too little too bloody late but you know I've now come to realise that it wasn't all bad at Secondary school and at the end of the day I am who I am because of these events and like I've said throughout this book 'what doesn't kill you makes you stronger'!

I met many interesting characters; some became good friends and some not but that's fine as I see it as we all had our own ways in which we passed through our teenage years and for me it took some time to become less serious and less prone to taking things to heart.

Now let me tell you all about work.

Chapter Nineteen

From A Jack To A King...

Asides communal clean ups and the occasional carpet washing at home my first job I suppose, was working as a paper lad from a shop in Wavertree. I know it's not technically a job but I was paid and I had responsibility and I had to do something!
I wasn't looking for work I had tagged along with Alan and Brad who put their names down in several shops. I did to but only because it seemed the right thing to do. I heard recently on the news that the willingness of kids to work on a Saturday or delivering papers has declined by over fifty per cent in the last fifteen years. Is that because kids are lazier these days relying upon the bank of Mum and Dad or is this due to a lack of opportunity in these harder economic times and the falling-off of newspapers?
Anyway I called in a week or so later and the owner offered me the round before Alan and Brad, I think this was because I was taller and he'd surmised there would be less chance of me being mugged and by then my voice had broken and I probably sounded older than Alan and Brad. There's a band called Sparks and they sum up wonderfully the changing tones us lads go through with the lines from their track *'Armature Hour'*; I cant print them for fear of copyright infringement but take a look and you will see what I mean. I'm seeing them in concert in November 2012, can't wait.
Alan and Brad were not pleased and didn't speak to me for a week, the cruellest of punishments to inflict on a mate. What was I to do, should I have remained loyal, should I have told the owner to stuff his job on the off chance they would then offer the job to either Alan or Brad. Also, whom would he choose, assuming he did and would the other side with me and shun the other and give them the coldest of shoulders? All very complicated so in the end I just took the job.
I was only paid a few quid and I had to deliver the Liverpool Echo up and down Woodcroft and Thornycroft Roads amongst others during the week and the Sunday rags at the weekend, which meant a heavier bag.

356 David Griffith

The sack would be heaving, don't think it would be so heavy these days with the Internet and like I said before I got a bike, which made the job less of an effort and so much faster.
I do confess to negotiating with Mum that I would pay her two quid towards the catalogue where she got the bike from but after a few weeks I conveniently forgot. Sorry Mum, I still owe you but in my defence I didn't get pocket money as times were always hard instead I would offer to go the shop so as I could keep the change.
I was into fashion and music big time by then not to mention Dunny's disco so, taking giving a nod to the Pretenders track, guys got to have '*Brass in Pocket*'.
I did this for a few months over the summer but it became tiresome and tedious by December but I knew Christmas would bring much needed bounty in the form of tips so I stuck it out. I did indeed reap the rewards and got many tips, people can be so generous during the festive season, but I gave the job up in January as did Alan and Brad who after all their moans and groans had managed to find their own paper rounds at a local rival shop not long after I started. That's just sparked off another guilty pleasure of mine that I loved to sing in the shower sometimes and I was never 'sick and tired' of it, '*January*' by 'Pilot'.
Now remember I had lost interest in school and I had no idea what lay before me. The country was in deep recession and adults were struggling to find work so I knew, as a spotty faced youth with an art O'Level that I would really struggle in the adult world. I had no idea what I wanted to do, I was set adrift thinking I could do better but accepting that I wouldn't have the opportunity.
At school I remember sitting with the PE teacher who doubled up as a careers adviser, his name was Mr Stewart and he was also into Rugby, to talk about what I wanted to do when I left school. I'm glad to see that in this day and age kids have a personal connexions worker and are given sound advice about what route to take and what courses best suit their aspirations but back in the early eighties, no such luck. You were either clever, had rich parents, parents or relatives who owned their own business or you knew someone who would give you a start.
Nepotism was rife, it had to be as jobs were hard to find so I felt hopeless and thought my only hope was to follow my Dad into the building industry. I'd taken woodwork but failed my O'Level and considered myself to be a decent artist so stands to reason that I'd make a passable builder.
After my 'careers advice', if I can call it that, I then got a letter some weeks later requesting that I attend this interview to discuss the building

trade and what opportunities were out there. I attended and from there I then had an interview for a Youth Training Scheme (YTS) to start in the September with an organisation called CITB or Construction Industry Training Board.
I got through the interview, which wasn't hard and was told to report to this site in Speke, ironically near to where my parents lived when they first met. My Dad prepared me by taking me on a bus journey so as I knew how to get there by myself and I caught the number seventy-seven bus mainly used by workers travelling to the Fords Factory.
Over the summer holidays my Dad was labouring, a cash in hand job, for this builder who needed an extra pair of hands. I was just sitting round the house doing little and my Dad mentioned me so I got a start. Now that reminds me of the track *'Up The Junction'* by the superb 'Squeeze'.
I got the lilac coloured single and I memorised every word from the Smash Hits Magazine and here's a bit of trivia for you. Do you recall Squeeze's tongue in cheek performance on TOTP in which the band members played the 'wrong instruments'? Singer Glenn Tilbrook drummed whilst Jools Holland tried to look proficient at the guitar. This track is about an unplanned pregnancy and if you know the words the daughter would have been born at 5.20am, go on work it out, but interestingly we never got to know her date of birth or her name, or indeed the mother's name only that she ended up with a soldier. Great track though.
I digress. Each morning my Dad and me would evade prying eyes as my Dad was on benefits and we would take a long walk to the other side of Newsham Park to the site and to save bus fare but this job didn't last very long. My Dad yearned for full time paid work but no one was hiring which is why so many left the north to seek work down south. My Dad and me would dig trenches and carry bricks and blocks around the site, it was really hard graft and although my Dad is smaller and lighter than me, I just couldn't match his physical prowess. The site Forman noticed too and finished me up after a couple of weeks. I left with sixty pounds in my pocket and it taught me a lesson, without doubt labouring was not for me and I knew I needed to focus on acquiring a trade. I bought myself a nice shirt though.
I started my twelve month YTS in earnest and met a gang of other lads who didn't really want to be there. It was like being back at school, similar pecking order bullshit and I made some friends but this time I was determined not to ruin the opportunity, as I wanted to learn a trade and prove I could make it in the adult world.

At the start I took an IQ test and afterwards the manager said that I should focus on surveying or being a draughtsman as I had the intelligence but sadly I never took his advice or indeed knew what to do! I was still lacking in confidence as a sixteen-year-old youth.
For the first few weeks we tried various trades, joinery, painting and decorating, plastering and bricklaying. I enjoyed being taught by teachers who had amassed many years in the trade and I believed I was good at them all but I chose painting in the end. I did this for two simple reasons; firstly I knew this was the least popular and therefore least likely trade to be disrupted by lads 'hell bent' on trouble and disrupting the lessons. Secondly, there was little cleaning up involved once you had finished your work.
In both bricklaying and plastering classes you had the laborious task of scraping the cement like mixture off the wall or the bricks to then be reused. Very messy, very cold and disheartening after standing back to admire ones work knowing it had to be demolished, if not by you then the rest of the pack when the tutor wasn't looking!
I learnt how to sand and prepare woodwork for undercoating and glossing. I leant how to emulsion walls and to hang wallpaper and I really enjoyed this part of the course. I remember one time larking about balancing along the walls that divided the rooms that we practiced in. This smaller kid slid down a trestle that was leant against the wall and I followed him as it was a quicker way to get down. The trestle slipped and the next thing I remember is being at the bottom with a very saw bottom but thankfully I had kept my hands from underneath the trestle, as I would have lost my fingers. I was sent to accident and emergency at Garston hospital for a tetanus jab in my thigh. I remember having to sit side ways on the bus all the way home as if I was about to let out an enormous fart.
Mum would look after me, I would give her ten pounds from my twenty five pound wage for 'keep' as they say not realising that this didn't even cover the cost of my lunch as Mum would make me my lunch everyday, sometimes sandwiches but often a Pot Noodle.
Did you know this 'taste sensation' was first launched in 1977, the classic convenient food for drunks, students and builders everywhere wanting a snack. Beef and tomato was my favourite closely followed by chicken and mushroom and it felt like the future, felt like one was on a space station, pots of taste, pots of flavour, pots of choice as the advert went.
We were kitted out with our own tools, boots and overalls and as part of the scheme we were sent out on work experience to local firms to test out how to be a decorator in the real world and to hopefully secure a

permanent apprenticeship with the firm, if you were lucky. I enjoyed this as it felt like proper work, with mature men lucky enough to be in work but like I said before it also felt like cheap labour.

I worked for this firm called Liverpool Decorators, an established firm in Liverpool and we painted the outside of council houses in Dovecot. My music tastes were rather odd around this time and I had a repertoire of tracks that I would holler on high from the top of the ladder.

See painting can be very monotonous and I would sing to pass the time away. I would sing *'From A Jack To A King'* a country and western track by Ned Millar and I liked the soulful *'Hurt'* by the Manhattan's, *'Always and Forever'* by 'Heatwave' was a must sing track and I loved *'You've Lost That Loving Feeling'*, but the 'Human League' version. I would bellow out the superlative *'Unchained Melody'* by the Righteous Brother's' and I guess I must have really annoyed the occupants particularly those who had worked nights.

I remember it being very cold and wearing my brown sheepskin mitts to paint in that matched my 'sheepy' as we called them, a beige sheep skin jacket. I remember chatting to this girl who lived at one of the houses, she had made me a brew on occasion and I had a fling with her for a few weeks. Years later in my role as a social worker I had yet another school reception encounter and sat next to this girl, now a woman of course, as I was there for a meeting; she was seemingly with her daughter. She didn't recognise me of course, I wasn't wearing my give away mitts and I decided not to introduce myself, it didn't seem appropriate. She looked so much older but I could see my old fling in her pale blue eyes, yes those eyes reveal so much?

We worked in small gangs and after work on a Friday the men would go the pub; this was customary. I didn't really get involved as I usually had my own plans but one Friday I relented and I was introduced to the very potent Barley Wine. It was still light outside but soon the afternoon became a daze as I was intoxicated and I vaguely recall the two men I was with successfully deciphering from my drawl where I lived. They took me home, that was very good of them and I was nauseous for the rest of the weekend. Saved a few quid as I recall, as I wasn't up for drinking for days, the smell of alcohol knocked me sick.

After returning to the training site, to be reacquainted with my fellow trainees, we were sent out on work experience a few weeks later and this time I was with this other outfit in North Liverpool; again painting the outside of council houses. Just thinking this wouldn't happen now with the advancement of double glazed plastic windows, as they don't need painting, a blessings some might say.

Anyway I worked with a lad called John who attended my old school strangely enough but not 'scon head'. John and I became good mates and we soon began to question what opportunities were available and we realised that we were being exploited, so we rebelled. It was the 12th July 1983, I'll tell you why I know the exact date in a bit but me and John decided to go to Freshfields for a laugh, it was a hot summer unlike nowadays it seems and we decided to take a sickie.

We caught the train from Moorefield's in town to Southport. The train was heaving and we had no understanding why? We sat there idling the time away talking about how much we hated our job when the boss's son got on at Seaforth and he sat next to us! He was all right but we knew we were in trouble as the boss was always talking about deadlines, we were bang to rights and we had no way out.

We hopped off the train at Freshfields and decided to enjoy ourselves and face the consequences the next day. We had a good day actually and we even went for a dip in the Mersey, very cold despite the warm July sun and I've just thought of a terrific track that reminds me of our day splashing around in the sea; *'Waves'* by the band Blancmange.

The next day John and I were painting away sheepishly, was I wearing those mitts again, no it was July, when the boss pulled up and beckoned us over. 'Oh no this is it were sacked we thought', we didn't really care but no, he shook our hands and said 'lads you should have told be you wanted the day off to attend the annual Lodge day out. Now John and me were Catholics, very much lapsed but we certainly weren't Protestants but he wasn't to know and he thought we were in the Orange Lodge and that we had attended the annual 12th July day out! Pure coincidental but funny chain of events and we went the pub afterwards and laughed over a pint of bitter. John's favourite tipple.

Despite getting along with the boss from that day forward this work experience didn't last long; we complained to CITB that the firm was flouting health and safety regulations by asking us to climb ladders without proper instruction or guidance. They probably weren't but we then found ourselves reassigned with a more professional outfit called Tompkins Decorators.

John and I were separated, probably because of our determination not to be misused and I was sent to St Julie's school in Everton and I became the 'can lad' for thirty odd men decorating the school. I enjoyed this role but never learnt much about painting as the can lad's role was to run around making tea for everyone at break using this huge urn, to wash up afterwards and to take orders and to get lunch.

I worked alongside another lad who was fortunate to have an apprenticeship with the firm and it become common knowledge that he took home double the money I was on so some of the old guys objected to this social injustice and it became the norm for the men to throw fifty pence in an old paint tin for me at the end of the week to make up the shortfall. I felt rich, so I would often buy another shirt.
All things come to an end and after spending a week cleaning brushes I was sent back to head office, as did John. They needed muscle; they should have called Dad, as the firm had a lucrative contract to spray paint hundreds and hundreds of girders for the Mersey Tunnel.
Did you know the second Mersey Tunnel, the Kingsway, opened in 1971 whilst the first Tunnel, the Queensway, with its entrance near the bottom end of William Brown Street opened to traffic in 1934? Stick that in your memory and Dad would tell me that by now we should be able to use the tunnels without paying, as this was the original plan.
Anyway seems like the Tunnels required on-going maintenance and John and I became small contributors for a while. We would turn the music up high and we would stack the girders in neat rows and we would spray them various black coats. John loved David Bowie and we'd stop for breaks of course but we were motivated as the firm treated us with respect. We were allowed a pint of milk a day, something to do with the harmful effects of lead in paint and they provided us with overalls and steel cap boots.
This was hard work but enjoyable and gratifying and for our efforts the firm kept us on after our scheme had ended after twelve months, to carry on with the girders contract. This was fantastic news as jobs were hard to come by like I said, Mum and Dad were chuffed and we were offered a three year apprenticeships with a guaranteed job at the end. It was September 1983 and we worked four days a week and the other day was spent on a day release college course; John and I were 'overjoyed' and a few weeks later we decided to have a night out in town to celebrate.
We met on the High Street in Wavertree for a couple of pints. I donned a blue leather box jacket with a matching blue leather tie, trust me it looked contemporary at the time and fashionable, I bought it second hand from Derek. I'll explain how I remember so much detail in a bit so stick with me. John mirrored the leather look but he was in brown and off we went to town.
We drank heavily, John was strictly a pint of bitter man like I said and I had to match him sip for sip, to prove I had the stomach for such masculine exploits. I was well oiled by the end of the night and to help soak up all the alcohol swishing around our swollen bellies, John

suggested we go for a Chinese on London Road he had been to in the past.
John said he was a regular and we both ordered chicken and sweet corn soup followed by chicken fried rice and a side portion of chips. We had a few more beers, half's this time and John set me a drunken dare, a dare that was to have far reaching consequences.
John explained that he had taken the salt and the soya sauce from this restaurant but never the vinegar. It never crossed my mind to ask why; did his Mum often run out of condiments? I knew it was wrong but he dared me to put the vinegar in my leather jacket pocket, hence my good memory and to my shame I nervously did. Now I'm not exactly known for being a thief, aside the occasional Yorkie Bar but I was young and very drunk before you go casting any aspersions in my direction so stop moralising.
We paid up and stumbled down the three steps that led away from the restaurant and I could hear Chinese voices behind me, was Lesley's Dad out to revenge his daughter's reputation? They were probably not shouting at me to come back but I wasn't concentrating and I fell over awkwardly; I had to sit and nurse my sore ankle. That bloody ankle again!
We were beat by then, drunk on merriment and full up, so John decided that should go home and he hailed a taxi and off we went. John lived in Childwall so he was last out and I gave him a five-pound note to go towards his fare.
The next morning I woke up with a terrible pain in my leg, my ankle to be precise, it had swollen and I was in agony. I somehow squeezed into a new pair of expensive Levi jeans and my Mum took me to the Royal Hospital accident and emergency department, ironically up the road from the Chinese, could have saved myself the taxi fare if I had slept in a doorway?
I had an X-ray to find that I had fractured my right ankle. They asked several questions about what I had been up to and the Doctor could probably smell last nights alcohol on my breath and I told him half truths, that I'd fallen over a step but decided I shouldn't tell him I had stolen a bottle of vinegar. Oh the indignity.
To rub it in further the hospital had to cut my jeans from the knee rather than squeeze them over my 'plastered ankle'. A very expensive dare was about to get even more expensive! Within hours I had been 'plastered' in town to then find myself being 'plastered' in hospital!
The next day I phoned work to tell them I'd be off for at least six weeks because I'd fractured my ankle. I could tell the boss wasn't pleased, who

could blame him and the firm paid me for a couple of weeks but then finished me as I was taken on to complete the girder contract. Now because the girder contract was a two-man job, John was also finished up. So there you have it kids, never ever steal from Chinese restaurants no matter how drunk you are and go without vinegar.

Having a fractured ankle did have some fringe benefits. One night I was hobbling home from Derek's down Lawrence Road when this girl called Mary interrupted my poetry recital and asked if I needed any help. I'd seen her around but we had never spoken before. We talked for a while and the next thing I know I'm propped up against this wall in a back entry smooching away whilst taking care not to fall over. I remember Mary telling me to prop my crutches up against the wall as I had them wrapped round her back and I guess you had to be there to understand how this makes me giggle thinking about this now.

So there I was, seventeen, with no job, no money and no immediate prospects. I felt lost in the wilderness not sure what to do then Derek got talking to this bloke called Jimmy at the badminton club we attended. I mention Jimmy a few times in this book, he was the one who suggested I go up the High Street when travelling back from Wembley, he was a short stout man with a beard, looked a lot like a hirsute Popeye and he had his own decorating firm.

He was on the look out for 'a new lad' and I had the obligatory scraper, brush and overalls from my YTS days; so he gave me a week's trial. Needless to say I showed a degree of competency in using a brush so I was once again in gainful employment.

I say employment but not the legal kind as Jimmy was a tight so and so. He paid me thirty five pounds a week cash in hand, more than what I earned on the YTS but in his mind I was on an acceptable wage as he would factor in what the government paid me for being out of work, my dole money, my benefits.

Here's an interesting snippet of information. I was watching an antiques programme on telly and I now know where the phrase 'dole' originates from. Apparently people who couldn't support themselves would take food from the 'dole cupboard', which would be stocked by altruistic members of the gentry and placed on roads and bridges.

Every two weeks, no matter where I was in Liverpool, I had to 'sign on' and I would have to clean my hands and wear clean clothes, hope I don't get into trouble writing this down? I must have stunk of turps, surely a dead give away and I would live in constant fear that someone would grass me up as people were encouraged to dob on dole scrounges. I hated the whole experience, I wasn't purposely cheating the system, I

wasn't a scrounger but like my Dad I just couldn't get a job!
I remember painting this blokes kitchen, an insurance number and he taped me the album 'Reckless' by Bryan Adams. He had it on one day, every track stood out in their own right and I particularly liked *'Summer of 69'*, *'Run to You'*, *'Somebody'* and the beautifully melodic track, *'Heaven'*. A song with heavenly guitar strings that flow and ebb across a bed of pure, blood warm mercury; I adored this track and still do. It may interest you to know that this album came out in 1984 and won sacksful of awards but that was his pinnacle as far as I was concerned for the Canadian. Never liked him from there on in.

Talking of all things celestial, *'Just Like Heaven'* by the Cure is a track that I also liked a lot and I am of the view that Robert Smith is a modern day poet. Don't believe me then take a look at the lyrics, God I hate this intellectual ownership crap. Heart pounding superb track don't you think, makes me sea sick but in a nice way and the lyrics moves me every time.

Jimmy was so tight, even tighter than me, which is why he lived in a decent semi detached house in leafy Childwall. He'd park his little red van out of sight of any passing traffic warden as he refused to pay his car tax and probably his insurance and at the weekend his wife, who worked in a high paid IT job in town as I recall, would paste paper for him! He was always thinking of scams and how to save money.

The owner of the badminton club bought houses to rent to students and Jimmy had the job of painting them to make them liveable. This usually meant literally throwing wood chip paper up on every interior wall to hide cracks and damp, then every room would be finished off with magnolia emulsion and white gloss woodwork.

When busy Jimmy would be out and about pricing other 'jobs' leaving me to my own devices so I would sit back and listen to music. I knew Jimmy couldn't be in two places at once as he would be doing his 'I'm a tradesman mam' on the more exclusive bits of work and would only introduce me if he needed to show off his prodigy as if to demonstrate that he had a growing empire.

I could complete most small terraced houses in a couple of weeks and I did this for nearly three years. Jimmy was raking it in, he was paid around eight hundred pounds cash for each house so after buying the materials and paying me my 'top up money', I figured he was earning in excess of six hundred pounds whilst also earning money on the jobs he was doing. But strangely he always cried poverty!

He was certainly a shrewd character our Jimmy, he was an Evertonian so some redeeming factors but he did exploit me and I remember many a time singing the track by Aha, *'Take on 'Me'* in an attempt to persuade him to make my employment legal.

Lets just pause a beat to recount yet another lyrical gaff of mine, the track would build to a falsetto crescendo and I thought Morton Harket would sing 'I'll be gone in a jiffy'. I realise my scouse twang had got it wrong when Sue heard me singing in the shower years later but 'in a jiffy' means to do something quickly to us scousers, so it made sense to me. Morton was after all from Norway where many a kopite lives?

Seemingly my singing fell on deaf ears thankfully, this was probably a good thing as I needed to move on, I knew I could make a better life for me, I knew I had the brains but I just needed a boost to my confidence. I had learnt how to decorate which has always been a bonus but I found this type of work mind numbingly boring. Brush in hand I would drift off and I would daydream about a better life and better opportunities.

The highlight of the day, the only time Jimmy and I slowed down was to listen to Simon Bates on Radio one in the morning. I think this occurred on every building site up and down the country and we'd take bets on who would make the next brew by guessing the year on the 'Golden Hour'.

Then we'd listen to other peoples terrible personal tragedies known as 'Our Tune' and Jimmy and me would be unusually quiet listening as Mr Bates summed up and ended with a poignant tearjerker song. *'Careless Whisper'* by George Michael was a popular choice.

By this time I was in a long-term relationship with Julia whom I mentioned before, the girl I met after returning from Wembley with Jimmy. I say long term as most relationships of mine lasted weeks; this had gone beyond a year, it was becoming serious so I decided to end my job with Jimmy. I had ambition and he pleaded with me to stay, I wonder why and I enrolled at Mabel Fletcher College on this Social Welfare course.

I had decided on a career in care work for the strangest of reasons. See, I had seen so many factories close like my Dad's with the introduction of modern technologies so I intellectualised that a robot could never replace a care worker. A job for life so I thought.

The course was interesting as I was with adult learners and this was the first time I was introduced to social and psychological concepts but I viewed this as a means to an end as I was desperate to work. I did earn extra money on occasion; sometimes I helped Jimmy out when he was really busy but my most memorable earner occurred after talking to this lad at college who wanted to shift a load of sheepskin coats.

Those 'sheepies' again and oh the eighties stereotype I hear you shout, scousers and sheepskins but I did a deal with him and thus perpetuated the image.
He delivered about three-dozen coats to my Mum's, they took up all the living room and for every coat I sold I made twenty pound profit. Mum helped and I would model the coats for her workmates at her school, word spread and I must have been good or perhaps the coats were a solid bargain, as I sold all the coats. Nice little earner that.
Let me digress slightly. I was aged seventeen and this adult male who lived in our street with his Mum who claimed to be a lecturer at Liverpool University needed someone to proof read his work. Word spread and we were cautious but Joey being a bit older offered to help him out and he was paid fifteen to twenty pounds as a I recall to read pages and pages of hand written material. Easy money!
Joey and me were suspicions of course and questioned his credibility, the work came across as a rouse as his spelling was awful, worst than mine and when it did make sense it looked like he had copied it straight from a book.
We weren't stupid and I remember talking to Joey about this bloke and warning him that he 'fancied him' but Joey was very much aware of this and we both thought 'if he's foolish enough to pay then that's his loss'.
For all I know he might have just been some lonely guy with no other motives but he tried the same thing with me after Joey lost interest but I refused as he came across as a bit creepy but I mention this because he did give me a number when chatting to me on the field about a course he had taken in sports leadership and a few months later I enrolled on the course and on the back of this got a job in youth clubs.
I would work as a youth worker at night whilst working for Jimmy and this was yet another government scheme for people who had been out of work for over a year. I worked as a Youth Leader at St Dunstan's and Paddy comp, which mainly involved taking subs and putting out the badminton nets. An easy job for me as I attended both clubs most nights and my boss was Glynn from Wales, money for old rope as they say.
Alan was the caretaker and most days we would play footy in the hall when we should have been cleaning and twice a week we had to get toys out from under the stage at Dunny's for a mother and toddler group.
I remember Alan and me being asked by June's sister to watch her and a mate practice this dancing routine in Dunny's Hall. How could we resist and they did this sexy number as they had been asked to perform for the troops in some way off land. We sat there trying not to get all giggly.
The second scheme I did as a youth worker was at Harthill Youth Club

in Wavertree and although part time I was paid fifty pounds a week and again it never felt like work and I actually became a decent footballer as we played hours and hours of five a side with the older kids.
Pool was another favourite and we'd play games against each other for ten pence bets. I had to work nights however so a slight draw back, but it was fun and I ended up running the bingo for the old ladies. All the fours droopy drawers!
We would take the kids away on trips to North Wales and I guess I had by then taken on the same role as the Vic as me and the other workers were the adults although sometimes that was debatable as it got a bit mad and I was only a few years older than some of the kids.
My relationship with Julia ended not long after I'd accomplished all this but those are the breaks and thanks for having faith in me when I needed it most. As for the welfare course I never completed it as I ended up getting my first full time job on the back of doing this course as a care worker at this hospital school in Surrey.
I remember asking this girl in college out on a date as I had a party to attend the night before I was due to leave Liverpool. Brad was with Jean and I needed a partner. I can't remember her name to my shame but she said yes and we arranged to meet up the next night. I ended up taking her back home to my house, which didn't happen very often, it was cold and I put my jacket that I had bought from 'Next' around her bare shoulders. Always the gent.
Again I recall this because some days later I remember looking at my jacket and thinking how did it get ripped as there were small rips on the collar. Well I tell you how; my date with no name had only gone and chewed my collar. Was she a hungry vampress, 'fangs' for the memory in any event?
The other thing I remember about this girl was my Mum and Dad's face as they came downstairs to see me off on my journey down south. It was early, I had packed my case the day before and I was lying on the couch with this blonde girl in my arms. They didn't know what to say.
I kept in touch with the vampire for a few weeks but she was a bit vague to be honest. I later learnt that some lad from the youth club had told her I was gay which is why I had moved south to find a boyfriend. I think one of them had his eye on her and I certainly never sung *'its not the leaving of Liverpool that Grieves me but my darling when I think of thee!'*
So my first full time job if you discount my brief apprenticeship as a decorator was a job as a Houseparent working with children who suffered with epilepsy and other neurological disorders and I lived in a hostel with other twenty something's.

I had my own room and I adorned it with images of home to stamp my own identity on the place, bands I liked and football posters of course and we would eat in this large canteen that reminded me of school.
The Hospital School was in the middle of nowhere by Lingfield Racecourse and doing your weekly shop was a task in itself as the nearest shop was half an hour away by foot and that was across fields and streams. I didn't drive then.
I remember being amazed at the night sky as the stars sparkled very brightly, my mates would have loved it, the lanes and fields were very dark and although I was accustomed to walking around the inner city of Liverpool I was very weary of walking down creepy lanes believing some huge beast was making its marauding way to the London tube, waiting behind the hedge to rip my 'bleeden' head off.
I had friends and I ended up living with a girl for a few years on the back of not being able to use the washing machine. She helped me understand the dials you see and later that night we got speaking at the local pub. I was 'a fish out of water' and although I thought I was mature and independent I clearly wasn't and I had to learn to fend for myself for the first time without the back up of my family.
I now realise I was seeking comfort as I was lonely and we ended up living together eventually relocating and buying property in Glasgow then Liverpool and this was the girl who translated Glaswegian to Scouse for me that I mention elsewhere.
The relationship ended some five years later, we got engaged so it was serious and although this relationship is something I now wish to forget I did learn many things not least it made me grow up quickly and I got on the property ladder much earlier than I would have if left to my own devices. Always look to the positives is a mantra I try and adhere too.
As time moved on I drifted away from my childhood friends perhaps due to not having mobiles and the likes and because I worked every weekend I stopped following Everton.
I became mates with people from all four corners of the United Kingdom and Ireland but my best mate's were two scouse lads; Dave an Evertonian, Nick a Liverpudlian and Mark who supported Middlesbrough.
I remember it being May 1987 so I was twenty-one and we were all on a day off the following day so we decided to go and watch a match. Mark had a Ford Capri and the choices were Everton against Norwich in the final game of the season to clinch the league title, or a mid table match between West Ham and Southampton.
We worked out that the distance from Lingfield to Norwich and to

Southampton was roughly the same and the night before we had a few beers to decide on what match we should see. Now of course Dave and I voted for the Everton match but the other two fancied the boring mid table encounter.
We protested and stated our case and we told Mick he was a bigoted red but knowing we would have felt the same if the tables were turned. We ended up tossing a coin and the next day there I was driving to the south coast to sullenly stand with the cockney Inter City Firm cheering on West Ham. Dam you Nick, Everton won the league and this goes down as one of my biggest regrets, should have asked 'best out of three' when we spun that bloody coin.
I would travel to Liverpool during the school holidays and I would be over the moon as I was home. Then it would be time to return to my self-imposed exile and in contrast to the inward journey the train would pass through Edge Hill Station and Wavertree as it shunted along the track making its way South.
I would sit and stare at places all too familiar to me, the gas works tower, Botanic Park, the iconic Littlewoods building, Picton Bridge, the High Street, the Mystery Park, Penny Lane and I am not ashamed to say this but often I would turn away from prying eyes and a tear would run down my cheek. God I hated leaving Liverpool.
I missed my street terribly you see and I missed the sanctuary of home and I could see the sun glisten on the rooftop of my house from the train which added to my heartache. I missed my area, I missed my family and I missed the friends I had made and I hated the feeling of the train as it pulled away and meandered down the line but I had a job unlike some and I realise this initial exploration into the adult world set me up for the rest of my life and I may not be who I am today if I hadn't embarked on this journey.
The tracks of my years would have been so different I am guessing and after all the people and the places we encounter serve to enrich life's tapestry!
Before I move on a few more lines about my time living down South which I did for two and half years in total. I remember being pally with a girl from Stoke called Debbie and she lived with a friend from Surry and I was watching telly in their flat one night and the soap Brookside came on.
The story line was about a body found on a railway track and the scene was filmed at Edge Hill Station and surrounding area. It looked different on telly, more urban but I guess that's because I had become accustomed to the trees and fields where I was living at the time but I jumped up

with excitement and exclaimed 'that's my home!'
I will always remember this, the girl from Surry looked horrified, she pointed and sniggered, 'it looks like a right dump'. I knew she was posh unlike Debbie, the kind of girl who wore oil soaked farming jackets and probably had a pony called Sally back home.
She judged me there and then and from that day her attitude towards me was different but I was okay with that, and I told her my home was a rough area but it was my home and I would never trade places with her no matter how comfortable her life had been. Silly 'plum in your mouth' cow.
Another time I was in the local village and I was talking to one of the young people about what we were having for tea. This old lady touched my arm and enquired in a croaky voice, 'are you from Liverpool my dear?' I know I have a scouse accent but it was stronger and more abrasive when I was younger and I remember thinking, 'here we go another person waiting to judge me based on my accent'.
I'm glad to say I was wrong; she had actually been born in Liverpool but left as a young girl to live in Surrey but before doing so she had lived by Sefton Park.
This felt very surreal; here was I reminiscing with a little old lady buying a loaf for toast later that night, a lady who was well into her eighties who spoke with a Southern accent about another area some two hundred and fifty miles or so away in a place that was socially and culturally as diverse as the Artic is to the Sahara.
She was a lovely old dear though and we talked for a few minutes and her face lit up when I told her about the boating lake, the Palm House and the caves, caves she once played in herself when she was a girl.
I felt a sense of pride and she certainly restored my faith in humanity and I have always remained steadfastly proud of my city and my background and I have always held my chin up high and sod everyone who thinks less of scousers or any other people with accents. They're by the grace of God so sod you Debbie's mate and lest hope you lost thousands when the stock market collapsed. Do I sound bitter and twisted?

Chapter Twenty

Living in the past...

I think its time I wrapt up this book and draw matters to a close, I think I'm becoming too grumpy in spite me still being in my forties and too sentiment at times but I guess I'm simply warn out remembering things and you're probably warn out too!
So how do I got about it, well, my clever mate Neil likes to read, he's an educated so and so and he bought himself a Kindle like so many have it seems these days, apparently sales have boomed because some women like reading the saucy 'Fifty shades of Grey' for some reason, I believe chapter seven is where it gets rather saucy.
I'm not suggesting Neil's read the Fifty Shades of course but I do have this image of Neil wearing a cravat whilst holding a single malt whisky without ice of course and bemoaning 'with my reputation young fellow' and quoting famous people from literature.
See, he told me during a round of golf recently that Ernest Hemingway asserts that the definition of a true man is someone who has achieved the following. Now forgive the male bias again, I thought I'd parked that in the first chapter, sorry about that and for any Hemmingway purists out there I also apologise if I get this woefully wrong but this apparently involves, fathering a son, planting a tree, wrestling a bull and writing a book.
Not sure in what particular order such tasks should be achieved but let's see if I pass Mr H's definition, not that I need to prove my manliness of course but simply for fun and I think it's a nice way to conclude this book.
I have two sons so double ticks awarded thus far and no more on the way thankfully and for that matter I can happily board the train without a care in the world as to whether I get off at Edge Hill, Lime Street Station or any Station for that matter?
I'm not sure if this counts as another tick but I planted five conifers when Kieran was born, they form a neat hedge at the front of my house should you have Google street map and at a stretch I think I'm okay to stake a

claim to them being trees, so surely five ticks awarded! That bloody competitive streak strikes again dear reader!
As for wrestling a bull, this is a tricky one as there was never much call for Spanish matadors round Edge Hill, I guess they got off elsewhere, but if any Taurean's out there fancy a wrestle sometime, a ram versus a bull, now there's a thought, then please do form an orderly queue. Time to think! No offers then, thankfully not as I hate fighting like I said, so how's about this somewhat spurious link to appease Mr H's theory.
I have big goalkeeper hands and fingers to match and I tend to 'wrestle' with the pulley on a can of 'Red Bull'. Ouch, that was painful I concede and a terrible link I know, so one tick deducted I hear you shout but let's face it I have chatted some 'cock an bull' throughout this book, so surely one tick restored! All this is making me dizzy but I think that now makes seven!
I'll stop now with this game of bull tennis but it conveniently links me to Mr H's final manly element, writing a book. Well, this may not be the best book ever written or the most interesting, true, a little saucy at times I know and I somehow don't see Neil getting all whimsical about my words jumping out of his Kindle and it is no doubt riddled with spelling mistakes and poor punctuation and some inaccuracies but it is a book. This book, if I may call it that is a personal and self-indulgent book and at times self-defecating, a collection of my memories and life experiences that I repeat sometimes and I'm guessing my words are only of interest to family and close friends. Now there's confidence for you.
You may indeed think less of me after reading this book, you may feel I've been disloyal to you or to people you know or have known and you may wonder what the bloody hell is going on in my mind. Has he gone mad?
You may not know me of course or my family or my area so whoever you are I really hope you enjoyed my journey into the seventies and a little beyond but if you didn't then that's fine and mercifully not long now before I draw all this drivel to an end.
Before I do though, I feel the need for some psychoanalytical Freudianesque self-reflective exploration is needed. Like I said I am very worried that I might have offended people with memories from the past but I remind you that this is about my perceptions and not necessary based on reality.
People who know me will know that I have changed most names, which was a task in itself but I've come to realise that everyone sees the world slightly differently, conditioned by our upbringing like the Jesuit monks proclaimed, our surroundings, our environment and this book has

demonstrated to me that I am who I am because of who I once was, some mucky kid from Edge Hill, unsure about life and what direction to take and this book has certainly taught me so much about myself.

Life is indeed an education and it's the things we said yesterday and to quote from the Beatles, the *'Things We Say Today'* and what we say tomorrow that enrich and formulate our memories over the passage of time.

I've learnt that I'm a flawed individual, I have selfish degenerative traits and I am annoyingly impatient and impetuous at times. I've taken a rueful look at love and loss and I've learnt that I like flying carpets and giving away pencil cases.

You may think I had a one 'track' mind, that I had 'tunnel vision' as I had several relationships as a young person, some of them involved trains but many not and in my defence I was a pubescent Sir Lustalot on a quest, a horny toad if you like, looking for love but never really finding it back then and I have other encounters that I shall keep under wraps for now?

I was better at keeping goal than scoring goals, I am better with my hands than my feet, I've learnt that I have week ankles, that I should never climb trees under the influence of alcohol, I should never write to lost cockney romances, I can walk on cracks without worrying about luck and for karma reasons I should never steal, vinegar bottles are a big no!

I suffer terribly with motion sickness and I get sick in the bath but I think I have passible motion moves on the dance floor and I really should have ditched those chat up lines. I'm really good at balancing stuff, I can canoodle using crutches, I have good stamina and recovery prowess, I can run for miles and I can never do a three sixty on a skateboard but I can do an impressive wheelie.

I like playing golf and badminton and because of my childhood I am fiercely competitive at most things as were my friends but I think this has lessoned as I get older and I can be very deep and a little intense and morose at times.

That aside I believe I am a sensitive and caring individual and I guess this is why I have ended up drifting into social worker as a career, as I am generally a good listener and I like to help others and I think that was due to good old Mum and Dad and chatting outside pubs with my mates counselling those who had been ditched or sometimes searching for ones own answers in the mirror of life.

I hate bullying based on my own experiences and I strive to tackle injustice. I'm the kind of person that will stand up and shout for their rights and the rights of others and I am far more confident as an adult than I ever was a child. I literally wish I knew then what I know now! I hate fighting and I have wimpish tendencies and I was bullied as a kid, I can see that now, I'm not ashamed of that otherwise those who bullied me have perhaps won and I know this is because I hadn't learnt the ability to laugh off criticism with banter and repartee and if I had my time again I would try and avoid wearing this old heart of mine emblazoned on my sleeve.

I have one of those faces that easily reveal my inner emotions; yes I would be crap at poker or spying for that matter.

I've learnt that I like stupid facts and stupid jokes too and I use humour as a defence mechanism when I feel cornered and I think I can be both quick witted at times but also slow on the uptake. I talk relentlessly when I feel nervous and I sometimes say things that should stay in this old brain.

Perhaps my education is splattered with one poor excuse after another and I really should have applied myself better at school, certainly my secondary education but I've also leant to be resilient, to never give up and if determined you can achieve most things in life if you have ambition and drive but most of all people who have faith in you, which reminds me of another brilliant Billy Bragg track, *'I Keep Faith'*; from the superb 'Love & Justice album.

Inner resilience is achieved when someone takes you under his or her wing and I can recall several individuals such as the Vic, Geoff, Danny and Glynn who guided me and offered me opportunity when I was a teenager and I am forever indebted to them wherever they may be and I wish them well from the bottom of my heart. I also include Neil in this list, as he has always been a good reliable mate over the years, we are different in so many ways but he knows me and I know him like the brother neither of us had.

I realise Primary School was a happier time for me and I felt connected and settled, Senior School stripped away my self-assurance down to the bone and it has taken me a fair few years to beef up again. I sometimes wish I had been some big dumb kid blessed with the courage to rise and shine, to stand up to those hell bent on harming me but fighting just wasn't and isn't in my nature. I have no idea why, Dad was a tough role model but always fair and caring at the same time so I guess it has something to do with the street as well.

I also admit to being gullible at times as I see the good in people but that said and having been reared on the mean streets, entries and wasteland of Edge Hill, I have a street wise cautious streak running through my

bones. I am careful in strange places and generally very sceptical of people and I sometimes have issue with trust but if I welcome you into my heart then I can be a very loyal friend and someone with whom you can rely upon in the long term.
That said I tend to think people will do me wrong in time and because of that I struggle to sustain friendships and I push people away, I sometimes try too hard.
I don't mean too but I have an innate suspicious side to my character and I wish I could shake that particular weight off my shoulders. It's a huge salty chip drenched in stolen vinegar weighing me down and I rarely allow people to totally understand me and seldom have I allowed people to venture into my soul or my heart, as I continually fear rejection like a penetrating dagger wishing to avoid the accompanying hurt that goes with the loss and I've come to realise that some people relish sucking on your dreams like emotional vampires.
I wish I had made more of an effort to keep in touch with people who have walked along my life's crooked line, so if you know someone who knew me, then tell them I'm doing fine and say hello and ask them to give me a call sometime. I need to start trusting folk and I really should arrange a reunion to coincide with the next time Grant visit's these shores.
Edge Hill is a 'tough' area for a kid to embark on life's path but I've come to realise that coming from humble beginnings when Dad was unemployed most of the time and in a decade full of social, political and cultural changes is character building and I am a better person for experiencing the highs and lows that impacted on my family in the seventies and I wouldn't change a single thing. It was indeed a *'Wonderful Life'*, thanks to the Felice Brothers for this linked track.
As for other tracks, *'In my Life'* by 'The Beatles' is a fitting track to mention at this stage due to it being full of lovely lines that tap into my seventies experiences and my childhood. For fear of copyright infringement I haven't written them but did you know John Lennon penned the original lyrics based on a bus route he took in Liverpool naming various sites along the way but he thought this was boring so he made the track less personal.
It wouldn't have been boring to me and I think he should have penned two versions and it may also interest you to know that the line that refers to someone who has died is reputedly about his art school pal, Stuart Sutcliffe. There you go my final fact and before I move on I must also mention *'In my Life'*, another track by 'The Felice Brother's' as it echoes similar memoire sentiments for me and I urge you to give it a listen,

bloody marvellous, Ian Felice has this gravel enriched tone to his voice that touches my soul.
God I nearly said 'give it a spin' but that would imply 'vinyl' which is something now sadly resigned to the static past but who knows vinyl may have its day again?
I realise now that the seventies were my kingdom of days and I would happily pop in to see every now and then if I had the Tardis. I've leant that we never had much when I was a kid compared to what I have now and my Dad taught me to wear a jumper during cold nights and just in case there is any doubt the tree in the garden has sadly remained devoid of money all my life.
I've learnt that you reap the rewards in life if you work hard and I thank my Dad for the work ethic he instilled in me, through adversity comes the drive to make ones life better than what came before so as you have more in the future and more for your decedents I guess.
That said I will always remain overly cautious when it comes to spending money and in fact I am often lambasted for having a 'thrifty' disposition in work and by my mates when in truth I can be generous but because of my past I despise unnecessary waste and I deplore being ripped off believing I am always being ripped off. 'Count your pennies and the pounds will look after themselves', is another one of Dad's favourite phrases.
We may have had very little and less tangible things but significantly more important ingredients to what constitutes a happy upbringing such as family, friendships, cooperation, community and connectivity.
I realise that we had freedom to explore our environment without too much concern, we suffered failure, we celebrated some successes and above all we had responsibility and we learned how to deal with it all!
In fact I feel compelled to teach my kids about being a seventies child as they can't climb, walk along a wall, throw a ball, juggle a ball with their feet, knock a conker out a tree or ride a bike with confidence on its back wheel and whilst they can teach me a thing or two when it comes to gadgets, kids have lost the ability to play out, to think of games using imagination, they now rely upon some geeks image of the world, a realistic world but a virtual world. I find that sad.
I realise that music has been a constant thread that has run through my tapestry and I have really enjoyed researching and reminiscing about tracks stored in the recess of my mind, some I thought were long forgotten and some should be forgotten I hear you cringe. I hope you enjoyed the many varied tracks I have talked about and I think I might just create my own special playlist on I Tunes should I feel the need to

reminisce during long cold winters when I'm old and grey supping on some gin and tonic.

I really hope I haven't infringed some lyricist intellectual copyright so I've used italics to show that I am quoting a track by name and I have clearly referenced the track in the appendix.

I chose the tremendous *'Living in the Past'* by 'Jethro Tull' as the heading to this concluding chapter because I like the track of course but also because for this past year or so I have selfishly jettisoned back in time without the help of the Dr searching for memories to record, I have literally lived in the past. Just pausing for a beat, I think Ian Anderson is hysterical with his contorted facial antics and he's the only flute playing lead singer I've ever came across. Very cool!

I've come to realise that I have wore retro specs, now there's a good name for a punk tribute band but it's high time I moved on and looked forward to the future.

I am forty six years of age after all, my hair grows greyer by the day and my waist line spills slightly above my belly, I feel old and past it but I guess I have the rest of my life to look forward too.

So let me now disembark from the nostalgic train that stands magnificently at Edge Hill Station to board the seventy-nine bus back to where I live, the same bus that runs through Edge Hill. To unashamedly quote directly from the stupendous 'Steely Dan' track, I've been *'Reeling in the Years'* but now I need to move on and I guess this is the first day of my life, so let me doth my cap to my seventies past and say so long old bean, its been a dream, it was a blast.

So back to Mr H. This is a book by anyone's definition and although I am guilty of massaging my own ego in writing this book I do feel very proud of myself. Not least because of my dedication and the pledge I made to myself to complete this book at the onset as it would take up large chunks of my free time but also because of the cathartic sense I am left with having embarked on this journey, chronicling my childhood for the betterment of my family I hope.

The things the children and the grandchildren should know like I said at the very beginning and I thank my family for their fortitude and patience as they have shared this experience too.

God this sounds like an acceptance speech but I have to say a big thank you to my Dad for by passing Edge Hill Station, as I wouldn't be here and of course Mum as she clearly played her part in that particular journey!

Perhaps in a parallel universe Dad got off, perhaps Mum and Dad never kissed outside the pub, perhaps Betty was home that fateful night,

perhaps I was never conceived, perhaps Mum and Dad missed that particular Liverpool Echo advertising seventeen Galloway Street, perhaps I never had my appendix removed and passed my elven plus, perhaps I had never fractured my ankle and carved out a career as decorator Dave running up and down ladders singing the tracks of my years...so many probabilities, so many sliding doors, 'A Simple Twist of Fete' as Bob Dylan would say!
This is an absolutely mind-boggling philosophical concept when you think about it and I guess for every living soul conception is an action and for every action there then follows a lifetime of reactions that enables life to continually ricochet through the cosmos beginning with the Big Bang and yes I must apologise for the last obvious innuendo.
I'm going to windup now but I also want to apologise to Adam as I have denied him many an opportunity to use the I Mac, much to his annoyance, so Adam, this dinky futuristic keyboard is now yours and I await your memories when I'm 'older' and 'greyer' as I pass through my declining years, less ricocheting but more stumbling and promise me one thing kids, share my book with your children, assuming you have any of course.
Yes the bittersweet tang of aging and who knows what the future will look like but one thing is for certain, society evolves, nations evolve, technologies evolve, I evolve, you evolve and the future will look and feel so different to now, so start remembering Adam and Kieran and carry the story on but I am guessing you wont be using a keyboard but mind controlled typing!
Who knows what technological wonderments are around the corner, perhaps the time travelling Tardis and if so I look forward to doing this all over again and again and you know, I wouldn't change a bloody thing ha! X

The Tracks of My Years!

Leaving of Liverpool – Sailors song circa 1885. How Much is that Doggy in the Window - Lita Roza 1953. **Singing The Blues – Guy Mitchell 1956.** From A Jack To A King - Ned Millar 1957. **A Hard Rains A Gonna Fal – Bob Dylan 1962.** In My Liverpool Home - The Spinners 1962. **The Monster Mash - Bobby 'Boris' Pickett 1962.** I Remember You - Frank Ifield 1962. **Return to Sender – Elvis 1962.** On Top of Spaghetti – Tom Glazer 1963. **Puff the Magic Dragon - Peter, Paul and Mary 1963.** Downtown - Petula Clarke 1964. **Things We Said Toady – The Beatles 1964.** Subterranean Homesick Blues – Bob Dylan 1965. **Unchained Melody - The Righteous Brother's 1965.** In My Life – The Beatle s1965. **The Sun Ain't Gonna Shine Anymore – The Walker Brothers 1966.** I Heard it Through the Grapevine - Marvin Gaye 1966. **Yellow Submarine – The Beatles 1966.** Eleanor Rigby – The Beatles 1966. **A Day in the Life – The Beatles 1967.** Penny Lane – The Beatles 1967. **Magical Mystery Tour – The Beatles 1967.** Hey Jude – The Beatles 1968. **Little Arrows - Leapy Lee 1968.** There's a Kind of Hush (All Over the World) – The Carpenters 1968. **White Horses – Jacky Lee 1968.** Honey - Bobby Goldsboro 1968. **Helter Skleter – The Beatles 1968.** Suspicious Minds - Elvis 1969. **Sugar Sugar - The Archie's1969.** Bad Moon Rising - Credence Clearwater Revival 1969. **Living in the Past - Jethro Tull 1969.** Where Do You Go to (My Lovely) - Peter Sarstedt 1969. **Come Together – The Beatles 1969.** Cavantina (AKA The theme from the Deer Hunter) – Stanley Myers 1970. **I Hear You Knocking – Dave Edmunds 1970.** Our House – Crosby, Stills and Nash 1970. **Instant Karma – John Lennon 1970.** Lola – The Kinks 1970. **Lets Work Together – Canned Heat 1970.** Knock Three Times - Tony Orlando 1970. **The Ballard of Sir Frankie Crisp (Let it Roll) – George Harrison 1970.** The Pushbike Song - The Mixtures 1970. **Shaft – Isaac Hayes 1971.** My Sweet Lord - George Harrison's 1971. **Son of My Father - Chicory Tip 1972.** Crazy Horses – The Osmond's 1972. **Sealed With a Kiss - Bobby Vinton 1972.** My Ding-a-Ling - Chuck Berry 1972. **Changes – David Bowie 1972.** Ziggy Stardust – David Bowie 1972. **Billy the Mountain - Frank Zappa 1972.** American Pie - Don McLean 1972. **Avenue and Alleyways - Tony Christie 1972.** Where's Your Mamma Gone - Middle of the Road 1972. **Season in the Sun - Terry Jacks 1973.** Do the Bump - Kenny 1973. **Yesterday Once**

More – The Carpenters 1973. Summer (The First Time) - Bobby Goldsboro 1973. **Like Sister & Brother – Drifters 1973.** Reeling in the Years – Steely Dan 1973. **The Ballroom Blitz - Sweet 1973.** Cum On Feel The Noize - Slade 1973. **When Will I See You Again -The Three Degrees 1973.** The Most Beautiful Girl in the World - Charlie Rich 1973. **Seasons in the Sun – Terry Jacks 1973.** Forever Young – Bob Dylan 1974. **Billy Don't Be A Hero – Paper Lace 1974.** This Town Aint't Big Enough For Both Of Us – Sparks 1974. **Amateur Hour – Sparks 1974.** Everybody Was Kung Fu Fighting - Carl Douglas 1974. **Sugar Baby Love - The Rubettes 1974.** This Year I'm Off to Sunny Spain – Sylvia 1974. **That's the Way I like It - KC and the Sunshine Band 1975.** Bye, Bye, Baby – Bay City Rollers 1975. **Love to Love You Baby – Donna Summer 1975.** Movie Star – Harpo 1975. **January – Pilot 1975.** Seventeen - Janet Ian 1975. **Love is the Drug – Roxy Music 1975.** Simple Twist of Fete – Bob Dylan 1975. **(Don't Fear) The Reaper - Blue Oyster Cult 1976.** Moonlight Feels Right' – Starbuck 1976. **New Rose – The Dammed 1976.** Year of the Cat – Al Stewart 1976. **The 'Rubberband Man - The Detroit Spinners 1976.** You Just Might See Me Cry – Our Kid 1976. **From New York to LA - Patsy Gallant 1976.** You To Me Are Everything - The Real Thing 1976. **Float On – The Floaters 1977.** Ma Baker – Bony M 1977. **If I had Words - Yvonne Keeley 1977.** Native New Yorker – Odyssey 1977. **Moondance - Van Morrison 1977.** Substitute – Clout 1977. **Romeo – Mr Big 1977.** Yes Sir I Can Boogie - Baccara 1977. **In the City – The Jam 1977.** Watching the Detectives – Elvis Costello and the Attractions 1977. **We are the Champions – Queen 1977.** Chanson De Amore - Manhattan Transfer's 1977. **Ca Plane Pour Moir - Plastic Bertrand 1977.** God Save the Queen – Sex Pistols 1977. **Peaches – the Stranglers 1977.** Always and Forever - Heatwave 1977. **Boogie Nights – Heatwave 1977.** The Passenger – Igg Pop 1977. **All Around the World - The Jam 1977.** Spanish Stroll – Mink De Ville 1977. **Is She Really Going Out With Him – Joe Jackson 1978.** Lay Your Love on Me- Racy 1978. **Down in the Tube Station at Midnight – The Jam 1978.** A Little bit of Toast – Streetband 1978. **Dancing in the City - Marshall Hain 1978.** Copacabana – Barry Manilow 1978. **Take A Chance - ABBA 1978.** If I Can't Have You - Yvonne Ellerman 1978. **Boogie Oogie - Taste of Honeys 1978.** Blame it on the Boogie - The Jackson's 1978. **Don't Cry For Me Argentina - Julia Covington 1978.** Tommy Gun - The Clash 1978. **Oliver's Army - Elvis Costello and the Attractions 1978.** Teenage Kicks - The Undertones 1978. **Promises – Buzzcocks 1978.** What Do I Get – Buzzcocks 1978. **Denis (Denee) – Blondie 1978.** Jilted John – Jilted John 1978. **Germ Free Adolescent's - X Ray Specs 1978.** Lucky Number - Lena Lovich 1978.

Getting Off At Edge Hill – The Tracks Of My Years

Cant Stand Loosing You – The Police 1978. Reunited - Peaches & Herb 1978. **Being Boiled – The Human League 1978.** Warm Leatherette - Daniel Miller 1978. **I Love the Sound of Breaking Glass - Nick Lowe 1978.** I am the Fly - Wire 1978. **Hit Me with Your Rhythm Stick - Ian Drury and the Blockheads 1978.** Hong Kong Garden - Siouxsie and the Banshees 1978. **Top of the Pops – The Rezillos 1978.** The Staircase (Mystery) - Siouxsie and the Banshees 1979. **Into the Valley - Skids 1979.** TV Stars – Skids 1979. **Masquerade – Skids 1979.** Working for a Yankee Dollar – Skids 1979. **Don't Stop Till You Get Enough - Michael Jacksons 1979.** Sunday Girl – Blondie 1979. **Heart of Glass – Blondie 1979.** Jimmy Jimmy – The Undertones 1979. **My Perfect Cousin – The Undertones 1979.** Ever Fallen In Love (With Someone You shouldntve) – Buzzcocks 1979. **Boys Keep Swinging – David Bowie 1979.** The Sound of the Suburbs - The Members 1979. **Cool For Cats – Squeeze 1979.** Up The Junction - Squeeze 1979. **Ring My Bell - Anita Ward 1979.** Dance Away – Roxy Music 1979. **Hersham Boys - Sham 69 1979.** Making Plans For Nigel – XTC 1979. **Something Else - Sid Vicious 1979.** Rock Lobster – B52's 1979. **Time For Action - Secret Affair 1979.** Green Onions – Booker T and the M.G.'s re- released 1979. **Gangsters – The Specials 1979.** Strange Town – The Jam 1979. **Eton Rifles - The Jam 1979.** Babylon's Burning - The Ruts 1979. **Video Killed the Radio Star – Buggles 1979.** Bang Bang - B.A Robertson 1979. **Oops Up Side Your Head - The Gap Band 1979.** D.I.S.C.O. by Ottowan 1979. **One Step Beyond – Madness 1979.** The Prince – Madness 1979. **My Girl – Madness 1979.** Rescue - Echo and the Bunnymen 1979. **Sleeping Gas - The Teardrop Explodes 1979.** Are Friends Electric – Tubeway Army 1979. **Down In The Park- Tubeway Army 1979.** Cars – Tubeway Army 1979. **Another Brick in the Wall – Pink Floyd 1979.** Empire State Human – Human League 1979. **You've Lost That Loving Feeling - The Human League 1979.** Transmission – Joy Division 1979. **Baggy Trousers – Madness 1980.** I Die You Die – Tubeway Army 1980. **Crocodiles – Echo and the Bunnymen 1980.** Villiers Terrace - Echo and the Bunnymen 1980. **Pictures on my Wall - Echo and the Bunnymen 1980.** All that Jazz - Echo and the Bunnymen 1980. **Too Much Too Young – The Specials 1980.** Whip It - Devo 1980. **Echo Beach - Martha and the Muffins 1980.** Going Under Ground – The Jam 1980. **7teen - The Regents 1980.** To Cut A Long Story Short - Spandau Ballet 1980. **Games Without Frontiers - Peter Gabriele 1980.** Geno – Dexy's Midnight Runners 1980. **Two Pints of Lager and a Packet of Crisps Please – Splodgenessabounds 1980.** Fade to Grey - Visage 1980. **Turning Japanese The Vapors 1980.** When I Dream - The Teardrop Explodes 1980. **Treason (Its Just A Story) - The**

Teardrop Explodes 1980. Messages - Orchestra Manoeuvres in the Dark 1980. **Electricity - Orchestra Manoeuvres in the Dark 1980.** Enola Gay - Orchestra Manoeuvres in the Dark 1980. **Sleepwalk - Ultravox 1980.** Vienna – Ultravox 1980. **Underpass – John Foxx 1980.** Is Vic There - Department S 1980. **Fashion – David Bowie 1980.** I Can't Stand up for Falling Down – Elvis Costello and the Attractions 1980. **Feels Like I'm in Love - Kelly Marie 1980.** Brass in Pocket – Pretenders 1980. **Beautiful Boy (Darling Boy) – John Lennon 1980.** (Just Like) Starting Over – John Lennon 1980. **A Song for Under the Floorboards – Magazine 1980.** Love Will Tear Us Apart – Joy Division 1980. **Romeo and Juliet – Dire Straits 1981.** Jealous Guy – Roxy Music 1981. **Centrefold - The J Geils Band 1981.** New Life – Depeche Mode1981. **Just Cant Get Enough – Depeche Mode 1981.** She's Leaving - Orchestra Manoeuvres in the Dark 1981. **Joan of Arc - Orchestra Manoeuvres in the Dark 1981.** Maid Of Orleans - Orchestra Manoeuvres in the Dark 1981. **Ghost Town – The Specials 1981.** African and White – China Crises 1981. **Ghost Town - The Specials 1981.** Bermuda Triangle – Barry Manilow 1981. **Don't Stop Believing - Journey 1981.** Souvenir – Orchestra Manoeuvres in the Dark 1981. **Can You Feel It - Jackson 5 1981.** Papas Got a Brand New Pigbag – Pigbag 1981. **Get Down On It - Kool and the Gang 1981.** It's My Party - Barbara Gaskin 1981. **Planet Earth - Duran Duran 1981.** Girls on Film – Duran Duran 1981. **One in Ten' – UB40 1981.** Passionate Friend - The Teardrop Explodes 1981. **Reward – The Teardrop Explodes 1981.** The Model – Kraftwerk 1981. **Einstein a Go Go - Landscape 1981.** (We Don't Need This) Fascist Groove Thang – Heaven 17 1981. **Play to Win – Heaven 17 1981.** The Height of the Fighting – Heaven 17 1981. **Open Your Heart – The Human League 1981.** The Sound of the Crowd – The Human League 1981. **Love Action (I Believe in Love) – The Human League 1981.** Don't You Want Me Baby – The Human League 1981. **Let's Groove Tonight – Earth Wind and Fire 1981.** Love Plus One – Haircut One Hundred 1981. **Art of Parties - Japan 1981.** Quiet Life – Japan 1981. **Visions of China – Japan 1981.** One in Ten – UB40 1981. **A Promise – Echo and the Bunnymen 1981.** Oh Superman - Laurie Anderson 1981. **I Could Be Happy – Altered Images 1981.** Happy Birthday – Altered Images 1981. **Over the Wall – Echo and the Bunnymen 1981.** Zoom - Fat Larry's Band 1982. **See You - Depeche Mode 1982.** All of my Heart – ABC 1982. **Tiny Children - The Teardrop Explodes 1982.** Glittering Prize - Simple Minds 1982. **Party Fears Two - The Associates 1982.** Club Country - The Associates 1982. **Say Hello and Wave Goodbye – Soft Cell 1982.** I Ran (So Far Away) - A Flock of Seagulls 1982. **The Day Before You Came – Abba 1982.** Invitation – Shakatak 1982. **Inside Out –**

Odyssey 1982. Our House - Madness 1982. **Talk Talk - Talk Talk 1982.** Only You - Yazoo 1982. **Go Wild in the Country - Bow Wow Wow 1982.** John Wayne is Big Leggy - Hazi Fantazee's 1982. **Nellie the Elephant - the Toy Dolls 1982.** The Story of the Blues - Pete Wylie 1982. **A Night to Remember - Shalamar 1982.** Rip it Up - Orange Juice 1982. **The Look of Love - ABC 1982.** In the Name of Love - The Thompson Twins 1982. **The Message - Grand Master Flash and the Furious Five 1982.** Should I Stay or Should I Go - The Clash 1982. **The Back of Love - Echo and the Bunnymen 1982.** The Cutter - Echo and the Bunnymen 1983. **Everyday I Write the Book - Elvis Costello and the Attractions 1983.** Pal of my Cradle Days - Ann Breen 1983. **Burning Down the House - Talking Heads 1983.** True - Spandau Ballet 1983. **Relax - Frankie Goes to Hollywood 1983.** Just Be Good To Me - SOS Band 1983. **Let the Music Play - Shannon 1983.** Wherever I Lay My Hat (That's My Home) - Paul Young 1983. **Red Red Wine - UB40 1983.** Many Rivers to Cross - UB40 1983. **Please Don't Make Me Cry -UB40 1983.** Oblivious - Aztec Camera 1983. **We Could Send Letters - Aztec Camera 1983.** Walk Out to Winter - Aztec Camera 1983. **Ain't Nobody - Rufus & Chaka Khan 1983.** Dolce Vita Ryan Paris 1983. **All Night Long - Lionel Richie 1983.** Sunday Bloody Sunday U2 1983. **Slippery People - Talking Head 1983.** Thriller - Michael Jackson 1983. **Tour De France - Kraftwerk 1983.** Sweat Dreams (Are Made of This) Eurythmics 1983. **Cherry Oh Baby - UB40 1984.** West End Girls - Pet Shop Boys 1984. **Hello - Lionel Richie 1984.** She's Strange - Cameo 1984. **William, It Was Really Nothing - The Smiths 1984.** Self Control by Laura Brannigan 1984. **Reckless - Bryan Adams 1984.** Summer of 69 - Bryan Adam 1984. **Run to You - Bryan Adams 1984.** Somebody - Bryan Adams 1984. Heaven - Bryan Adams 1984. **Careless Whisper - George Michael 1984.** Single Life - Cameo 1985. **Imagination - Belouise Some 1985.** Take On Me - Aha 1985. **Tarzan Boy - Baltimora 1985.** Rock Me Amadeus - Falco 1985. **She Sells Sanctuary - The Cult 1985.** Don't You (Forget About Me) - Simply Minds 1985. **Live It Up - Mental As Anything 1985.** Move Closer - Phyllis Nelson 1985. **Alive and Kicking - Simple Minds 1985.** Break Out - Swing Out Sister 1986. **The Final Countdown - Europe 1986.** Living on Prayer - Bon Jovi 1986. **Misfit - Curiosity Killed the Cat 1986.** Shoplifters of the World Unite - The Smiths 1987. **Just Like Heaven - The Cure 1987.** There She Goes - The La's 1988. **Lullaby - The Cure 1989.** Free as a Bird - The Beatles 1995. **Small World - Roddy Frame 2002.** The Things the Grandchildren Should Know - The Eels 2005. **Blinking Lights (For Me) - The Eels 2005.** In My Life - The Felice Brothers 2006. **Copper Coin - Mark Olson 2007.** World Without End - A.A Bondy 2008. **Wonderful Life - The Felice**

Brothers 2008. One Day Like This – Elbow 2008. **Whiskey in My Whisky** – The Felice Brothers – 2008. I Keep Faith – Billy Bragg 2008. **Rollin Sea** – Vetiver 2009. Kids – MGMT 2011. **Never Buy the Sun** – Billy Bragg 2011.

Printed in Great Britain
by Amazon.co.uk, Ltd.,
Marston Gate.